D1739692

Varieties of World-Making
Beyond Globalization

STUDIES IN SOCIAL AND POLITICAL THOUGHT 14

STUDIES IN SOCIAL AND POLITICAL THOUGHT
Editor: Gerard Delanty, *University of Liverpool*

This series publishes peer-reviewed scholarly books on all aspects of social and political thought. It will be of interest to scholars and advanced students working in the areas of social theory and sociology, the history of ideas, philosophy, political and legal theory, and anthropological and cultural theory. Works of individual scholarship will have preference for inclusion in the series, but appropriate co- or multi-authored works and edited volumes of outstanding quality or exceptional merit will also be included. The series will also consider English translations of major works in other languages.

Challenging and intellectually innovative books are particularly welcome on the history of social and political theory; modernity and the social and human sciences; major historical or contemporary thinkers; the philosophy of the social sciences; theoretical issues on the transformation of contemporary society; social change and European societies.

For a complete list of titles in this series, visit www.liverpool-unipress.co.uk

Varieties of World-Making

Beyond Globalization

Edited by
NATHALIE KARAGIANNIS
and PETER WAGNER

LIVERPOOL UNIVERSITY PRESS

First published in 2007 by
Liverpool University Press
4 Cambridge Street
Liverpool L69 7ZU

Copyright © 2007 Liverpool University Press

The right of Nathalie Karagiannis and Peter Wagner to be
identified as the editors of this work has been asserted by them in
accordance with the Copyright, Designs and Patents Act, 1988.

All rights reserved. No part of this book may be reproduced,
stored in a retrieval system, or transmitted, in any form or by any
means, electronic, mechanical, photocopying, recording, or
otherwise without the prior written permission of the publishers.

British Library Cataloguing-in-Publication data
A British Library CIP record is available

ISBN 978-1-84631-019-5 cased
     978-1-84631-020-1 limp

Typeset in Plantin by XL Publishing Services, Tiverton
Printed and bound in the European Union by Biddles Ltd, King's Lynn

Contents

Part 2: The Bonds that Make a World

Part 3: Framing a World

List of contributors

Gurminder K. Bhambra, University of Keele
Dipesh Chakrabarty, University of Chicago
Michael C. Davis, Chinese University of Hong Kong
Nancy Fraser, New School University, New York
Charlotte Girard, Université de Rouen
Nilüfer Göle, Ecole des hautes études en sciences sociales, Paris
Sandra Halperin, Royal Holloway, University of London
Manfred Henningsen, University of Hawai'i, Honolulu
Nathalie Karagiannis, University of Sussex, Brighton
Friedrich Kratochwil, European University Institute, Florence
Jorge Larrain, Universidad Alberto Hurtado, Santiago de Chile
Angelos Mouzakitis, University of Patras
Eugenia Siapera, Leicester University
Peter Wagner, European University Institute, Florence, and University of
    Warwick

Acknowledgments

The contributions to this volume were first presented at the conference 'Varieties of world-making: Europe in global context', which took place at the European University Institute in Florence on October 14–16 2004. Organized by the editors, together with William Outhwaite (University of Sussex) and Bo Stråth (EUI), this conference brought two more long-term intellectual concerns together. The final step in the research programme 'The modernity of Europe: towards a comparative-historical and politico-philosophical re-assessment', which Bo Stråth and Peter Wagner have been conducting at the European University Institute over the past four years, coincided with the beginning of a year of seminars in the Social and Political Thought programme at the University of Sussex. The editors would like to thank William Outhwaite and Bo Stråth for their smooth and fruitful support and cooperation; and Anwen Elias, Aidan O'Malley, Thomas Roberts and Jonathan White for help with the linguistic editing of the contributions, as well as all the contributors for the ease, diligence and speed of their work.

Melana, July 2005

Introduction
Globalization or World-Making?

Nathalie Karagiannis and Peter Wagner

Ways of Conceptualizing World-Making

An artist living at the end of the twelfth century in France contributed to the miniature illustration of the *Bible de Souvigny* by painting the creation of the world. Until the sixth day, everything is in order: day after day, God creates light, the firmament, the earth, the animals. The first deviation by the artist from the Biblical text concerns the seventh day when, instead of resting – as he should, according to Genesis – God creates Adam and Eve. Even less predictably, the miniaturist adds an eighth day to the creation of the world: it is the day of the original sin when, having eaten the fruit of the tree of knowledge, Adam and Eve realize that the Garden of Eden is only one possible world. This example immediately confirms what any historian of Christian art knows: that representations of the making of the world by God may tell us more about the artist's experience of the world surrounding her (or, more usually, him) than about the Book of Genesis. Furthermore, this representation also demonstrates the plurality of ways of world-making. World-making takes place in at least three different ways here: the creation of the world by God, the discovery of another world by humans, and the expression of the world of art. For our purposes, this example frames three fundamental, interrelated questions that are posed once our perspective on the world focuses on the making of the world:

> Can a world be made?
> Can several worlds coexist?
> Can we know a world?

This book proposes positive answers to all of these questions. Broadly, each question corresponds to one aspect of life in common. The first is the political

1

question. The second is the social question, asking how human beings always already are in the world, and in more than one world. The third is the epistemological question. It is possible to read each question in the light of a specific thinker.

First, Hannah Arendt (1958) has famously theorized the world as a man-made stabilizer between 'man's subjectivity' and 'nature's sublime indifference'. The world objectifies, that is, it allows different human beings to relate to each other through its objects. And at the same time, the world is that which separates human beings and keeps them at a distance from each other. The Arendtian world is an in-between that unites and separates human beings. Deriving from this conception, the idea of worldliness is the idea of the common human existence in the world; its constant rebirth (or natality) is the characteristic of political action, the creation of a political space through Logos, that is, through the others.

Second, Jean-Luc Nancy's (2002) theorizing of the common is related to Arendt's philosophy via Martin Heidegger. The emphasis here, countering liberal individualism, is on community and on the idea that human beings are always in the world, always together and facing each other. It is thus not possible to think of 'individuals', but rather one should think of singular human beings whose singularity arises out of the common to which they belong. Such singularity points, consequently, to a plurality of beings and, by extension, to a plurality of worlds that these beings experience, traverse and live in.[1]

Third, in his *Ways of Worldmaking*, Nelson Goodman insists on the different operations that are involved in the perception, representation and description of the worlds of art, philosophy and the sciences: composition and decomposition, weighing, ordering, deletion and supplementation are ways of making world. Emphasizing that the human universe is made of a plurality of ways that describe a world or worlds, Goodman (1978: 4) points out that, from the viewpoint of the philosophy of sciences, 'many different world-versions are of independent interest and importance, without any requirement or presumption of reducibility to a single base'.

At a first glance, it may appear as if each of these perspectives put an accent on a very different quality of the human life in common, as if each of them alluded to a different understanding of the world. Whereas the first stresses the vital political need and struggle for the creation of the world, the second relies on the social givenness of, and interaction in, the world, and the third sees in the world

---

1 Connecting the concern for the common with the constitutive plurality of human social life, Jacques Rancière (1999: 42) writes: 'Politics is not made up of power relationships; it is made up of relationships between worlds.'

the constant activity of the human mind. Accordingly, the relation between the possibility of making a world (or worlds) rather than receiving a world (or worlds) is seen in different terms in each approach. And, maybe most fundamentally, even the emphasis on the uniqueness or the multiplicity of the world(s) varies across these approaches and their specific mode of enquiry – politico-philosophical, socio-philosophical or epistemological.

From the viewpoint that this volume aims to put forward, however, these perspectives can also be seen as converging in important respects. They all attribute the existence of the world to the human capacity for creating it. They all see human beings as making and remaking their own universe. The accent may be more (in the case of Arendt and Goodman) or less (in the case of Nancy) voluntaristic; more (in the case of Goodman) or less (in the case of Arendt and Nancy) constructivist; and more (in the case of Nancy) or less (in the case of Arendt) communitarian. But in all cases, humans are experientially and normatively tied to the world.

Furthermore, all three thinkers would subscribe to Goodman's phrase: 'Worldmaking as we know it always starts from worlds already at hand; the making is a re-making' (1978: 6). Thus, Arendt's historical references to the passage from worldlessness to worldliness and the other way around, Nancy's understanding of the novelty that each human interaction introduces into the already existing tissue of social interactions, and Goodman's mapping of the operations of amendment to pre-existing frameworks of representation, all point to the changing of the world on the basis of more or less existing worlds.

The Impasses of Globalization Theory

Current debates on globalization seem to have little use for such thinking, which has long pre-existed them. Even worse, the sense of a common world threatens to get lost in the rather futile debates taking place among the proponents of globalization, its critics, and those who predict the unavoidable clash of mutually exclusive civilizations. Across all those views, globalization is seen predominantly as an anonymous, actorless process, against which a defensive reaction is at best possible. By contrast, the purpose of this volume is to move the attention towards the idea of diverse projects of giving meaning to the world as unity, and the accompanying idea that there is a valuable plurality of ways of knowing these projects. Since the term 'globalization' dominates much of the current discussion, it seems worthwhile briefly to review this debate in the light of our purpose.

When it widely surfaced almost two decades ago under this title, the topic of globalization was a disturbing one. It questioned established wisdom in intellectual life as much as in the realm of political action. Associated with the diagnosis of the decline of the nation state and the dissolution of boundaries in all walks of social and political life, globalization even challenged the very idea of human agency, be it individual or collective. Action seemed to presuppose an actor, who somehow stands out from the world upon which s/he acts, and a world of rather solid structure, so that any intervention into it would have somewhat predictable effects. By contrast, the world of globalization appeared fragmented, at best in a disorderly way and at worst permanently fluid and beyond grasp. In turn, the inhabitants of that world, who had been seen as easily identifiable members of a class, a nation or a gender, were now seen as 'individuals', in the radical sense that they could be certain neither about the ties they have towards other human beings, nor about their own self and identity.

Such a world, however, is an uninhabitable one. And that insight seems to be the main reason why this early, disturbing perspective on globalization has gradually given way to a somewhat more orderly, intellectual landscape. Very broadly, we may distinguish a debate in political philosophy – which starts out from the idea of the alleged decline of the form of the democratic polity, the nation state and its sovereignty and circles around the idea of cosmopolitanism – on the one hand from a more sociological debate about processes that transform the social fabric – most importantly those of globalization and individualization.

From a politico-philosophical perspective, a renewed interest in cosmopolitanism expressed a double need: on the one hand to uphold the normative commitment of modernity to democracy, which was hitherto incarnated in the nation state as the organ of societal self-determination, most succinctly expressed in the idea of (state and popular) sovereignty; and on the other, to expand the horizons of human community towards a multicultural understanding of humanity, expressed in politico-legal terms as international multilateralism.

The first need is consistently upheld in all cosmopolitan theorizing, where an often encountered urge to argue for the freedom of all human beings from oppression and for self-realization is invariably accompanied by strong claims to equality. Clearly, however, when considerations of access to knowledge, justice and care are taken into account, complications immediately arise, because human beings today are obliged to face different institutional contexts, or because of related issues of representation (of who can speak for whom). Hence, although the earliest, Stoic versions of cosmopolitanism had a rather practical, political orientation – which is often overlooked – recent cosmo-politanisms struggle hard to deal with the need for political anchoring.

Furthermore, regarding the second need, cosmopolitanism clearly inscribes itself in a tradition that opposes communitarianism. However, specific belongings that human beings may not wish to forego pose a theoretical question to cosmopolitanism, a question that it is difficult to avoid answering in terms other than those of varying degrees of proximity and corresponding levels of obligation (Anthony Appiah). Thus, despite the doubtless morally compelling and often very elegantly argued claims to a widening of human beings' horizons (Martha Nussbaum or Jürgen Habermas), cosmopolitanism leaves too many questions hanging, which is the reason why more sociologically oriented thought has often ignored it (with one, notable, exception, to which we turn below).

In this volume, the contributions by, in particular, Michael Davis, Nancy Fraser, Friedrich Kratochwil and, on politico-economic issues, Sandra Halperin, take up the debate on the role of the nation state and cosmopolitan orientations in the current era of a plurality of competing world-making projects.

In sociological debate, there are three major ways of diagnosing the global constellation that started to emerge after colonialism and after the end of the Cold War. Most closely associated with the very meaning of the term 'globalization', first, there are observers who hold that we are in the process of creating actual global structures for all major social practices – most importantly an effective world market for many products and a relatively homogeneous global (mass) culture. This view is held in two versions, an affirmative and a critical one. The former is dominant among proponents of neo-liberal deregulation projects; the latter points to an increasingly globalized resistance to such projects, perhaps most prominently in the works of, for example, Michael Hardt and Antonio Negri.

Second, other diagnoses insist on the persistence of cultural particularity in the world, often even suggesting that globalization tendencies may provoke the crystallization of such cultural forms. As used to be the case with theories of nationalism and the nation state, such reasoning is most often accompanied by the idea that cultural communities should give themselves a political form. The rise of communitarianism in political theory pre-dated the globalization debates and, at its outset, did indeed constantly address national communities. From the early 1990s, however, this theme was integrated into a new culturalist diagnosis of the time, finding its most widely debated contribution in Samuel Huntington's idea of a 'clash of civilizations'. While this concept has rightly been criticized as intellectually and politically conservative, more innovative uses of – broadly understood – cultural thinking have also emerged in the context of the globalization debate, the most interesting one probably being Johann Arnason's renewal of civilizational analysis in his recent *Civilizations in Dispute*. Furthermore, a variety of 'culturalist' approaches, often from anthropology or post-colonial studies, rejected the idea of crystallization of pre-existing cultural forms and focused instead on cultural reconfiguration, under terms such as 'hybridization' (Homi Bhabha), 'cultural complexity' (Ulf Hannerz), or 'multilocal cultures' (Marshall Sahlins).

With the emphasis on reconfiguration, these latter approaches resonate with a third position that, while culturally rather blind, emerged as the globalist turn of the sociological debate about reflexive modernization, which is most strongly associated with the names of Anthony Giddens and Ulrich Beck. In this perspective, modernity was seen, following the sociological tradition, as an institutional constellation that had set off a particular dynamic of societal development. Deviating from the sociological tradition, however, these authors recognized that this institutional constellation did not incarnate modernity tout court, but could itself undergo further transformations. Significantly, some recent transformations were seen as a reinterpretation of the modern project in the light of the preceding experiences with the institutionalization of the modern self-understanding: the term 'reflexivity' became central in this diagnosis.

Thus, the otherwise so-called decline of the nation state was regarded as part of the general reflexive reinterpretation of modernity, though that part may have touched the institutional pillar upon which the original modern project was erected, and the boundaries by which it was protected and made viable. Rather than see this development as a mortal danger for the modern project, however, the theorem of reflexive modernization accepted the idea of social bonds increasingly being constructed and reconstructed through flexible networks rather than formal organization. After its globalist turn, the theorem of reflexive modernization has become, in political terms, something like the intellectual wing of global social democracy. The position it takes is critical of neo-liberalism and 'neo-culturalism', and thus of numerous powers that be. At the same time, however, its acceptance of the diagnosis of boundary dissolution and 'flexibilization', moderate as it is in comparison with some other recent diagnoses of the time, has also entailed an increasing vagueness in the way in which key questions of social and political philosophy can be addressed.[2]

In this volume, the question of specific social and cultural bonds between human beings is addressed in ways that aim to avoid the conceptual alternatives: the idea of long-term fixation of those bonds and, thus, the creation of rather closed sociocultural containers; and endless fluidity and malleability associated with high confidence in the human capacity for collective sociocultural creation.

---

2 To put it very crudely, the globalist version of reflexive modernization theory marks a politico-intellectual position with which one can too easily agree from too numerous particular viewpoints, because it is both broadly reasonable and at the same time insufficiently precise. That is why it has gained many followers and has turned into an intellectually mainstream position.

The contributions, in particular, by Angelos Mouzakitis, Nathalie Karagiannis and Peter Wagner aim to lay the foundations for a view that starts out from world-creation through interpretation, but keeps in view the institutional results of collective interpretation and the limits they may impose on re-creation.

World-Making under Contemporary Conditions

Shifting the emphasis to world-making means insisting that the *challenges* that globalization poses to the human condition need to be thought through and talked about much more and in different contexts. Is it humanly possible to live in a world that consists of nothing but widely extended flows, by constantly monitoring and reflexively reconsidering one's own position in it and linking up flexibly to whatever other beings and objects there are in that world? Would not human agency and creativity under such conditions need to aim at world-making in all the senses mentioned above: open the space of possibilities by creating a plurality of representations; reading one's social situation in terms of possible community; and acting in common with a view to creating a world as a space in between?

In sociological terms, the promise of globalization resides in individualization seen as the liberation from socio-institutional constraints. In politico-philosophical terms, the same promise could, for brevity, be called the hope for freedom within a cosmopolitan order. One may accept those ideas in their broad terms, but from there one would need to elaborate what may be termed a dialectic of globalization by emphasizing that human beings are more able to open themselves up to others the more they are embedded in a world that is meaningful for them. Thus, the central philosophical issue of globalization concerns not merely the boundaries – or boundlessness – of societies and polities, but mainly the individual's need for both freedom and meaning (see, for a related perspective, Safranski 2005). If one insists that human beings can be thought about only in the plural, then this view entails the need to situate oneself in a world with others, that is, to establish one's own existence in relation to time on the one hand and to other human beings on the other. In other words, one would need to ask simultaneously about the ways in which the singular human being is always embedded in the world and also takes reflexive distance from the world.

Every singular human being situates his/herself reflexively in the world and will always find his/herself at a particular position in the world. The era of globalization should not be thought of as that epoch in world history in which all human beings will see themselves in the same, indistinct situation. There will always be some need to understand one's own situation by drawing a boundary and conceptualizing 'otherness'. Rather than assume that the condition of particularity can be overcome, and that the era of globalization is the one in which it potentially will be overcome, our attempts to grasp the contemporary human condition should aim at finding ways of thinking specificity without characterizing others as enemies to be annihilated, and ways of drawing boundaries without the assumption that any crossing of them would lead to a clash of civilizations.

In other words, striving for recognition in a globalized context is not a violation of the modern commitment to equality, but part of being human. And situating oneself in comparison to others should not be seen as a traditional habit of human beings that will be overcome in times of globalized practices. The generally valuable return to cosmopolitanism in political theory contains the potential for reconstituting the political in a truly modern way, by means of democracy, market and publicity, as Kant hoped. But this will be the case only if we do *not* assume that democracy today demands all-inclusive individual membership of a single global polity; or that markets today should create a homogeneous global network of competitive commercial practices; or that the call for global publicness should level all particularity of intellectual and cultural exchange.

The need to make distinctions and to draw boundaries is today often seen as a conservative demand, and in some forms it certainly is. The claim, however, that every human being in the world could reflexively and flexibly relate to every other in the creation of a homogeneous world order is not only unrealistic but also undesirable, because of some features of humanness that a reflection about 'globalization' in terms of world-making can unveil. Such a philosophy of globalization would – unlike conservative positions – be based on a commitment to freedom. The concept of freedom, however, should not be an abstract one, as one finds in much political theory, but rather one of 'situated freedom' (as Charles Taylor would put it) and of solidarities of a novel kind.

It is in this sense that the approach we aim to elaborate in this volume, 'world-making', is directed against the dominant idea of neo-liberal and mass-cultural globalization as running its course, against the revival of theories of conflicts between closed cultural communities, but also against any empty insistence on a combination of flexibility and reflexivity that will easily catapult humanity into a free and peaceful cosmopolitan future. In contrast to any idea of dissolving or hardening social bonds, this volume starts out from a systematic rethinking of the ways in which human beings relate to others and to the world – by emphasizing the plurality of bonds between human beings, of their experience and their interpretation – and it applies this perspective to the varieties of ways in which the contemporary global situation is interpreted in major regions of the world today. Thus, we come back to our opening questions and aim to answer them from the new angle: Can several worlds coexist? Can a world be made from human social bonds? How to frame a world in common?

The Coexistence of Several Worlds

Part 1 of this volume illustrates the possibility and the actuality of coexistence of different worlds by looking at regional varieties of worlds that come about and recreate themselves by contact with another world, including at the global level. First, the North American (US) and Latin American experiences and the interpretations attached to them are created in contact and by contrast with European thought and experience. Manfred Henningsen points to a possible inversion of the North American and the European ways of world-making in Chapter 1. The US began as a federated republic at a time when Europeans created nation states that often competed aggressively with each other, developed a relation of domination to other parts of the world through colonization, and remained for a long time in forms of ancien régime. Today, by contrast, Europe is engaged in a process – with yet uncertain outcome – of creating a federation of democratic republics having solidarity with each other, while the US may increasingly develop an imperial and despotic relationship with other parts of the world.

The US and Europe are also present in Chapter 2, Jorge Larrain's contribution, but from the angle of the Latin American ways of world-making. In his analysis of the historical transformations of Latin American modernity, he underlines the historically variable ambivalence between democratic self-constitution and the attempt to create a self-sustained model of economic organization. Through the need to arrive at an interpretation of this ambivalence that is adequate to Latin America, Europe and the US have served as points of orientation, with the US now sometimes seen as an imposed model and Europe in terms of the hope for an alternative to the US.

While chapters 1 and 2 take up the challenge of identifying regionally specific ways of world-making and their transformations, in Chapter 3 Gurminder K. Bhambra reviews the debate on multiple modernities in the light of the assumption that such varieties emerge in territorial forms. There is a double risk in this debate: first, by focusing on such territorially circumscribed plurality and often assuming for these forms a certain degree of historical constancy, the debate could lead to a culturalism in a new guise, as briefly discussed above. Second, by distinguishing the common features of such world-making projects as 'modern' and, therefore, general, from the specific features of any particular social configuration, there may be a residual Eurocentrism in the debate.

However, there are various ways of practically and effectively avoiding Eurocentrism. To insist on the simultaneous coexistence of the Chinese, the American and the European world views and their consequences may be a first, practical step in this direction. In Chapter 4, Michael Davis argues that it is through the observation of the types of wars waged by big powers in our global era (wars linked to humanitarian interventions, and security-related wars) that we can grasp the world views at the root of different world-making projects. These world views are attached to distinct understandings of 'sovereignty': if the US is characterized by 'new sovereigntism' and Europe by 'transnationalism', it is 'old sovereigntism' that marks China. Evidently, none of these views can solve global conflicts on its own; a regional perspective is thus proposed.

Placing different ways of knowing Europe in the centre is another, effective step against Eurocentrism. After reviewing the problems inherent in the usual modes of knowing Islam – theological, sociological, post-colonial – Eugenia Siapera argues in Chapter 5 for a dynamic, interactive apprehension of the bond that Islam forms between the religious and the political. She shows that it is in the encounter between Islam and the Internet that one can fully grasp Islam's remarkable creative potential as political and social experience and the various ways in which it reconfigures, and is reconfigured by, European sites. Preparing the ground for Part 2, Siapera argues for the rejection of a modernity exclusively premised on secularism and for its redefinition to include the religious bond.

The Bonds that Make a World

Part 2 focuses on the bonds that keep a world together, the links that cause people to conceive of themselves as belonging to a common world. It begins with Chapter 6 and Dipesh Chakrabarty's review of the shift in the understanding of what constitutes the political bond that occurred in India with the transition from colonial sovereignty to national, democratic sovereignty. This account traces the different forms of politics that were considered legitimate in different eras, and the inclination towards domination (that is, rule through fear and the resignation to it) that colonial sovereignty had. Domination was resisted through legitimate 'disorder' or lawbreaking – by contrast with the early post-independence understanding of disorder as not belonging to 'everyday politics', but also with the highly disciplinary form of power prevailing in Western liberal democracies.

Contrary to the classical definition of the political bond as constituting community, the economic bond has often been seen as dissolving social bonds and, thus, community. Standard critical analyses of global capitalism accordingly posit the existence of a regionally based centre of advanced capitalism that dissolves community on the periphery. However, Sandra Halperin shows in Chapter 7 that economic bonds often stretch through extended trans-local networks, and it is the transformation of those networks that should be at the centre of studies of economic 'globalization'.

The transformation both of the bonds that make the world and of our ways of knowing them is at the root of Chapter 8, which is devoted to the social bond. Retrieving a genealogical outlook on solidarity, Nathalie Karagiannis argues that the concept, tied to an unreflective understanding of modernity, is understood too 'thinly' or too 'thickly'. Instead, solidarity can be seen as the recurrent specification of social bonds with a political view. This perspective opens up the possibility of grasping the evolution of the concept up to its various uses by the nation state as its organized container, or by the social movements that have increasingly resisted the nation state.

The final contribution to Part 2 critically reviews the idea of a religious bond between human beings, which has moved back into the centre of scholarly and public attention due to the weakening of national and class bonds. The observation of the increasing presence of Islam in Europe poses the question of the transformation of a space that is actively insisting on its secular self-definition by its inclusion or rejection of the religious bond. In Chapter 9, Nilüfer Göle presents two cases that have led to wide public debate in Europe: Islamic women wearing headscarves; and the question of Turkey's membership of the European Union. She demonstrates how the concept of a secular republic, which is particularly strongly held in France, and the idea of Islam, are both transformed in the course of such public debates.

Framing a World

In Part 3, the creative but also critical coexistence of several worlds, and the variety of bonds for world-making, pose anew the question of how to make a common world possible when it emerges from a diverse set of founding assumptions. In Chapter 10 Nancy Fraser tries to show that 'framing' the world in terms of justice and posing the question of a post-national global justice seem urgent necessities in the face of the weakening of the nation state as the site in which claims for justice could be effectively raised. This site determines the subject of justice, so justice cannot be taken for granted any more; the change necessitates a questioning of the way in which philosophers have relied on social-scientific assumptions up to now. More fundamentally, this upheaval entails the questioning of the way in which the decision is taken about how to determine the frame of justice.

In Chapter 11, Charlotte Girard poses the same question at the European level, with particular regard to the recent debate about the European Constitution and thus to the problem of founding something in common. This document openly commits itself to the double objective of diversity and community. From the viewpoint of the philosophy of law, therefore, it cannot but raise basic issues of legal and political poetics.

Framing world-making in a novel fashion also requires superseding conventional wisdoms of contemporary political philosophy, in particular the idea that the human being is a knowing subject and a political actor, who should be conceived of as an individual who maintains instrumental relations to the world and to others. In Chapter 12, Angelos Mouzakitis takes a first step in criticizing those assumptions by reading the philosophies of Martin Heidegger and Hans-Georg Gadamer in terms of a concern for the 'worldhood' of the world. The concepts of 'being-in-the-world' and 'tradition' both refer to a primary embeddedness of the human being in the world, while not denying the possibility of and the need for reflexively relating to the world of which one is an inextricable part.

A second step is taken in Chapter 13 by Peter Wagner, who identifies the sources of individualism and instrumentalism in European intellectual history, while additionally offering a sketch of the current intellectual landscape, in which individualism and instrumentalism are dominant in the US and their criticism is more strongly rooted in Europe. To counter the risk of losing a sense of a common world, which would come with the wholesale adoption of individualism-cum-instrumentalism, one needs to review politico-philosophical alternatives that sustain a sense of the common without falling into any a priori notions of community. With some qualification, the European attempt at world-making can be read in the light of such a search.

Another effort in novel framing is the rapprochement of the disciplines of sociology and international relations in a way that underlines their common endeavour and their common perplexity vis-à-vis the question of a globalized world. Friedrich Kratochwil argues in Chapter 14 that, in the face of the several phenomena subsumed under the word 'globalization', the first temptation was to consider that most actors were left with no space of choice; and, correcting the first, the second temptation was to insist on 'governance' and the appearance of a 'world society'. However, there is a widening gap between the ideal of a global civil society and the reality of the different 'worlds' present in international relations, and the actual functioning of rather restricted and closed world fora, where diffuse interests and democratic commitment to debate and consensus-seeking are likely to be captured by stronger and fewer stakeholders. Thus, the universalizing features of the inherently liberal perspective that promotes this ideal act as a foil against the recognition of valuable, local 'social' processes and of the structural deficiencies of larger sites.

References

Arendt, Hannah, 1958, *The Human Condition*, Chicago, The University of Chicago Press.

Arnason, Johann P., 2003, *Civilizations in Dispute: Historical Questions and Theoretical Traditions*, Leiden, Brill.

Goodman, Nelson, 1978, *Ways of Worldmaking*, Indianapolis, Hackett Publishing Company.

Nancy, Jean-Luc, 2002, *La création du monde ou la mondialisation*, Paris, Galilée.

Rancière, Jacques, 1999, *Disagreement. Politics and Philosophy*, Minneapolis, University of Minnesota Press.

Safranski, Rüdiger, 2005, *How Much Globalization Can We Bear?*, Cambridge, Polity.

PART 1

THE COEXISTENCE OF SEVERAL WORLDS

CHAPTER 1

Republic or Empire?
On the American End and the European Beginning of Politics

Manfred Henningsen

The Centre of US Power after September 11 2001

When in 2000 Michael Hardt and Antonio Negri published their book, *Empire*, it became an instant best-seller in anti-globalization circles around the world. The major thesis of the authors was that an empire-like regime with no territorial boundaries was presiding over 'an irresistible and irreversible globalization of economic and cultural exchanges. Along with the global market and global circuits of production has emerged a global order, a new logic and structure of rule – in short, a new form of sovereignty.' The empire they saw 'materializing before our eyes' (Hardt and Negri 2000: ix) reverted to the more familiar imperial Gestalt after September 11 2001. In response to the bombing attacks on targets of American power by Muslim radicals, whose resentment of Western modernity and its cultural and political formation is indistinguishable from that of violent European fascists of the 1920s and 1930s, the US, under the leadership of a president whose existential legitimacy had been in doubt since the unusual circumstances of his election in 2000, emerged as the global hegemonic regime. All questions about the territorial location of the hegemonic regime became answered in a straightforward way. The surviving superpower of the Cold War lost all symbolic inhibitions against the use of violence and began to behave as the empire it had become since the collapse of state socialism in the Soviet Union in 1989–91 or, as some have argued, had been since its founding (Bacevich 2002) and during long stretches of recent history (Johnson 2004). Whatever evidence can be produced to support any of these claims, history has invalidated Hardt and Negri's notion of empire as metaphor and reintroduced the perspective of a territorially identified sovereign agent. The dimension of imperial sovereignty has become even more obvious since the war against Iraq in 2003 and its aftermath.

Since the beginning of the war in Iraq the imperial tendencies of American politics have become obvious to people of radically different backgrounds. For the liberal political scientist Chalmers Johnson, the new career of empire means the 'end of the Republic' (Johnson 2004), whereas his conservative colleague Claes Ryn (2003) detects a neo-Jacobin mindset in the foreign policy elites of the post-September 11 period. The detailed investigative reports by journalists and insiders about the decision-making process that led to the war are even more suggestive. They hint at a Machiavellian design of imperial power. President Bush assured Bob Woodward: 'I haven't suffered doubt' (Woodward 2004: 420). Unlike Paul Wolfowitz, for whom 'Saddam's Baathist party was a Nazi-like organization of gangsters and sadists' and their removal 'an essential stage in the march toward human freedom, democracy and the defeat of terrorism ...' (Woodward 2004: 426–27), Bush had a more detached and long-range vision: ' "History," he said, shrugging, taking his hands out of his pockets, extending his arms out and suggesting with his body language that it was so far off. "We won't know. We'll all be dead".' (Woodward 2004: 443). The uncertainty about the judgment of history did not affect the certainty about the need for war against Iraq. Richard Clarke remembers the atmosphere of White House meetings on September 11 and 12 when he reports (2004: 30):

> I walked into a series of discussions about Iraq. At first I was incredulous that we were talking about something other than getting al-Quaeda (sic). Then I realized with almost a sharp physical pain that Rumsfeld and Wolfowitz were going to take advantage of this national tragedy to promote their agenda about Iraq.

Whereas Vice President Dick Cheney impressed Secretary of State Colin Powell as being in 'a kind of fever' over Iraq (Woodward 2004: 175), President Bush addressed a small group of people in the White House Situation Room on September 12: ' "Look," he told us, "I know you have a lot to do and all ... but I want you, as soon as you can, to go back over everything, everything. See if Saddam did this. See if he is linked in any way" ...' (Woodward 2004: 32).

The fixation on Saddam Hussein, which had its primary origin in the first Gulf War, became frequently reinforced by the comparison with Hitler and Nazi Germany. Sometimes the reference to the Holocaust took on competitive forms. In the first meeting on Al Qaeda in April 2001, Clarke compared Al Qaeda to the Nazi movement and added:

> '... (as) with Hitler in *Mein Kampf,* you have to believe that these people will actually do what they say they will do'. He regretted this reference when

Wolfowitz picked up on it: 'I resent any comparison between the Holocaust and this little terrorist in Afghanistan.' Clarke's response: 'I wasn't comparing the Holocaust to anything. I spoke slowly! I was saying that like Hitler, bin Laden has told us in advance what he plans to do and we could make a big mistake to ignore it.' (Clarke 2004: 232)

Clarke did not realize that the upper echelon of the Bush administration had already settled on Saddam Hussein as being the equivalent of or counterpart to Hitler.

Elie Wiesel sealed this identification when he dropped by at the White House on the February 27 before the war and provided the President with his confirmation of the comparison. As Woodward reports the encounter:

> Wiesel told president Bush that Iraq was a terrorist state and that the moral imperative was for intervention. 'If the West had intervened in Europe in 1938', he said, 'World War II and the Holocaust could have been prevented. It's a moral issue. In the name of morality how can we not intervene?' (Woodward 2004: 320)

Bush was impressed by Wiesel's arguments and complained to him about France's lack of co-operation: 'The killer sees the protests of respectable people and thinks they are for him. If the French had put pressure on him, he'd be gone. I read your views on Auschwitz in Michael Beschloss's book.' Bush's reasoning became quite clear when he said to Wiesel: 'If we don't disarm Saddam Hussein, he will put a weapon of mass destruction on Israel and they will do what they think they have to do, and we have to avoid that.' The journalist sums up the Wiesel episode persuasively:

> In the face of such evils, neutrality was impossible, Wiesel said. Indecision only promoted and assisted the evil and the aggressor, not the victims. 'I'm against silence.' In the days after, Bush routinely repeated Wiesel's comments. 'That was a meaningful moment for me', he recalled later; 'because it was a confirming moment. I said to myself, Gosh, if Elie Wiesel feels that way, who knows the pain and suffering and agony of tyranny, then others feel that way too, and so I am not alone.'(Woodward 2004: 320–21)

The Neoconservative Revisioning of the US

The moral certainty about evil powers planning to humiliate and even attack the United States of America drove the cadre of neoconservatives in the administration to action. Richard Clarke suggests in his account of the workings of the inner circle (2004: 243) that there was not much interest in analysis:

The problem was that many of the important issues, like terrorism, like Iraq, were laced with important subtlety and nuance. These issues needed analysis and Bush and his inner circle had no real interest in complicated analyses; on the issues that they cared about, they already knew answers, it was received wisdom.

Clarke does not elaborate on what he means when he says that 'received wisdom' permeated the 'inner circle' of the administration. Yet the important role that the neoconservatives played in the preparation, selling and execution of the march on Baghdad leaves no doubts about the membership of the circle. Before the presidential election of 2000, the neoconservatives were connected from coast to coast in a network of think tanks and foundations planning and designing a conservative revolution in American domestic, foreign and defence policies. Having been forced by the questionable circumstances of the election to put their radical plans for change on hold, the events of September 11 gave them the green light. Along with the emergency measures of the Attorney General and the creation of a Department of Homeland Security, existing plans for the solution of international crisis scenarios became activated.

These plans had been developed during the Clinton years in conservative think tanks and reflected a political mentality that was closer to the historical European state-centred 'decisionism' than the Anglo-American type of political thinking. The constitutional constraints that have traditionally limited the behaviour of the state in the US seemed suddenly very elastic. The connection to continental political thinking runs from Leo Strauss, the philosopher of German-Jewish background. Strauss had a tremendous impact on graduate students of political science at the University of Chicago in the 1950s, when the social sciences in general and political science in particular became intellectually impoverished by positivism in its most reductionist behavioural version. In her book on the Strauss school, Norton (2004: 28) rightly emphasizes, 'Chicago was a place where intellectual passions ran unchecked.' According to her, these passions stay with Straussians, inside and outside the academy, for life. 'It is one of their great virtues.' She presents the intellectual profile of the school and concludes: 'American political discourse at home and overseas has been influenced by a succession of Straussians. The speeches of Republican presidents, vice presidents and secretaries of defense have been written by Straussians' (Norton 2004: 18). The impact of Strauss on the students in Chicago was never fully appreciated by American journalists who, while in their college years, were instructed by positivists, but were certainly not taught the major texts of Western political philosophy that Leo Strauss put at the centre of his teaching. In many journalistic accounts Strauss becomes presented, either in a mocking[1] or serious manner,[2] as an obscure and reactionary German scholar. Any liberal academic detractor could have written Earl Shorris's characterization of Strauss and his school, which he published under the title 'Ignoble Liars. Leo Strauss, George Bush, and the Philosophy of Mass Deception'. He writes in a combination of irony, analysis and deep-rooted anti-Platonic prejudices about the master thinker:

> Strauss was content to write books in obscurity and to convey the ideas in them to a few students here and there over the years. The students carried on the work, teaching Strauss to their students, creating a growing network until there are now Straussians on the faculty of many universities. Since Straussians revel in the difficulty of the master's work they attract very bright students, many of whom will remain in the academy, producing other Straussian scholars, writers, activists, and members of the government at every level, a cadre that will soon begin to think itself as a class, that class for which Plato could find no better name than gold. (Shorris 2004: 67)

Like most of the journalists and public intellectuals, Shorris misses Strauss's connection with the famous legal theorist of the Nazi regime, Carl Schmitt. Norton recognizes the importance of the relationship, but does not speak about the glimpse it provides of the mindset of the Straussians in power. Strauss considered Schmitt a creative political thinker, whose essay, *The Concept of the Political*, he reviewed sympathetically in 1932 in a German academic journal (Meier 1995) a few months before having to leave Germany. Norton (2004: 39) captures this connection beautifully when she writes: '... Catholic and Jew, one who will rise only to fall, and one who will fall only to rise. The man of faith, the jurist of the Prussian State Council, meets the reasoning son of the covenant.' Schmitt's political philosophy was unequivocally clear in asserting that: 'The specific political distinction to which political actions and motives can be reduced is that between friend and enemy.' This affinity defines the existential core of all political relationships, preceding all other commitments: 'The distinction of friend and enemy denotes the utmost degree of intensity of a union or separation of an association or dissociation' (Schmitt 1996: 26). He insists:

> The political enemy need not be morally evil or aesthetically ugly; he need not appear as an economic competitor, and it may even be advantageous to engage with him in business transactions. But, he is, nevertheless, the other, the stranger; and it is sufficient for his nature that he is, in a specially intense

---

1 Atlas (2003) is a mix of satire and analysis. The accompanying cartoons and collage of pictures highlight the absurd.
2 Drew (2003) indicated her incomprehension of Strauss.

way, existentially something different and alien, so that in the extreme case conflicts with him are possible. (Schmitt 1996: 27)

Schmitt left no door open for interpretation: 'The friend and enemy concepts are to be understood in their concrete and existential sense, not as metaphors or symbols, not mixed and weakened by economic, moral, and other conceptions' (1996: 27–28).

In his review of Schmitt's essay, Strauss (in Schmitt 1996: 84) argues that liberalism has failed. By negating the political it did not eliminate it, but has 'hidden' it.

[Liberalism] has led to politics being engaged in by means of antipolitical mode of discourse. Liberalism has thus killed not the political but only understanding of the political, sincerity regarding the political. In order to remove the smokescreen over reality that liberalism produces, the political must be made apparent as such and as simply undeniable. The political must first be brought out of the concealment into which liberalism has cast it, so that the question of state can be seriously put.

Strauss is writing here about the crisis and beginning of the collapse of the Weimar Republic, which will bring Schmitt to intellectual power in the Third Reich and force his Jewish reviewer into exile. The 'antipolitical mode of discourse' Strauss is referring to as a kind of 'Ersatzpolitik' applies to the Nazis and the Communists alike. Both were engaged in destroying the constitutional regime of the Republic. Neither Schmitt nor Strauss defends the liberal legitimacy of Weimar. As Hobbesians, they are watching anti-liberal movements create a state of nature, i.e., a state of war, on the ruins of the social contract that had been produced after the First World War and the self-destruction of the imperial and monarchical order of political things in Germany.

Schmitt's friend-enemy concept, though, aimed as much at the domestic as the international realm. People may hope that the Hobbesian transformation of American political discourse in recent years is only a temporary aberration – but Anne Norton removes all doubts about the policy implications of the thinking of the Straussians. Some treat Strauss's major work, *Natural Right and History* (1953), as a sacred text, whose meaning can be narrowed down to the point, as Norton indicates (2004: 76), that nature 'has but one form. That form is simple and certain, stable and secure. Nature ... is the realm of certain and self-evident truths.' Following this understanding of nature in a literal sense, it becomes a 'realm of certainties', which have to be enforced by policy measures of an authoritarian type. Norton summarizes her understanding of the Straussian policy expectations in an unequivocal, maybe slightly exaggerated, way when she writes (2004: 87): 'Nature ... authorizes totalitarianism. All of life – eating, dining, sex, marriage, children, happiness, mourning, and death – is natural.' This certainty about the meaning of nature that Norton detects in the body of the Straussian discourse evokes frequently religious associations. Christian fundamentalists use this language in order to empower themselves with the inerrancy of divine pronouncements in both parts of the Bible, the Old and the New Testament, whenever they fight back the temptations of modernity. Schmitt sympathized with this counter-revolutionary and anti-Enlightenment mode of resistance in his early books, *Political Romanticism* (1919/1925) and *Political Theology* (1922). Leo Strauss avoided in almost all of his writings inroads into the religious texts. Not being anti-religious in any sense (see, e.g., Deutsch and Nicgorski 1994), he made it quite clear that:

> Philosophy and Bible are the alternatives or the antagonists in the drama of the human soul. Each of the antagonists claims to know or to hold the truth, the decisive truth, the truth regarding the right way of life. But there can be only one truth: hence, conflict between these claims and necessarily conflict among thinking beings; and that means inevitably argument. (Strauss 1993: 223)

The Straussians, however, have not resisted the blurring of philosophical and revelatory language in their service of the born-again president. As a result of this discursive blurring of philosophy and revelation, a striking configuration has emerged.

The peculiar similarity in the symbolic representation of the two major warring sides in the post-September 11 confrontations has not escaped some observers. Anne Norton (2004: 110) quotes the Israeli Gershon Shafir, who told her in a conversation 'that the world is currently divided between followers of Leo Strauss and the followers of Sayyid Qutb'. Unlike Strauss, Qutb was an intellectual activist, whose radical critique of Western modernity informed insurrectionist Islamic movements, including the Taliban in Afghanistan and the insurgents in Iraq. His Islamic fundamentalism and the rigid exclusionary politics it legitimated clashed with the nationalist modernization strategy of Nasser in Egypt, and he was hanged in Cairo in August 1966. Ever since his death, Qutb's fame has grown. His book, *Social Justice in Islam*, was ironically published in the US in the same year (1953) as Strauss's critique of Western modernity, *Natural Right and History*, appeared. It presents many of the arguments against the West that Osama bin Laden, who was one of his students, has expressed against Western modernity, including the justification of terror against Arab modernizers and the collaborators with the Western Enlightenment project. This direct connection of Qutb to terror is at the centre of Paul Berman's book, *Terror and Liberalism* (2003), though he recognizes at the core of the critique of modernity a longing for an authentic Islamic past. Still, the thrust of his reading was encapsulated by the headline of an article he published in the *New York Times* Magazine (March 23: 2003): 'The Philosopher of Islamic Terror'. Before September 11, Roxanne Euben had written about Qutb's genuine political vision in a book that makes the connection with the Straussians even more ominous, though she mentions Strauss only in passing and uses Hannah Arendt in order to make Western readers understand why the uproar in the Islamic world is not all that removed from visions of anti-modernity in the West. Euben (1999: 132) identifies Qutb's cure for the ills of modernity in this way:

> The authority that accrues to "those who know" is underwritten by no less than God. In this sense Qutb exemplifies the literal meaning of the word 'fundamentalism': a return to and excavation of indisputable foundations that are taken to exist in a realm beyond human power and interpretation.

Sayyid Qutb shares some of Schmitt's contempt for the liberal West, a contempt that lasted until Schmitt's natural death in 1985. Schmitt followed with eager anticipation the growing polarization in West German society. The violent actions by, for example, the Red Army Faction/Baader-Meinhof Gang in the 1970s and the response of the Social Democratic chancellors Willy Brandt and Helmut Schmidt made him believe, as Jan-Werner Müller (2003: 181) describes it, 'that liberalism could not hold a state together in the face of a determined challenge unless it betrayed its own ideals'. This polarization became visible in the US between 2001 and 2005 and was confirmed by the presidential election in 2004. The 'Great Political Divide' that the *New York Times* highlighted in a front-page article (July 25 2004) on voter attitudes defines American political life since the election. Schmitt's critique of Weimar parliamentarianism, which appealed in the 1920s to the German intellectual left and right, gained a new lease of life in the 1970s, when the West German Bundestag passed authoritarian measures of the state, with support from all parties, to protect society against violent 'left fascists'. The German philosopher, Jürgen Habermas, had already, in 1967, begun to speak of extreme groupings within the student movement as 'left fascists' (Albrecht et al. 1999: 323). For Schmitt, who did not like the West German constitutional regime because it had refused, among other things, to reinstate him in a university position, there were expectations about a new paralysis of the liberal regime. 'Schmitt's desperate hope', writes Müller (2003: 170), 'for a resurgence of friend–enemy relations against the technocratic universalism of both the US and the Soviet Union seemed to make him put faith in any radical movement – even the student left'. He suggested in a letter to another anti-liberal writer with great national and international appeal, Ernst Jünger, that, as Müller (2003: 170) paraphrases it:

> substance might be restored to politics, if a radicalized Left could recreate real enmity. Such polarization would also lead representatives of the state back to Schmitt's thought on emergency powers – especially once parts of the student rebellion had become radicalized as terrorism.

Reading Müller's exploration of the 'dangerous mind', Carl Schmitt, and his lifelong obsession with the empowerment of the state to subdue civil society, the question may be raised whether this German trench war substitution for politics is applicable to the US? Does the polarization in American political culture over issues and values that has intensified since September 11 lend existential support to the imperial transformation of the Republic? Has a sea change taken place in the American political self-understanding, so that the Hobbesian fear of violent death has begun to cannibalize the social contract on which the republic was built? Do the two presidential elections in the new millennium underscore the watershed? The first sentence of Schmitt's book, *Politische Theologie* (1922), seems to define very well the mind of the Straussians in power: 'Sovereign is he who decides on the state of exception.'

The Liberal Swan Song of the Republic

Unlike the Straussian critique of American politics and their Schmittian affirmation of an authoritarian security regime, which claims to bypass international law and agreements in making and pursuing war, i.e., by declaring a state of exemption, there exists another critical perspective on the dramatic transformation of the Republic that comes from within the liberal persuasion. An articulate representative of this persuasion is Sheldon Wolin, who taught political theory for many years at Berkeley and Princeton. He promoted in his scholarly and general intellectual publications an understanding of American political thought as having its own patterns and continuities, which were not simply European derivatives. He blamed American intellectuals and activists for their inability, in reflection and action, to connect with and build on the creative founding experience. His struggle with the overwhelming influence of European paradigms on American vision was especially directed against the various versions of reading Marx instead of invoking American interventions. He celebrated a democratic radicalism born in the US. In a way, his magisterial work on de Tocqueville, which was published in 2001, but written before the watershed of September 11, is the swan song of the democratic republic. Wolin sees the Gestalt of empire, which Bacevich, Johnson and others have almost exclusively located in global reach, and which became identified by the 'Anonymous' CIA author as 'imperial hubris' (Anonymous 2004), as being the consequence of democratic self-destruction.

Wolin (2001: 5) revisits de Tocqueville's report on Jacksonian America because he sees de Tocqueville as possibly the 'last influential theorist who can be said to have truly cared about political life'. The journey 'convinced him that he had witnessed the future of Western societies'. Whatever can be critically said about the statement on de Tocqueville as theorist, the prediction for the future was certainly wrong. The conditions of equality that de Tocqueville anticipated had to wait a century or more to be realized on the European continent. De Tocqueville (see Tocqueville 1969: 12) felt that 'the gradual progress of equality is something fated' and that the 'new political science' he was inaugurating with his book was envisaging it. His prediction was: 'It seems to me beyond doubt that sooner or later we, like the Americans, will attain almost complete equality of conditions.' However, he made this concession: 'But I certainly do not draw from that the conclusion that we are necessarily destined one day to derive the same political consequences as the Americans from the similar social state' (Tocqueville 1969: 18). Even accepting this critical admission, it is doubtful whether de Tocqueville would have been prepared for the macro-criminal detours Continental European history took via the communist and fascist revolutions in the early twentieth century, until in 1989, after the fall of the Berlin Wall, it finally reached the plateau of departure the US had reached more than a century earlier.

This statement about the American plateau of equality has, of course, to be considerably qualified. After all, the original inhabitants of the land were killed or removed to places that were not in the way of development. And the black slaves who had worked the land since 1619 were kept, after their formal emancipation in 1865 and temporary granting of male citizenship, in unequal conditions until the civil rights legislation of the 1960s. These inhumane, almost proto-fascist conditions under which natives and blacks lived for two centuries have to be factored in when talking about American democracy from the publication of the two volumes of *De la démocratie en Amérique* in 1835 and 1840 to the 1960s. This qualification is important because even the radical liberal Wolin does not recognize this distorting dimension of the American political formation when he speculates about the postmodern political regime. He writes:

> The Tocquevillian answer is: very possibly a despotism. That answer naturally invites reference to Hitler and Stalin and to their mass support and seems proof of Tocqueville's prescience. What could be clearer instances of

democratic despotism, of what one acclaimed study labeled 'totalitarian democracy'? [The reference is to Jacob Talmon's *The Rise of Totalitarian Democracy.*] Or what could be more misleading? Tocqueville's conception depended on precisely what was absent in the prior history of both the Soviet Union and Nazi Germany: prolonged exposure to the experience of democracy, not simply to its catch words or to a brief and thin experience of Weimar electoral politics and cultural experiment. Despotism in Tocqueville's formulation signifies simultaneously the conquest of democracy and the mimicry of it. (Wolin 2001: 569)

But the intellectual recognition of historical fate and political failure comes with the concluding sentences of the book:

At home, democracy is touted not as self-government by an involved citizenry but as economic opportunity. Opportunity serves as the means of implicating the populace in antidemocracy, in a politicoeconomic system characterized by the dominating power of hierarchical organizations, widening class differentials, and a society where the hereditary element is confined to successive generations of defenceless poor. Democracy is perpetuated as philanthropic gesture, contemptuously institutionalized as welfare, and denigrated as populism. (Wolin 2001: 571)

The depressing finale for the American Republic in Wolin's view does not only exist in the imperial bid for global hegemony. This American endgame would not have been possible without the people in its majority practising political apathy, applauding the march of empire and remaining silent about all the gory details of the military and post-military campaigns, e.g., the prohibition of 'any enemy body counts' (Woodward 2004: 327) and the refusal to connect the criminality and obscenity of the treatment of prisoners in Afghanistan, Guantanamo and Abu Ghraib with the upper echelon military and political leadership of the war by dismissing it as 'aberration committed by a few soldiers' (Manzetti 2004). An independent four-member panel concluded in August 2004: 'Defense Secretary Donald Rumsfeld and the Joint Chiefs of Staff failed to exercise proper oversight over confusing detention policies at US prisons in Iraq and Afghanistan' (Aldinger and Dunham 2004). The reports about the deaths of captives, torture of prisoners and other abuses have not stopped since that panel report was issued. They now include revelations about 27 'victims of homicide or suspected homicide' (Manzetti 2005) among at least 108 people who died in US custody in Iraq, Afghanistan and Guantanamo. Stories of Guantanamo detainees that have surfaced in law court papers indicate that the imperial disregard for international law is widespread. In a transcript, the unidentified president of a US military tribunal exclaimed: 'I don't care about international law. I don't want to hear the words "international law" again. We are not concerned with international law' (Yost and Kelly 2005; see also Danner 2005).

All of this reporting about violent acts in Iraq, Afghanistan and Guantanamo did not have a dramatic impact on the US. The American electorate showed in 2004 its indifference about these signs of a security state in action. After 228 years, American history returns to an almost pre-constitutional beginning, a beginning of Hobbesian fear and Schmittian decisionism. This time, however, to quote the language of the Declaration of Independence, it may be Europeans who 'dissolve the political bands which have connected them with another, and to assume among the powers of the earth the separate and equal station to which the Laws of Nature and of Nature's God entitle them'.

A Pretentious Europe at the Gates?

In 1788, twelve years after the Declaration of Independence, Alexander Hamilton commented on the European–American relationship in a way that needs only a slight role reversal in order to be applicable to the present situation: He wrote in *Federalist* No. 11:

> The world may politically, as well as geographically, be divided into four parts, each having a distinct set of interests. Unhappily for the other three, Europe, by her arms and by her negotiations, by force and by fraud, has in different degrees extended her dominion over them all. Africa, Asia, and America have successively felt her domination. The superiority she has long maintained has tempted her to plume herself as the mistress of the world, and to consider the rest of mankind as created for her benefit.

He elaborated on the 'arrogant pretensions of the European', who dismissed the American continent as place of 'degeneration' and then called upon the Americans 'to vindicate the honor of the human race, and to teach that assuming brother moderation'. He promised that '[union] will enable us to do it ... Let Americans disdain to be the instrument of European greatness!' (in Madison et al. 1987: 133).

The question at the beginning of the twenty-first century is not whether the Europeans, through their union, will reject being an object of American hegemony, but whether they will overcome the disabling memory of their imperial pasts by exercising political will in creating something entirely new. Dipesh Chakrabarty articulated the European problem somewhat differently when he unknowingly echoed Hamilton's American complaints about Europe's 'arrogant pretensions'. Chakrabarty's post-colonial plea for 'provincializing Europe' calls for the liquefaction of the pretentious Europe, which 'is an imaginary figure that remains deeply embedded in clichéd and shorthand forms in some everyday habits of thought ...' Yet in order to navigate in the modern world, which has lost many of its traditional moorings, it is, as Chakrabarty (2000: 4) insists:

> impossible to think of anywhere in the world without invoking certain categories and concepts, the genealogies of which go deep into the intellectual and even theological traditions of Europe. Concepts such as citizenship, the state, civil society, public sphere, human rights, equality before the law, the individual, distinctions between public and private, the idea of the subject, democracy, popular sovereignty, social justice, scientific rationality, and so on all bear the burden of European thought and history. (Chakrabarty 2000: 4)

The Europe that Chakrabarty invokes is the birthplace of the meta-narratives of modernity. They have empowered Europeans over the last 200 years as much as they were abandoned or violated by them. As a consequence of this chequered record of actualization, Europeans have lost the exclusive rights of civilizational ownership in them. They have to compete with the rest of the world to earn the distinction of actually living them. The transformation, though, of the basically economic European Community in 1992 into the European Union (EU) has given Europeans the rare opportunity to redefine themselves before the backdrop of an ever more consolidated and shared political economy.

This re-visioning of Europe as a civilizational entity is challenged not only by the presence of the US in the old world and its imperial designs for NATO. The nostalgia for the national past that plays a role from England to Poland, from Denmark to France and the Netherlands undermines the attempt to create a truly transnational political union. However seriously the newly liberated societies of Eastern Europe are engaged in the retrieval of national mentalities, the mature nation states of Northern and Western Europe lend credibility to these irrational flights of imagination. The presence and continuing 'in-migration' of non-European people contribute to the identity Angst of Europeans. The North African immigrants in France, the immigrants into Great Britain from South Asia and the West Indies and the Indonesian and Surinamese expatriates in the Netherlands remind the metropolitan people of their colonial pasts. The post-colonial anger that characterizes some of these communities has sometimes found a symbolic medium of expression in religion, especially Islam, and uses it to legitimate attacks on the metropolitan culture, e.g., in France and the Netherlands. This tension, however, is not limited to post-colonial populations. The Turkish minority in Germany, which began to arrive in the 1960s, after the surplus labour supply from Italy, Greece, Spain and Yugoslavia dried up, shows similar, if less violent, symptoms of a clash of meaning.

Until the beginning of negotiations between the EU and Turkey concerning Turkish membership of the Union, the clash of meaning had only a remote connection with Samuel Huntington's famous prediction of a 'clash of civilizations', since it happened within societies and did not involve the countries of origin or larger civilizational terrains. With the possibility of the entry of Turkey and its 70,000,000 people into the EU, this issue has changed. Suddenly, the EU has to face the question of meaning seriously. The headscarf issue had created the impression of French Muslim girls using the headscarf as a badge of rebellious otherness against the patriarchal Western state. Now the question of meaning has left the schoolyard and become recognized for what it has always been, namely, connected with the God question. Because of the intellectual unwillingness to deal with the God question, it is now aiming at the core of the EU project itself.

Contrary to Friedrich Nietzsche's proclamation that 'God is dead', for many people God and the spiritual meta-narratives that are connected with his existence are very much alive. For example, the German theologian Friedrich-Wilhelm Graf (2004), speaks about the 'return of the gods' in modern culture. As deplorable as the behaviour of many true believers may be, in many countries they are considered to be the keepers of the moral codes and have tremendous influence in dictating what is acceptable and what is not. The hegemonic power of the modern world system, the US, is populated with more than 2,000 Christian churches of various sizes and denominations. In the last decades it has also become the world's most religiously diverse nation (Eck 2001). Although the 'God question' is kept out of the draft of the EU Constitution, that has not silenced the intellectual and political debate. It was not only Pope John Paul II who insisted on including Christianity in a legitimating prologue to the constitution (probably supported by then-powerful Cardinal Ratzinger, who is now Pope Benedict XVI). Seven member states of the EU (Italy, Portugal, Poland, Lithuania, Malta, Slovakia and the Czech Republic) sent a letter in May 2004 to the then President of the EU Council, the prime minister of Ireland, insisting on an amendment to the draft that would explicitly spell out the 'Christian roots of Europe' (Sciolino 2004). The newspaper account does not report how or whether the Irish President of the EU Council responded. His own constitution would have tied his hands, since the Preamble of the Irish Constitution proclaims its Christian allegiance in no uncertain terms, invoking the Holy Trinity and recognizing Irish obligations before Jesus Christ, though commemorating his support in fighting back English persecution.

Even if the anti-English slant gives the preamble an almost insurrectionist connotation, the Catholic invocation of the Holy Trinity, which one finds also, Greek Orthodox style, in the Constitution of Greece, favours neither an American nor a French answer to the God question in the EU. Since many, if not most, European countries look back at institutionalized relations between state and Church, they could not adopt an American non-establishment clause. This clause meant that the political regime should never support the establishment of a state religion. It did not mean the prohibition of any religious communities or their presence in the public sphere. On the contrary, the founders were aware of the Christian, particularly Protestant, identity of the citizenry. In a way, the founders unleashed with the constitutional clause the expansion of religious movements and empowered their public activism for the next two centuries. This American constitutional provision is, therefore, different from the second article of the French constitution, which states, 'France is an indivisible laicistic, democratic and social Republic. It guarantees the equality of all citizens before the law without difference of origin, race or religion. It respects all faiths.'

This radical separation of state and religion, which goes back to the Declaration of Human and Civil Rights of August 1789, ran into trouble when a law was passed by the National Assembly in February 2004 to ban all religious symbols, from Islamic headscarves to Jewish skullcaps and large Christian crosses, in public schools. The uproar in the Islamic community in France and the Islamic world at large was extraordinary, though there were some Jewish and Catholic protests also. Most critics, including liberal Americans who prided themselves on their tolerance of religious diversity, did not appreciate that French laicism is anchored in a deep-rooted historical resentment of the influence of the Catholic Church on the monarchical state. The French distaste for religious fundamentalism preceded the mass arrival of North African Muslims by centuries. Whether all other EU member states share this constitutional indictment is questionable. After all, the Lutheran Church performed the functions of certifying birth, marriage and death in Scandinavian societies until recently. The state in Germany still collects taxes for the churches and provides for religious instruction of students in schools. Very soon 700,000 Muslim students will receive Islamic instruction in German public schools (Schenk 2004). A potential EU law that mandated a strict enforcement of separation of state and religion would therefore run into opposition in many member states.

The European difficulties with religion on the institutional level reflect the larger issue of religion as part of the core of the meaning of civilization. The English political scientist Larry Siedentop has expressed the counter position to the laicistic conviction of modern French political culture in an assertive Christian way. He wants Europeans to accept as the basis for their 'moral identity' a story we can tell ourselves about the origins and nature of our beliefs. And such a story is available. Europeans have only to pick up the pieces of their past in order to become aware of important moral continuities. For him, the European achievements Chakrabarty listed as universal property have a Christian origin. As Siedentop (2001: 193) defines it: 'Christianity provided the moral foundation of modern democracy, by creating a moral status for individuals – as children of God – which was eventually translated into a social status or role.' Against ancient Israel's 'primarily tribal ... outlook', he insists (2001: 194), 'the Christian conception of God provided for what became an unprecedented type of human society'. In Siedentop's daring rewriting of history (2001: 197), Christian teaching gave Europe its 'original constitution, a foundation provided by the egalitarian norms of Christian morality, with their implications for the role of conscience and a private sphere ...' (Siedentop 2001: 192–93).

Siedentop's Christian identity project for the EU adds support to the opposition against the membership of Turkey. The German historian Hans-Ulrich Wehler grasped early on the mood against admission in a polemical article in the German weekly *Die Zeit* under the headline 'Das Türkenproblem'. The arguments he expressed covered the catalogue of human and civil rights deficiencies the EU had presented to Turkey and which it had mostly, though not completely, corrected at the time of the EU summit in December 2004. Wehler was adamant that Turkey, like the North African states and Israel, did not belong in the EU. As for the Ukraine, Belarus and Russia, it was even more obvious to him that they were not part of Europe and should never be admitted to the EU. They have not been 'shaped by the Jewish-Greek-Roman antiquity, the Protestant Reformation and the Renaissance, the Enlightenment and the scientific revolutions' (Wehler 2002). Why Italy and Germany still belonged to that Europe, though they had indulged in fascism and National Socialism despite these foundations and roots, Wehler does not explain. And Siedentop's medieval Christian frame is totally absent from Wehler's understanding of Europe, a peculiar deletion of major features of European history by a German historian.

Still, Siedentop's truly foundational reading of European meaning makes sense for the period after the Second World War, when the nations of Western Europe were trying to recover from the terror of one totalitarian regime and to prevent the expansion of another. In a way, Siedentop's medieval vision of Europe's future lies at the roots of the beginning of the European Coal and Steel Community (ECSC) in the early 1950s, which was the brainchild of Christian

Democratic politicians in the six member states. The EU that came into being after the fall of the Berlin Wall in 1989 and, primarily, in response to the fear of a reunited Germany resonates in that respect with those beginnings. Still, the pacification of Germany at the centre of a peaceful European continent has relativized those fears to such an extent that even Siedentop as a representative of an insular English political class sees France now as the driving force of a political union. How much the negative outcome of the French and Dutch referenda on the EU constitution will change the political dynamic in the future remains an open question.

Siedentop does not explain why the anti-European prejudices of the English political class have not changed since the Second World War and why he would not find any support for his medieval Christian design in that class or any other European political class outside the Vatican. As anti-French as this English intellectual may be, deep down in his cultural guts he is as anti-German as the rest of the English political and intellectual class, not to mention the English press. Contemplating a failure of the EU, he envisions this alternative future:

> What seems most likely is that France, after flirting with a right-wing alternative, will turn to the left, while Germany will turn towards the right – not least, with the impulsion of public opinion in the provinces which previously formed part of the German Democratic Republic and have had only minimal experience of the disciplines required for representative government. (Siedentop 2001: 225)

This ever-present suspicion of Germany harbouring the makings of a 'Fourth Reich' belongs as much to the arsenal of anti-EU prejudices as the assertion that France exploits Germany's Nazi guilt in order to further its own national agenda in dominating Europe. Germany and France cannot change this use and abuse of history for the purpose of undermining the EU project. Recognizing this means that there may exist an Anglo-American opposition to the creation of a continental republic and that it is up to the major countries of Continental Europe to push the constitutional process of the EU forward, even after the setback in 2005 in France and the Netherlands. In 2004, the *New York Times* published an article under the revealing headline: 'America has second thoughts about united Europe'.[3] American historians and social scientists went further than the *New York Times* when indicating that the US under Clinton and Bush was trying 'to translate Cold War victory into sustainable hegemony over

---

3 Cohen 2004. The author did not mention the British reservations about a Continental republic.

Western Europe'. Thomas McCormick (2005: 83) reaffirms the appreciation of the new Europe when he writes:

> Whatever the present failings of the European Union, and however uncertain its future course, it has already achieved something of a miracle, not only in political and economic integration but in its collective consciousness and worldview. The continent that gave the system two world wars, fascism, and the holocaust now offers itself as a role model of how to build a new system on the ashes of a moribund one.

The US had once an interest in seeing Western Europe integrated. With the collapse of East European state socialism and the USSR, this interest has become superseded by the notion of provincializing Europe, not to make its civilizational achievements universally accessible but to turn it into regional and docile provinces of the empire. Niall Ferguson, the English historian laureate of the American empire, adds ridicule to his dismissal of the EU when he writes in *Colossus*: 'Europe's, in short, is a curious kind of a federation without ever quite becoming one. It has an executive, a legislature, an upper house, a supreme court, a central bank, a common currency, a flag and an anthem.' Quoting Siedentop and other biased English intellectuals, he can't quite make up his mind whether the EU 'threatens to become a "Fourth Reich", not only dominated by Germany, but German in its institutional structure' or whether 'it is the French who really run the union in the style of their own less than accountable bureaucracy, preventing its evolution into an American-style United States' (Ferguson 2004). The embarrassing part about Ferguson's understanding of the EU is that he not only invents institutions, like the upper house of parliament, that do not exist, but also that he does not seem to realize that the German constitutional vision for the EU is exactly what he alleges the French fear most, namely, a United States of Europe. Ferguson has a limited vision when it comes to the political imaginary on the European continent, even if he registers correctly irrational prejudices against the EU and actually welcomes them as signs of support for the imperial 'Pax Americana'.

Something must be wrong with this reading of the place of the EU on the map of global politics if the American political scientist Charles Kupchan can come to an almost opposite strategic conclusion. He boldly predicted in 2003 'the end of the American era' in a book of the same title, and he did it before the Anglo-American war in Iraq and the failed politics for that country and the whole region unfolded. Kupchan (2003: 28–29) indicated that the EU was on the way 'to build a military force capable of operating without US participation. These moves will make Europe', he predicted, 'more autonomous and less willing to follow America's lead. Along with an integrating Europe, Russia, Japan

and China will gradually emerge as counterweights to American strength.'
Kupchan's geopolitical placement of the EU in a multipolar world goes, as he
himself confessed, 'against the grain of conventional wisdom'. Yet he did not
base his global mapping on military and other conventional data. He introduced
two assumptions. First:

> Europe will soon catch up with America not because of a superior economy
> or technological base, but because it is coming together, amassing the
> impressive resources and intellectual capital already possessed by its
> constituent states. Europe's political union is in the midst of altering the global
> landscape. (Kupchan 2003: 119)

His second and much more dramatic assumption is that 'the EU and the United
States might part ways ...' As Kupchan admits (2003: 119) 'for most
policymakers and scholars alike, amity among the Atlantic democracies is a fact
of life, an unalterable product of their common history and values'. But to him,
'the EU is thriving, and Europe had better realize that it may well be on its own'
(Kupchan 2003: 215).

Europeans, in large majorities, do not believe any more that America's 'cause
is the cause of all mankind'. One of the master thinkers of the Bush
administration, Robert Kagan, quotes this symbolic claim by Benjamin Franklin
in his book, *Of Paradise and Power. America in the New World*, and calls it the
'enduring American view of their nation's exceptional place in history, their
conviction that their interests and the world's interests are one'. He believes that
'it is reasonable to assume that we have only just entered a long era of American
hegemony' (Kagan 2003: 88). In a later article in the journal of the American
foreign policy establishment, *Foreign Affairs*, Kagan sounded less convinced
when he pointed to 'a darker reality'. He wrote:

> A great philosophical schism has opened within the West, and mutual
> antagonism threatens to debilitate both sides of the transatlantic community.
> At a time when new dangers and crises are proliferating rapidly, this schism
> could have serious consequences. For Europe and the United States to come
> apart strategically is bad enough. But what if their differences over world order
> infect the rest of what we have known as the liberal West? Will the West still
> be the West? (Kagan 2004: 66)

Kagan (2004: 67) recognizes that this infection has already spread: '[For] the
first time since World War II, a majority of Europeans has come to doubt the
legitimacy of US power and of US global leadership'. Kagan prefers the
American view of a world that is threatened by dark forces. Most Europeans, he
notes, believe 'that the United States exaggerates international security threats'.

35

Kagan demurs: 'After September 11, 2001, most Americans fear they haven't taken those threats seriously enough.' For Kagan (2004: 87) herein lies a tragedy: 'To address today's global dangers, Americans will need the legitimacy that Europe can provide, but Europeans may well fail to grant it.' Postmodern Europe might succeed in 'debilitating the United States'. Europeans 'are betting that the risks posed by the "axis of evil", from terrorism to tyrants, will never be as great as the risk posed by the American leviathan unbound.' Kagan's American self-interpretation captures probably fairly well the idea of America that Bush and his supporters identify with. It is an America that is righteous, virtuous and powerful. Yet, contrary to their beliefs, this America does not represent any longer the hopes of Europe. It still gets applause, though, in recently empowered states on the periphery of Russia, states such as Georgia, the Ukraine and the Baltic republics.

The EU will not take over America's symbolic role, even if there may be some geopolitical strategists who contemplate an alternative role for the EU. At this point, the EU's unique promises lie somewhere else. Despite the fiscal crisis of the welfare state in almost all European societies, they will not abolish it, but rather attempt to sort out the essential from the peripheral pieces in the social safety net. For Europeans, the idea of the good life continues to include health coverage for all, heavily subsidized public education from first grade to university level, protection in old age, including long-term care insurance in some countries, paid vacations of at least two weeks for all employees, and paid maternity leave of varying length, etc. It also includes major public funding of cultural venues that the modern republics inherited from the monarchical states. In most EU member states, the national treasuries fund grand opera, ballet companies, national theatres, symphony orchestras, art and other museums. The peoples of Europe are still supporting the public funding of high culture.

The uneven distribution of the benefits of the traditional welfare state across the EU, however, will have to be confronted in light of the fiscal crisis in most European societies. The move from benefits to social rights remains a limited accomplishment primarily for the Scandinavian member states. Étienne Balibar's critique can be interpreted as a political challenge for the EU:

> To say that European unification depends on the possibility of inscribing a progress of citizenship in a "constitution" means to emphasize the following radical dichotomy: either Europe will institute social citizenship on more solid and broader bases than ever before, or it will in the long term become impossible. (Balibar 2004: 165)

This balancing act applies to all of Europe, but especially to the integration of the peoples of the former state socialist societies. The deep resentments that surfaced in 2004 in East Germany against the reform package of the SPD/Green government in Germany, which contributed to early new elections in Germany in September 2005, are an indication of the failure of communication within one country. This political failure in Germany may be also understood as a lack of communication within the EU. Still, Balibar does not only point to the West–East division over social rights. When he speaks about a 'refounding of Europe on the basis of a "Congress of European Peoples", or at least a conference of their governments, that could draw up a balance sheet of the consequences of the Cold War and the problems left behind …' (Balibar 2004: 167), he also thinks of the new immigrant proletariat that has been left out of the fragile social contract. He remarks:

> European citizenship is presented as the mechanism that includes some of the populations historically present in the space of the community while rejecting others, most of which are long established and contribute equally to the development of the civil society of the new organism. Foreigners have become *metics* or second-class citizens whose residence and activities are the object of particular surveillance. (Balibar 2004: 171)

Whoever belongs to this constituency deserves to be granted equal citizenship rights. The EU should not emulate the model of the US, which did not grant the people who were the slave labour force from 1789 to 1865 equal citizen rights until 100 years after emancipation. The refounding of Europe has to begin with the reinvention of active citizenship for all, whether they are native-born, foreign-born, immigrant or surplus labour from the periphery of the world economic system.

The EU has not begun to think about the political integration of the external proletariat that it will need to retain its level of productivity and standard of living. Despite the growing indications of resentment in the core states of the EU about this integration of immigrant populations, Europeans have not much choice. With declining birth rates and a growing percentage of older people in all societies, the demographic rejuvenation of the EU can only come from outside its present boundaries. Rigid border controls, therefore, make demographic sense only with the existence of fluid immigration policies. Without these policies and the evolution of transnational and Continental citizenship, the EU will fall victim to 'EU-sclerosis'. The announcement of the withdrawal of American troops from the Continent may be the necessary impetus for the people of Europe to take charge of their own affairs.

The imminent closing of military bases in Europe reflects primarily a new geostrategic thinking in the US and only secondarily dismay about a widespread European disenchantment with unilateral American power behaviour. However, the signs of political irritation on both sides of the Atlantic have been registered around the world. The Chinese political class especially has become intrigued by this development and the impact it may have on a multipolar world order. The Chinese scholar Lanxin Xiang (who teaches in Washington, DC, Geneva and Shanghai) envisions a 'Eurasian experiment' for China. He claimed in 2004 that the 'EU is at the top of the Chinese leadership's agenda' (Xiang 2004: 113). This unusual Chinese interest in other regions of the world is partly caused by the rising tensions in the Pacific. According to Xiang, 'the geopolitical instinct of the Beijing leadership tells it that a Eurasian orientation is safer for its foreign policy than a Pacific one. In the Pacific, potentially explosive issues are abundant ...' China would prefer to 'avoid dangerous entanglements'. The political class considers 'integrating into the current international system' and hopes that the EU will 'provide an alternative political and foreign policy model to the US'. Following Xiang's line of argument, Jacques Chirac and Gerhard Schröder's attempts at lifting the EU weapons embargo appear in a different light. They seem to respond positively to enquiries that have not registered on the public radar screen.

As important as this Chinese interest in the role of the EU in an emerging new world may be, equally, if not more important, is the notion that the Chinese political class looks at the constitutional process of the EU as a model for the necessary transformation of its own growingly unmanageable, centralized political system. The Chinese want the EU, as Xiang (2004: 118) writes, to succeed and 'put its own house in order'. The EU is considered an 'inspiration to the new generation of the Chinese leaders who are the heirs of China's revolutionary past' (2004: 117). The hope that the Chinese political class has invested especially in French leadership may have become damaged by the negative outcome of the referendum in May 2005. Still, looking at the America-Europe competition from a Chinese perspective, the Continental European republic may already have defeated the American empire in the realm of political imagination. What is to be done now is to translate the imaginary into political, and that means also constitutional, reality.

References

Albrecht, Clemens, et al., 1999, *Die intellektuelle Gründungsgeschichte der Bundesrepublik. Eine Wirkungsgeschichte der Frankfurter Schule*, Frankfurt/New York, Campus Verlag.

Aldinger, Charles, and Will Dunham, 2004, 'Rumsfeld, Officers Share Blame, Panel Says', *Washington Post*, August 24.

Anonymous, 2004, *Imperial Hubris. Why the West is Losing the War on Terror*, Washington, DC, Brassey's.

Atlas, James, 2003, 'A Classicist's Legacy: New Empire Builders', *New York Times*, May 4.

Bacevich, Andrew J., 2002, *American Empire. The Realities and Consequences of U.S. Diplomacy*, Cambridge, MA, and London, Harvard University Press.

Balibar, Étienne, 2004, *We, the People of Europe? Reflections on Transnational Citizenship*, Princeton, NJ, and Oxford, Princeton University Press.

Chakrabarty, Dipesh, 2000, *Provincializing Europe. Postcolonial Thought and Historical Difference*, Princeton, NJ, Oxford, Princeton University Press.

Clarke, Richard, 2004, *Against all Enemies. Inside America's War on Terror*, New York, Free Press.

Cohen, Roger, 2004, 'America Has Second Thoughts About a United Europe', *New York Times*, Sunday May 4, 'Week in Review', 3.

Danner, Mark, 2005, *Torture and Truth. America, Abu Ghraib and the War on Terror*, London, Granta.

Deutsch, K. L., and W. Nicgorski (eds), 1994, *Leo Strauss.. Political Philosopher and Jewish Thinker*, Lanham, MD, and London, Rowman and Littlefield.

Drew, Elizabeth, 2003, 'The Neocons in Power', *New York Review of Books*, June 12.

Eck, Dian L., 2001, *A New Religious America. How a 'Christian Country' Has Become the World's Most Religiously Diverse Nation*, San Francisco, Harper Collins.

Euben, Roxanne L., 1999, *Enemy in the Mirror. Islamic Fundamentalism and the Limits of Modern Rationalism*, Princeton, NJ, Princeton University Press.

Ferguson, Niall, 2004, *Colossus. The Price of America's Empire*, New York, The Penguin Press.

Graf, Friedrich-Wilhelm, 2004, *Die Wiederkehr der Götter. Religion in der modernen Kultur*, Munich, C. H. Beck.

Hardt, Michael, and Antonio Negri, 2000, *Empire*, Cambridge, MA, and London, Harvard University Press.

Johnson, Chalmers, 2004, *The Sorrows of Empire. Militarism, Secrecy, and the End of the Republic*, New York, Henry Holt.

Kagan, Robert S., 2003, *Of Paradise and Power. America in the New World*, New York, Knopf.

Kagan, Robert S., 2004, 'America's Crisis of Legitimacy', *Foreign Affairs*, May/April.

Kupchan, Charles, 2003, *The End of the American Era. U.S. Foreign Policy and the Geopolitics of the Twenty-First Century*, New York, Knopf.

Madison, James, Alexander Hamilton and John Jay, 1987, *The Federalist Papers*, ed. J. Krammick, New York, Penguin Books.

Manzetti, Mark, 2004, 'Army Deems Prisoner Abuse "Aberration"', *Honolulu Advertiser*, July 7.

Manzetti, Mark, 2005, 'Army Admits to Homicide in Detainee Deaths', *LA Times*, March 26.

McCormick, Thomas, 2005, 'American Hegemony and European Autonomy', in L. Gardner and M. B. Young (eds), *The New American Empire*, New York and London, The New Press.

Meier, Heinrich, 1995, *Carl Schmitt and Leo Strauss. The Hidden Dialogue*, Chicago and London, University of Chicago Press.

Müller, Jan-Werner, 2003, *A Dangerous Mind. Carl Schmitt in Post-War European Thought*, New Haven, CT, Yale University Press.

Norton, Anne, 2004, *Leo Strauss and the Politics of American Empire*, New Haven, CT, Yale University Press.

Ryn, Claes G., 2003, *America the Virtuous. The Crisis of American Democracy and the Quest for Empire*, New Brunswick, NJ, and London, Transaction Books.

Schenk, Armfried, 2004, 'Allah an der Tafel', *Die Zeit*, June 9.

Schmitt, Carl, 1996, *The Concept of the Political*, trans., intro. and notes George Schwab, with notes by Leo Strauss on Schmitt's essay, foreword by T. B. Strong, Chicago and London, University of Chicago Press.

Sciolino, Elane, 2004, 'God's Place in Charter is Dividing Europeans', *New York Times*, May 26.

Shorris, Earl, 2004, 'Ignoble Liars. Leo Strauss, George Bush, and the Philosophy of Mass Deception', *Harper's Magazine*, June.

Siedentop, Larry, 2001, *Democracy in Europe*, New York, Columbia University Press.

Strauss, Leo, 1993, 'The Mutual Influence of Theology and Philosophy', in *Faith and Political Philosophy. The Correspondence Between Leo Strauss and Eric Voegelin, 1934–1964*, ed. P. Emberly/Barry Cooper, University Park, PA, The Pennsylvania State University Press.

Strauss, Leo, 1996 [1932], 'Notes on Carl Schmitt's "Der Begriff des Politischen"', in Carl Schmitt, *The Concept of the Political*, trans., intro and notes by George Schwab, foreword by T. B. Strong, Chicago and London, University of Chicago Press.

Tocqueville, Alexis de, 1969, *Democracy in America*, ed. J. P. Mayer, Garden City, NY, Anchor Books.

Wehler, Hans-Ulrich, 2002, 'Das Türkenproblem', *Die Zeit*, September 17.

Wolin, Sheldon, 2001, *Tocqueville between Two Worlds. The Making of a Political and Theoretical Life*, Princeton, NJ, and Oxford, Princeton University Press.

Woodward, Bob, 2004, *Plan of Attack*, New York, Simon and Schuster.

Xiang, Lanxin, 2004, 'China's Eurasian Experiment', *Survival*, vol. 46, No. 2, Summer.

Yost, Peter, and Matt Kelley, 2005, 'Papers Detail Guantanamo Hearings', *Honolulu Advertiser*, April 9.

CHAPTER 2

Latin American Varieties of Modernity

Jorge Larrain

Following Castoriadis, I shall understand by 'modernity' the conjunction of two key significations: autonomy and control. Autonomy refers to the freedom of a society to make its own laws; control has to do with the expansion of rational mastery over the world of things, including the development of science and technology and their application to production and the control of nature (Castoriadis 1990: 15–17). Peter Wagner has developed this idea more precisely into an 'interpretative approach', which focuses on the responses that human beings give to certain basic *problématiques* of social life, responses that change with the onset of modernity. These *problématiques* are, first, the search for true knowledge (the epistemic *problématique*); second, the construction of a viable and good political order (the political *problématique*); and third, the way in which the satisfaction of needs is organized (the economic *problématique*) (Wagner 2001: 7). Responses to these *problématiques* do not lead to the same institutional solutions everywhere. For instance, Wagner distinguishes North American interpretations of rationality as instrumental rationality, and of autonomy as individual autonomy, from other interpretations that conceive of collective autonomy as collective self-determination and favour non-instrumental kinds of rationality (Wagner 2001: 17, 20). This is why it is possible to speak of different trajectories of modernity.

The first theories of modernization in the 1960s understood the combination of autonomy and rational control as realized solely and definitively in the institutions that emerged in Europe and the US. This led them to confuse a particular historical interpretation of modern principles with a general feature of modernity. As a result, modernization in newly developing countries was understood as an imitation of that which had occurred in more advanced countries. If it is accepted that the institutional solutions stemming from the projects of autonomy and control may vary from one place to another, and that they constitute neither a copy nor part of a process that follows a pre-established path, then the idea of there being different routes to modernity seems justified indeed.

This is the backdrop to the idea that modernization is an interpretative field, a disputed field of meanings, where a struggle takes place to institutionalize the imaginary significations of modernity in some specific sense. A country or region's basic structure of symbolic forms, its central cultural tendencies, have a crucial impact on the manner in which that country or region shapes its institutional responses to the imaginary significations of modernity. To study modernity in Latin America is, therefore, to study the cultural parameters that guide the institutional expressions of the three *problématiques* referred to by Wagner.

Nevertheless, in order properly to understand the way in which cultural factors influence the institutional responses to these *problématiques* of modernity, there is a clear need to avoid essentialist conceptions of culture and of cultural identity that fix symbolic meanings once and for all and ignore the possibility of cultural change. Essentialism is the source of many traditionalist positions in Latin America which are distrustful of modernity and find it incompatible with Latin American culture and identity. It is also the source of equally mistaken pro-modernist positions which assume that, in order to become modern, Latin America should substitute for its own cultural identity a new one imported from Europe.

Cultural Determinants of Latin America's Projects of Autonomy and Control

Although Latin America, Europe and the United States have embraced broadly similar imaginary significations of autonomy and control and have all tried to respond to the three *problématiques* of social life that structure the transition to modernity, it is important to explore to what extent the cultural differences between these regions have led to different institutions and therefore distinct paths to modernity.

Although the principal modernizing processes in Latin America started rather late, with the achievement of independence, there is no doubt that the cultural features that evolved during three centuries of colonial rule (1492–1810) have conditioned these processes ever since. Claudio Véliz has argued that in Latin America there have been four key historical absences, which mark substantial differences with European modernity: the absence of feudalism, the absence of religious dissidence, the absence of an industrial revolution and the absence of something similar to the French Revolution (Véliz 1984: 15–16).

If we put this in positive terms, i.e., in terms of what effectively existed in the place of these absences, we could say that there was, first, political centralism unchallenged by local powers; second, a Catholic religious monopoly unchallenged by Protestant denominations or popular religious movements; third, an economic drive, initially oriented towards the export of raw materials and subsequently towards limited state-promoted and state-controlled industrialization, which did not create strong and independent industrial bourgeoisies and proletariats; and finally, a principle of authoritarian political power which gave way to a top-down version of democracy without bourgeois or popular underpinnings and was, therefore, markedly non-participatory. All these elements point to a strong centralist cultural tradition in Latin America.

The project of autonomy in Latin America began as a consequence of an external historical development – the Napoleonic invasion of Spain – more than as a consequence of any endogenous liberationist movement within the colonies themselves. Although this may explain the serious limitations of the emerging democracies, there is no doubt that the quest for autonomy, this key imaginary signification of modernity, both in its political and epistemic dimensions, emerged during the nineteenth century after the victorious wars of independence. As regards the project of control, the situation was somewhat different: the ruling landowning oligarchies were not interested in the development of industry and industrial capitalism of the kind that, in Europe, was so crucial for the expansion of rational control over nature. In Latin America the ruling classes chose to export the products of their haciendas, and, far from rationalizing production or introducing technology, they increasingly imposed extra-economic forms of coercion upon their peasants, showing little concern for their low productivity.

Capitalism slowly began to emerge in Latin America during the second half of the nineteenth century. Arguably this means, therefore, that in Latin America the project of autonomy (self-government) has taken priority over the expansion of rational control. While the latter also developed, it did so later and more weakly. The development of industrial production, science and the control of nature has always been less dynamic in Latin America than in Europe or North America. In my view, while this imbalance has not been enough to prevent the development of modernity in Latin America, it has led to its being institutionalized in a distinct manner.

Several authors have analysed this imbalance as the cause of economic underdevelopment and authoritarian forms of government in Latin America. Aníbal Pinto, for example, compares the advanced political and social organization of Chile with its very meagre and feeble economic base and reads this disjuncture as the cause of the country's underdevelopment (Pinto 1962: 129–30). Nicos Mouzelis has elaborated a similar thesis for the wider context of the semi-periphery, taking in Latin America, Greece and the Balkans. For him, the semi-periphery has typically experienced political and social development before economic development. The adoption of liberal ideas and parliamentary institutions contributed to the early mobilization of non-oligarchic political groups and the broadening of political participation before the advent of industrialization. This mobilization, in the absence of strong bourgeoisies and working classes and in the absence of a firm economic base, led to the formation of populist political movements, the accentuation of economic contradictions and, eventually, to authoritarian forms of government (Mouzelis 1986: 6–7, 13–15).

In turn, Claudio Véliz links this imbalance to the nature of Latin American Baroque identity, which in his view has engendered systematic cultural resistance to modernity. For as long as a cultural identity derived from the Catholic Counter-Reformation is maintained, the inevitable consequence will be the failure of modernity. According to Véliz, this identity is averse to change and risk-taking, it distrusts the new, it accords too much respect to the ascribed status of individuals, it prefers stability and central control to transformation and freedom and, therefore, it is inherently inimical to a modern economy (Véliz 1994: 180, 198). In Véliz's view, modernity requires a cultural identity similar to the Anglo-Saxon one, but only since the 1990s has Latin America started to rid itself of its Baroque identity under the impact of commodities born of Anglo-Saxon industrial capitalism.

The theses of Pinto and Mouzelis about the impact of this imbalance upon the projects of autonomy and control are plausible. The delay of industrialization until the beginning of the twentieth century has something to do with the economic underdevelopment of Latin America. As Hinkelammert has argued, the very technological revolution that conditioned the industrialization process in the twentieth century made the industrialization of new countries much more difficult, since they could not initiate it with their own traditional technology (Hinkelammert 1972: 82). It is also plausible to maintain that a situation in which weak economies are incapable of satisfying the demands of highly organized social movements, which are mobilized and legitimized by a more advanced democratic political system, can lead to authoritarian breakdowns when social pressure overwhelms the political capacity to deal with it. In respect of Véliz's thesis, however, important doubts arise, given that he seems to advocate the substitution of an Anglo-Saxon cultural identity for the Latin American one in order for modernity to develop. This is not only highly problematic and unlikely in itself, but it also mistakes a particular cultural feature of Anglo-Saxon modernity for a general feature of any modernity.

It is important to understand this original weakness of the control project in Latin America, not as a permanent technological incapacity, or as a culturally determined, once-and-for-all alternative orientation to instrumental reason. In contrast to Véliz, who at least believes that a radical change in Latin American identity is possible and desirable, other religiously oriented, essentialist conceptions of Latin American identity argue that the instrumental rationality heralded by European enlightened modernity definitely does not form a part of Latin American identity, which is more oriented towards traditional wisdom and aesthetic-religious knowledge than to scientific knowledge, and more inclined to dramatic representations than to logical and abstract discourse (Morandé 1984: 144–45). These visions have no plausible justification and become a kind of cultural determinism which would impede the progress of any project of control in Latin America.

The Autonomy Project in Latin America

The autonomy project in Latin America has differed in several regards from the trajectories of North America and Europe. Its centralist and authoritarian features and the absence of a strong bourgeoisie give a special character to democracy and to the first attempts at epistemic autonomy in Latin America. Even if the birth of modern nation states and their democratic institutions in Europe entailed a process of centralization, what is understood as centralism in Latin America is different, in that it is not associated with a process of industrialization or with a revolutionary political tradition of nationalist and egalitarian character (Véliz 1984: 19). Latin American centralism was consolidated before independence and industrialization upon the basis of a legalistic and authoritarian bureaucracy imposed by the Spanish kings. This kind of centralism included very extensive religious powers.

With independence, the project of autonomy started in earnest in Latin America. But it was strongly conditioned by authoritarian and centralist features as much as by the deeply ingrained Catholic religion, inherited from three centuries of colonial rule and unchallenged by real revolution. In relation to the epistemic *problématique*, religious, press and educational freedoms were established in most countries. Many newspapers emerged, which took upon themselves the mission of spreading republican and liberal ideas. Responses to the political *problématique* initially contemplated a series of liberal constitutional projects designed to establish democratic governments and to build decentralized federal republics. Most of them established the separation of state powers, thus creating judiciaries and parliaments with free elections at the national and local levels, introduced declarations of human and citizens' rights and guaranteed a free press.

But all of these changes were riddled with ambiguities. Without doubt, the responses to the epistemic *problématique* were initially very weak. Education was restricted to a tiny segment of the population and other religions had little real chance to expand, since Catholicism remained the official state religion in most countries. The weight of what Catholicism considered to be the truth was still overwhelming and was disseminated through its control of virtually all available education. After independence, the press suffered the consequences of the anarchistic struggles for power and the political instability that ensued in many countries. It became highly militant, partisan and ephemeral, and was thus repressed by the governments of the day.

On the political side, responses were stronger and more institutionalized, but, all the same, ambiguous. Three characteristics of the first constitutional attempts should be highlighted. First, they were imitative in character: most of them very closely copied European or North American models. As Hartlyn and Valenzuela show, 'in a very short period, from 1811 (Chile, Colombia, Venezuela) to 1830 (Uruguay), seventeen countries promulgated republican constitutions which to a greater or lesser extent were inspired on the document drafted in Philadelphia in 1787' (Hartlyn and Valenzuela 1997: 19).

Second, they tended to be ephemeral and unsuccessful: very few survived. The 1823 Chilean Constitution proposed by Juan Egaña lasted exactly one year. In many cases during the first half of the nineteenth century, the new republics fell under dictatorships such as that of Santa Anna in Mexico or Rosas in Argentina, or at least under authoritarian governments such as those of Rivera in Uruguay, Páez in Venezuela and Santander in Colombia. As Hale has argued, liberal ideas were applied in an environment that was 'resistant and hostile', 'in countries which were highly stratified, socially and racially, and economically underdeveloped and in which the tradition of centralised state authority ran deep' (Hale 1986: 368).

Third, they managed to achieve only a very limited amount of popular participation. The right to vote was limited to a male, literate and high-income minority, which excluded between 90 and 95 per cent of the population. Restrictions on those who could be elected were even more strict. Electoral fraud was frequently resorted to in order to secure elections (Bushnell and Macaulay 1988: Chapter 2). A growing gap appeared between the liberal and democratic principles expressed in constitutions and laws on the one hand and political practice on the other. Even so, the creation of representative democratic institutions and elections, for all their imperfections, constituted a notable advance of the autonomy project in comparison with that which existed in colonial times.

Even if there was clear progress, an original weakness of the political project of autonomy can be detected: it was not underpinned by movements of sufficient social base, nor was it led by a well-consolidated bourgeois class. Its foundation was rather an alliance between: a) the military chiefs who, after fighting for independence, became landowners; and b) an enthusiastic but very small, liberal, pro-European intelligentsia. This narrow base allows one to speak of an 'oligarchic modernity' emerging in the course of the nineteenth century.

With the triumph of liberal ideas during the second half of the nineteenth century, the responses to the epistemic *problématique* became more solid. Liberalism did not express itself in a collective project of autonomy emphasizing political and economic democratization, but rather in struggles to liberate citizens from religious tutelage in matters such as marriages, births, cemeteries and education. A powerful anticlericalism emerged which, although not necessarily anti-religious in character (the great majority of people continued to be Catholic), sought to do away with the ecclesiastical privileges through which the Church had exercised its power over common people. Liberal and radical parties fought major battles with the Catholic Church during the second half of the nineteenth century in order to achieve these objectives.

In this way, the state assumed control of education, lay cemeteries and civil registries of births, marriages and deaths. Clerical judicial privilege was abolished. The separation of the state and the Catholic Church was introduced everywhere. All this contributed to the completion of a significant part of the autonomy project: the end of the religious monopoly of the Catholic Church and, above all, the consolidation of epistemic autonomy. The foremost nineteenth-century intellectuals struggled for 'mental emancipation', as the Mexican Gabino Barreda called it (Barreda 1983: 26). Political independence was not enough: it was also necessary to change old habits of thought, to renovate customs, and to abandon colonial attitudes. Under the idea of 'mental emancipation', Barreda advocated three kinds of emancipation: scientific, religious and political.

The Chileans Bilbao and Lastarria were other important examples of intellectuals committed to this process. The former called for the de-Hispanicizing and de-Catholicizing of Chile and Latin America (Bilbao 1993: 58); the latter maintained that '*the emancipation of the spirit* is the great objective of the Hispano-American revolution'. He considered the Spanish tutelage barren and exhorted Latin Americans to reconstruct social science as the Anglo-Americans had done (Lastarria 1993: 499, 505). These visions manifested themselves in attempts to refashion higher education so as to form a new elite.

New institutions were created to become centres of modern science: in Mexico the *Escuela Nacional Preparatoria*, inspired by Barreda; in Argentina the *Escuela Normal de Paraná*, formed by Sarmiento; in Chile the *Instituto Pedagógico* of the University of Chile, created by Letelier; and in Brazil the *Escola Militar* managed by Constant (Hale 1986: 384–85).

Sarmiento's famous antithesis of civilization and barbarism also falls into this tradition. He and his followers rejected the Hispanic tradition and hoped that North American or European policies (aided by white immigration and education) could be put into practice to compensate for the inherent deficiencies stemming from the racial inferiority of the Latin American ethnic inheritance. But the contradictory nature of these projects of epistemic autonomy is obvious: they sought to free the mind from traditional Spanish culture only in order to embrace French and North American culture. They did not see any problem in substituting one foreign cultural legacy for another, something that rather confirms the extroverted and imitative character of the process.

The Widening of the Political Autonomy Project and the Beginnings of the Control Project

The struggle for autonomy against Catholicism and Hispanic culture not only had imitative and extroverted features but also it increased the centralist features of Latin American democracies, as the state took control of education and other cultural institutions. It is not surprising, then, that during the first half of the twentieth century, when the export crisis brought about the downfall of the oligarchic governments, it was the state that played a central role in two substantial advances of modernity: first, the expansion of political autonomy in a collective sense by the widening of the franchise (thereby allowing the middle and working classes to participate in the political system from which they had been so far excluded); and second, the introduction in the 1930s of import substitution as a means to industrialization, which advanced the project of control.

While Europe was living through a crisis of liberal industrialism, in Latin America it was the predominant export-oriented aristocratic and oligarchic system that was entering its terminal phase. The political crisis of the old system that ultimately led to new national populist regimes and to a partially successful process of import substitution was precipitated by economic collapse. Populist movements sought to initiate a process of transformation that widened voting rights and democratized the political structures which, until then, had been totally under the control of the oligarchy. In order to gain political power, they sought the support of the masses by offering them new employment and new forms of welfare state and social legislation, and even by taking steps to organize them. Peron in Argentina and Vargas in Brazil organized trade unions from within the state.

The widening of the autonomy project, with the incorporation of the middle classes into political power and the implementation of social legislation, was not free of authoritarian tendencies and transformations. As Véliz has shown, 'during the three years that followed the Great Depression of 1929, seventeen governments of twelve Latin American countries were overthrown by force' (Véliz 1984: 273). In several cases, it was these military interventions that gave rise to the populist and nationalist regimes that widened political participation and established numerous social laws from above and against the conservative forces entrenched in parliaments.

Thus, between 1930 and 1970 a form of modernity that widened the project of autonomy and began to make progress in the project of control with industrialization came to be consolidated in Latin America. Industrialization was realized with heavy state protection and investment which survived practically until the end of the 1970s. The incipient bourgeois class that was created was a result of these state promotion policies, not prior to them, as in Europe. But even so, it could be argued that the general orientation of the modernizing process in Latin America at this time had more of a European imprint than a North American one, in the sense that the centralism typical of the region favoured a project of collective autonomy over the North American model of individual autonomy. This determined the creation of welfare states and forms of social legislation comparable to European models.

Notwithstanding this, important differences remain between the European tradition of collective autonomy and the Latin American one. The principal difference concerns the more decentralized character of European modernity. This affects the project of autonomy as much as the project of control. While the parliamentary system in Europe tends to distribute power more evenly, the presidential system in Latin America concentrates power. Whereas the British industrial bourgeoisie is born far away from the centres of power and the state, in small provincial workshops, the Latin American industrial bourgeoisie is created by state action and has always been much more dependent on state aid to exist and prosper. A second important difference has to do with the practical efficacy of citizens' rights. While in Europe there is a greater correspondence between citizens' rights and their respect in practice, in Latin America the rights embodied in constitutions and laws often lack guarantees and accessible procedures to protect them in practice.

The consequences of this are important. First, Latin American presidentialism is an important source of serious conflicts between the executive and legislative powers – more than in European parliamentary regimes. This factor has contributed to the political instability of Latin America, since both presidents and parliaments claim popular legitimacy and tend to blame each other for their problems (Hartlyn and Valenzuela 1997: 23). Second, state fostering of entrepreneurial classes has led these classes to interfere much more actively in politics in order to achieve favourable conditions, something that is also destabilizing and potentially increases the chances of corruption. Third, 'the majority of subjects experience the insecure and unpredictable character of their rights' (Whitehead 1997: 69) and are often defenceless in the face of the enormous power of the state and of entrepreneurs. This is related to what O'Donnell has called 'a democracy of low intensity citizenship', which occurs when the state is unable to enforce the rule of law, not so much in the area of political rights as in the area of civil rights: 'peasants, slum-dwellers, Indians, women, et al. are often unable to get fair treatment in the courts, or to obtain from state agencies services to which they are entitled, or to be safe from police violence ... etc.' (O'Donnell 1993: 16).

The big gap that sometimes exists in Latin America between a clearly established legal system and its practical enforcement is also related to a cultural feature that derives from colonial times and which is well captured by the saying '*se acata pero no se cumple*' (it is obeyed but not implemented). This is a kind of double standard, whereby the practical unwillingness to comply with a norm does not question its validity or legitimacy, but, on the contrary, proclaims respect for it. Principles are transgressed, but in such a way that they are simultaneously recognized, thus keeping the appearance of respect for authority that is so important in Latin America. The saying was coined to deal with royal edicts that the conquerors found impractical. Similarly, the Indians forced to convert to Catholicism under duress publicly accepted the new religion but secretly continued to practise their own.

Some authors have expressed the difference between Europe and Latin America by means of a distinction between polycentric and concentric structures (Mascareño 2000; Leiva 2003). European modern societies are seen as polycentric because their diverse and differentiated systems of politics, law, economy, religion, science and art have 'a high level of autonomy and capacity for self-organization' which impedes the possibility 'that one of them assumes the control of the others and puts itself at the centre of society' (Mascareño 2004: 68–69). By contrast, in Latin American concentric societies, although there is functional differentiation this has not impeded the primacy of the political system over the other systems which it instrumentalizes and uses, imposing upon them its own logic (Mascareño 2004: footnote 15). In other words, the autonomy of politics is realized at the cost of the autonomy of the other spheres.

In contrast to the modernity of Europe and North America, Latin American modernity suffers from a 'voracity of politics which swallows everything and behind which everyone seeks protection or justification: equally entrepreneurs, intellectuals, universities, trade unions, social organizations, clerics, the armed forces' (Brunner 1988: 33). As a consequence of the enormous pull of politics and the state, civil society in Latin America is weak and highly dependent upon state political dictates.

Modernity in the Neo-Liberal Stage

The stage of protected and centralized modernization came to an end in the 1970s when, in the context of international crisis and under the threat of increasingly radicalized left-wing urban movements, a new wave of military coups hit Latin America. Right-wing dictatorships were established, which were not only more durable than those of the 1930s but also had longer-term social and economic impacts, associated with the application of new liberal economic policies. What is interesting and what confirms trends already present in the nineteenth century is that the renewed liberal character of the economy was able to coexist with political authoritarianism.

This had two important effects on the modernizing processes: the reaffirmation of the authoritarian centralist tendency in conflict with the rule of law; and a shift from the influence of the European model of collective autonomy to the influence of the North American model of individual autonomy. The common element of these two effects was the expanding presence of the United States. There is little doubt that the authoritarian centralist tendency in Latin America was compounded by the logic of the Cold War. The increasingly open intervention of the United States in order to prevent countries going communist was certainly related to the new wave of military takeovers. But it also influenced the way in which social and economic policies were increasingly modelled on the United States example of individual autonomy.

Reaffirmation of Authoritarian Logic and Concentric Modernity

A general overview of Latin American history cannot but see repeated breakdowns of democracy and the recurrent presence of dictatorships. In the twentieth century alone there were three periods in which a good number of Latin American governments were overthrown by force: 1930–1933, 1948–1954 and 1964–1980. What was relatively new about the period 1964–1980 was the context of heightened Cold War tensions and the more or less open intervention of the United States beyond Central America.

True, since 1990 there has been a massive return to democracy and dictatorships have not recurred in Latin America. But political instability has been growing since 2000 in countries such as Peru, Bolivia, Argentina, Venezuela, Colombia and others. The failed coup attempt against Chavez in Venezuela, the swift succession of resigning presidents in Argentina (five presidents in two weeks), the resignation of Fujimori in Peru and Sanchez de Lozada in Bolivia, and the precarious positions of Toledo in Peru and Meza in Bolivia, are symptoms of political systems in which the rule of law is frequently bypassed.

Even if the last series of military coups in the 1970s was related to the Cold War, there is also another factor that is producing instability in the post-Cold War period. In this respect a comparison with Europe is telling. It could be argued that the greater stability of European modernity is due to a kind of compromise between the political system and the legal system whereby each respects the autonomy of the other in such a way that decisions taken within the political domain are always processed by means of the law and help to enforce the rule of law in every sphere of society. On the contrary, it can be shown that Latin American political instability is due to a mismatch between the political and the legal systems, such that there is a tendency for political decisions to be implemented through sheer power but not properly processed via the legal system (Mascareño 2004: 65).

This can be explained again by the concentric character of Latin America's modernity, in which politics has acquired primacy over other spheres and often violates the rule of law, or rather bends it to its own interests, or prevents it from fulfilling its role in other spheres. Given the character of Latin American culture, the overriding of the rule of law is almost always accompanied by a strong nominal legalism which seeks juridical justifications. But ultimately the point is that the trade-off between power and legality is weaker in Latin America, given the cultural centrality of power and authority. The European polycentric structure, on the contrary, guarantees that politics, even if it also plays a central role, respects the autonomy of the rule of law and avoids flouting it.

More recently, there has been a tendency for some authors to argue that even if the concentric character of Latin American modernity has not changed in the sense of evolving towards a polycentric pattern, it has certainly evolved in the sense that the economy displaced politics as the main axis or central system. Not only did the market acquire autonomy in relation to the political system, but, according to these authors, it also instrumentalized politics by imposing its own logic (Mascareño 2000: 194–95; Cousiño and Valenzuela 1994: 17; Garretón 2000: 165; Leiva 2003: 270–72).

It is true that the economic system has been gaining autonomy in Latin America since the 1990s, with the arrival of neo-liberalism and its market-oriented economic policies, but this does not mean that the economic system has replaced politics in a concentric pattern, or that it has acquired the same weight as politics. The autonomy of the economic system continues to be very fragile and frequently threatened by decisions of political intervention. Power politics continues to be the central element that has been unable fully to subject itself to the law in Latin America. There have been numerous examples where arbitrary decisions from above have interfered with the autonomous operation of the economy. It cannot be maintained that the autonomy of the economic system has displaced the preponderance of the political system.

From Collective to Individual Autonomy
The second effect of changes that have occurred since 1970 in Latin America has been the transition from an orientation towards a European model of collective autonomy and state intervention to an orientation towards a North American model of individual autonomy and lesser state intervention. This has meant in variable degrees the privatization of public education, health and social security, the sale of state public services, the loss of power of trade unions and social organizations and, generally, the conceptualization of citizens as individual consumers of goods and services in the market. It has also meant the end of a series of interventionist economic policies.

True, it could be argued that the same is happening in Europe; but the welfare state, public health and education, as outcomes of the exercise of collective autonomy, even if trimmed and cut here and there, have not been and will not be dismantled to the extreme extent that they were, for example, in Chile during Pinochet's dictatorship. Besides, economic policies in Europe have been coordinated, harmonized and regulated by the European Union for all the member states, which up to a point implies a larger degree of intervention in the project of control.

Summing up, in Latin America during the nineteenth century we have the pre-eminence of the project of autonomy over the project of control; when the project of control takes shape in the twentieth century, it develops in a highly centralized and state-dependent way. When the project of autonomy breaks down in the 1970s with the military takeovers, the project of control acquires a more liberal character, following more closely the North American model. Democracy returns in the 1980s with a more individualistic character and without having overcome the tendency for political power to go beyond the rule of law. Thus it can be seen that one of the main differences between Latin American and European modernities is the type of articulation between politics and the economy. Whereas in Europe there seems to be greater consistency between a collective project of autonomy and a project of control regulated by the state or the European Union, in Latin America there is a coexistence between individualistic and authoritarian features in politics and liberalism in economics.

Is there a contradiction in the notion that Latin America starts to move in the 1970s towards a more individualistic, North American model of autonomy while retaining centralist and authoritarian features? I do not think so. What an individualistic model does is cut the incentives for collective projects and favour the atomized vote of the consumer citizen. But this does not necessarily have to do with the cultural role of authority. In the United States an individualistic project of autonomy coexists with a certain decentralization of power and a rather strict attachment to legal mechanisms. By contrast, in Latin America the increasingly individualistic autonomy project coexists with centralism and tendencies to exceed the law.

An argument could be made that somehow this situation is related to the role of Catholicism in Latin America. Not just Catholicism in the general sense, but a particular version of it with strong cultic leanings that favours external rituals over deep conversion. It is a more traditional and defensive kind of Catholicism, which harks back to the Counter-Reformation and displays an undisguised longing for the era of Christendom when the value of authority and the right of the hierarchy to uphold Christian values for the whole of society were unchallenged. By contrast, the European and North American trajectories to modernity were influenced by a Protestant ethic that values democracy and the rule of law and the scientific and rational control of nature. The Latin American trajectory to modernity has been influenced by traditional Catholicism and by authoritarian and centralist forms of government, and has had a less marked orientation towards the rational control of nature and towards technology. The enormous cultural weight of traditional Catholicism in Latin America has no doubt been related to the great success and acceptance of Hayek's brand of neo-liberalism in the region.

What Hayek proposed was a conservative liberalism, opposed to the social liberalism of Mill, Voltaire and Rousseau, which emphasizes liberty, democracy and equality. Hayek highlighted three elements of his kind of liberalism, which fit perfectly with the Catholicism of the region: first, an evolutionist interpretation of culture and an inherent respect for tradition; second, a full understanding of the limitations of reason and, consequently, a distrust of all attempts at constructing a social order by means of planning; and third, a separation of liberalism from democracy. According to Hayek, democracy accords absolute power to the majority and thus there is the possibility that it could become anti-liberal (Hayek 1978: 161).

Weber's classic thesis linked Calvinism and Protestant Puritanism with the rationalist spirit of capitalism. Traditional, cultic Catholicism appears to have a greater affinity with Hayek's type of neo-liberalism. In his conception, religion, authoritarianism and the free market become fused. This could help explain the greater ease with which an overwhelmingly Catholic Latin America has adopted a more radical sort of neo-liberalism, while in Protestant countries a stronger bond survives between Protestantism, democracy and rational constructivism.

The supremacy of neo-liberalism in Latin America is also related to the renewed weakness of the control project. After almost half a century of state-protected and state-promoted industrialization, the new policies of openness to the international market and of state non-intervention mean the abandonment of industrialization and attempts to acquire new productive technologies. The unquestioned dominance of the theory of comparative advantage has given a rationale to the idea that some countries will never industrialize in so far as others have accumulated comparative advantages in that area. With the exception of Brazil and Mexico, this could be the case in the majority of Latin American countries, which basically continue to export raw materials.

Free trade and neo-liberal economic policies have brought about a considerable diminution of industrial production and employment in Latin America. Only Mexico and Brazil have managed to expand their industrial exports. The rest have managed only to diversify the export of primary products, thus making more permanent the low level of industrial production and employment. In this respect, the Latin American trajectory to modernity has been very different from the Asiatic one, where the state took an important role in the acquisition and adaptation of state-of-the-art technologies and in the promotion of industrial exports (Gwynne 1996: 220, 228–29).

Latin American Modernity and Varieties of World-Making

In spite of some macroeconomic gains like the control of inflation, the influx of foreign capital and fiscal stability, the social impact of radical neo-liberal policies in Latin America, plus the results of the economic crisis that began in 2000, have been on the whole very negative: a steady rise in unemployment, downward pressures on real wages, reduction in the minimum wage, increased inequalities in the distribution of wealth and a substantial increase in poverty (Gwynne and Kay 2004: 253–60). These negative results have brought about strong resistance to the model practically everywhere in the region, but the lack of clear-cut alternatives, due partly to the ideological success of neo-liberalism and partly to the collapse of socialist policies, makes the resistance less powerful and significant. Besides, resistance varies from place to place. Three patterns seem to be emerging. A first group of countries, including Venezuela, Bolivia, Argentina and Uruguay, have been hit so hard by an economic and political crisis that their political stability is threatened and their governments and populations are increasingly disaffected with globalization and the leadership of the US. A second group, including Peru, Ecuador and Colombia, also in deep crisis, suffer from an important split between the populations, which are mostly disaffected and disillusioned, and the governments, which still want to pursue American-led globalization as the means to recovery. Finally, there are Chile and Mexico which, in spite of certain difficulties, have managed to grow and have fully embraced American-sponsored globalization. Popular resistance to globalization in these countries is far less marked. Brazil does not seem to fit well into this classification and may be in a category of its own. It is more stable politically and more orthodox in its economic policies than the countries of the first group. Its people are not as disaffected with the government as are the populations of the second group. Yet it is far less keen on United States-led globalization than Chile or Mexico.

It is difficult, therefore, to generalize for the whole of Latin America. Still, two features brought about by the neo-liberal stage seem to affect most countries in the region. First is the renewed weakness of the control project, prompted by free trade and liberal policies which have resulted, barring two exceptions, in a process of deindustrialization. Second is a weakening of the political autonomy project: throughout the region a relative depoliticization of society and political instability have been growing. True, democracies have managed to survive since the 1990s, but increasing resistance to the system manifests itself in growing problems of governance and disaffection in respect of parties, politicians and even democracy itself, especially among the young.

These two effects represent a sea change in the process of modernization. The neo-liberal stage has brought about a process of deinstitutionalization of the responses to the political and economic *problématiques* that had been predominant during the first seventy years of the twentieth century. In respect of the economic *problématique*, commercialism, trade and financial strategies concerned with primary products and services have come to replace the goal of technologically advanced industrial production. As for the political *problématique*, democratic institutions have survived, but people are deeply disaffected with them and seem not to believe in them any more. In the economic realm there is at least a new neo-liberal institutional framework emerging; in the political field, the old institutions have lost the support of the masses, but no new ones are emerging. This is extremely dangerous for the future. Without a strengthened project of control and the rejuvenation of popular support for democracy, the future of modernity in Latin America looks uncertain.

The shift towards a project of individual autonomy modelled on North American institutions, which has made such inroads into Latin America, is nevertheless, up to a point, counterbalanced by a growing perception that a balkanized Latin America will not be able to face up to the challenges of a globalized world. This is where the example of the European Union's world-making, with its collective autonomy project, still exercises considerable appeal in Latin America (even if European social democracy is in crisis). There is the political intuition that Latin America badly needs a similar kind of union to be able to have a say in the regulation of a globalized world. It is true that in many respects the North American-inspired neo-liberal programme is still stronger in the region, and there does not seem to be enough political will to implement anything remotely similar to the European Union. But this is precisely the challenge of the future and it is what Latin America will have to decide in order to make its own world-making count in an increasingly complicated world.

References

Barreda, Gabino, 1983, 'Oración Cívica', recited on September 16 1867, in O. Terán (ed.), *América Latina: Positivismo y Nación*, Mexico, Editorial Katún.

Bilbao, Francisco, 1993, 'Iniciativa de la América. Idea de un Congreso Federal de las Repúblicas', in Leopoldo Zea (ed.), *Fuentes de la Cultura Latinoamericana*, vol. 1, México, Fondo de Cultura Económica.

Brunner, J. J., 1988, *El Espejo Trizado*, Santiago, FLACSO.

Bushnell, D., and N. Macaulay, 1988, *The Emergence of Latin America in the Nineteenth Century*, Oxford, Oxford University Press.

Castoriadis, Cornelius, 1990, *El Mundo Fragmentado*, Buenos Aires, Altamira.

Cousiño, C., and E. Valenzuela, 1994, *Politización y Monetarización en América Latina*, Santiago, Cuadernos del Instituto de Sociología, Universidad Católica de Chile.

Garretón, M. A., 2000, *La sociedad en que vivi(re)mos, Introducción sociológica al cambio de siglo*, Santiago, LOM.

Gwynne, Robert, 1996, 'Industrialization and Urbanization', in D. Preston (ed.), *Latin American Development*, Harlow, Longman.

Gwynne, R., and C. Kay, 2004, 'The Alternatives to Neoliberalism', in R. Gwynne and C. Kay (eds), *Latin America Transformed, Globalization and Modernity*, London, Arnold.

Hale, Charles, 1986, 'Political and Social Ideas in Latin America, 1870–1930', in L. Bethell (ed.), *The Cambridge History of Latin America*, vol. 4, Cambridge, Cambridge University Press.

Hartlyn, J., and A. Valenzuela, 1997, 'La democracia en América Latina desde 1930', in L. Bethell (ed.), *Historia de América Latina*, vol. 12, *Política y Sociedad desde 1930*, Barcelona, Grijalbo Mondadori.

Hayek, Friedrich, 1978, 'The Principles of a Liberal Social Order', in F. Hayek, *Studies in Philosophy, Politics and Economics*, London, Routledge and Kegan Paul.

Hinkelammert, Franz, 1972, *Dialéctica del Desarrollo Desigual*, Valparaíso, Ediciones Universitarias de Valparaíso.

Lastarria, José Victorino, 1993, *La América*, fragments in Leopoldo Zea (ed.), *Fuentes de* la *Cultura Latinoamericana*, vol. 2, México, Fondo de Cultura Económica.

Leiva, Felipe, 2003, 'Consideraciones en torno a la intervención política en la constitución que nos rige como forma especial de situarnos en la modernidad', *Persona y Sociedad*, vol. XVII, no. 3.

Mascareño, Aldo, 2000, 'Diferenciación funcional en América Latina: los contornos de una sociedad concéntrica y los dilemas de su transformación', *Persona y Sociedad*, vol. XIV, no. 1.

— 2004, 'Sociología del Derecho', *Persona y Sociedad*, vol. XVIII, no. 2.

Morandé, Pedro, 1984, *Cultura y Modernización en América Latina*, Santiago, Cuadernos del Instituto de Sociología, Universidad Católica de Chile.

Mouzelis, Nicos, 1986, *Politics in the Semi-Periphery*, London, Macmillan.

O'Donnell, Guillermo, 1993, 'On the State, Democratization and Some Conceptual Problems', Working Paper no. 192, April, Kellogg Institute, University of Notre Dame.

Pinto, Aníbal, 1962, *Chile, un caso de desarrollo frustrado*, Santiago, Editorial Universitaria.

Véliz, Claudio, 1984, *La tradición centralista de América Latina*, Barcelona, Ariel.

— 1994, *The New World of the Gothic Fox: Culture and Economy in English and Spanish America*, Berkeley, University of California Press.

Wagner, Peter, 2001, 'Modernity, Capitalism and Critique', *Thesis Eleven*, no. 66, August.

Whitehead, Laurence, 1997, 'Una nota sobre la ciudadanía en América Latina', in L. Bethell (ed.), *Historia de América Latina*, vol. 12, *Política y Sociedad desde 1930*, Barcelona, Grijalbo Mondadori.

CHAPTER 3

Multiple Modernities or Global Interconnections: Understanding the Global Post the Colonial

Gurminder K. Bhambra

The colonial encounter has been a defining moment in the making of the contemporary world. It has *made* a particular world and established cognitive patterns for *knowing* the world, yet the colonial encounter is missing in most sociological accounts of modernity. In recent times, increasing significance has been given to global phenomena. Acknowledging the complexity brought by globalization and interdependence has led theorists to contend that a new approach to modernity is needed. A shift from the singular trajectory of modernity to multiple modernities has been recommended (Arnason 2000; Delanty 2004; Eisenstadt 2000, 2001, 2004; Eisenstadt and Schluchter 1998; Wittrock 1998, 2000). However, I argue that a more thoroughgoing analysis is still needed: one that reappraises the underlying assumptions upon which the discourses and practices of modernity are premised and one that addresses colonialism and other interconnections within a truly global social inquiry.

Globalization: The Universalization of Western Particularities

This chapter contends that the worlds we inhabit, just like the worlds that have been inhabited in the past, are the products of historical flows of people, goods and ideas that intersect and transcend particular localities. Cultural forms and social practices are both *interconnected* and constituted in those interconnections. There are no entities that are not hybrid, that are not always and already hybrid. Yet, as Trouillot (2003) argues, our understandings of the world are rarely posited in these terms. Indeed, as the Introduction to this volume highlights, the sense of living in a common world is increasingly lost in discussions between those in favour of globalization and those against it – as if the world were not already global (and, in fact, has been so for a very considerable time) but only in the process of becoming global. This understanding of the world as *becoming global* points to a particular way of understanding that world where what is under discussion is the extent to which something has become global – rather than whether the world is global or not. And the thing that is driving the process of 'becoming global', whether mentioned explicitly or not, is generally 'Europe', or 'the West' at large, and its *impact* on the rest of the world.[1] With globalization commonly being regarded as a synonym for 'modernization' or 'Westernization', it requires no great leap of the imagination to see that the global is then equated with the modern, or the West or, then, with the modern West. In this sense, the global is not the global world, as a world inhabited in common, but rather the projection of a spatio-temporal fraction of the world as the definition of that world in common. Globalization, then, becomes understood as *both the universalization of a particular and the purported transcendence of particularisms.*

Drawing attention to the always already existing interconnectedness of the world – the common world – requires us also to reconsider the theoretical paradigms that have permitted the extrapolation of universal significance from a partial history. Much academic scholarship rests on an implicit understanding of the West as being 'the sole legitimate site for the universal, the default category, ... of all human possibilities' (Trouillot 2003: 2). The focus of academic deliberations is largely placed on the experiences, stories and histories of privileged men in the West; the 'other' – be it the class, gendered, or post-colonial other – has only recently begun to inform theoretical debates and sociological analyses. Understandings of the global are similarly parochial, with Europe being taken to embody the values and norms that are seen to be, usually without question, those that will be, or at least ought to be, universalized. Ascribing universal significance to a partial experience is only possible through the insistence on the silence of all others, in that their contribution has already been presumed to be predicated on categories previously available. The projection of a socially and historically limited experience onto the world stage, with no due recognition of that experience being partial and situated, excludes and delegitimizes other experiences and knowledge claims (Nelson 1993; Trouillot 2003).

With the universal being equated with the global and with the modern, it is with the modern, or modernity more precisely, that this chapter is concerned.[2]

---

1 The terms 'Europe' or 'Eurocentric' are used in this chapter as continuous with central aspects of North American social and political undertakings. For distinctions between Europe and North America within the West, see Henningsen: Chapter 1; Wagner: Chapter 13; and Larrain: Chapter 2.

2 I use the term 'universals' here to associate what would normally be termed 'universals' in normative theory with 'general categories' in explanatory theories. The process of the elision of the particular and the universal (or general) is similar in normative and explanatory theory.

It also addresses the relationship between the idea of modernity and the form of the social sciences: a relationship that Wittrock (1998), among others (e.g., Heilbron 1995; Wagner 2001), suggests arises with the emergence of the social sciences as a form of reflection on the processes of modernity. Theorists, not just in the West but across the world, have used the concept of modernity to frame the standard methodological problems posed by social enquiry and the explanations posited in resolving them. Equating modernity with Europe, at least in the first instance, has reinforced a fundamental assumption of much academic thought today: that particular structures, emerging first in the West, would become universal. With the development of this paradigm, the future was no longer seen as being about the reproduction of the present but was considered to be a space for the further development of projects and trends (Burke 1992). These trends and projects were to be the trends and projects of modernity itself, where modernity could also be understood as, in Habermas's (1996) words, an *unfinished project* – one that was not yet realized but that could be used as a normative framework with which to legitimate social movements.

The 'unfinished project', however, is the bringing to fruition of what is already predicated in the Western experience. Ideas of evolution and progress were fundamental to the interest in the future and, for many, the history of the West was seen as foreshadowing the future of the non-West. Our understandings of modernity are integral to how we think about the social sciences and, more importantly, the use to which we put them. Where the problem with the concept of modernity has been defined in terms of its failure to address the experiences of peoples and societies outside Europe and the West, this failure can only be remedied by taking them into account *and* by rethinking the previous structures of knowledge from which they had been omitted. While dominant understandings of modernity have been challenged by postmodern and post-colonial scholars alike, and there is increasing hesitancy in equating Westernization with progress, it is my contention that the West is still seen as the leader, or 'signifier', of change. In orienting its focus around the relationship between modernity and Eurocentrism, this chapter challenges the continual privileging of the West as the maker of 'universal' history, and thus understandings of the global, and seeks to develop alternatives from which to begin dealing with the questions that arise once we reject this initial formulation.

From Evolutionary Modernization to the Multiplicity of Modernities

It was in the aftermath of the French Revolution that academic scholarship in Europe came to be characterized by the emphatic endorsement of its own history as the central historical experience for humanity. The modern world that was seen to come into existence through the twin events of the French and Industrial revolutions was understood as fundamentally different from all other civilizations and cultures, and the history of Western civilization was writ large as the history (and future) of humanity. The social scientists of the nineteenth century mostly operated with an idea of modernization that endowed historical development with coherence (Iggers 1997); and modernization was seen to be the *imitation* of the modern, a matter of entering the established trajectory of the way of *becoming modern*. Sociology's explanations of the processes of modernization, for example, were primarily located in the context of a historical understanding of the social, whereby each form of social organization was deemed to be superseded by a progressively higher one. Traditional, or pre-modern, societies were put forward as objects of comparison with societies already deemed to be modern and the problem was posed in terms of accounting for the historical transition from one to the other. The general conceptual understanding of the modern world was thus premised on the idea of modernization as 'a process of the global diffusion of Western civilization and its key institutions' (Wittrock 1998: 19); and patterns of modernization in other parts of the world were understood to be greatly influenced by 'the original Western project' that formed 'the basic reference point for others' through its 'historical precedence' (Eisenstadt 2000: 2, 3).

Modernization theory, as it emerged in the post-Second World War period in Anglo-American social science, typically operated 'with a "before-and-after" model of the society under consideration' (Bendix 1967: 309). Scholars such as Lerner (1958) and Rostow (1960) – identified by Bendix (1967) as key theorists within the debates – believed that Western modernization should be used as a model of global applicability and other societies classified in terms of their relative modernization in comparison with this model; that is, other societies were to be studied in terms of the extent to which they approximated the characteristics of Western industrial societies. This not only set up the Western experience as the model of comparison for other societies, but also projected it as defining the future trajectories of those societies. According to Bendix (1967: 324–25), modernization theory rested on three related assumptions: first, an understanding of 'tradition' and 'modernity' as mutually exclusive; second, social change occurring as a consequence of phenomena internal to the society changing; and third, a belief that modernity would eventually replace tradition and, in doing so, would have the same effects across the globe. In this sense, modernization theory is regarded as resting on a notion of *convergence*, whereby the difference of other societies – constituted through their traditions – would be erased through the process of the global diffusion of Western institutions.

In recent decades, theorists have moved from a conceptual language of modernization to that of *modernity* and, more recently, to *multiple modernities*. This shift reflects an unease with the idea of a singular, uniform trajectory applied to the current diversity of contemporary societies within the global world. As Eisenstadt and Schluchter (1998) point out, the hegemonic and homogenizing tendencies attributed to the project of modernization have not borne out convergence, not even in the West itself. For them, the idea of linear historical progress associated with modernization should give way to pluralized understandings of multiple modernities. Similarly, Delanty (1999) has argued that the historical model of transition from traditional society to modern society is no longer viable and social theory ought, instead, to focus on the dissolution of the modern, from a single pattern into various trajectories. The notion of 'multiple modernities', then, has been put forward in an attempt to rectify the erroneous assumptions of standard theories of modernization and to highlight the importance of 'specific cultural premises, traditions, and historical experiences' (Eisenstadt 2000: 2) that had previously been neglected. However, as I shall show, the distinction elaborated by Eisenstadt to this end – between the common institutional framework of modernity and the different cultural premises (or cultural codes) that articulate with it – is problematic as a solution to the deficiencies of modernization theory.

Institutional Commonality and Cultural Diversity

In the introduction to a special issue of *Daedalus* on 'Early Modernities', Eisenstadt and Schluchter (1998) suggest that in developing a new approach to the question of modernity and its global instantiations, two fallacies are to be avoided:[3] the first, that there is only one modernity; and the second, 'that looking from the West to the East legitimates the concept of "Orientalism"' (Eisenstadt and Schluchter 1998: 2). While Eisenstadt and Schluchter point to the problem of Eurocentrism, then, they do so at the same time as asserting the necessary priority to be given to the West in the construction of a comparative sociology of multiple modernities. I take issue with their claim that this avoids Orientalism.[4]

With regard to the first fallacy, Eisenstadt and Schluchter (1998: 2, 3) suggest that the global expansion of modernity ought not to be viewed 'as a process of repetition but as the crystallization of new civilizations'; albeit new civilizations that take as their reference point 'the original Western crystallization of

---

3 Eisenstadt and Schluchter (1998) do mention a third fallacy, that of postmodernity, but write that it is not of crucial importance for them.
4 I am using Orientalism and Eurocentrism as interchangeable terms.

modernity'. This reference point is not a singular, uniform trajectory around which there is convergence, but one from which others are understood to deviate or diverge and thus the reference point establishes a multiplicity of modernities. In their view, this is sufficient to avoid the second fallacy of Orientalism. Nonetheless, for Eisenstadt and Schluchter (1998), multiple modernities are derived from the creative appropriation, by those that followed, of the institutional frameworks of modernity that originated in Europe.

The literature on multiple modernities, and that of modernization theory more generally, identifies modernity with 'the momentous transformations of Western societies during the processes of industrialization, urbanization, and political change in the late eighteenth and early nineteenth centuries' (Wittrock 1998: 19). As such, modernity is understood simultaneously in terms of its *institutional constellations*, that is, its tendency 'towards universal structural, institutional, and cultural frameworks' (Eisenstadt and Schluchter 1998: 3), as well as a *cultural programme* 'beset by internal antinomies and contradictions, giving rise to continual critical discourse and political contestations' (Eisenstadt 2000: 7).

Understanding modernity in this way allows scholars to situate European modernity – seen in terms of the conflation of the institutional and the cultural forms – as the 'originary' modernity and, at the same time, allows for different cultural encodings that result in *multiple* modernities. The idea of multiple modernities, then, is consistent with the idea of a common framework of modern institutions – for example, the market economy, the modern nation state and bureaucratic rationality – which originated in Europe and was subsequently exported to the rest of the world.[5] This explains the apparent paradox that Eisenstadt and Schluchter (1998: 5) can disassociate themselves from Orientalism at the same time as apparently embracing its core assumptions, namely, 'the Enlightenment assumptions of the centrality of a Eurocentred type of modernity'.

This focus on different non-European civilizational trajectories is based on the assumption that, even if these trajectories did not lead to an 'originary' modernity, as in Europe, they did, nevertheless, lead to complexity in institutional patterns and cultural codes. As Wittrock (1998) also argues, these

---

5 This is not to deny diversity among the core institutions of state, market and bureaucracy – for example, Hall and Soskice (2001) refer to varieties of capitalism, distinguishing Anglo-American, German and Japanese varieties, among others – but to identify the way in which it is cultural difference that is believed to produce diversity within the institutional complex. The purpose of this chapter is to criticize the separation of the institutional complex and the cultural programme, and the way in which this separation is then used to argue for a European origin of the institutional framework and the separate development of cultural traditions within which that framework can become inflected.

societies were not stagnant, traditional societies but were developing and transforming their own institutional and cultural contexts prior to the advent of Western modernity. However, it was not until the institutional patterns associated with Western modernity were exported to these other societies that multiple modernities emerged within them. It was the conjunction of the institutional patterns of the Western civilizational complex with the different cultural codes of other societies that created various distinct modernities.

The challenge posed to modernization theory by the approach of multiple modernities is substantial but it is less fundamental than its advocates suppose.[6] Particularly welcome is its deconstruction of the dichotomy, favoured by modernization theory, between the traditional and the modern, where the former has generally been understood in terms of stagnation and backwardness and the latter as dynamic and progressive. With their parallel focus on developments in other parts of the world and an acknowledgement of existing cultural dynamics within those societies, theorists of multiple modernities provide a necessary corrective to previous analyses based on ideas of a stagnant, stultifying East, which only awoke from its slumber *after* encounters with the West. Their basic premise, questioning the dominant assumption of convergence and its corollary idea of one trajectory to modernity, is also recognized as an important qualification to modernization theory. What is significant in its omission, however, is the failure to address adequately the way in which the West remains the point of reference, and the assumption of internal civilizational dynamics that developed in isolation until the point of contact with Western modernity. The inability to take a point of view *other* than from the West does constitute a form of Eurocentrism. While theorists of multiple modernities may sometimes make reference to *connected and entangled histories*, the adequate conceptualization of such histories is fundamentally weakened by a comparative approach based on the internal dynamics of civilizations, one with a trajectory leading to modernity and others with trajectories that do not but which then later adapt to it.

Non-European Origins of Different Modernities

As presented above, theorists of multiple modernities address modernity in terms of two aspects, its institutional framework and its cultural codes; and in this part of the chapter I want to explore this distinction and its implications in

---

6 It should be recognized that many of the arguments advanced by theorists of multiple modernities were also present in the heyday of modernization theory – for a contemporary critique, see Bendix (1967).

more detail. This separation of the institutional and the cultural allows the former to be understood as that which is common to the different varieties of modernity – and thus allows all types of modernity to be understood as such – while the cultural, being the location of crucial antinomies, provides the basis for variability, and thus the divergence that results in multiple modernities.

Eisenstadt (1998: 5) argues that central to the cultural programme of modernity, as it originated in Europe, 'was an emphasis on the autonomy of man', on emancipation from traditional forms of authority, and a focus on 'reflexivity and exploration' and the 'active construction and mastery of nature, including human nature'. The conjunction of these developments, he continues, highlighted the openness of the modern political arena and the possibility of contestation within it with the fundamental tension existing 'between an emphasis on human autonomy and the restrictive controls inherent in the institutional realization of modern life' (Eisenstadt 2000: 6); that is, a continual tension between a move towards totality on the one hand, as contrasted with more pluralistic tendencies on the other. The internal antinomies and contradictions of modernity were thus focused on the relations and tensions between the premises of modernity and 'between these premises and the institutional developments in modern societies' (Eisenstadt 2001: 325). These antinomies were understood to lead to political contestations around issues such as the relations between state and society and the patterns of collective identity resulting in the variations of modernity that were seen subsequently to come into being.

Eisenstadt (2000: 13) argues that the first radical transformation of 'modernity', of European cultural premises – in fact, the first instance of a *multiple* modernity – takes place 'with the expansion of modernity in the Americas'. Other distinct alternative models of modernity are the communist Soviet types (see also Arnason 2000)[7] and the fascist, National Socialist types. Even within Europe, then, there was no *one* modernity but rather, as Wittrock (2000: 58) argues, 'an empirically undeniable and easily observable *variety* of institutional and cultural forms' (my emphasis).[8] These differences, these multiple modernities, were thus seen to have developed first in Europe and then continued with modernity's expansion into the Americas, Asia and Africa.

Not only modernity, then, but multiple modernities too have their origin in Europe or, following Eisenstadt (2000), in 'the Western civilizational framework' at large. He believes it to be significant that multiple modernities

---

7   Arnason (2000) attributes to modernization theory the belief that communism is not truly modern, and himself argues for its distinctive modernity as one of modernity's multiples.

8   This is also argued by Therborn (1995), who highlights the intra-European cleavages for and against modernity.

developed first, not in Asia 'or in Muslim societies where they might have been attributed to the existence of distinct non-European traditions, but within the broad framework of Western civilizations' (Eisenstadt 2000: 13). Multiple modernities are thus seen to emerge from the encounters 'between Western modernity and the cultural traditions and historical experiences' of other societies: a conjunction whose first occurrence was in Europe itself (Eisenstadt 2000: 23). The apparently non-Orientalist point of view of the West now establishes the West both as the *origin of modernity* and as the *origin of multiple modernities*.

What, then, is the contribution of non-European civilizations within this new approach? Among the different multiple modernities originating in the West, as discussed above, are those associated with totalitarian forms – communism, in a line stretching back to Jacobinism, and fascism, connecting to ethnic nationalism. These tendencies are then seen to be movements away from the fragile master Enlightenment code of modernity, understood in terms of the autonomy of man and mastery over nature. As such, the space given to codes that develop in other civilizations is in contrast, or even opposition, to the precepts of autonomy, freedom, pluralism and participation associated with the central form of European modernity. The emergence within multiple modernities of fundamentalist and communal religious tropes, often ostensibly in opposition to modernity and, particularly, European modernity, are seen to 'evince distinct characteristics of modern Jacobinism ... and share with communist movements the promulgation of totalistic visions' (Eisenstadt 2000: 19).

Despite their other differences, Eisenstadt (2000, 2001, 2004) suggests that communist and fundamentalist movements share, at the very least, a preoccupation with modernity and an engagement with its central ideological problem, that of pluralism versus non-pluralism. The only space given to the codes of other civilizations, then, is to be aligned with the deeply problematical codes of totalitarian modernity, that is, communism and fascism. In line with their Weberian heritage, theorists of multiple modernity present an implicitly pessimistic view of the possibilities confronting global societies, namely, that totalitarian forms are not abnormal or aberrant (see Arnason 2000, 2003) in contrast to the 'optimistic' view of modernization theory.[9] What is also clear is that their analysis provides no reason for being optimistic about what might be *learnt* from other civilizations.

---

9 Therborn (2003: 297) writes that even though modernization theory ignored the effects of colonial and imperial history, it nonetheless 'struck a more optimistic liberal note of programmatic change'.

Paths to Modernity – Parallel or Interconnected?

As Dirlik (2003: 285) argues, by identifying 'multiplicity' with the cultural aspect, 'the idea of "multiple modernities" seeks to contain challenges to modernity by conceding the possibility of culturally different ways of being modern'. However, it does nothing to address the fundamental problems with the conceptualization of modernity itself. As was suggested earlier in this chapter, the inability to take a point of view other than *from the West* does constitute a form of Eurocentrism. This will now be dealt with in more detail by first addressing the problematical nature of the comparative approach.

Eisenstadt and Schluchter (1998) believe that accounting for the internal dynamics of other civilizations is sufficient to overcome the charge of Orientalism. Furthermore, they justify maintaining the gaze from the West to the East in the belief that this is necessary for an adequate comparative approach to modernity. This comparative approach is advanced through a methodology of 'ideal types' of different civilizational trajectories placed in comparison with each other and, more importantly, with the West. The advantage of 'ideal types' over the evolutionary approach associated with modernization theory is, according to them, that it allows differences to be understood as deviances: 'deviances not from a norm but from an ideal type used only for heuristic purposes' (Eisenstadt and Schluchter 1998: 7). Furthermore, they argue that the ideal type of Western modernity serves as *a common denominator* against which to analyse other civilizations and to ensure that it is possible to say more than simply 'everything is distinct and therefore different' (Eisenstadt and Schluchter 1998: 7). However, it is the very nature of ideal types that the processes they represent are internal and separate from those of other ideal types.[10]

In maintaining its focus on the internal dynamics of *separate* civilizations, I argue that the comparative approach exacerbates the problem of Eurocentrism by ignoring (and even actively excluding through its use of ideal types) the connected and entangled histories that constitute the basis of an adequate understanding of modernity. In particular, I take as a starting point the argument made by Gyan Prakash (1999: 12), in which he suggests that the erroneous assumption, perpetuated by many theorists, is that the West 'had forged its characteristic commitment to modernity *before* overseas domination' as opposed to *through* it. In other words, modernity has to be understood as formed in and through the colonial relationship – colonization was not simply an outcome of modernity, or shaped by modernity, but rather modernity itself, the modern

---

10 See Weber, 1949; Kalberg, 1994.

world developed out of colonial encounters. As Barlow (1997) has argued, the colonial core of European modernity is as indisputable as the modernity of its colonies. Indeed, these colonial encounters have also constituted the circumstances for the emergence of the fragile emancipatory codes of modernity at the same time as modernity has been separated from its origins in the colonial relationship, and has been regarded as a resource for the emancipation of others.[11]

Although theorists such as Wittrock (1998, 2000) and Arnason (2003) do point to the importance of interconnections, global conjunctions and connected and entangled histories in understanding the development of modernity, rarely do they incorporate what is *learnt* from a reading of these histories into their conceptual analyses. Wittrock (1998: 38), for example, argues that during the 'long period of early modern societies in Eurasia, there was a constant flow of cultural, political, and commercial contacts and interactions between different civilizations'. However, nowhere in the rest of his article does he develop this point, but rather iterates repeatedly the *differences* between early modern societies and their *separate* trajectories, not their interconnections. When Wittrock does discuss interconnections in more depth, these interconnections are related to processes that are all located *within* Europe. Explicitly following a Weberian tradition, he suggests that it is possible to see 'the formation of modernity in *Europe* as the result of a series of basically continuous processes where political, economic, and intellectual transformations mutually reinforced and conditioned each other' (Wittrock 2000: 40; my emphasis).[12] Furthermore, only the trajectory of early modern European society is regarded as being able to develop to modernity without interaction with other societies. All other societies are believed to have 'gained' their modernity in relation to what Wittrock calls the momentous transformations within Western societies. There is no substantive discussion or engagement with the question of how the multiplicity of early societies may have shaped the development of modernity.

In discussing the importance of widening the perspective 'to include the experiences of civilizations outside of Europe' (Wittrock 1998: 27) it is clear that what is meant is to lay the experiences of the civilizations outside Europe in parallel to Europe, not to discuss the connections between them. Indeed, as Wittrock (1998: 28) goes on to argue, these other experiences are 'comparable

---

11 The example of the Haitian Revolution is illustrative here, in that the clause abolishing slavery in the French Declaration of Human Rights was only included after a deputation from the colony of Saint Domingue went to France in 1794 and made the argument to the Constituent Assembly (see Fischer, 2004, and Trouillot, 1995, for more details).

12 Therborn (2003: 299) similarly locates the emergence of modernity in the 'conflicts internal to Europe'.

with, yet radically different from those of Europe'. Arnason (2000: 63) also points to 'the particular importance of the Western path to modernity' which, he believes, 'can be acknowledged without denying *parallel* (even if more partial) developments in other regions and with due allowance for distinctive versions of patterns first invented but not unilaterally imposed by the West' (my emphasis). Where the commonplace meaning of parallel implies no relation, interconnection or influence it is clear that Arnason follows Wittrock in asserting the importance of developments in 'other' places without taking their importance into account in the conceptual schemes that are then developed, except in terms of separate ideal types. While acknowledging developments *outside Europe*, then, Wittrock and Arnason see them as emerging, developing and existing in isolation to developments *in Europe*. Although the recognition of difference is an important corrective to the dominant universalizing tendencies within social science, simply recognizing difference is not a sufficient address. 'Difference' also has to *make a difference* to the assumptions that informed the initial enquiry: in this case, the endogenous origins of modernity in Europe.

As Subrahmanyam (1997: 737) argues, it is important 'to delink the notion of "modernity" from a particular European trajectory' and to understand it, instead, as 'a more-or-less global shift with many different sources and roots'. This would require scholars to focus not only on the different sources and roots, but also on the ways these interacted and intersected over time, leading to global shifts as opposed to shifts in particular areas which became global. There is an urgent need to address the *interconnections*[13] as opposed to reifying the entities that are supposed to be connected (that is, civilizations), all the while keeping in mind, as Subrahmanyam (1997: 748) argues, 'that what we are dealing with are not separate and comparable, but connected histories'. The point is to see modernity *historically* as 'a global and *conjunctural* phenomenon' (Subrahmanyam 1998: 99). And, I would underline, not as one that *became* global but rather one that *was* global in its institution.

Varieties of Modernity as Multiple Co-Presences

In a global context, the colonial experience has been one in which contact and communication between human societies multiplied and intensified. The social

---

13 A difficulty with the term 'interconnected' (as with 'hybrid') is that an assumption of previous purity can be read into it. I want to assert here that the way in which I use the terms 'interconnected' and 'hybrid' is in the sense of the world always already being so. That is, I believe that interconnectedness/hybridity is the condition of the world. The problem with ideal types is that they separate entities from their complex relations and build hypotheses and analyses around internal connections abstracted from wider interconnections.

interactions that ensued from this process radically transformed the configurations of what was known and how it was known. The cognitive patterns that became embedded in social actions and representations through the colonial process need to be addressed, then, if we are to understand how knowledge is produced today (Mignolo 1995). Failing to challenge the ethnocentrism implicit in both historical and socio-theoretical understandings allows the perpetuation of a line that flows from the *denial of subjecthood* in history and social theory to *subjection in the present* (Nandy 1987). In contesting Eurocentrism, I contest the 'fact' of the 'originary' 'specialness of Europe' – both in terms of its culture and its events; the 'fact' of the autonomous development of events, concepts and paradigms; and, ultimately, the 'fact' of Europe itself as a coherent, bounded entity giving form to the above. The new approach of multiple modernities persists in the error of identifying particular values (for example, autonomy and control) as European and then linking these 'European values' with the development of a particular institutional framework, the conjunction of which is believed to lead to modernity. Against this, I argue that it is possible to understand modernity as a shift of global dimensions and, at the same time, to recognize that its consequences in different places varied in their local manifestations. These different manifestations are not the multiple, cultural variants of an original European modernity but rather they constitute multiple co-presences of modernity.

By contrast, discussions of modernity being identifiable in other places and peoples continue to locate those 'others' in terms of the general categories already identified, where the 'other' is understood as representing a tradition that has an integrity separate from the traditions of 'oneself'. In this way, the other is left as the other and there is no sense that we might learn from them and reconstruct our categories of understanding as a result of the new knowledge gained (Holmwood and Stewart 1991). Thus, while purporting to offer new ways of understanding the concept of modernity, theories of multiple modernities continue to rest on assumptions of an original modernity of the West, which others adapt, domesticate, or tropicalize. *Their experiences make no difference to the pre-existing universals.* Interrogating the colonial inheritance is not only about arguing for a critical perspective on European forms of knowledge; it is also about problematizing the very assertion of forms of knowledge as European. In the process, nothing is lost except a certain insularity.

Acknowledgments

I should like to thank John Holmwood and William Outhwaite for their helpful comments on this chapter. I would also like to thank the ESRC for its financial support, through the Postdoctoral Fellowship scheme, during the period of writing.

References

Arnason, Johann, 2000, 'Communism and Modernity', *Daedalus: Multiple Modernities*, 129(1), 61–90.
— 2003, 'Entangled Communisms: Imperial Revolutions in Russia and China', *European Journal of Social Theory*, 6(3), 307–25.
Barlow, Tani, 1997, *Formations of Colonial Modernity in East Asia*, Durham, NC, Duke University Press.
Bendix, Reinhard, 1967, 'Tradition and Modernity Reconsidered', *Comparative Studies in Society and History: An International Quarterly*, IX, 292–346.
Burke, Peter, 1992, *History and Social Theory*, Cambridge, Polity Press.
Delanty, Gerard, 1999, *Social Theory in a Changing World: Conceptions of Modernity*, Cambridge, Polity Press.
— 2004, 'Multiple Modernities and Globalisation', *ProtoSociology*, vol. 20, 162–82.
Dirlik, Arif, 2003, 'Global Modernity? Modernity in an Age of Global Capitalism', *European Journal of Social Theory*, 6(3), 275–92.
Eisenstadt, Shmuel N., 2000, 'Multiple Modernities', *Daedalus: Multiple Modernities*, 129(1), 1–29.
— 2001, 'The Civilisational Dimension of Modernity: Modernity as a Distinct Civilisation', *International Sociology*, 16(3), 320–40.
— 2004, 'An Interview with S. N. Eisenstadt: Pluralism and the Multiple Forms of Modernity', interviewed by Gerard Delanty, *European Journal of Social Theory*, 7(3), 391–404.
Eisenstadt, Shmuel N., and Wolfgang Schluchter, 1998, 'Introduction: Paths to Early Modernities – A Comparative View', *Daedalus: Early Modernities*, 127(3), 1–18.
Fischer, Sibylle, 2004, *Modernity Disavowed: Haiti and the Cultures of Slavery in the Age of Revolution*, Durham, NC, Duke University Press.
Habermas, Jurgen, 1996, 'Modernity: An Unfinished Project', in M. P. d'Entreves and S. Benhabib (eds), *Habermas and the Unfinished Project of Modernity: Critical Essays on The Philosophical Discourse of Modernity*, Cambridge, Polity Press.
Hall, Peter A., and David Soskice (eds), 2001, *Varieties of Capitalism: The Institutional Foundations of Comparative Advantage*, Oxford, Oxford University Press.
Heilbron, Johan, 1995, *The Rise of Social Theory*, Cambridge, Polity Press.
Holmwood, John, and Alexander Stewart, 1991, *Explanation and Social Theory*, London, Macmillan.
Iggers, Georg G., 1997, *Historiography in the Twentieth Century: From Scientific Objectivity to the Postmodern Challenge*, Middletown, CT, Wesleyan University Press.
Kalberg, Stephen, 1994, *Max Weber's Comparative-Historical Sociology*, Cambridge, Polity Press.
Lerner, Daniel, 1958, *The Passing of Traditional Society*, Illinois, The Free Press.
Mignolo, Walter D., 1995, *The Darker Side of the Renaissance: Literacy, Territoriality, and*

Colonisation, Ann Arbor, MI, University of Michigan Press.

Nandy, Ashis, 1987, *Traditions, Tyranny and Utopias: Essays in the Politics of Awareness*, New Delhi, Oxford University Press.

Nelson, Lynn Hankinson, 1993, 'Epistemological Communities', in Linda Alcoff and Elizabeth Potter (eds), *Feminist Epistemologies*, London, Routledge.

Prakash, Gyan, 1999, *Another Reason: Science and the Imagination of Modern India*, Princeton, NJ, Princeton University Press.

Rostow, W. W., 1960, *The Stages of Economic Growth: A Non-Communist Manifesto*, Cambridge, Cambridge University Press.

Subrahmanyam, Sanjay, 1997, 'Connected Histories: Notes Towards a Reconfiguration of Early Modern Eurasia', *Modern Asian Studies*, 31(3), 735–62.

— 1998, 'Hearing Voices: Vignettes of Early Modernity in South Asia, 1400–1750', *Daedalus: Early Modernities*, 127(3), 75–104.

Therborn, Goran, 1995, *European Modernity and Beyond: The Trajectory of European Societies, 1945–2000*, London, Sage Publications.

— 2003, 'Entangled Modernities', *European Journal of Social Theory*, 6(3), 293–305.

Trouillot, Michel-Rolph, 1995, *Silencing the Past: Power and the Production of History*, Boston, Beacon Press.

— 2003, *Global Transformations: Anthropology and the Modern World*, New York, Palgrave Macmillan.

Wagner, Peter, 2001, *A History and Theory of the Social Sciences – Not All That is Solid Melts into Air*, London, Sage.

Weber, Max, 1949, *The Methodology of the Social Sciences*, trans. and ed. Edward A. Shils and Henry A. Finch, New York, The Free Press.

Wittrock, Bjorn, 1998, 'Early Modernities: Varieties and Transitions', *Daedalus: Early Modernities*, 127(3), 19–40.

— 2000, 'Modernity: One, None, or Many? European Origins and Modernity as a Global Condition', *Daedalus: Multiple Modernities*, 129(1), 31–60.

— 2001, 'Social Theory and Global History: The Three Cultural Crystallisations', *Thesis Eleven*, May, no. 65, 27–50.

CHAPTER 4

Europe, America, China: Contemporary Wars and their Implications for World Orders

Michael C. Davis

The operative paradigm of the current world order reflected in the UN Charter has proved a troubled one in the post-Cold War era. Differences over principles of sovereignty and military intervention have divided the world, especially the three critical strategic actors addressed in this essay: the United States, China and Europe. I characterize their competing notions of sovereignty as 'new sovereigntism', 'old sovereigntism' and 'transnationalism', respectively.[1] These three views, while clearly colliding with each other, are also in many respects mutually constitutive. In the shrinking world addressed in the Introduction and various chapters of this book, the challenge for international relations scholars and international lawyers is to find common cause in very differently constructed worlds, while preserving sufficient levels of local autonomy. Recently, the collision of these world views has been more in evidence than the accommodation. These three views have collided in the UN Security Council, and the UN has become the venue for attempted resolution of this conflict. A late-2004 UN report, *A More Secure World: Our Shared Responsibility*, discusses at length the condition of the international regime on the use of force and makes policy suggestions for improvement (see UN 2004). The UN Secretary-General (UNSG) adopted these policy suggestions and recommended action in his March 21 2005 Report to the UN General Assembly (see UN 2005). The

---

1 In this chapter, the concept of sovereignty being advanced by various protagonists will generally be apparent from its context. The classic 'Westphalian sovereignty', advanced by the 'old sovereigntist' perspective, has emphasized the exclusive control of states over their internal affairs. At the other extreme, an internationalist or transnationalist perspective tends to emphasize participation over exclusivity (Krasner 1999). Constructivists have emphasized the intersubjective understanding of sovereignty as an 'artifact of practice' (Wendt 1992: 412–13).

question of international intervention offers a fruitful and focused venue for comparing the world views of these three key strategic actors, and for evaluating avenues to mutual accommodation in ways consistent with underlying values of mutual respect, embodied in a deeper cosmopolitan project.

These three world views have been worked out in a global order in which fundamental values were shaped in the UN Charter by the horrors of the Second World War. With such a pedigree, the UN Charter simultaneously offers a defence of sovereignty and a federation of free states with a commitment to human rights and peace. States are not to intervene in the internal affairs of other states. In simple terms, the Charter advances the principle of non-intervention, while preserving the right to individual and collective self-defence and providing an institutional commitment to maintain peace under the control of the UN Security Council.[2] The Charter regime (see UN Charter: Chapters VI, VII; Article 51) has been historically plagued by the conceptual difficulties of its statist design (UN Charter: Articles 33, 39), political difficulties embodied in the veto power of the permanent members of the Security Council, and by a reluctance of its members to commit the resources necessary to its success. Concerned parties facing a humanitarian crisis at the regional level – if confronted with UN Security Council (UNSC) immobility – may feel the urge to bypass the UNSC approval required for regional action (UN Charter: Articles 52–54). As discussed below, the recent UN reports have responded to these various difficulties by invoking a 'responsibility to protect', while still retaining the veto power of the existing permanent members. The reports have given very little attention to improving regional regimes. If it is indeed our project to accommodate different world orders within a broader order, then the foundation of this effort may better rely on regional efforts, which may, in turn, influence each other, even when global agreement is out of reach.

Two recent kinds of wars have defined the post-Cold War international security situation. Military interventions for humanitarian purposes came earlier, most notably in the former Yugoslavia, Rwanda and East Timor – and more recently in Liberia and Darfur. For such humanitarian crises, the United Nations framework proved inadequate (Kristof 2005). Wars primarily based on claims of national security, in the face of extreme violence and terrorism, have grabbed our attention since September 11 2001. While each of these kinds of wars brings its own set of challenges to human rights and global institutions,

---

2   The dual commitment of the UN Charter is reflected in the Preamble and Article 1, paragraph 3. Article 2, paragraph 7 highlights the role of the non-intervention principle in the peace and security regime, but provides that 'this principle shall not prejudice the application of enforcement measures under Chapter VII'. Article 51 preserves the 'inherent right of individual or collective self-defence'.

they generally have common origins in common problems of state failure and collapse (Holsti 1999: 291, 294). They also appear to have underlying causes in structural problems that plague the world at large – underdevelopment, poverty and communal conflict (UN 2004: Part 2, 21–56).

The recent aggressive posture of the United States in the Iraq War has proven a grave challenge to the international security regime and to America's partners. The 'new sovereigntists' of the Bush administration see the path to international security through proactive projection of American power, rejecting international legal and institutional constraints. While multilateral interventions in Kosovo and Afghanistan appeared to stretch the international intervention regime, the notion of 'preemptive self-defense', suggested in the September 2002 National Security Strategy of the United States and applied in the Iraq War, has stretched this intervention regime to breaking point (see United States 2002). This has posed a challenge to 'old sovereigntists' around the world, including especially China, who favour a strong non-intervention norm. But it especially challenges the 'transnationalist' agenda of those who favour a strong multilateral regime to constrain the use of force – a view shared by prominent Continental European leaders and by the UN Secretary-General and his advisers.

The thesis developed in this paper favours a two-track approach. On the one hand, we should focus on developing the global UN-based regime, with a normative commitment to a 'responsibility to protect', along the lines suggested by the UN reports. This includes reform of UN institutions. This project seems most consistent with common values. On the second track, at the regional level, we should pursue a 'constitutive approach', embodying regional human rights and security agreements consistent with this global normative commitment on the one hand and regional traditions and structural constraints on the other. These regional agreements should embody pre-commitment strategies for avoidance of and quick response to humanitarian crises and other security concerns. It is envisioned that this constitutive approach will increasingly build human rights and democracy into the non-intervention norm. The mutually constitutive character of cross-regional experience opens up to the creation of common global norms in a more egalitarian dialogue. Because of different levels of economic development, the development of this two-track effort depends greatly on a proactive and complementary effort in the Atlantic Alliance.

Differing Perspectives on Sovereignty and Intervention

A richer sense of the different perspectives of major players on the world scene seems essential to crafting or just anticipating future solutions to the continuing problems of intervention. There is a need to anticipate how proposed solutions are likely to be perceived in different regions and to take advantage of regional differences and experiences in a project of mutual constitution. Developments after the end of the Cold War have revealed a global incapacity to respond adequately to the pressing security and humanitarian concerns noted above – in Eastern Europe, Central Asia, Africa and the Middle East. Neither Europe, China nor the United States can afford to allow these dysfunctional circumstances to persist. There is a need to appreciate the challenges and offer regionally sensitive solutions.

The United States
US foreign policy has long included contending forces of isolationism and multilateralism. The isolationist strain has sometimes revealed a distrust of international law and institutions and anxiety about the diminution of 'democratic sovereignty' (Drezner 2001). Much of the multilateralism of the current age was, nevertheless, built on earlier US regional and global multilateral initiatives. American President Woodrow Wilson took the lead in promoting the League of Nations, though Congressional rejection of Wilson's proposal bears out the contending isolationist strain. The UN Charter after the Second World War signalled an embrace of Wilson's multilateralist vision, though the Cold War certainly long undermined the full realization of this vision and fostered a distrust of ineffectual multilateral institutions. In spite of these obstacles, multilateralism grounded in the mobilization of soft power flourished in the twentieth century. Multilateral institutions have arisen under a range of treaties related to human rights, social order, security and trade. Even where the US was sometimes reluctant to sign on, US fingerprints were usually all over the founding documents. These fingerprints and their underlying values are important fixtures of the processes of mutual constitution across the world orders considered herein. As will be seen below, the competing isolationist values have likewise shared common ground with the other world views under discussion.

The current US policy has veered sharply towards a robust projection of unilateral power. This 'new sovereigntist' view argues that the US 'pick[s] and choose[s] the international conventions and laws that suit its purpose and reject[s] those that do not' (Spiro 2000). Critic Peter J. Spiro notes:

New Sovereigntism delivers three flawed lines of attack. The first impugns the content of the emerging international legal order as vague and illegitimately intrusive on domestic affairs. The second condemns the international lawmaking process as unaccountable and its results as unenforceable. Finally, New Sovereigntism assumes that the United States can opt out of international regimes as a matter of power, legal right, and constitutional duty. (Spiro 2000: 2)

Many commentators associate the new sovereigntism with the so-called 'neoconservative' influence on US foreign policy (Wallace 2001). In this neoconservative view, compliance with international law is a matter of maximizing national interest. Using a rational choice analysis, Jack L. Goldsmith and Eric A. Posner argue that international law does not (and should not) pull states towards compliance contrary to their interests. They urge, 'Powerful states may do better by violating international law when doing so shows that they will retaliate against threats to national security' (Goldsmith and Posner 2005: 103). Critics may question whether the Bush administration has narrowed its conception of American interest too much, undervaluing the importance of the soft power engaged by international institutions (Nye 2004). From the standpoint of jurisprudence, some may question whether this viewpoint of simple rational choice may under-appreciate the moral and collective policy choices reflected in international legal norms, the authority attached to processes for deriving rules, the mutual constitution of interests and identity, and the legitimacy that attaches to a reputation for compliance.

The trend of projecting American power to advance some perception of the common good, with uncertain regard for international obligations, was, it should be acknowledged, already on display in the Kosovo action of the Clinton administration. Many have questioned the unsanctioned NATO action and the legality of the war in Kosovo (Chinkin 1999). Some have split hairs, labelling it 'illegal but legitimate' (Falk 2003). The trend of challenging international constraints was again evident in the early Bush rejection of the Kyoto accord and the ICC. The Iraq War has elevated this concern dramatically – this time with the language of terrorism and pre-emptive self-defence replacing the Kosovo humanitarian concerns. Even UN Secretary-General Kofi Annan characterized the 2003 Iraq invasion as illegal (Tyler 2004).

While the US administration spoke of weapons of mass destruction and terror links in its Iraq policy, statements from administration supporters before the invasion seem to suggest a policy guided by some vision of 'Pax Americana' – what some scholars have labelled the 'new American imperialism' (Ikenberry 2004, 2002; Jervis 2003; Mallaby 2002). One scholar sent around the world to promote the Bush administration view stated that 'Baghdad was on the road to Palestine', arguing that forceful use of American power in Iraq would lead the US to solve the Palestinian question (Doran 2001; Hirsh 2002). This view may have underestimated the potential for increased Arab resistance to the US hegemonic agenda (Lynch 2003; Ajami 2003; Rubin 2002).

The overall view of the new sovereigntist appears to be that America is the only superpower and it should use its power in a proactive way towards its security objectives. International law and related institutions are profoundly distrusted in the security equation. Other long-established commitments to transparency are also under challenge. Even before Iraq, the US Defense Department had advocated a lesser commitment to truth. In the interests of security, public disinformation was acceptable policy. On the humanitarian front, this disregard for international law seemed to produce disregard for human rights constraints and the Geneva Conventions in the treatment of prisoners in Afghanistan and Iraq. This no doubt contributed to the lax view of ordinary soldiers at Abu Ghraib. As was evident in the last presidential election, the American people appear to be divided over these issues. Only time will tell whether this new sovereigntism becomes the established American world view or just an unconventional view within a single US administration (Kagan 2002). Whichever it is, it has clearly influenced contesting views from other key strategic actors.

China

China presents the case of the 'old sovereigntism'. Its views are profoundly shaped by its historical circumstances and by the other, competing views it confronts. This legal positivist nineteenth-century form of sovereignty emphasizes non-intervention. While historically suspicious of multilateralism, China has become a skeptical convert to a kind of multilateralism it sees as a counterweight to American hegemony (Yuan 2005: 109). China's role as a permanent member of the UN Security Council (UNSC), with veto power, largely explains its conversion to limited multilateralism. Its fear of American encroachment and its consequent commitment to multipolarity have likewise encouraged a more robust multilateral engagement at the Asian regional level. This has included cooperative agreements with ASEAN, conducting naval exercises with India and Pakistan and the founding of the Shanghai Cooperation Organization, engaging several countries in Central Asia (Van Ness 2004: 41). China perceived itself a target of the US national missile defence strategy prior to 9/11, but this concern has eased as the 'war on terror' has taken centre stage in US defence policy. But even in this new strategic environment, sovereignty and non-intervention remain the primary guiding values of Chinese foreign policy. China's views in this regard are representative of a number of developing countries in Asia, most prominently those included in ASEAN, for whom a central organizational premise is non-intervention.

The central plank of Chinese foreign policy since the founding of the current regime has been to defend aggressively a very robust notion of sovereignty and

79

non-intervention on nearly every occasion when it has been at issue. Throughout much of the post-war period, this has meant great distrust of foreign intentions and multilateral institutions. Human rights treaties were looked upon with suspicion and human rights intervention consistently condemned. Until the emergence of the Bush doctrine, security arrangements were unilateral and always emphasized non-intervention. There were no multilateral trade arrangements until well after the open policy began in the early 1980s, and these were negotiated only with great difficulty – with negotiations over WTO entry taking over fifteen years.

China's commitment to non-intervention appears to be grounded in a colonial experience of outside intervention and humiliation of China. In the late colonial period, this spawned what was described as 'anti-foreignism'. This was still manifest in the early communist period in closing the PRC off from the outside world during its first couple of decades. By the 1980s, as China's open policy kicked in and anti-foreignism became moderated, there remained a great deal of suspicion concerning foreign human rights and intervention policies. China's suspicions in this regard have shown some signs of easing in the past decade, with the signing of human rights treaties, the above-noted security initiatives, and the signing up to the WTO. The Hong Kong agreement has likewise displayed a more nuanced stance. But the Chinese world view remains substantially defined by distrust of outsiders' intentions and an emphasis on sovereignty and non-intervention. Even the five principles of peaceful coexistence, the most fundamental principles of China's foreign policy, are essentially five versions of non-intervention.[3]

Much of China's testy relationship with the outside world may be attributed to its authoritarian system of governance. Most multilateral initiatives of the twentieth century are concerned with human rights and a more transparent and democratic world order. These ideals may rarely be realized, but they do have an ideational force in international affairs. The values of the emerging international human rights and humanitarian order are fundamentally at odds with the Chinese system of governance. In the United Nations General Assembly, when Secretary General Kofi Annan advanced his thesis that 'state sovereignty is being redefined by the forces of globalization and international cooperation' as part of his argument for a more interventionist response to humanitarian crises, China took the lead in resisting this notion (Annan 1999). Until more substantial political reform occurs in China, it is doubtful whether

---

3 These five principles include: (1) mutual respect for sovereignty and territorial integrity; (2) mutual non-aggression; (3) mutual non-interference in internal affairs; (4) equality and mutual benefit; and (5) peaceful coexistence (Kim 1994: 428).

one will see a fundamental change in the Chinese official world view.

Beyond the colonial experience and issues of authoritarian governance, China has been faced with challenges to its territorial claims. For many, China appears an old empire in the clothing of a modern state. There are doubts about the quality of its territorial claims to historical tributary states in Central Asia and the island of Taiwan. These doubts have generally put Beijing on the defensive in international relations. A regime with tenuous claims to legitimacy has vigorously resisted outside censure or challenges to its territorial claims. The Taiwan issue factors into nearly every exercise of diplomacy. The recent Chinese enactment of an Anti-Secession Law targeting Taiwan is yet another demonstration of the centrality of this issue (Kagan 2005). On the UN Security Council, China will rarely use its veto power unless the Taiwan issue lurks behind an intervention question.[4] There is a seeming fear that if a broad norm of humanitarian intervention were to emerge, it might justify a similar intrusion if China were to use military force against Taiwan. At the same time, the regime's weak international standing and the above issues of trust have meant that China places great value on its international reputation. Any response of disapproval will normally just be abstention. The task of reconciling these competing concerns has preoccupied Chinese foreign policy.

China would surely object to international efforts to enforce autonomy arrangements, or even to the emergence of standards in this regard. In the case of Kosovo, China signalled its objections up front and NATO simply did not approach the UNSC. In East Timor, China had similar objections until Jakarta consented to intervention. This suggests the general principle that interventions in respect of internal conflicts will be supported only if the sovereign power consents, or with severe constraints. Currently the most prominent problem arises out of the alleged genocide in Darfur, Sudan. As in the previous cases of East Timor and Liberia, it seems that the best strategy to gain Chinese concurrence for any humanitarian intervention will be to gain the Sudanese regime's consent – an entirely feasible option given existing acceptance of African Union forces in Sudan. China has abstained in the passage of three intervention resolutions before the UNSC. China's willingness to support interventions in respect of cross-border conflicts is somewhat broader. Such interventions are acceptable if they meet the espoused principles of self-defence, or have the clear approval of the UNSC.

China's preoccupation with reconciling competing concerns with non-

---

4 In the first twenty years of its UN membership, China appeared to use its veto four times, twice in 1972 and twice in 1997–99, largely with a Taiwan concern lurking in the background (Morphet 2000).

intervention and its reputation has been especially manifest in respect of peacekeeping operations. Its concern with its international reputation has meant that in recent years it has become involved in international peacekeeping operations approved by the UN, though generally at a token level. This token engagement marks a significant step from China's nearly total disengagement of thirty years ago. China has served on the UN Special Committee on Peacekeeping Operations and has contributed about 1 per cent of its budget. From 1989 to 2000 China contributed around 650 military observers and 800 engineers to peacekeeping operations (see China 2002; Gill and Reilly 2000). It recently volunteered to send 125 security personnel to Haiti to help with law enforcement. Some suspected that this was an effort to reach out to Haiti, which had diplomatic relations with Taiwan.

It seems that without resolving its fundamental contradictions at the national, regional and global level China will be unable to resolve this underlying tension. Though China's neighbours in Southeast Asia appear to share China's 'old sovereigntist' views, they may also share among themselves an ambivalence about China. Its neighbours appear to see it as a needed but not necessarily trusted partner. The perceived shield of US security engagement still features prominently in the region. In ASEAN in particular, many members seek to include China in the development of regional alliances while still maintaining security relations with the US. The big risk for China of not being fully engaged in efforts to develop both global and regional norms for humanitarian intervention is that it will be marginalized and its voice left out. Given the importance of the same set of issues that concern Europe and the United States – in Central Asia, Eastern Europe and the Middle East – such disengagement will surely be at a price.

The European Union

The European Union presents a stark contrast to both China and the United States. European views on sovereignty and intervention have generally embodied a refined notion of 'transnationalism', including substantial engagement in a range of supranational and multilateral institutions. For a variety of reasons, this transnationalism has been characterized by a high level of intervention on multiple non-military channels within Europe – leading John Ruggie to describe Europe as a 'multiperspectival polity likely to remain international' (Ruggie 1993). This has been accompanied by robust relations in trade and aid, but a rather timid approach to military intervention beyond Europe's borders. Debates over the development of the 'Eurocorp', a transnational EU military force, have revealed a Europe that is sensitive about its weak military posture, but strongly oriented towards non-military channels of interaction (Cimbalo 2004). This has allowed Europe to make a significant contribution to peacekeeping and peace-building in several areas in Africa, the former Yugoslavia and Afghanistan. In many ways, Europe has taken up the defence of UN norms previously promoted by the US.

At its highest ideal, the European vision, which favours putting out fires before they occur (conflict prevention) and after they have raged (peacemaking and state-building), might offer a needed counterweight to the currently more aggressive US. With some moderation of the US stance, as suggested above, the continued value of the Atlantic Alliance to address development and peace-building concerns in areas vital to the US and Europe is apparent (Asmus 2003). Andrew Moravcsik has suggested that Europe and its American partners abandon the notion of military competition and focus on 'complementarity' (Moravcsik 2003). By this he means a partnership that emphasizes European attention to development, peacemaking and peace-building and American military intervention as appropriate under multilateral constraints. This would seem to take the project of mutual constitution to a highly conscious and complementary level. European support has long lent legitimacy and public credibility to American policy. At the same time, American participation tends to make European initiatives – such as the current negotiations with Iran – more forceful. In the absence of such American support, neoconservatives in America have often been happy to portray Europe as lacking backbone. This criticism often fails to appreciate the more genuine European commitment to the global regime. As reflected in the recent UN reports, in many ways the European transnational approach is the UN approach.

Accordingly, a positive response to the UN reform agenda is critical to the European vision and to evolving any notion of complementarity. Europe needs to develop a strategy for advancing the UN reform agenda while also advancing complementarity strategies within the Atlantic Alliance. For Europe, this may require more active engagement on security matters and more earnest coordination with its allies with respect to allocation of peace-building and state-building resources. For example, lifting its current arms embargo against China for certain trade opportunities does not seem very prudent, given the volatility on the Taiwan Strait (see *International Herald Tribune* 2005) At the same time, the coordinated effort to negotiate nuclear non-proliferation with Iran is very productive, as would be strategic development of military capacity that directly targeted peace- and state-building (Sciolino 2004). On the American side, more genuine consultation with Europe is vital. One would hope that, after the Iraq disaster, American leaders gain a new appreciation of multilateralism. It would certainly be advantageous to both sides to revitalize the Atlantic Alliance.

The tension in the Atlantic Alliance was most prominently on display over the Iraq War, when a multilateralist Europe, led by France and Germany, contested the largely unilateralist policies of the United States and Britain. The presence of Britain and other European countries on the American side of this dispute signals that – as in America – the European stance is far from monolithic. This dispute displayed a palpable difference in world views across the Atlantic. While America appears to envision multilateralism in European acceptance of American hegemony, Europe questions the value of alliance on such terms (Kagan 2004). Before one exaggerates the differences it is important to recall that leading European protagonist France was not always committed to multilateralism. During the Cold War it long displayed a cantankerous go-it-alone approach to security (Menon 1995). The French commitment to multilateralism appeared to ratchet up at the end of the Cold War with the unification of Germany and the emergence of an independent Eastern Europe. With the drafting of the European Constitution and the expansion of the EU to twenty-five members or more, it is difficult to be European today without a substantial regard for transnationalism and substantial commitment to consensus-building on a wide range of issues (Nicolaidis 2004).

Europe has not, however, been able to come up with a security consensus. Philip H. Gordon has contrasted the 'intergovernmentalist' vision of Europe's future, offered by Britain, with a 'functionalist' view, more committed to building common institutions and interests, led by France and Germany.[5] Kalypso Nicolaidis characterizes the latter camp as supranationalist, emphasizing greater purposefulness than mere functionalism (Nicolaidis 2004). A truly European version of international security has been largely stillborn. Efforts at building a common foreign and security policy within the EU have been hamstrung by the competing politics of its members and, at its base, by a lack of commitment to building European military power.

On this basis, Europe has been cast in a largely reactive position to the more aggressive United States. While the tragic consequences of America's aggressive policies in Iraq may serve to reinvigorate transnationalism, more traction in Europe's transnational security commitments will surely be essential. This might better be targeted towards peacekeeping efforts. European work to build a more forceful intervention regime to deal with humanitarian crises will surely advance this effort. A common ground with liberals in America and a dialogue with Asia will be essential. Without more forceful engagement, Europe risks its own marginalization in the growing intervention debate. If China is also marginalized, the danger that the United States will continue to go it alone on

---

5 The basic vision of functionalism is that people enter into agreements for functional economic purposes, but there is a spill-over into politics (Gordon 1997/98).

the development of intervention norms is great.

Europe's combination of robust multilateral capabilities and weak military projection capabilities may put Europe at odds with the United States on the issue of intervention, but in a somewhat ambivalent posture towards China. In this triadic relationship, both Europe and China tend to have their primary relationship with the United States, though they may occasionally play each other off against the United States in trade areas when it proves convenient. One can see in this delicate balance some opportunity for the Atlantic Alliance to be turned in the direction of a more substantial liberal multilateral intervention regime. At a global level, this might emphasize the 'responsibility to protect', as discussed in the next part of this chapter. It will also greatly implicate a commitment to more robust regional institutions. With this in mind, it is important to consider leading options to transform the intervention regime.

Mutual Accommodation: A 'Constitutive Approach' and the Two-Track Solution

The effort at bridging these contesting world orders embodied in the 'responsibility to protect' was first articulated in the 2001 report to the UNSC submitted by the Canadian International Commission on Intervention and State Sovereignty (see Canada 2001; Evans and Sahnoun 2002). This blue chip panel of leading international experts recommended shifting the emphasis in the humanitarian intervention debate from a negative focus on exclusion to a positive emphasis on the responsibilities that attach to principles of sovereignty and non-intervention. This is done by first emphasizing the responsibility of individual states to protect their own citizens. It is recognized that only when there is a failure in this respect, by the state harming its own people or failing to protect them from violence perpetrated by others, that the international community should become involved in exercising the responsibility to protect. This international collective responsibility is to be exercised where possible by UN institutions, in accordance with the UN Charter. This suggestion in some ways combines the old sovereigntism, European transnationalism and collectively more affirmative intervention – in a sense embracing elements of all three world views now under discussion.

The 'responsibility to protect' thesis has now been taken up in the 2004 UN Report and advanced as a formal proposal in the 2005 Report of the UNSG to the General Assembly (see UN 2004, 2005). The 2004 Report was the product of a blue chip commission appointed by the UNSG, a response to the perceived crisis of confidence in the UN after the Iraq debacle. While the scope was broadened from the humanitarian crises focus of the Canadian Report (see

Canada 2001) to the broader issue of international security, it largely concurs in the Canadian recommendations. Both the 2004 and 2005 UN reports emphasize that the principle of non-intervention cannot be used to protect genocidal acts or other atrocities (UN 2004: paragraph 200).

The 2004 UN Report lists five criteria to be considered in authorizing an intervention: seriousness of the threat, proper purpose, last resort, proportional means and balance of consequences (UN 2004: paragraph 207). It further includes a recommendation for reform of the UNSC, either by creating a second tier of permanent members or by expanding the overall non-permanent membership – in both cases increasing the overall membership to twenty-four.[6] These recommendations are all taken up in the 2005 UNSG Report. The problem is that the UN reports appear timid in not altering the veto powers of the existing five permanent members – one of the chief sources of UN immobility. At the same time, the seeming expansion of regional options to sometimes go around the Security Council, as suggested in the Canadian Report (Canada 2001), is not sufficiently developed. Fortunately, the reports hold the line on US efforts to amend Article 51 to expand the notion of self-defence – a stance to which the US has already objected (UN 2004: paragraph 188). For 'preventive' defence from future attack, the reports suggest control by the UNSC (UN 2004: paragraph 189). The UN reports do make a number of helpful operational recommendations, including the establishment of a new Peacebuilding Commission (UN 2004: paragraphs 261–65). The UNSG has even suggested the replacement of the UN Human Rights Commission by a more expert and proactive human rights council. The current Human Rights Commission, which is made up of state members elected from the General Assembly by region, has been captured and largely neutralized by several of the most serious human rights violators. Overall, the UN reports provide a more thorough analysis of the causes of conflict and offer the most feasible reform agenda now likely, with some persisting limitations. This points to the merits of the two-track solution suggested in this essay: global reform at the UN level in accordance with the reports; and a regional constitutive initiative.

In the face of the persistent limitations of the UN reform agenda, the development of more proactive regional alliances seems imperative (Doyle 1986; Tesón 1997; Fielding 1995; Wippman 1995). Preserving the integrity of

---

6   Two models in the alternative are advanced. Model A would create six new permanent members (in addition to the existing five) with no veto, and three new two-year-term, non-permanent seats for a total of 24. Model B provides for no new permanent members, but creates a new category of eight four-year, renewable-term seats and one new two-year, non-permanent (and non-renewable) seat for a total of 24 (United Nations 2004: paragraphs 252–53).

regional orders likewise decreases the chance that well-meaning global solutions might convert into new forms of hegemony. Projects to construct a common order continually face the need to preserve the local – a form of what in the EU context may be called subsidiarity. As the long-term American experiment with federalism demonstrates, such local effort – what we are calling regionalism on a global scale – also preserves alternative venues of experiment and, ultimately, avenues of mutual constitution. States in several regions have already agreed in considerable detail on regional standards of behaviour respecting human rights and their enforcement. A 'constitutive approach' looks to build regionally on such multi-dimensional regimes. Regional agreements may specify concerted responses and ostracism for state regimes within the regional community that overthrow existing democracies. Such agreements may eventually set up specific regional standards for intervention that relate sovereign rights of non-intervention to the maintenance of democracy and human rights – in whatever form it is understood and implemented locally. Soft intervention may more typically be specified, but such agreements may go further, specifying the possibility of military intervention in the face of humanitarian crises. Such a 'constitutive approach' frames in advance the conditions for addressing urgent regional concerns and crises in ways that take account of regional history and structure.

Such a constitutive approach may embody the notion of a 'responsibility to protect' and specifically address regional standards for humanitarian intervention when that responsibility is not satisfied. Such standards may also require democracy and human rights, as these norms are the contemporary embodiment of the more classic notion of self-determination that underlies the non-intervention principle. In some ways, this constitutive approach recognizes the concerns of all three camps discussed in this chapter. It both specifies a basis for non-intervention and constructs a multilateral community for proactive responses to crises and security threats. With its higher level of political and economic development, the Atlantic Alliance could be in the forefront of this development, refining its own regional norms and assisting others to do so. It is imagined here that, as long as the global system is unable to achieve significant reform, the UN and the regional communities may both find opportunities to address seemingly intractable problems through regional initiatives and experimentation. Those communities that are more developed in this regard may provide useful models for those regions still lagging behind – the conscious avenue to mutual constitution of world orders.

References

Ajami, Fouad, 2003, 'The Falseness of Anti-Americanism', *Foreign Policy*, 82(5), 52–61.

Annan, Kofi, 1999, 'Secretary-General Presents His Annual Report to the General Assembly', September, press release SG/SM/7134/GA/9596.

Asmus, Ronald D., 2003, 'Rebuilding the Atlantic Alliance', *Foreign Affairs*, 82(5), 20–31.

Canada, 2001, International Commission on Intervention and State Sovereignty, *The Responsibility to Protect*, Ottawa, International Development Research Centre.

China, 2002, China's National Defense White Paper.

Chinkin, Christine M., 1999, 'Kosovo: A "Good" or "Bad" War?', *American Journal of International Law*, 93(4), 841–47.

Cimbalo, Jeffrey L., 2004, 'Saving NATO from Europe', *Foreign Affairs*, 83(6), 111–20.

Doran, Michael Scott, 2001, 'Palestine, Iraq, and the American Strategy', *Foreign Affairs*, 82(1), 19.

Doyle, Michael W., 1986, 'Liberalism and World Politics', *American Political Science Review*, 80, December, 1151–69.

Drezner, Daniel W., 2001, 'On the Balance Between International Law and Democratic Sovereignty', *Chicago Journal of International Law*, 2(2), 321–36.

Evans, Gareth, and Mohamed Sahnoun, 2002, 'The Responsibility to Protect', *Foreign Affairs*, 81(6), 99–110.

Falk, Richard A., 2003, 'What Future for the UN Charter System of War Prevention?', *The American Journal of International Law*, 97(3), 590–98.

Fielding, Louis, 1995, 'Taking the Next Step in the Development of New Human Rights: The Emerging Right of Humanitarian Assistance to Restore Democracy', *Duke Journal of Comparative and International Law*, 5, 329.

Gill, Bates, and James Reilly, 2000, 'Sovereignty, Intervention and Peacekeeping: The View from Beijing', *Survival*, 42(3), 41–59.

Goldsmith, Jack L., and Eric A. Posner, 2005, *The Limits of International Law*, New York, Oxford University Press.

Gordon, Philip H., 1997/98, 'Europe's Uncommon Foreign Policy', *International Security*, 22(3), 74–100.

Hirsh, Michael, 2002, 'Bush and The World', *Foreign Affairs*, 81(5), 18–43.

Holsti, K. J., 1999, 'The Coming Chaos? Armed Conflict in the World's Periphery', in T. V. Paul and John A. Hall (eds), *International Order and the Future of World Politics*, New York, Cambridge University Press, 283–310.

Ikenberry, G. John, 2002, 'America's Imperial Ambition', *Foreign Affairs*, 81(5), 44–60.

—2004, 'Illusions of Empire: Defining the New American Order', *Foreign Affairs*, 83(2), 144–54.

International Herald Tribune, 2005, 'Setting Limits on Weapons for China', February 26.

Jervis, Robert, 2003, 'The Compulsive Empire', *Foreign Policy*, 82, 83–87.

Kagan, Robert, 2002, 'Power and Weakness', *Policy Review*, 113.

— 2004, 'America's Crisis of Legitimacy', *Foreign Affairs*, 83(2), 65–87.

— 2005, 'Those Subtle Chinese', *Washington Post*, March 10, A21.

Kim, Samual, 1994, 'Sovereignty in the Chinese Image of World Order', in Ronald St. John Macdonald (ed.), *Essays in Honor of Wang Tieya*, London, Nijhoff, 425–45.

Krasner, Stephen, 1999, *Sovereignty: Organized Hypocrisy*, Princeton, NJ, Princeton

University Press.

Kristof, Nicholas D., 2005, 'The Secret Genocide Archive', *New York Times*, February 23, A31.

Lynch, Marc, 2003, 'Taking Arabs Seriously', *Foreign Affairs*, 82(5), 81–94.

Mallaby, Sebastian, 2002, 'The Reluctant Imperialist: Terrorism, Failed States, and the Case for American Empire', *Foreign Affairs*, 81(2), 2–7.

Menon, Anand, 1995, 'From Independence to Cooperation: France, NATO and European Security', *International Affairs*, 71(1), 19–34.

Moravcsik, Andrew, 2003, 'Striking a New Transatlantic Bargain', *Foreign Affairs*, 82.

Morphet, Sally, 2000, 'China as a Permanent Member of the Security Council, October 1971–December 1999', *Security Dialogue*, 31(2), 151–66.

Nicolaidis, Kalypso, 2004, 'We the People of Europe', *Foreign Affairs*, 83(6), 97–110.

Nye, Joseph S., 2004, 'The Decline of America's Soft Power', *Foreign Affairs*, 83(3), 16–20.

Rubin, Barry, 2002, 'The Real Roots of Arab Anti-Americanism', *Foreign Affairs*, 81(6), 73–85.

Ruggie, John, 1993, 'Territoriality and Beyond: Problematizing Modernity in International Relations', *International Organizations*, 46, Winter, 139.

Sciolino, Elaine, 2004, 'Iran and Europeans Open New Round of Negotiations', *New York Times*, December 14.

Spiro, Peter J., 2000, 'The New Sovereigntists: American Exceptionalism and Its False Prophets', *Foreign Affairs*, 79(6), 9–15.

Tesón, Fernando R., 1997, *Humanitarian Intervention: An Inquiry into Law and Morality*, 2nd edn, Irvington-on-Hudson, NY, Transnational.

Tyler, Patrick E., 2004, 'U.N. Chef Ignites Firestorm by Calling Iraq War "Illegal"', *New York Times*, September 17, A11.

UN, 2004, 'A More Secure World: Our Shared Responsibility', Report of the Secretary-General's High-level Panel on Threats, Challenges and Change, www.un.org/secureworld

— 2005, 'In Larger Freedom: Towards Development, Security and Human Rights for All', Report of the Secretary-General to the UN General Assembly (A/59/2005), March 21.

United States, 2002, *The National Security Strategy of the United States of America*, www.whitehouse.gov/nsc/nss.html

Van Ness, Peter, 2004, 'China's Response to the Bush Doctrine', *World Policy Journal*, XXI(4), 38–47.

Wallace, William, 2001, 'Europe, the Necessary Partner', *Foreign Affairs*, 80(3), 16–34.

Wendt, Alexander, 1992, 'Anarchy is What States Make of It: The Social Construction of Power Politics', *International Organizations*, 46(2), 391–425.

Wippman, David, 1995, 'Treaty-Based Intervention: Who Can Say No?', *University of Chicago Law Review*, 62, 607–87.

Yuan, Jing-dong, 2005, 'Chinese Perspectives and Responses to the Bush Doctrine', in Mel Gurtov and Peter Van Ness (eds), *Confronting the Bush Doctrine, Critical Views from the Asia-Pacific*, London, Routledge Curzon, 108–29.

CHAPTER 5

Islam Online:
The Internet, Religion and Politics

Eugenia Siapera

The historico-political developments following September 11 2001 have raised the profile of Islam and its political relevance. From a secular and liberal perspective, religious/transcendental struggles should be confined to the private domain and should concern individual consciences. However, the forceful entry of Islam as a topic into the public domain post-9/11 represents a questioning of the secular/liberal world. This raises broader questions about the links between religion and politics and the relevance of religious interpretations for our life in common and in the commons, that is, in the public domain. At stake here are the common elements and bonds necessary for socio-political and public life. These issues as specifically applied to Islam are confounded by the inability of dominant constructions to understand it adequately without falling into the trap of essentialism. The closures imposed by modes of approaching Islam must, therefore, be outlined before any attempt is made to understand the role of Islam and, more broadly, of religion in political life. Three dominant modes of theorizing Islam will be critically reviewed here: the theological mode, exemplified by the Quran and other sacred texts of Islam; the social scientific mode, exemplified by the work of Max Weber; and the cultural mode, exemplified by the work of Edward Said.

The closure and other problems involved in these modes of presenting Islam prohibit a dynamic understanding of the religion and its role in politics. We must, therefore, develop a new mode, which should remain open to the nuances and dynamism of Islam while recognizing its specificities and acknowledging the possibilities for its public role. This is, admittedly, a daunting task, to which this effort can only hope to contribute through refocusing and rearticulating the issues involved. As a starting point, this chapter will focus on the articulation of

Islam on the Internet. Given the current interest in the political role of Islam, the public character of the Internet makes it a relevant focus of analysis. The centrality of the public sphere in politics has been well documented (Habermas 1989) and although there is no agreement regarding how it should be conceived, the link between the public and the political is one of the central premises of theorizations of the political. Indeed, to the extent that the political requires a space in which to take place, this space is a public one, in being – at least in principle – open to all.[1] Looking at public Islam, then, enables a discussion of the issues concerning Islam and politics. The analysis of Islam online will, therefore, seek to articulate the links between the public experiences and practices of Islam on the Internet and the domain of the political.

Knowing Islam

Thinking about Islam requires knowledge of it and knowledge is, as Foucault argues (1980), a crucial domain for power. In other words, knowing Islam means having some form of power over it. The three forms of knowledge reviewed here posit a different set of claims over Islam and are always implicated in power arrangements and, hence, in politics. This first part of the chapter will summarize these three forms, namely theological, sociological and cultural modes of knowing Islam, and will seek to identify their implications for Islam and/in politics. The discussion will adopt a historical perspective, beginning with theology, moving on to discuss the sociological knowledge of Islam and, finally, considering the cultural mode.[2]

Positing the existence of distinct forms of knowledge, such as the above, does not imply that they are mutually exclusive or unrelated. Rather, they emphasize different relationships within and focus on different aspects of the worlds of Islam. Thus, the cultural mode of knowledge privileges identity and a semantic

1 This is premised on a democratic understanding of politics, although it should be noted that the public should not be reduced to the political: the public may contain elements that are not directly or always politically relevant. At the same time, however, the political must always remain public, that is, enacted in a common space and open to participation by all. This understanding of the public may sidestep some problems involved in the modern publicity process, which requires the ceaseless churning of information and the associated domain of secrecy (see Dean 2001).
2 This argument has a lot of affinities with the work of Salvatore (1997), as they are both premised upon a Foucauldian theorization of discourse. Yet there are also several differences. Salvatore views the different discourses on Islam as involved in the historical production of Islam, while the current perspective theorizes these discursive modalities as involving different sets of rules of formation (Foucault 1972), hence each produces a different Islam. Nevertheless, the author acknowledges the influence of Salvatore's work when thinking about and writing the argument presented in this chapter.

interpretation, in which Islam 'becomes' through its relationship with other such entities, notably the 'West'. The social scientific mode focuses on structure, and emphasizes relationships between Islam as an analytical category and the other categories seen as comprising society, such as politics, the economy and society itself. The theological form privileges an internal understanding of Islam, focusing on the Quran and other sacred texts. Theological Islam necessarily involves dogma, a centre or an essence, which can then be seen as constituting its uniqueness and tradition.

The theological mode provides an understanding from 'within', as it were, from the perspective of the religion itself, of its dogma, values and morality. It is here that we see the unity or identity of Islam, that which sets it apart from other religions. At the same time, however, we can also witness here the multiplicity and diversity of Islam, derived from the varied interpretative possibilities of its scriptures and traditions. It is arguable that this mode of thought is a privileged one, compared with the other forms cited above, in that it comes from an internal point of view. It is a reflexive mode that looks to Islam from within, which attempts a substantive understanding of it, and which seeks to capture its determinate forms. Nevertheless, this mode is not without its problems. The multiple theological interpretations of Islam imply an ordering and a certain hierarchy, hence an asymmetry and a difference within Islam. These cannot be resolved theologically, since all these interpretations can successfully claim the same relationship to truth, as there is no arbiter or criteria that can be applied to resolve differences – at least in this world. This implies that this inside-oriented mode must, in the end, be complemented by an external orientation.

Understanding Islam theologically requires a (re)turn to its origin, namely the scripture, because this contains the knowledge that constitutes Islam as a theology.[3] Theologically, through the Quran and the Sunnah, Islam shows the way to attain the ideal, thereby enabling Muslims (believers) to come closer to, or to know, God. Herein lies the problem, however. Although the Quran and the Sunnah provide guidance, there is considerable difference in the interpretation not only of these texts, but also of the historical events that have influenced the development of Islam. The appointment of Abu Bakr as Caliph, successor of the Prophet and ruler of Islam, has been interpreted as usurpation by an important part of Islam, which considers Ali the rightful 'heir' of Islam. The subsequent assassination of Ali and the massacre of his son Hussein and his supporters in Karbala marked a significant shift within Islam: a schism

---

3   Theology is understood here literally, as a discourse on the divine.

between Shia and Sunni Islam. For the Shias, the death of Hussein represents a pivotal moment, with succession passing from those who rightly deserved it to the usurpers. In contrast, Sunni Muslims believe that leadership should be in the hands of the Muslim community at large, thereby giving rise to legalistic interpretations of the scripture. The subsequent development of Sufism could be understood as opposition to the legal-minded and formal interpretations of the Quran. For Sufism, God can be known through intuition and love, and through direct communion via one of the mystical methods.

These doctrinal differences and their spill-over into the political domain[4] indicate the problems with the theological construction of Islam. Although it offers crucial insights into Islam, it ultimately falls short of knowing it in all its diverse forms, a problem common to the other forms of knowledge also. The theological mode takes Islam seriously, in that it takes it literally as it is, a set of discourses on the divine, and a means of living in a manner that pleases God. As such, this mode of knowledge is firmly oriented towards the 'inside' of Islam, towards a determination of what the scriptures and the descriptions of the life of the Prophet mean. For the good Muslim, only one type of world is worth pursuing, that is, the world that brings one closer to God, and which allows one to emulate the attributes of the Prophet. Political opposition, therefore, would only make sense for the Muslim believer when the politics that it contests are directed explicitly against Islamic values. However, this merely displaces the question of the precise world that brings believers closer to God, which relies on the nature of the interpretation of the scriptures and the parables. Therein we encounter the problem of theological knowledge: that while it can provide us with interpretations, it cannot provide us with the means of discerning or choosing between them. Theology seems unable to give us the tools by which we can decide. This inability implies a polarization that cannot be resolved theologically and that has led to violence and to religious wars. On its own, this theological mode of knowledge is, in political terms, dangerous.

The problems involved in knowing Islam theologically may be sidestepped if another reflexive form of knowledge is applied, that of society looking back at itself. In sociology, Islam is studied as one of the 'religions'. It is understood in terms relative to other religions and other categories of society, including politics, the economy and society itself. The goal of the sociology of religion, as proposed by Weber (1991 [1922]), is to formulate an understanding of religion and to draw parallels between religion and other forms of self-regulation. Weber's perspective focuses on the subjective experience of religion, its

---

4 This domain is narrowly understood as concerning questions of leadership and statehood.

'meaning' or substance, which is then linked to other systems, including other religions. The sociological or social scientific mode of knowing Islam is, therefore, a comparative exercise which seeks to relativize, rather than polarize, religions and other social systems or categories. As such, it may be more appropriate for understanding Islam and politics. The discussion here will focus on Weber, whose work on religion has truly defined the field.

For Weber, Islam is characterized by a warrior ethic, since at its inception the main carrier of Islam was a warrior group. This, Weber argues, shows that Islam is a religion that seeks to accommodate the world rather than master it, and whose religious ordinances have a 'political' orientation. In other words, Islam as a religion enables the warrior caste to acquire a position of prominence through proscribing war until it 'should rise to the top of this world's social scale, by exacting tribute' (Weber 1991 [1922]: 262). Hence, rather than seek to change, order and shape the world methodically, Islam has sought to conquer it.[5] At the same time, it (re)adapts doctrine to preserve and regulate the community as a whole. 'Political' here means concerning the fate of the community, and it is, therefore, antithetical to the individualistic, inner-directed quest for salvation that characterizes Christianity, and Protestantism in particular. In addition, this prioritization of the community of believers in Islam implies that any potential conflict between religious ethics and socio-political life is unlikely to arise, in so far as one is a believer. Non-believers are subjugated but tolerated, as Islam does not practise universal conversion by coercion, but at the same time justifies domination over unbelievers. Islam appears both as a political religion par excellence, since it enables the more or less peaceful coexistence of different groups, and as an anti-political religion, as it does not seem to accept the possibility of a secularized politics, or a politics without religion. Politics must always be secondary to religion. Finally, this warrior ethic coupled with Islam's belief in predestination in the form of 'kismet' eventually gives rise to fatalism, which then opens the door for the reinsertion of magic. Ultimately, therefore, the rationalization of Islam was stinted and Islam could not modernize, as it lacked the dynamism or drive of religions oriented towards mastery.

The gist of Weber's account is evident: Islam has failed to produce a secular, rational and methodical view of the world. A so-called 'value-free' sociology appears to have collapsed into an Orientalist discourse. As Turner (1991)

5 Although accommodation to and conquest of the world might appear contradictory, in Weber's terminology they are compatible in so far as this conquest does not radically alter the world, but merely replaces its ruling class. For Weber, the opposite of accommodation is the rational mastery of the world, changing the world according to a group's requirements rather than finding a niche within it.

observes, Islam is characterized by a set of absences, by what it does not have, by what it has not developed, and by what it lacks. The canon is set by the modern, secular, rational West, which then becomes the measure of everything, judging Islam as traditional, irrational (or insufficiently rationalized), and static, notwithstanding that the actual factual basis of Weber's Islam is erroneous (Turner 1974). It is arguable that the problem with a sociological account of Islam is a broader one, however. Pushed towards generalizations and system-atization, and unaware of its own modalities, social scientific thought is bound to run into problems of Eurocentrism. Furthermore, evaluative judgment masked as value-free examination leads, in the end, to the application of social science as a means of control. Thus, even nuanced and sensitive accounts such as Weber's interpretative sociology appear unable to deal with such accusations. This is not to preclude all forms of sociological enquiry or theorizing, but merely to point to its limitations, to the fact that it is bound to remain a few paces behind its object of study, and that it must be aware of its limited applicability in terms of time and scope. This type of reflexive and historicized social science continues to be relevant today,[6] as the appeal of certain aspects of Weber's work shows. Specifically, his focus on interpretation, on how concepts or ideas are interpreted and then put into action by social agents themselves, and the view that horizons of ideas inform actions in multiple ways, can all give renewed impetus to a sociological understanding of Islam.

Nevertheless, this sociological Eurocentrism, the fact of its long unquestioned nature, and the focus on European modernity as the measure of all things, constitute the themes of Edward Said's critique (2003 [1978]). Said views this sociology as a cultural product and examines it, along with the products of European culture more broadly, from a highly critical perspective. He tries to show how colonial Europe constructed a set of ideas enabling and justifying its rule over Islam. However, in seeking to expose not only the complicity of (European) culture but its actively productive role in dominating the Orient, Said's work generates two unfortunate and unintended consequences. Firstly, it reduces Islam to its European construction of it, seen primarily as a form of European alter ego. Secondly, at the same time, Islam and Europe are both essentialized, since any dynamism, internal struggle and possible resistance is ignored. In addition, the contribution of this work to the construction of a particular Islam (static, reactive, almost perennial, unresisting) must also be taken into account. To his credit, Said sought to address some of these criticisms in his subsequent work (1994). Nevertheless, these efforts were bound to fail,

6 For the continuous relevance of a 'reformed' social science, see Wagner (2001).

because of the particular characteristics of cultural production around which this mode of knowledge evolves. For Islam, this means that any quest to rewrite an authentic Islamic culture is problematical from the outset, and the politics it might lead to is suspect.

Thus, notwithstanding the great insights offered by Said and his account of the continuous European construction of the Orient and Islam, it is precisely this focus on European culture that is creating problems for this mode of knowledge. Said's attempt to 'deconstruct' European/Western Orientalism has the effect of creating a singular Europe, from its classical roots in Greece through to the Renaissance, to colonial industrial Europe and to post-war Europe and the West. It is not only Islam and the Orient that are essentialized in this Orientalist discourse, but also Europe, whose multiplicity, its internal contradictions and differences and its ambivalences have all disappeared. Thus, Said's account constructs, paradoxically, an essential Europe/West/Occident, as well as an image of Islam as a mere reflection of the European imagination. Moreover, his work overlooks Islamic cultural production and its construction of Islam, the Orient and the Occident – the so-called Orientalism in reverse (al-'Azm 1981). In this context, Said's insistence that Islam must have its own voice lends credence to arguments mobilizing a politics of authenticity, and to a surge of 'nativism' (Moghadam 1989).[7] While authenticity is problematic in that it masks the multiple dialogues in which Islam is involved, internally and with others, the ideological affinities of nativism with fundamentalist movements render it politically suspect.

This polarization between an essential Orient and an equally essential Occident, the disregard of internal divisions, multiplicities, positions and so forth, the implication that only certain voices are authorized to speak, and, equally importantly, the polysemy of cultural texts and the different contexts of production and reception, all constitute crucial and unsolvable problems for this mode of knowledge. While the first three criticisms are discussed in the literature, the importance of the latter is often downplayed. However, it is the constitutive polysemy of cultural texts, as well as the multiple contexts of their reception, that pose impossible obstacles for knowing/constructing Islam in cultural texts. In other words, this mode must find a way to incorporate the multiple meanings of texts (and ideas) and their contexts of reception. For example, Aeschylus's *Persians*, which for Said marks the beginning of Orientalism in glorifying Greece/Europe at the expense of a defeated Orient,

---

7   Moghadam defines 'nativism' as the binary opposition between the authentic and the alien, while
    Tavakoli-Targhi (1994) holds that Iranian nativism in particular has given rise to discourses of
    gharbzadegi ('westoxication'), where the West is seen as poisonous, inferior and corrupt.

might also be interpreted as dealing with the problem of human hubris. It may also show the ambivalence of war, and that it is precisely at the point of victory that war wreaks more havoc. Which meaning shall we choose? And would it have the same meaning if staged and presented in, say, modern-day Iran? At best, therefore, this mode can give rise to fertile works such as Said's and, at worst, to essentialist abstractions (for example, Huntington 1997). The politics to which this form of knowledge vis-à-vis Islam can be linked ranges from a politics of authenticity, in which only certain persons or groups are entitled to speak of and for Islam, to a politics of separatism, as is evidenced in the surge of nativist discourses, and a fundamentalist politics, which prioritizes 'core beliefs' over everything else.

Experiencing Islam: the Internet and Islam

Some of the inadequacies and problems of the above modes of knowledge may be traced to their disregard of Islam as a lived experience – and hence as a dynamic world – and to their attempt to pin down their 'object' in dogmatic, structural and conceptual terms. Focusing on Islam as an experience may, in turn, provide an important means by which we can understand its relevance for political life without positing a static or essential Islam. Furthermore, this theorization comes from the inside, from within, while also remaining open, because it considers experiences of Islam, rather than Islam as an already constituted category. Of importance here is to point out that this mode of knowledge is not revisiting a politics of authenticity: Islam is equally experienced by believers and non-believers, by practising and 'lapsed' Muslims, by Hindus, Buddhists, Christians, Jews and atheists. They all contribute to knowing/ constructing Islam. It is because of this emphasis on the plurality of voices, the widening of participation and the focus on openness, that the Internet becomes a crucial site for Islam. Islam and the Internet has been the subject of several fascinating and insightful studies. Employing their findings, this part of the chapter will seek to provide an alternative interpretation.

Most of the existing accounts of online Islam seek to theorize it in terms of the public sphere discourse, and analyze the implications of a religion entering the public domain. For instance, Eickelman and Anderson (2003) argue that online Islam has led to the emergence of a new Muslim public sphere, dispersed across both Muslim-majority and Muslim-minority countries, and fragmented along class, gender, national and other lines. For Eickelman and Anderson, the new media, including the Internet but also satellite television, mobile telephone technology, fax machines and so forth, have created new forms of communities, which revolve around shared communications and which bind together 'new people'. This refers to those who have benefited by the expansion of mass education and the widening circles of literacy, and who are the main users of this new technology. This combination of new media and new people has created a new type of thinking about Islam, which Eickelman and Anderson understand to be a re-intellectualization of Islam. In other words, Islam, its doctrine and discourse, are presented in accessible and vernacular terms leading to inevitable changes, reinterpretations and even doctrinal challenges, based primarily on the practical experiences of believers.

With a similar focus on Islam as a religion, Bunt (1999, 2003) views the role of the Internet as one of diffusing religious authority. While religious authority was traditionally concentrated in the hands of the ulama and was disseminated mainly through the madrasas, or universities, the Internet has had the effect of dispersing this authority and the channels for conveying it. Thus, the Internet has now become a major source of fatwas, or religious opinion, not necessarily offered by qualified persons. Sites offer services such as 'Ask the Imam', where people pose questions concerning dilemmas encountered in their everyday experiences. Often, however, questions are posted in online forums, in which case the responses come from other Muslims and not from any religious authority. This may be read as a challenge to traditional religious authority and could, in turn, represent a struggle within Islam. At the same time, however, Bunt notes that religious authorities have themselves taken advantage of the Internet, a sign of their unwillingness to relinquish the power they hold. They themselves have appropriated this new media, offering, for instance, MP3 and other audio files with sermons and religious teachings.[8] Furthermore, the Internet is used for activism, or 'e-jihad', which often assumes a disruptive form through the hacking, or otherwise sabotaging, of websites considered appropriate targets.[9] The fact that these new forms of activism have not met with the approval of authoritative figures is a further indication of the internal diversity within Islam.[10] The results of such activism are not yet clear but, overall,

8 Bunt (1999, 2003) and others have noted that, due to the relatively high incidence of illiteracy in (some) Muslim societies, cassettes and other auditory means of dissemination are crucial in Islam.

9 One of the best-known Muslim 'hactivism' incidents was against Ariel Sharon's Election Campaign website, which was hacked by the World's Fantabulous Defacers. The original format of the site was kept intact but the image and text changed to include horrific photos of an injured Palestinian child and the statement 'Long live Hizballah! Long live Palestine! Long live Chechnya, Kashmir, Kosovo and Bosnia!' (Bunt 2003: 43). In the ensuing cyber-war in 2002, visitors to the Hamas website were diverted to porn sites, which was allegedly the work of Israeli hackers.

10 For instance, the now dead leader of Hamas, Sheikh Yassin, was quoted as saying in 2000 that 'We will use whatever tools we can – email, the Internet – to facilitate jihad' (Bunt 2003: 49). In contrast, Sheikh Faisal Mawlawy, the Vice President of the Islamic European Fatwa Council,

the Internet seems to have opened up new opportunities for political action.

This is precisely the point raised by Mandaville (2001), who argues that the Internet's relationship with Islam raises new possibilities. He points to the digitalization of Islam, with religious texts, including the Quran, being published online, in English as well as in Arabic and other languages. Citing conflicting opinions as to the effects of this on Islam, Mandaville argues that this poses serious challenges to traditional Islamic religious authority. Moreover, just as Eickelman and Anderson (1999/2003) point to the creation of new Islamic intellectuals, Mandaville identifies the outcomes of the wider availability of and access to religious material. These involve the development of new outlooks on Islam, the possibility of generating online fatwas, and contributions to a new way of thinking about Islam. The obvious parallel here is with the impact of the printing press on Christianity,[11] which is linked to the Reformation and to new and radical ways of thinking about religion and society.

Of equal importance is the function of the Internet in distributing and disseminating Islam. Therein, argues Mandaville, lies its main political potential, namely that its transnational reach, coupled with its ability to more or less successfully evade controls, may lead to important challenges to authorities in the Muslim world. In addition, communicating Islam and writing/arguing about Islamic issues across borders may lead to greater mobilization and participation among Muslim communities. In this manner, argues Mandaville, just as print capitalism has led to the formation of 'imagined communities' (Anderson 1981) so have new technologies led to the development of new grass-roots support for Islamist movements. There is, of course, a caveat here, to which Mandaville points, concerning the question of access to new media and the various digital divides affecting the Muslim world. Mandaville concludes by arguing that the mediation of Islam has led to a 'politics of authenticity', where different groups vie for authority to write on/about the 'authentic' Islam.

The insights offered by these authors are indeed fascinating. The relationship between Islam and the Internet emerges as one full of possibilities. These are interpreted primarily in positive terms, in that the Internet allows for a critique of traditional authorities, supports alternative viewpoints, and widens participation in an Islamic public sphere. However, all these studies focus on the Internet as a medium or tool. They consider its implications for Islam as encountered in the offline world, thereby positing a dichotomy between a virtual

---

has issued an online fatwa, in which any hacking attacks were strongly prohibited (Bunt 2003: 46).

11 This argument is put forward by Anderson (1997).

and a real Islam. At the same time, they fall prey to the criticism of essentialism, at least in so far as they speak of Islam in the singular. This appears to be the case, for instance, in arguments that the Internet is a means of democratizing Islam, through the creation of an online public sphere. Additionally, employing the public sphere discourse may not be appropriate given its rootedness in European modernity. What seems to be missing here is an argument regarding the implications of a dynamic and multiple online Islam for political life more broadly or globally. In placing online Islam at the centre of our enquiry, we can trace not merely the political consequences of the Internet for Islam, but also make a wider argument regarding Islam online specifically and its political relevance in its own right. This view considers the Internet not as a tool, but as an inseparable aspect of Islam(s), [12] one of its many articulations with wider implications that need to be clearly outlined.

An alternative interpretation might begin with a view of online Islam as a type of experience. The concept of experience requires further elaboration, particularly as it is understood here. Linked to phenomenology, experience points to a subjective or subject-based understanding of life. It prioritizes an anthropological perspective, in which, crucially, experience is linked to practice and to action: experiencing Islam implies practising or performing it. Given that experience is a broad and multifaceted concept, the focus here will be on one aspect, that of performance, which is theorized and elaborated more extensively. Moreover, it offers an entry point into a broader discussion of how Islam is achieved, beyond its dogmatic or scriptural centre, its conceptual/cultural bases, and the analytical/structural impositions on it. Performance and performativity are drawn from Butler's work on gender (1990, 1993). Although Butler aims to show how subjects are involved in the replication of power, she also seeks to provide a space for resistance. Performativity captures this dynamic very eloquently, in showing how subjects both (re)produce and embody gender identities, as well as in leaving a space for creative reappropriation of elements involved in these identities. This is the result of the internal dynamic of performativity, which requires both a structural stability that enables performances to be reproduced in different contexts, and yet also a semantic instability which points to the polysemy of performances (Butler 1997). Additionally, gender performances are not linked to specific genders, but require the collaboration of all genders. These aspects of performativity, its context-free

---

12 This rather inelegant plural form of Islam is used to point to Islam understood as dispersed across its various practices, performances and experiences – including those of online Islam – which bind it to the domain of the practical and experiential, displacing or deferring its transcendental aspects.

operation but context-bound meaning(s), as well as its collaborative basis, are crucial in understanding online Islam in performative/experiential terms. From this perspective, the focus shifts from a narrow one on Islam as a religion seen as becoming more open or public in its encounters with the Internet, to one that acknowledges Islam as a fluid, dynamic, shifting set of performances. Since these performances are always collaborative, and geared towards functioning in this world, Islam can then be placed firmly on the plane of the social, the experiential and the practical, hence displacing its transcendental aspects.

The current argument is, then, to consider Islam as co-authored by these online performances. In these terms, the online fatwas,[13] the MP3 files with sermons, the hypertexted and fully searchable Quran, the electronic Quran reciter,[14] the online teachings by imams, the online fiqh[15] and Hadith, and the prayer time downloads, all denote an online performance of Islam, which then *becomes* in these performances. Indeed, Islam and the performative may be linked through an argument that Islam is orthopraxic in focusing on correct or proper practices or rituals (Cantwell-Smith 1957[16]). This focus prioritizes action, practice or performance, as opposed to, for instance, the orthodox character of Christianity with its focus on dogma and beliefs. Nevertheless, the argument put forward is that these performances help recreate and re-enact Islam. From this perspective, it is not the 'orthopraxia'[17] of Islam that is denoted by its performativity but the obverse: performativity denotes the instability and dynamism of its practices, and creates or opens up new spaces in every performance. This occurs through reiteration or repetition. Thus, using Derrida's reading of Austin, Butler argues that performativity operates through a reiteration and repetition that frees it from its context and enables it to operate more broadly. It is this repetition in the performance of Islam that then

---

13 The site www.fatwa-online.com offers free software, FatwaBase v4.21, which can be used by Muslims to get fatwas on subjects of concern.

14 The Islamic Assembly of North America is currently offering the Reciter 2.0 version in English, Arabic and French – see www.reciter.org

15 Islamic jurisprudence, and the rulings of Islamic scholars on matters of Muslim life.

16 Cited in Hermansen (2004).

17 Orthopraxia insists on the correctness of practices or actions. Although it shares an affinity with the current view in prioritizing action, it nevertheless opposes it in focusing precisely on the correctness of these actions. The aim here is to show that it is through this constant questioning and instability of action, practice and performance that Islam enacts its dynamism. While it may be tempting to argue that Islam's orthopraxia privileges performance and action, such a view risks presenting Islam as having an essence, something that this chapter tries to avoid. Additionally, the extent of difference and separation between *doxa* and praxis can be questioned, given their necessary reliance on language.

reproduces it. Islam is only possible because it can be repeated and re-enacted all over the world and in different contexts, the mosque, the street and the Internet. At the same time, however, these performances of Islam destabilize it, as it necessarily borrows elements from the iterative contexts within which it finds itself.

The relevance and importance of the Internet here are crucial. It provides new and multiple contexts for the re-enactment of Islam, which can be beyond or bound to geography; beyond or bound to ethnicity, gender and other lines of division. These are the factors that determine Islam in its and in their plurality. And since it is the context that structurally enables the subversion, or at least multiplication, of the dominant or hegemonic aspects of Islam, the Internet becomes a critical site. Bunt's (1999, 2003) findings on the undermining of traditional religious authority are a case in point. More broadly, however, these different contexts give rise to a multi-vocal Islam that contains both convergences and divergences, commonalities but also irreducible differences. Moreover, they bring together a disparate set of authors/performers, which further contribute to Islam's dynamism.

In this manner, what appears as a prosaic Muslim online engagement acts as a means by which Islam achieves convergence or unity. One literal example of such a unity is found in the numerous Muslim matrimonial sites, where Muslims can search for marriage partners. Similarly, Muslim business takes place online, creating an online market place where Muslims can buy halal products, trade with Muslim countries, and can bank with 'Shariah compliant' financial institutions.[18] One can add here the numerous debating sites, in which Islam is debated by Muslims and non-Muslims alike. These 'thematic' discussions enact an Islam that is convergent in being an object of thought, debate and deliberation.[19] Finally, for the non-Muslim or the non-practising Muslim, online Islam provides ample opportunity for learning about the scriptures, Islamic practices, and the Muslim outlook more generally, and often issues invitations for non-Muslims to join. The Islam that is performed here is a unitary one, anchored in the scriptures and religious practices, and drawing on the Muslim/non-Muslim distinction.

This unity, however, is made problematic by other instances, in which a divergent and different Islam is performed. In offering online Islamic tools, as both Bunt (1999, 2003) and Mandaville (2001) have observed, we witness a struggle for authority, for the right to speak for Islam. Whose fatwas are right?

---

18 For example, Alburaq, a subsidiary of the Arab Banking Corporation – www.alburaq.co.uk
19 Such debates correspond to the concept of *ijtihad* found in the Quran, or independent thinking. Hence these debates are enacting an aspect of theological Islam.

Which fiqh should one follow? Which pronunciation of the Quran is the appropriate one? Which of the Hadith collections is the definitive one? Another instance of a divergent Islam is found on the websites of the different strands of Islam, such as, for instance, the Shia Islam homepage,[20] in which the performance and presentation of Shia Islam recreates its specificity. Moreover, the performances of 'e-jihad', hacking, the so-called 'inter-fada', as well as instances of flaming[21] also enact a divergent Islam. Furthermore, such a divergence is evident in the online environments where Muslims encounter non-Muslims. Here, the performance of Islam often enacts an Islam that is misrecognized by both. For instance, the sites 'Answering Islam' and 'Answering Christianity'[22] establish themselves in confrontation one against the other, with the result of recreating a polarized Islam. Islam is then dispersed across these performances, which constantly move on a multiple and shifting terrain, while also aiming at unity.

However, this online Islam, if considered an inseparable formation, has important political ramifications. To understand these and the wider relationship between online Islam and politics, the work of Göle (1997, 2002), which focuses on the public performances of Islam as a means of publicly expressing and embodying the constitutive ambiguities of (non-Western) modernity, provides a good starting point. However, unlike their offline counterparts, the online performances of Islam are not corporeal. They do not concern or involve the body, at least not in the first instance. Göle argues that the corporeality or embodiment of performances is crucial in constructing gendered Islam. For Göle, the body provides the crucial link between non-verbal and/or implicit practices and the public or visible domain, and in so doing entails a deliberate choice. This presupposes visibility, the possibility to see and be seen. None of these conditions – corporeality and visibility – is present online, at least not in the same form. The performances of Islam online acquire, therefore, a different significance which needs to be understood. If we consider the body to correspond to the sensory and emotional register (Göle 2002), then its absence may be taken to denote the obverse: the mind or the intellect.[23] Furthermore, a

---

20 www.shia.org
21 Flaming refers to aggressive postings in online environments that allow for user participation. Such flaming is not uncommon in Muslim fora, often perpetrated by non-Muslims, but there are also flaming instances by Muslims who post aggressive messages towards both non-Muslims and Muslims with whom they disagree.
22 www.answering-islam.org.uk and www.answering-christianity.com
23 This should not be read as a revival of the body/mind dualism in its rigid form, but rather as a heuristic means by which to understand the specificity of the Internet. The body is present online as much as the mind is present in public performances.

103

(relative) lack of visibility may be linked to obscurity or lack of clarity. Taken together, the online performances of Islam occur under conditions of intellectualization and obscurity. These, in turn, denote a primacy of the intellect and an emphasis on attempts to clarify or to shed light. The online performances of Islam might then be interpreted as efforts to render Islam visible, not to the eyes, but to the mind. This appears to be an intellectualization of Islam, as Eickelman and Anderson (1999/2003) have argued, but one that is not narrow in the sense that it concerns only the intellectuals of Islam. Rather, since online participation and practices are much wider, this intellectualization points to an engagement with Islam either reflexively, when it involves believers, or from the 'outside', by those who seek to understand Islam, or even actively to disagree with it. The mediation of Islam by the Internet may, then, be understood as an intellectual and public engagement with Islam, even in its more extreme and negative forms, such as hacking and flaming. Indeed, in the absence of the corporeal, such instances may be understood as the 'acting out' of actual violent conflicts and wars, or another performance and form of public engagement.

Islam Online and the Political: Against Secularism[24]

Having discussed theorizations of Islam in the earlier parts of this chapter, and having argued that online Islam involves public engagement, this last part will conclude by approaching the issue from the perspective of the political. Despite worthy attempts at capturing the political, it remains notoriously elusive. For instance, Mouffe (2000) understands it as the domain of irreducible antagonisms, while Habermas (1998), admitting the difficulties of a substantive understanding of the political, seeks to encapsulate it in formal terms, focusing on rules and procedures. Given the difficulties in capturing the political, we may instead begin with its conditions of possibility. The relevance of publicity for the political has already been alluded to, and this can be seen as one of its conditions. A second, crucial condition is that of indeterminacy. Drawing on a particular strand of political theory associated with Castoriadis (1991, 1997) and Lefort (1988), we can understand the political (in democracy) as occurring under conditions of indeterminacy, privileging no single source of knowledge, discourse, signification or practice.[25]

---

24 This section is inspired by Connolly (1999), who calls for an ethos of public engagement.
25 Lefort (1988) considers the political as part and parcel of society, as the 'form' of society. Castoriadis (1991: 156) defines it as 'a dimension of the institution of society pertaining to explicit power', and views politics proper as the 'collective activity which aims at being lucid (reflective and deliberate) and whose object is the institution of society as such' (Castoriadis 1991: 160).

From this perspective, to reject a place for Islam(s) in the political would be to impose a certain determination in a domain that should be kept indeterminate. Indeed, that is precisely what secularism appears to be doing. To the extent that it leads to an irrevocable and compulsory closure of the political, it must be understood as undemocratic. Thus, although secularism might have been radical in resisting the theological determination of society, it has now itself become a determination calling for resistance. The radical aspects of certain forms of Islam may, then, be seen as resistant to this determination from a fundamentalist theological perspective: an equally problematical attempt towards a singular determination. Reinstating Islam(s) in the public domain must, therefore, be accompanied by a movement towards ensuring the indeterminacy of the political. This requirement points to the necessity of politicizing Islam(s), not in the sense of privileging it as a source of state power, but in the sense of accepting a dynamic and plural Islam as having a legitimate claim to participate in attempts to shape and change society. This is, in turn, premised on a public engagement with(in) Islam(s), which takes a plural Islam seriously, acknowledges its concerns as legitimate, and seeks to address them without repressing them or deeming them irrelevant.

It is the requirement for a public engagement that provides the link to online Islam. An online performative Islam, by displacing the body and visibility, by pluralizing the participatory basis of Islam, and by multiplying it through providing a platform for its diverse interpretations, enables a public engagement with it, without polarizing or reducing it to one dimension. Moreover, the suspension of corporeality in online Islam(s) privileges an intellectual engagement, which can take place in many forms, including inflammatory ones, without the costs that would otherwise be incurred. In addition, the displacement of geography shifts the focus from a territorial and localized engagement to a global one, providing a third space – the other two being the local/national and the international one – wherein a public engagement with Islam in its multiplicity might reinsert commonality and substance in a politics that is hitherto conceived either as antagonistic or in formal/procedural terms.

Lefort further considers that in democratic politics 'the locus of power becomes an empty place' (Lefort 1988: 17) and Castoriadis holds that the project of autonomy requires the constant questioning of any given truth. Both would, therefore, reject any transcendental source of truth and power as profoundly antidemocratic and heteronomous. This discussion of political theory (another form of knowledge) and religion must be left aside for the time being, but this emphasis on indeterminacy as a condition for democratic politics is borrowed for the purposes of the argument developed here.

References

Al-'Azm, S. J., 1981, 'Orientalism and Orientalism in Reverse', *Khamsin*, 8, 5–27.

Anderson, B., 1981, *Imagined Communities*, London, Verso.

Anderson, J., 1997, 'Globalizing Politics and Religion in the Muslim World', *Journal of Electronic Publishing*, unpaginated, available at: www.press.umich.edu/jep/archive/Anderson.html (accessed April 2005).

Bunt, G., 1999, *Virtually Islamic*, Cardiff, University of Wales Press.

— 2003, *Islam in the Digital Age*, London, Pluto Press.

Butler, J., 1990, *Gender Trouble: Feminism and the Subversion of Identity*, New York and London, Routledge.

— 1993, *Bodies that Matter: On the Discursive Limits of Sex*, New York and London, Routledge.

— 1997, *Excitable Speech: A Politics of the Performative*, New York and London, Routledge.

Cantwell-Smith, W., 1957, *Modern Islam in India*, Princeton, NJ, Princeton University Press.

Castoriadis, C., 1991, 'Power, Politics, Autonomy', in C. Castoriadis, *Philosophy, Politics, Autonomy*, trans. and ed. D. Ames Curtis, New York and Oxford, Oxford University Press.

— 1997, *The Imaginary Institution of Society*, trans. K. Blamey, Cambridge, Polity Press.

Connolly, W., 1999, *Why I Am Not A Secularist*, Minneapolis, MN, University of Minnesota Press.

Dean, J., 2001, *Publicity's Secret*, New York, Cornell University Press.

Eickelman, D., and Anderson, J., 2003, 'Redefining Muslim Publics', in D. Eickelman and J. Anderson (eds), *New Media in the Muslim World: The Emerging Public Sphere*, 2nd edn, Bloomington, IN, Indiana University Press, 1–18.

Foucault, M., 1972, *Archaeology of Knowledge*, trans. A. M. Sheridan Smith, London, Tavistock.

— 1980, *Power/Knowledge*, New York, Prentice.

Göle, N., 1997, *Forbidden Modern*, Ann Arbor, MI, University of Michigan Press.

— 2002, 'Islam in Public: New Visibilities New Imaginaries', *Public Culture*, 14(1), 173–90.

Habermas, J., 1989, *The Structural Transformation of the Public Sphere*, Cambridge, Polity Press.

— 1998, *Between Facts and Norms*, trans. W. Rehg, Cambridge, Polity Press.

Hermansen, M., 2004, 'Muslims in the Performative Mode: A Reflection on Muslim-Christian Dialogue', *The Muslim World*, 3, 387–97.

Huntington, S., 1997, *The Clash of Civilizations and the Remaking of World Order*, New York, Touchstone.

Lefort, C., 1988, 'The Question of Democracy', in C. Lefort, *Democracy and Political Theory*, trans. D. Ames Curtis, Cambridge, Polity Press.

Mandaville, P., 2001, *Transnational Muslim Politics: Reimagining the Ummah*, London, Routledge.

Moghadam, V., 1989, 'Against Eurocentrism and Nativism', *Socialism and Democracy*, 9, 81–104.

Mouffe, C., 2000, *The Democratic Paradox*, London, Verso.

Said, E., 1994, *Culture and Imperialism*, New York, Vintage.

Said, E., 2003 [1978], *Orientalism*, London, Penguin.

Salvatore, A., 1997, *Islam and the Political Discourse of Modernity*, Ithaca, NY, Ithaca Press.

Tavakoli-Targhi, M., 1994, 'Women of the West Imagined: The Farangi Other and the Emergence of the Woman Question in Iran', in V. Moghadam (ed.), *Identity Politics and Women: Cultural Reassertions and Feminisms in International Perspective*, Boulder, CO, Westview Press, 98–122.

Turner, B. S., 1974, *Weber and Islam*, London and New York, Routledge.

— 1991, *Religion and Social Theory*, London, Sage.

Wagner, P., 2001, *A History and Theory of the Social Sciences*, London, Sage,

Weber, M., 1991 [1922], *The Sociology of Religion*, trans. E. Fischoff, Boston, Beacon.

PART 2

THE BONDS THAT MAKE
A WORLD

CHAPTER 6

'In the Name of Politics':
Sovereignty, Democracy and
the Multitude in India

Dipesh Chakrabarty

The first of the great operations of discipline is [to] ... transform the confused, useless or dangerous multitudes into ordered multiplicities.

Michel Foucault, *Discipline and Punish* (Foucault 1979: 148–49)

'To take part in demonstrations and hooliganism *in the name of politics*' [my emphasis], said Jawaharlal Nehru, the first Prime Minister of India, speaking to a group of college students in the city of Patna in Bihar on August 30 1955, 'is, apart from the right or wrong of it, not proper for students of any country' (Nehru 2001b [1955]: 83). A 'minor' conflict between the students of the B. N. College, Patna, and the State Transport Employees had led to police firing on the students on August 12 and 13 1955. The Independence Day celebrations on August 15 were marred by 'desecration of the National Flag, student–police clashes and black flag demonstrations in Chhapra, Biharsharif, Daltonganj, and Nawada' (editors' note, see Nehru 2001b [1955]: 47). Nehru had gone to Patna to assess the situation. In retrospect, it is possible to read Nehru's speech as addressing a question that would be important for post-colonial India: what kind of political behaviour would be appropriate for the citizens of an independent nation? Nehru's expression 'in the name of politics' suggests that he did not see 'demonstrations and hooliganism' as the proper stuff of the politics that students could take part in.

Nehru deplored the police action: 'It is obvious that any incident that warrants firing is bound to be deplorable ...' But he could not 'tolerate' the violence and the trampling of the national flag. Violence in public life was something he saw as a sign of political immaturity: 'I cannot tolerate this at all. Is India a nation of immature, childish people ...? ... We must behave like an adult, mature,

111

independent nation.' Students must have interrupted his talk at this point, for the speech reads: 'Shouting and creating chaos will get you nowhere. I represent a mature nation. How can I have any respect for your intelligence ... if the students in this town do not have the patience to listen to me?' (2001b [1955]: 72). In another speech made at a public meeting in Guwahati, Assam, a few days earlier, Nehru had already made this point:

> No strong nation indulges in throwing stones and behaving like hooligans. Any fool can do that .... But why should an incident in Patna set off a conflagration all over Bihar, with trains being burnt and attacks on police and the railway officials and what not? The whole thing started with a small incident on a bus. Our students, particularly in Bihar, consider it beneath their dignity to buy tickets on buses or trains. What kind of a country are we building? (Nehru 2001b [1955]: 57

Nehru was not against students taking an interest in political matters. Such interest was part of the process that would make them into citizens: 'You have the right to belong to any political party that you choose. But one development which is wrong is the increasing interference of political parties in universities and colleges, generating great tension ... I do not say that you should not take part in politics. As citizens you must think about these things. But you must keep them out of universities and colleges.' Violence could not be a part of democracy: 'We have democracy in India ... We cannot get anywhere by beating up one another or breaking the laws' (2001b: 74). Politics in democracy must be based on discussions, debates and discipline. Nehru continued: 'The most crucial thing at this juncture is unity and discipline ...' (2001b: 74). He added: 'the moment we allow ourselves to behave like hooligans, we will lose control over ourselves .... The reins [of public life] then pass into the hands of goondas, the lawless elements ...' (2001b: 78).

Yet, in spite of his aversion to the violence of student action, Nehru could not but see that what the students in Bihar had done was not totally unfamiliar to him. Their actions were reminiscent of the anti-British nationalist movement of the pre-independence period. He conceded that the violence and indiscipline he regarded as 'improper' to politics could be 'the lot of students only in countries under foreign rule'. It was somehow acceptable when students of a country under foreign rule resorted to them. But they were 'not the sign of a free nation'. He challenged his audience: 'You can find out if such things happen in Great Britain, America, Soviet Union, Germany, Japan, China or any other country' (2001b: 83). Indeed, on other occasions in the 1950s, Nehru insisted on there being a real difference between the political methods used to achieve independence and the political methods suitable for an independent democratic country. Mentioning the agitation by Sikh leaders for the creation of a separate Punjabi Suba (province), Nehru once again pointed to the 'obsolete' nature of their political methods. Referring directly to the Gandhian technique of satyagraha (which, roughly defined, means 'passive resistance') Nehru said:

> I cannot say that nobody should ever do satyagraha. It is possible that it may be necessary sometimes. But to go on hunger-strike or undertake satyagraha over day-to-day problems, whether it is a political problem or an industrial or labour dispute, is absolutely wrong. I want you to realize that it weakens us politically ... This is worth considering because an independent nation which is advancing, and is no longer immature, has to adopt different methods of working. We must give up these ways ... Whatever it is, why don't we talk? ... Are we going to start a civil war in the country? That is absurd. (Nehru 2001a [1955]: 22–23)

He went on to mention a strike in Kanpur: 'A strike has been going on in the factories of Kanpur for the last two months or so. It has excited a great deal of passion. I feel that the time is gone when we could solve our problems in this way in India or anywhere else' (Nehru 2001a [1955]: 23–24).

Now, why was it that practices that were judged acceptable as political methods in colonial India – defying the law, staging satyagraha, even destroying public property, and so on – were no longer an appropriate language for politics in the post-colonial period, at least in Nehru's view? Why would Nehru now describe them as pure 'indiscipline', as signs of political 'immaturity'? I do not think the distinction Nehru drew between politics appropriate for fighting foreign rule and what was properly political for a democratic and sovereign India was merely self-serving. He had a point. The violent and the non-violent methods of political agitation used during British rule were techniques for challenging the sovereignty of the British in India. Anti-colonial political methods were all designed to challenge the capacity of the colonial rulers to make and enforce law. Breaking the law was central to Gandhian nationalism. Now that India was a post-colonial, independent state based on the democratic principle of representation through universal adult franchise, actions that called into question that sovereignty of the new state were necessarily illegitimate in the eyes of Nehru. In his speech to the students in Patna, he castigated the Communist Party of India – whose student followers, he suspected, were involved in insulting the national flag – for insisting 'that India was still a colonial country' (2001b [1955]: 72). Politics, for Nehru, had become a question of negotiating the day-to-day problems of development: 'The problems facing the country are mainly economic and in a sense the biggest issue is the Five Year

Plan ...' (Nehru 2001c [1955]: 6, 8). Crowd action was no longer political in Nehru's reckoning; it was merely an act of hooliganism carried out 'in the name of the political'. As he put it to the students in Patna: 'Now how do you think we can solve India's problems except through discipline?' (Nehru 2001b [1955]: 74). Or, as he put it in an earlier moment in the speech: 'We must try to solve our problems through discussion' (Nehru 2001b [1955]: 74).

The very transition from the colonial to the post-colonial state in India thus raised in turn an important question about Indian political life. What would constitute the limits of the political in independent, democratic India? How would politics in the country reflect in everyday life the idea of the popular sovereignty that underlay the parliamentary form of the government and that was enacted in the five-yearly ritual of universal adult franchise? How would politics become a mundane and quotidian part of development? In some ways, Nehru looked forward to a certain kind of diminution of the role of politics in national life: '[I]n today's world, an engineer has more value than an officer sitting in the secretariat. Similarly ... scientists are more valuable than our ministers' (Nehru 2001d [1955]: 19). 'I am fed up of [*sic*] politics,' he said in a public speech in Chandigarh in 1955. It was as if politics should end with the attainment of independence. Whatever politics remained should be harnessed in the interest of development: 'My entire life has been spent in politics and even now I have to give most of my time to it ... Ultimately, however, the real problem in front of us is the economic progress of India' (2001d [1955]: 33).

Nehru argued in the 1950s that any practice that in effect or by intention challenged the sovereignty of the new state fell outside the limits of the political. It became an unlawful activity deserving of punishment by the law (that is, by an act that asserted the sovereignty of the state). One could also read into Nehru's statements the idea that, on the attainment of independence, something like a sphere of 'everyday politics', where politics was part of the routine and process of development, should emerge in India: 'The behaviour of a free and independent nation is always different. It is not the way of constant friction and tension as in the days of British rule' (Nehru 2001c [1955]: 55).

Nehru was not alone in raising these questions. Well into the 1960s, commentators in India, writing in a Nehruvian vein on the problem of 'indiscipline' and violence in Indian public life, would point to the need to create an idiom of everyday politics in independent India that was different from the political language of the nationalist movement. In a collection of essays, published in the 1960s, on the issue of mass violence and its relationship to democracy in India, R. Srinivasan (1967: 67–68), a political scientist with the University of Bombay, would make this negative evaluation of the Gandhian tools of mass politics:

It is time we recognized that several of these undemocratic features have grown out of methods which we resorted to for attaining independence. Against the absolute right of *purna swaraj* [freedom; literally complete self-government] there could be no counter claims acceptable to the people under subjection. The method followed was that of satyagraha, peaceful agitation, and constitutional agitation, but with one difference. The "constitutional" agitation simultaneously undermined the basis of constitutionalism.

In writing the Foreword to the book in which Srinivasan's essay appeared, Dr. P. B. Gajendragadkar, then Vice-Chancellor of the University of Bombay, pointed to the 'danger' that mass violence posed to 'the democratic way of life' at a time when (in my terms) the sovereignty of the government was no longer colonial: 'Citizens who are disaffected against the Government *established by law* [my emphasis] have other remedies open to them and resort to violence ... by a group of people with the political object of ousting the Government in power is totally inconsistent with the true concept of democracy.' He also made a reference to the seemingly unfortunate legacy of the anti-colonial movement in this regard:

> It is true that even while Gandhiji started his Satyagraha movement, Mrs. Besant protested strongly against the whole philosophy of Gandhiji on which Satyagraha was founded. Mrs. Besant told Gandhiji 'that the day of victory for India would be the biggest day of defeat for Gandhi because the spirit of lawlessness, resulting in loss of respect for the law, which was inculcated through civil disobedience, would react against the Indian Government and people would disobey authority on the lines taught to them by Gandhi'. Some people take the view that the recent developments in India have proved Mrs. Besant to be a true prophet. (Srinivasan 1967: 7–8)

But this new call for mass behaviour that was properly political, as these quotations make clear, went against the history of what constituted the political in colonial India. We need to understand the colonial legacy of the political to see the ironical significance of Nehru's position that the political behavior judged appropriate in colonial India was no longer properly political after independence.

Colonial Sovereignty and the Nature of the Political under British Rule

It could be said, then, that it was only with the coming of independence that a question was raised in India about what 'everyday politics' should look like.

Politics could not be a 'routine' affair for Indians under colonial rule. For while the British allowed for a highly limited degree of constitutional and electoral politics during the 1920s and 1930s, the nationalist effort to rid the country of the British may be likened in its entirety to a war. Indeed, expressions such as 'freedom struggle' or 'national movement', popular among Indians and Indian historians, suggest that nationalist activity constituted, for Indians, something more than the routine, everyday politics that is meant to be the life of a democracy. For instance, it is significant that in independent India, politics is called politics (*rajniti*) and has no other exalted name, whereas it was known by many other names during British rule (in Bengali, expressions like *desher kaj*, 'to work for the country' or 'nation', *shvadhinata shangram*, 'freedom struggle', and *mukti shangram*, 'the struggle for liberation', were commonly used). This seems appropriate, for the aim of the nationalist movement was to challenge and bring to an end the sovereignty of the British. The overall non-violent nature of the ideology of the Indian leadership should not blind us to the fact that the forms of 'political action' developed during the 'freedom struggle' were like so many tactics of a battle, each of them aiming to challenge, symbolically or otherwise, the rule of foreigners. Hence, violent or non-violent, they all emphasized the overarching strategy of disobedience of the law.

At stake in all this was the nature of colonial sovereignty itself. British colonial rule in the nineteenth and twentieth centuries was a political arrangement, which, by definition, denied to Indians the principle of popular sovereignty. Indians were subjects, not citizens. The British were admittedly influenced by their own theories of liberalism and self-government. They never saw themselves as settlers in India, but rather as having taken on the altruistic responsibility of gradually instilling in Indians the political skills of self-government. They introduced into the colonial legislatures, through a mixture of motives that ranged from self-interest to ideological commitments, some very limited principles of representation, but even at the height of British colonial rule no more than approximately 13 per cent of the population voted. Anthony Low (1997) has described the British imperial attitudes in India as always carrying an 'imprint of ambiguity', resulting from their efforts to negotiate their liberal regard for self-rule as the best form of government and their vested interests in being imperial masters.

Colonial sovereignty may be likened to what Hobbes called 'acquired sovereignty' in his *Leviathan*. In chapters 18 and 20 of *Leviathan*, Hobbes (1976 [1651]: 228–29) developed a distinction between 'instituted' and 'acquired' forms of sovereignty. 'A *Common-wealth* is said to be *Instituted*', he wrote:

when a *Multitude* of men do Agree, and *Covenant*, *every one, with every one,* that to whatsoever *Man*, or *Assembly of Men*, shall be given by the major part, the *Right* to *Present* the Person of them all, (that is to say, to be their *Representative*;) every one, as well he that *Voted for it*, as he that *Voted against it*, shall *Authorise* all the Actions and Judgments, of that Man or Assembly of men, in the same manner, as if they were his own, to the end, to live peaceably amongst themselves, and be protected against other men.

From this Institution of a Common-wealth are derived all the *Rights*, and the *Facultyes* of him, or them, on whom the Soveraigne Power is conferred by the consent of the People assembled.

In other words, an instituted form of sovereignty is one where the myth of an original contract between men whereby they have agreed to invest sovereignty in their representatives is enacted in the everyday life of the polity. As against this, Hobbes explained another source and kind of sovereignty in Chapter 20: acquired sovereignty or 'A *Common-wealth by Acquisition*, is that, where the Soveraign Power is acquired by Force: And it is acquired by force, when men singly, or many together by plurality of voyces, for fear of death, or bonds, do authorise all the actions of that Man, or Assembly, that hath their lives and liberty in his Power'. He continued:

And this kind of Dominion, or Soveraignty, differeth from Soveraignty by Institution, only in this, That men who *choose* [my emphasis] their Soveraign, do it for fear of one another, and not of him whom they Institute: But in this case [i.e. in the case of acquired sovereignty], they subject themselves to him they are afraid of. (Hobbes 1976 [1651]: 251–52)

Hobbes would go on to make a crucial distinction between the nature of political obligation to obey the sovereign in the two cases, carefully distinguishing 'acquired sovereignty' from the despotism of the slave master. In the case of instituted sovereignty, the original contract resulting in the sovereignty is the ground for obedience in the everyday life of the polity. In the colonial case of acquired sovereignty, Hobbes is careful to point out that it was not conquest as such that created for the conquered the impulse to obey the sovereign, but his own act of submission to the victor, which takes the place of the contract of instituted sovereignty:

It is not therefore Victory, that giveth the right of Dominion over the Vanquished, but his own Covenant. Nor is he obliged because he is Conquered; that is to say, beaten, and taken, or put to flight; but because he commeth in, and submitteth to the Victor ... (Hobbes 1976 [1651]: 255–56)

Foucault explains this aspect of acquired sovereignty beautifully through a distinction he draws between 'Domination' and (acquired) 'Sovereignty'. If one state simply won a military victory over another, killed or extinguished the sovereign, and yet spared the lives of the population, who then agreed to pay the victors taxes and obey their laws, would we have a case of 'a relationship of Domination based entirely upon war and the prolongation, during peacetime, of the effects of war?' Foucault (2003: 95). Following Hobbes, Foucault clearly says 'no': 'Domination, you say, and not sovereignty. But Hobbes does not say that: he says we are still in a relationship of sovereignty. Why?' Here is Foucault's answer:

> Because once the defeated have shown a preference for life and obedience, they make their victors their representatives and restore a sovereign to replace the one who was killed in the war. It is therefore not the defeat that leads to the brutal and illegal establishment of a society based upon domination, slavery, and servitude; it is what happens during the defeat, or even after the battle, even after the defeat, and in a way, independently of it. It is fear, the renunciation of fear, and the renunciation of the risk of death. It is this that introduces us into the order of sovereignty and into a juridical regime: that of absolute power. The will to prefer life to death is what founds sovereignty ... (Foucault 2003: 95)

Hobbes argued (1976 [1651]: 252) that 'the Rights, and Consequences of Soveraignty, are the same' in both the instituted and the acquired forms. But Foucault helps us to see what an unstable structure colonial or acquired sovereignty would become once it was confronted by nationalism or even sentiments of anti-colonialism that aroused the vanquished to stake their lives in the fight for freedom. Perhaps the brief moment when the British rule enjoyed some form of acquired sovereignty in India was in the second half of the nineteenth century, when the imposition of a 'Pax Britannica' throughout the subcontinent indeed gave rise to an ideology and a feeling of loyalty to the Empire among many Indians. I do not mean to deny or denigrate the contribution of members of the Raj, official and non-official, who took their liberalism seriously and agonized over the contradiction between colonial rule and the precepts of liberalism. And there were, no doubt, large areas of life in which Indians were allowed some degree of self-rule within the parameters of British imperial presence, e.g., in municipal government, educational institutions, etc. But any time that Indians produced something like a 'disorder' or a rebellion that challenged British sovereignty, one important and undeniable part of the response of the colonial authorities was about reminding Indians of the need to be afraid of the power of the colonial state. The acts of revenge and retribution that followed the Great Rebellion of 1857 – literally blowing away individual offending sepoys by cannon fire, or even the illegal decision to deny the sovereignty of the last Mughal king, Bahadur Shah, and to try him – were based, as Lucinda Bell has very recently shown in her doctoral thesis (Bell 2004), on political calculations about instilling fear into Indians. Sir Cecil Beadon, Home Secretary to Canning, wrote on October 13 1857: 'to have … [the king] hung on the palace would have had the best effect throughout India just as our omission to do so will be assuredly attributed to fear' (Bell 2004: 142). Even the summary execution of the two sons of Bahadur Shah, Mirza Buktawur Shah and Mirza Mendoo, was prompted by the assumption that 'the execution of such men will strike terror, and produce a salutary fear through the Mahomedan population' (Bell 2004: 143). Clearly, the concern that Indians did not fear the British authorities enough could tip colonial sovereignty over into the sphere of domination.

Teaching Indians a lesson was therefore often a part – not the only element but an important part – of the response of the British to what they saw as acts challenging the sovereignty of the colonial state. A reader of the report of the sub-committee of the Indian National Congress appointed to investigate British military violence against nationalist mobilization in the Punjab during the April 1919 agitation against the so-called Rowlatt Act would be struck by the way the nationalists pitted the liberal language of procedural checks and balances against the imperial haughtiness of the colonial rulers. Thus, referring to police firing on rioting crowds in Amritsar on April 10 1919, the Congress sub-committee wrote:

> Our study of the evidence led before the Martial Law Commission, of the official evidence before Lord Hunter's Committee and the evidence collected by us, leads to the conclusion that there was no warrant for firing. The authorities omitted all the intermediate stages that are usually resorted in all civilized countries. There was no parleying, no humouring, and no use of milder force. Immediately, the crowd became insistent, the order to fire was given. In this country, it has become too much the custom with the executive and the military never to run any risk, or, to put it another way, to count Indian life very cheap. (India 1976a: 49)

Indeed, as this report pointed out, any act of 'disorder' that challenged the public symbols of the Raj or the authority of the British was immediately treated as a departure from the code of willing submission that constituted the core of colonial sovereignty. This was surely the spirit with which the British suppressed the Rowlatt Act agitation in the Punjab, where the military authorities often spoke to the residents of the city of Amritsar in the language of war: 'Do you people want peace or war? We are prepared in every way. The Government is all powerful. *Sarkar* [the government] has conquered Germany and is capable

119

of doing everything. The General will give you orders today. The city is in his possession ... You will have to obey orders' (India 1976a: 59).

Such a moment, when a challenge to the sovereignty of the colonial power had to be put down with violence, always contained a contradiction that was necessary to colonial sovereignty. One sees this clearly in the proceedings of the Hunter Commission, appointed by the government to enquire into the violence in Punjab in April 1919 when martial law had been promulgated. General Dyer, under whose order almost 400 unarmed civilians with no escape route were gunned down during the infamous massacre at Jallianwala Bagh, unintentionally made clear some of the constitutive contradictions of colonial sovereignty:

> Q. I take it that your idea in taking that action was to strike terror?
> A. Call it what you like. I was going to punish them. My idea from a military point of view was to make a wide impression.
> Q. To strike terror not only in the city of Amritsar but throughout the Punjab?
> A. Yes, throughout the Punjab. I wanted to reduce their *morale*; the *morale* of the rebels. (India 1976b: 189–90)

This reads like a statement about the code of conduct of an army officer. But there was more to it. The Commission's questions and Dyer's answers bring out the dilemma that British sovereignty faced in meeting popular and nationalist opposition to colonial rule. Dyer himself admitted that he thought it 'quite possible that [he] ... could have dispersed them [the people collected at Jallianwala Bagh] even without firing'. But his fear was that 'they would all come back and laugh at me, and I considered that I would be making myself a fool' (India 1976b: 191). Was this 'I' to whom Dyer referred that of a military officer who feared the loss of his official, military authority? Would Dyer personally make himself a fool? Or was he speaking of the authority of the European – a question that cannot ever be separated from the question of race – in colonial India? (The later decision of Dyer and his colleagues to force Indians to crawl through a lane where a European lady had been assaulted by a rioting crowd only shows that a considerable amount of race-consciousness was at play in the actions of the military.)

As is well known, Dyer's action at Jallianwala Bagh received immediate approval from the higher authorities, including the Lt Governor, Sir Michael O'Dwyer. But the Commission was deeply divided (along race lines) in its evaluation of the violence involved and there was no wholehearted approval of Dyer's action. Even the Majority report (from the European members) made it clear that Dyer's decision to fire without warning and for as long as he did fell into the category of 'error' (India 1976b: 45–47). The Minority report (from mostly Indian members) clearly said:

General Dyer thought that he had crushed the rebellion and Sir Michael O'Dwyer is of the same view. There was no rebellion which required to be crushed. We feel that General Dyer, by adopting an inhuman and un-British method of dealing with subjects of His Majesty the King–Emperor, has done great disservice to the interest of British rule in India. (India 1976a: 194)

This unease that both the Majority and the Minority authors of the official reports expressed with respect to the violent method of asserting sovereignty and the ambiguous nature of the authority that Dyer thought he was upholding points to a contradiction at the heart of the exercise of colonial power in the age of nationalism. Sheer conquest never by itself offered a formal basis for the sovereignty of British colonial rule. Yet the submission of the colonized in an age of nationalist movement demanding self-rule could not be sustained without the reassertion, from time to time, of the moment of conquest, or at least without a show of force that extracted only a forced submission. Unwilling obedience, however, made the exercise of sovereignty precarious. Colonial sovereignty, in other words, always risked becoming domination.

The Gandhian nationalist movement that started around 1919 and that continued to be the main strand of Indian nationalism through the 1920s, '30s and '40s, created a political domain for ordinary Indians: students, middle-class salary earners, the working classes and the peasants. This was a major part of the training in 'politics' that most Indians received before the country became independent. Because of the extremely limited franchise that the British instituted in the country, there was no everyday domain of constitutional politics in which the people could directly participate. Legislative politics was 'elite politics', even when it involved leaders of the low-caste or other subaltern constituencies. Colonial legislatures were based on the assumption that Indian leaders did not represent the masses they claimed to represent.[1]

Nationalists, on the other hand, clearly wanted both a representative form of government and an instituted form of popular sovereignty through universal adult franchise. But, denied any mechanism for electoral representation of the people and their will, nationalists had to work out other methods of demonstrating their claims to represent 'the people', methods more immediately visual than the abstract process of representation through legislatures. The nationalists' answer to the charge that the Indian political elites were not representative of the masses was to mobilize the masses in direct agitational programmes of the nationalist movement. That story is well known. But we

---

1 For the appreciation of this point at some depth, I am grateful to my student Arvind Elangovan's research on the 1919 constitutional reforms in India.

should note that what underwrote this anti-colonial but populist faith in the modern-political capacity of the masses was another European inheritance: Romanticism. It is, of course, true that the middle-class leaders of anti-colonial movements – this includes Gandhi – often expressed a fear of the lawless mob and saw education, both political and general, as a solution to the problem (Pandey 1988a). But the fear was qualified by its opposite: a political faith in the masses. In the 1920s and '30s, this Romanticism marked Indian nationalism generally – many nationalists who were not Communist or of the Left, for instance, would express this faith.

Francesca Orsini has recently excavated a body of evidence documenting this tendency. To take but some stray examples from her selection, here is Ganesh Shankar Vidyarthi (1890–1931), the Editor of the Hindi paper *Pratap*, editorializing on May 31 1915:

> The much-despised peasants are our true bread-givers [*annadata*], not those who consider themselves special and look down upon the people who must live in toil and poverty as lowly beings. (Orsini 2003 [translations by Orsini])

Or Vidyarthi again, on January 11 1915:

> Now the time has come for our political ideology and our movement not [to] be restricted to the English-educated and to spread among the common people [*samanya janta*], and for Indian public opinion [*lokmat*] to be not the opinion of those few educated individuals but to mirror the thoughts of all the classes of the country ... democratic rule is actually the rule of public opinion. (Orsini 2003 [translations by Orsini])

One should note that this Romantic-political faith in the masses was populist as well, in a classical sense of the term. Like Russian populism of the late nineteenth century, this mode of thought not only sought a 'good' political quality in the peasant but also, by that step, worked to convert the so-called 'backwardness' of the peasant into a historical advantage. The peasant, 'uncorrupted' by the self-tending individualism of the bourgeois and oriented to the needs of his or her community, was imagined as already endowed with the capacity to usher in a modernity different and more communitarian than what was prevalent in the West.[2] The contradiction entailed in the very restricted nature of franchise under colonial rule and the simultaneous induction of the peasant and the urban poor into the nationalist movement had one important consequence. The constitutional law-making councils instituted by the British and the street (or

---

2 For an excellent discussion of this point, see Walicki 1989: chapters 1 and 2, in particular the section under 'The Privilege of Backwardness'.

the field and the factory) emerged, as it were, as rival and sometimes complementary institutions of Indian democracy. 'In the [legislative] Councils and the Assemblies', wrote Shrikishna Datt Palival (1895–1968) in an essay in the Hindi monthly *Vishal Bharat* (February 1936), 'one meets power and wealth face to face [and] the rulers' rights are kept safe in a temple where [people's] representatives are denied entry, just like untouchables [in a Hindu temple]' (cited in Orsini 2003). The very restrictions put on constitutional politics then meant that the field, the factory, the bazaar, the fair and the street became major arenas for the struggle for independence and self-rule.

It is in these arenas, as several historians of the Subaltern Studies group have pointed out, that subaltern subjects with their characteristic mode of politics (including practices of public and collective violence that governments would call 'disorder') entered modern public life. The general characteristics of peasant insurgency – looting, destroying, burning, etc., which Ranajit Guha studied in his book on the subject – left their imprints on all of the three large mobilizations that occurred under Gandhi's leadership (often without Gandhi's approval): the Non-Cooperation movement of 1919–22, the Civil Disobedience movement of 1931–34, and the Quit India movement of 1942 (Guha 1983; Amin 1995; Pandey 1978, 1988a). The shadow of the 1857 Rebellion always fell over these movements whenever they acquired a violent pitch. As Max Harcourt wrote of the Quit India movement in Bihar: 'The whole procedure was very reminiscent of the rural disturbances accompanying the 1857 Mutiny.' His essay reproduces a large extract from a description of a 'fairly typical siege of a thana office' from the diary of the Collector of Ballia, with the comment that '[it] could well have been written by his counterpart 85 years earlier' (Harcourt 2005: 318; see also Pandey 1988b).

By thus appropriating into itself modes of public violence and 'disorder' characteristic of peasant insurgency, the nationalist movement did create something like an everyday language of politics for the people. But this was not in any way the kind of 'everyday politics' that Nehru would look for after independence. The nationalist means of street politics were like so many tactics of battle that all contributed to an overall strategy of a 'war', the ultimate aim of which was to put an end to the colonial sovereignty of the British. That is why most of these expressions, peaceful or not, of everyday politics of the people had to do with defying the laws the British had instituted, a practice that amounted to challenging colonial sovereignty. These practices came to prefigure the idea of popular sovereignty in independent India.[3] In addition, it has to be

---

3 Obviously not everywhere to the same degree. My statement would apply more easily to regions that had seen violent mass mobilization during British rule in India. These regions are mostly in the north.

remembered that, unlike the Chinese Communists, for instance, who set up revolutionary governments in areas they 'liberated' in the course of their revolution, the Indian nationalists did not create any alternative centre of instituted sovereignty while the nationalist battle to evict the colonial power was on. Whenever popular mobilizations were on hold, the Congress leaders and other politicians took part in the provincial and central legislatures the British had set up. On independence, the nationalists created a Constituent Assembly, wrote a democratic constitution and adopted the principle of universal adult franchise, granting citizenly rights to all eligible Indians with the stroke of a pen, but chose to work through the legislative and bureaucratic structures they had inherited.

Post-Colonial Sovereignty

It is an interesting fact of Indian politics today that no theorist of the political in India would remain content with either Nehru's or Gajendragadkar's bemoaning of 'indiscipline' in public life. The very question of what constitutes 'discipline' and why so would be under the microscope. If Nehru wanted everyday forms of popular politics to bolster governance of the country, it is generally conceded now that, if anything, politics in India has progressed in the opposite direction. In many parts of India – though not everywhere, it has to be said, and in uneven ways – politics has indeed become separate from the business of governance.[4] Whatever it was that in Nehru's judgment was politics only in name – actions that he thought were conducted only 'in the name of politics' – today makes up the very substance of much that is considered political by scholars who theorize contemporary India. My effort here is not directed to explaining how the change happened, but more towards gaining an understanding of the nature of the change.

Let me jump several decades ahead from the 1950s and begin with two rather recent 'everyday' instances of popular politics in contemporary India. Both of my examples come from the state of West Bengal, so that may very well make them somewhat atypical of the rest of India. The Communist Party of India (Marxist) has been in power in West Bengal for more than twenty-five years now. The forms of political action illustrated by these two incidents owe something to the forms of popular mobilization that the Communist and other political parties championed in the state. But they also help us to reflect, provisionally, on questions of political power and sovereignty in India today.

---

4 I owe this insight to conversations with many students of Indian politics and to reading their works. I may mention here Sudipta Kaviraj, Partha Chatterjee, Thomas Hansen, Awadhendra Saran, Yogendra Yadav and Pranab Bardhan, among others.

Here are the two events as reported in the newspaper the *Telegraph*, published from Calcutta.

Event 1:

Krishnagar, November 26 [2004]: A mob of over 100 people ransacked a ward office and *gheraoed* [surrounded] the superintendent of Chakdah State General Hospital last night for two hours after a patient died allegedly due to doctors' negligence and forced him to write an apology letter. Relatives of the patient said that 35-year old Polly Karmakar, gasping for breath, was admitted to the hospital in Nadia, 55km from Calcutta, around 11 am with complaints of chest pain. The doctor prescribed administration of oxygen and left as his shift ended. Karmakar continued to gasp for over three-and-a-half hours as the doctor on the next shift was absent. Finally, well after 2.30 pm, an ENT surgeon was brought in and arranged for oxygen. By then, Karmakar had breathed her last.

Health department bosses in Salt Lake reacted strongly to the incident. Director of health services ... said the doctor on duty should not have left the hospital without handing charge over to the reliever and ordered a probe. He also took strong exception to the superintendent's apology. Moloy Banerjee [the Superintendent] had no right to issue an apology letter without permission from higher authorities, he said.

...

When the news of the death spread, the Karmakar relatives and neighbours started agitating at the hospital and ransacked the ward office. They returned around 8 pm and *gheraoed* the superintendent. Despite intervention of the assistant CMOH [Chief Medical Officer (Health?)] of Kalyani, the protesters insisted on an apology letter and dispersed after they got the letter.

The Telegraph (Calcutta), November 27 2004

Event 2:

Burdwan, Feb. 21 [2005]: Nobel Laureate Amartya Sen was among thousands stranded on the tracks here this morning as a group of people turned a station some distance away into a battlefield. Train services in the Khana-Ranaghat section of the Eastern Railway were disrupted for over eight hours from 6.30 am as hundreds squatted on the lines at Bhedia station, 220 km from Calcutta, and fought police while pressing for a slew of demands.

Sen, on his way to Santiniketan, however, did not have to sit stuck for that long. The district administration ensured that he took a car home from Burdwan station.

...

The demands were many – from the construction of a footbridge at the station to erecting a platform shed and ensuring stops for three long-distance trains at Bhedia.

...

Tear-gas shells had to be lobbed and 12 rounds fired in the air to bring the situation under control. At least 20 policemen were injured ... A jeep was ransacked. District Magistrate Subrata Gupta said that the demonstrators demanded that senior railway officials from Howrah speak to them

The Telegraph, February 22 2005

Clearly, there are genuine grievances and particular histories at issue in both cases (details I cannot go into). They also speak of continuing problems with public utilities in West Bengal – hospitals and transport – and particularly so in the context of the move to liberalize the economy and privatize some of these critical services. It is also obvious that in both instances the language of protest involves breaking the law and causing public inconvenience. The incidents are typical of everyday occurrences in West Bengal; I have collected them at random from newspapers. The very fact that no political parties are mentioned in either report suggests the popularity and familiarity of these forms of protest: people are so well trained in these modes of expression of disaffection that they do not any longer need the leadership of organized political parties to stage such 'events'. Their 'routine' nature is also suggested by the fact that the railway authorities had made prior special arrangements to ensure that the prominent economist's travel was as little interrupted as possible. The incidents are a large part of what takes place today, not just 'in the name of politics' but rather as the very stuff of politics itself. But what do they suggest about the operation of post-colonial sovereignty?

Something happens in both of these incidents that would not have happened in colonial India. This is the fact of a rioting or violent crowd demanding, often successfully and as a climactic moment in their activities, to have senior officers, who normally would not deal with members of the public, come to see them, or insisting on an official gesture of apology. Both are rituals of humiliation of officialdom. The officials go along with it because it has become a practical and effective method of pacifying a violent crowd. It becomes a gesture of the government eating humble pie, something that a colonial government would have found difficult to perform. The politics of sovereignty in post-colonial India works in these cases by the officials of the state acting as though the state, for the moment, were ceding a share of its capacity to make and enforce laws to a direct and concrete form of popular mobilization, which, in effect, stands in for the abstract ideal of popular sovereignty.

The ritual of humiliating officials also speaks of a very particular form of power. The act of senior officials apologizing to a crowd or listening to their grievances is no necessary guarantee of future improvement in conditions. If anything, a ransacked hospital ward or interrupted traffic perhaps mean more, and not less, inconvenience for the public than before. Yet there is a certain pleasure and sense of authority in seeing the government lose face, in seeing its officers humiliated. Officials, on the other hand, willingly concede this pleasure as an expedient way of buying peace. The exercise of this kind of power is obviously helped by the fact that, contrary to what Nehru once said, the post-colonial, democratically elected government is seldom able to establish 'order' with a heavy hand for a number of reasons, including the fear of a massive political backlash. This power of the multitude is not a programmatic one. It spends itself in its execution. It is not oriented towards a future; nor is it the vehicle of any dialectic of history. Yet, at the moment when a crowd unleashes its power in a situation where the memory of repression has become remote, it creates a vision, however fleeting, of direct and popular control of governance. The democratization and dissemination of this kind of popular power – something that stands in for 'people's power' – suggests that one perhaps needs to see this very form of power and its associated pleasures as themselves constituting a 'good' that Indian democracy makes available to the people.[5]

How this has come to be so is a complex history that I will not attempt here, except to note that the question of the place of crowd action and the need for public order in India's democracy was debated throughout the 1950s and the early 1960s until, thanks to the unfolding dynamic of Indian democracy, the debate lost all political utility (i.e., the ruling classes lost the capacity to impose discipline). The legacy of what anti-colonial nationalism had created as 'everyday politics' of the people was clearly a factor. Looking at West Bengal politics alone in the early 1950s, it is obvious that many political leaders of the day did not look on the law as providing any kind of limit to political action, and particularly so in the context of the massive in-migration of refugees from East Pakistan. They would sometimes directly refer (in good or bad faith) to the nationalist movement as a source of inspiration. Thus, Sureshchandra Banerjee, a Socialist member of the West Bengal Legislative Assembly and a supporter of the cause of the refugees, made this speech in the Assembly in the early 1950s, drawing a Gandhian distinction between legitimate actions and the law:

---

5 I do not intend this statement to be an exhaustive or summative statement about Indian democracy. One would need to make distinctions between histories of governance in different regions. There are also other forms of power at work in India. I only have in mind the feature that Nehru would have called in the 1950s a problem of 'indiscipline in public life'.

As regards to laws, I would like to mention with all humility that under the leadership of the father of the nation we have been taught how to break lawless laws, and if need be we will break laws again ... To us life is more precious than legal forms ... we may be tear-gassed and there might be lathi [sticks issued to the police] charge, but it is a legitimate action to commit satyagraha. In a demonstration the people must have the right to violate the law. Peacefully, of course. If there is violence, it is because the government acts violently, not the people. Gandhi taught them this ... (cited in Srinivasan 1967: 70–71)

When the refugees began to occupy and claim land that legally belonged to others, leaders such as Prafullachandra Ghosh applied similar distinctions between law and legitimate actions to support the move. He was reported to have remarked that 'although such occupation might not be right in the eyes of the law, it could be morally justified on the ground that the Government itself had failed to rehabilitate these helpless people' (The *Statesman* (Calcutta), March 22 1951). A nationalist tradition of breaking the law in the name of a morality higher than that enshrined in the law was thus invoked and acted upon in independent India.

Also to the point would be instances in which political leaders moved to shame both provincial and central governments into passivity by building up a political culture of demanding judicial enquiries into most acts of police firing. The Nehru papers, for instance, contain a report from the *National Herald* (January 22 1955) about a debate that took place in the Subjects Committee of the All India Congress Committee that met at Avadi on January 21 1955. Trikamal Patel, a delegate from Gujarat, 'had urged in ... [a] resolution that a tribunal should be set up in every state, consisting of three judges of the District or High Court, to conduct enquiry into incidents of police firings resulting in death'. Nehru made a strong intervention opposing the resolution: 'It pains me whenever police resort to firing ... It is possible that a particular police firing may not be justified. Such a thing will certainly be subjected to a searching inquiry ... If any policeman or official resorts to firing without justification and this results in death, then such an official will be tried for manslaughter ...' (Nehru 2000 [1955]: 460–61). Nehru in these years would on occasions underscore the differences between colonial and national armies and the police force: 'We have our armed forces. They have fired upon Indians under British rule. But now they are a national army and so we treat them as our brave young comrades. The police should also be a nationalist force. We must not do anything to spoil this image' (Nehru 2001b [1955]: 79). But this time he was clear that 'the resolution is out of place', for order sometimes 'has to be restored with a heavy hand' (Nehru 2000 [1955]: 460–61).

How Nehru and his like came to lose this debate is a complex history that has not been researched yet. Besides, one might argue that the 1960s' commentators drew too straight and unbroken a line between the anti-colonial creation of a sense of 'everyday politics' and the problem of public violence or 'indiscipline' they encountered. If we get away, however, from their rather moralistic use of the word 'discipline' and take the word in the more sociological sense that, say, the work of Michel Foucault has lent it, it is possible to see that a large part of the 'everyday politics' of Indian democracy is marked by the operation of a form of power that works on principles opposed to those of disciplinary society. What does it mean to say that India has a sovereign, democratic polity in which power often refuses any deep engagement with disciplinary forms?

Here, it seems to me, Foucault's 1976 lectures, recently published as *Society Must be Defended*, offer us a clue: tentative, provisional, speculative, but a clue nevertheless. In discussing the emergence of disciplinary power as a main mode of domination in the modern West, Foucault triangulates three terms: sovereignty (Hobbesian), discipline and society. He acknowledges that sovereignty, which ultimately gives birth to the language of rights, and discipline, which works by proliferating mechanisms of surveillance and domination, started their careers initially as 'incompatible' modes of power. Yet, as sovereignty in Europe shifted from the monarch to 'the people', there also emerged a certain degree of fraught reciprocity between the two 'because the democratization of [popular] sovereignty was heavily ballasted by the mechanism of disciplinary coercion' (Foucault 2003: 37). Hence, in the nineteenth century, the theory of sovereignty, says Foucault, was 'a permanent critical instrument to be used against the monarchy and against all of the obstacles that stood in the way of the development of the disciplinary society'. Public sovereignty 'made it possible to superimpose on the mechanism of discipline a system of right that concealed its mechanisms and erased the element of domination ... involved in discipline, and which, finally, guaranteed that everyone could exercise his or her own sovereign rights thanks to the sovereignty of the state' (2003: 37). Foucault (2003: 39) goes on to characterize thus the contemporary West: 'In our day, it is the fact that power is exercised through both right and disciplines, that the techniques of discipline and discourses born of discipline are invading rights, and that the normalizing procedures are increasingly colonizing the procedures of the law, that might explain the overall workings of what I would call a "normalizing society".'

In Foucault's thinking, there is a third term that mediates the fraught relationship between discipline and (popular) sovereignty: 'society'. 'Society' is produced only when sovereignty is able to eradicate all private wars from the social body and banish them to the frontiers or the 'outer limits of the great State units'. War then ceases to be internal to a social body and exists 'only as a [possible or actual] violent relationship ... between states'.

> This led, broadly speaking, to the emergence of something that did not exist as such in the Middle Ages: the army as institution. It is only at the end of the Middle Ages that we see the emergence of a State endowed with military institutions that replace both the day-to-day and generalized practice of warfare, and a society that was perpetually traversed by relations of war. (Foucault 2003: 48–49)

Indeed, it would seem that in terms of Foucault's analysis the generalization of disciplinary mechanisms through the social body would have been impossible without the production of 'society', which, in turn, was made possible in Europe initially by the 'state monopoly' of war (i.e., by the sovereignty that Hobbes theorized).

Could one then say that the histories of sovereignty and democracy in India take a route rather different from the trajectory outlined by Foucault? There was a 'Pax Britannica' in the nineteenth century, but it lost its meaning once nationalism arrived on the scene. Colonial sovereignty, faced with nationalist demands for self-rule, was often reduced to domination. It could never eliminate from the social body its internal wars. If anything, it helped exacerbate some of them. Nationalism created an everyday sphere of politics, but the political methods of this sphere were, as I have said, like tactics in a war, the war to end colonial sovereignty. Without this larger goal in view, a simple and local act of breaking the law of the British would not have acquired any broad significance. The war, actually, was not always with just the British. There were 'wars' internal to Indian society, fought by contesting nationalisms. The same crowd action was also at work in the riots that did not have to do with the British but rather with Hindu–Muslim or caste or linguistic conflicts.[6] The point is, neither colonial rule nor the nationalist movement was in a position to produce a 'society' (in the Hobbesian sense) by banishing these wars to the edges of the social body. At the end of colonial rule, India – one could say, using Foucault's prose (2003: 49) – remained a social body 'perpetually traversed by relations of war'.

If my argument is right, neither colonial rule, nor nationalism nor democracy has been able to produce the form of sovereignty that is necessary for the construction of a 'society' amenable to disciplinary power and its politics. If one

---

6 To say this, I repeat, is not to deny the impact of colonial rule on the creation or exacerbation of some of these conflicts.

assumes that a liberal-capitalist society (for all its faults) is unworkable without some hegemony of disciplinary power, then Indian democracy furnishes an interesting case where the political task of creating the typically modern mix of 'sovereignty' (rights) and disciplinary domination arises not *before* but *after* the coming of a universal adult franchise and a democratic form of polity. This critical difference from the European or Western model is what makes Indian democracy both practically and conceptually challenging.

References

Amin, Shahid, 1995, *Event, Metaphor, Memory: Chauri Chaura 1922–1992*, Berkeley, University of California Press.

Bell, Lucinda Downes, 2004, 'The 1858 Trial of the Mughal Emperor Bahadur Shah II "Zafar" for "Crimes Against the State"', unpublished PhD thesis, Faculty of Law, University of Melbourne.

Foucault, Michel, 1979, *Discipline and Punish: The Birth of the Prison*, Harmondsworth, Penguin.

— 2003, *'Society Must be Defended': Lectures at the Collège de France, 1975–1976*, ed. Arnold I. Davidson, trans. David Macey, New York, Picador.

Guha, Ranajit, 1983, *Elementary Aspects of Peasant Insurgency in Colonial India*, Delhi, Oxford University Press.

Harcourt, Max, 2005 [1977], 'Kisan Populism and Revolution in Rural India: The 1942 Disturbances in Bihar and East United Provinces', in D. A. Low (ed.), *Congress and the Raj: Facets of the Indian Struggle 1917–47*, Delhi, Oxford University Press.

Hobbes, Thomas, 1976 [1651], *Leviathan*, ed. C. B. Macpherson, Harmondsworth, Penguin.

India, 1976a, *Punjab Disturbances 1919–1920: Indian Perspective*, vol.1, Report of the Commissioners Appointed by the Punjab Sub-Committee of the Indian National Congress, 1920, Delhi, Deep Publications.

— 1976b, *Punjab Disturbances 1919–1920: British Perspective*, vol. 2, Report of the Disorders Inquiry Committee 1919–1920, appointed by the Government of India to investigate disturbances in Punjab, Delhi and Bombay, Delhi, Deep Publications.

Low, D. A., 1997, *Britain and Indian Nationalism: The Imprint of Ambiguity, 1929–1942*, Cambridge.

Nehru, Jawaharlal, 2000 [1955], 'Judicial Inquiry into Police Firing', in *Selected Works of Jawaharlal Nehru*, 2nd series, vol. 27, ed. Ravinder Kumar and Y. T. Sharada Prasad, Delhi, Jawaharlal Nehru Memorial Foundation.

— 2001a [1955], 'Policy of India', in *Selected Works of Jawaharlal Nehru*, vol. 29, ed. H. Y. Sharada Prasad and A. K. Damodaran, Delhi, Jawaharlal Nehru Memorial Fund.

— 2001b [1955], 'Students and Indiscipline', speech at public meeting in Patna, August 30 1955, in *Selected Works of Jawaharlal Nehru*, vol. 29, ed. H. Y. Sharada Prasad and A. K. Damodaran, Delhi, Jawaharlal Nehru Memorial Fund.

— 2001c [1955], 'Tasks Ahead', in *Selected Works of Jawaharlal Nehru*, vol. 29, ed. H. Y. Sharada Prasad and A. K. Damodaran, Delhi, Jawaharlal Nehru Memorial Fund.

— 2001d [1955], 'Hard Work for Building a New India', speech at the plenary session of the third convention of the All-India Bharat Sevak Samaj, Nagpur, March 12 1955, in *Selected Works of Jawaharlal Nehru*, vol. 28, ed. Ravinder Kumar and H. Y. Sharada Prasad, 2nd series, Delhi, Jawaharlal Nehru Memorial Fund.

Orsini, Francesca, 2003, 'The Hindi Public Sphere and Political Discourse in the Twentieth Century', unpublished paper presented at a conference on 'The Sites of the Political in South Asia', Berlin, October.

Pandey, Gyanendra, 1978, *The Ascendancy of the Congress in Uttar Pradesh: A Study in Imperfect Mobilization*, Delhi, Oxford University Press.

— 1988a, 'Peasant Revolt and Indian Nationalism', in Ranajit Guha and Gayatri Chakravorty Spivak (eds), *Selected Subaltern Studies*, New York, Oxford University Press.

— 1988b, *The Indian Nation in 1942*, Calcutta, K. P. Bagchi for the Centre for Studies in Social Sciences, Calcutta.

Srinivasan, R., 1967, 'Democracy and the Revolt of the Masses', in S. P. Aiyer (ed.), *The Politics of Mass Violence in India*, Bombay, Manaktalas.

Walicki, Andrzej, 1989, *The Controversy Over Capitalism: Studies in the Social Philosophy of the Russian Populists*, Notre Dame, IN, University of Notre Dame Press.

CHAPTER 7

'Horizontal' Connections and Interactions in Global Development

Sandra Halperin

In order to consider fully the challenges and possibilities of world-making, it is necessary to understand the socioeconomic space that already exists across national boundaries and how it has been politically constituted and reconstituted over time. Nelson Goodman's observation, already cited by the editors in the Introduction to this volume, makes the point precisely: 'Worldmaking as we know it always starts from worlds already at hand; the making is a re-making' (1978: 6).

Discussions of the global era and how to navigate or shape it often fail to give sufficient consideration to the global socioeconomic order that pre-existed, and continuously worked to shape, the era of nation states. The era of nation states was forged within a global constellation which worked to unite dominant groups around the world, at the same time separating the masses that populated their local jurisdictions into culturally and politically bounded national collectivities. An understanding of the socioeconomic and political bonds that have long existed among dominant groups around the globe, and of the connections and interactions that constitute and reproduce these bonds, is necessary to any consideration of how to remake the world.

With this aim in mind, this chapter endeavours to bring into clearer focus the structure of global socioeconomic relations from the point of view of predominantly 'horizontal' bonds rather than 'vertical' ones contained by state institutions. More specifically, it explores the trans-local/cross-regional interactions and connections that, beginning in the late eighteenth century, brought about the synchronic and interdependent development of dynamic focal points of growth throughout the world.

Most perspectives assume that industrial capitalism developed during this period through a process of nationally organized economic growth and that, today, its organization is becoming increasingly trans-local or global. However, nationally organized economic growth has rarely been the case. From the start, capitalist development has been essentially transnational in nature and global in scope, involving not whole societies but the advanced sectors of dualistic economies in Europe, Latin America, Asia and elsewhere. This chapter endeavours, therefore, analytically to shift the axis of view from the vertical (states, regions) to the horizontal (classes, networks) and, in this way, to bring into view the synchronic and interdependent development of dynamic focal points of growth throughout the world shaped within and outside Europe by trans-local interaction and connection, as well as by local struggles and relations of dominance and subordination.

Most accounts of the development of capitalism begin with the 'rise of Europe'. The story they tell is that the 'lights went on' in Europe following the European dark ages (or certainly by the eve of Europe's 'industrial revolution') just as, or long after, they had gone out elsewhere in the world; and that, as a result of European exploration, settlement, colonization and conquest, lights of varied brightness and colour gradually appeared in non-European areas of the world over the course of the next two centuries.

However, this story is no longer convincing. As Janet Abu-Lughod (1989) and others have shown, the rise of Europe took place within an already existing system, stretching from Western and Southern Europe through the Middle East to China, and characterized by a prosperous and far-flung network of trade and intercultural exchange. European military expansion into this system did not displace or destroy it: when the 'lights went on in Europe' they remained on elsewhere in the world. Thus, after the 'lights went on in Europe', the actual pattern of economic expansion throughout the world resembled (to borrow an image from James Blaut [1993: 171]) 'a string of electric lights' strung across Asia, the Middle East, Africa, Latin America and Europe. These lights illuminated small islands of urbanized industrial society and export sectors in Asia, Latin America, Europe and elsewhere, each surrounded by traditional communities and institutions and by underdeveloped, weakly integrated local economies. This pattern developed around the world as elites and ruling groups, seeking to expand production while avoiding the social levelling required for the production of articles for mass local consumption, produced largely for external markets instead. As a result, *within* and outside Europe domestic markets remained weak and poorly integrated, and economic expansion proceeded through a trans-local/cross-regional exchange of capital and commodities among governments, ruling groups and elites.

Local Relations of Power

Distinctions are conventionally drawn between class structures in different European societies and, particularly, between those that were supposedly dominated by an indigenous, independent capitalist bourgeoisie, and those that were not.[1] This distinction is the basis of various schemas that define 'two roads' to industrial capitalism and democracy in Europe. One road, exemplified by Britain, is characterized by the emergence of a relatively open political space – the result of a bourgeois revolution having displaced the old landed aristocracy and the absolutist state. The second road, exemplified by Germany and other 'late' developers, is distinguished by its relatively closed political space, the result of the continuing dominance of an agrarian class able to block industrialization and resist democracy (Coates 2000; van der Pijl 1998; Moore 1966; Gerschenkron 1962). But nowhere in Europe was there a clear division between industrial and landed capital; everywhere, in fact, industrial capitalist development was characterized by their fusion. In Britain, as elsewhere, the nature of industrial capitalist development was shaped by the political convergence of a landed aristocracy and large capitalist manufacturers.

Many have argued that this elite had become 'bourgeoisified' by the eighteenth or nineteenth century. However, throughout the nineteenth century the most effective elites were traditional and aristocratic, landowning and rent-receiving, and oligarchic. Rosa Luxemburg got it precisely right: in England, there was no revolutionary changeover from medieval to modern society, but 'an early compromise which has preserved [into the twentieth century] the old remnants of feudalism'. The old forms of medieval England 'were not shattered or swept away, but filled with new content' (1976: 232).

It is assumed that the road to industrial development and democracy was made possible by the conflict between the new industrial capitalist classes in Europe and absolutist monarchs. However, the conflict between the 'new' bourgeoisie and absolutist monarchs involved only selective aspects of absolutism and, specifically, those that scholars have identified as 'enlightened' and 'liberal' (see, e.g., Gagliardo 1967). The leaders of the 'national' revolutions and revolts against absolutism were opposed to 'liberal' reforms and, particularly, price and wage controls, labour protections and national welfare systems that monarchs had introduced in Britain, France, and elsewhere,

---

1   The discussion that follows sometimes focuses on 'Europe', but often discusses only Britain. 'Europe' is indicated when the statement has general applicability – though qualifications are often noted. Britain is the focus of much of the discussion because it will likely be considered the 'hardest case', i.e., that for which arguments elaborated in this chapter would seem to be least applicable.

beginning in the sixteenth century. Their aim was to seize control of the state in order to privatize new sources and means of producing wealth, to dismantle much of what today would be considered socially enlightened in 'liberal absolutism', and to retain much of what was not in a new guise. Many of the revolutionary and progressive changes attributed to the emergence of nation states were aspects of liberal absolutism that survived the nationalist assault. For instance, the features of France that, in 1815, were thought to resemble a 'bourgeois' state – its centralized administrative apparatus, standing armies, national taxation, a codified law, and the beginnings of a unified market – were the work not of the Revolution but of the ancien régime. It was France's ancien régime that began the break-up of large estates into a multiplicity of small proprietorships.[2] Nor were the ideas and values supposedly born in the Revolution the product of a new and revolutionary class (Tocqueville 1955). As Immanuel Wallerstein notes, 'from a strictly French point of view, the balance sheet of the French Revolution is relatively meager' (1996: 12).

It is often assumed that in Britain the repeal of the Corn Laws marked the end of the power of the traditional landowning elite there. However, the Corn Laws were designed, not to shore up a declining sector, but to retain the high profits generated during the Napoleonic war years. For most of the nineteenth century, British agriculture remained the biggest branch of the economy by far in terms of employment. Moreover, until 1914, non-industrial Britain could easily outvote industrial Britain (Hobsbawm 1968: 196). Despite all that had been written about industrialists replacing landowners as the dominant element in the ruling elite, as late as 1914 industrialists 'were not sufficiently organized to formulate broad policies or exert more than occasional influence over the direction of national affairs' (Boyce 1987: 8). The traditional landowning elite formed the basis of Britain's 'capitalist class',[3] dominated the state apparatus, led Britain's capitalist development and channelled it into dualistic and monopolistic forms. As a result, industrial expansion in Europe was shaped not by a liberal, competitive ethos, as is emphasized in most accounts, but by feudal forms of organization, monopolism, protectionism, cartelization and corporatism, and by rural, pre-industrial and autocratic structures of power and authority.

2 Some students of the subject maintain that the number of landed proprietorships in France was scarcely smaller before 1789 than it is today (Johnson 1979: 155).
3 'Far from the bourgeoisie having overthrown the aristocracy, we have instead the aristocracy becoming the bourgeoisie' (Wallerstein 1991: 58).

The Trans-Local Structure of Industrial Capitalist Expansion

In the eighteenth century, 'absolutist' governments in England,[4] France, and elsewhere in Western Europe were regulating local markets, as well as controlling employment and settlement. 'Absolutism' was attacked by its opponents for its over-regulation. However, the aim of much of this regulation was to protect the local population against monopoly and speculation, shortages and high prices. Those in England who demanded 'freedom of trade' during the eighteenth century were actually demanding freedom from the requirement to trade inside open markets, by means of open transactions, and according to the rules and regulations that ensured fair practices and prices (Lie 1993: 283).

In Britain, wages rose throughout the eighteenth century and labourers were able 'to take on less work and spend more time at leisure without endangering their traditional standard of living' (Gillis 1983: 41). Because economies were based on local markets, workers were often able to exercise economic power as consumers as well. However, by the end of the eighteenth century these features became the target of a broad campaign to 'dis-embed' capitalist development, which, by expanding production largely for export, obviated the need to furnish labourers with sufficient means to buy what they produced and deprived them of the ability to exercise power through consumer choice or boycott. Land and industry became concentrated in fewer and fewer hands in the course of the century; and an unprecedented degradation and intensification of labour inside and outside Europe produced an increasing volume of goods and capital for circulation among a transnational network of property owners.

Europe's Transnational Industrial Expansion

States in Europe were built up within a pre-existing, region-wide system of social institutions, relationships and norms. For centuries, and with the Church acting as an international unifying agent, regulating economic life and political and class struggles across the region, political development, class struggles, social change, ideology and culture remained essentially trans-European.[5]

Because of the essentially transnational nature of European society and the similarities and interdependencies that it created among states, as the various economies of Europe began to expand in the nineteenth century, their advanced

---

4 Many historians assume that England did not experience a form of state corresponding to the absolute monarchies of the Continent because English monarchs could not take the property of their subjects without their consent in Parliament. But Continental absolutism was also based on the rights of property.

5 See, e.g., Mann 1988; Mattingly 1955; Pirenne 1969, 1958; Meynial 1926; de Tocqueville 1955; Stubbs 1967; Granshof 1970; Balch 1978; Strayer 1970.

sectors were tied more closely to those within the economies of other European countries than to the more backward sectors within their own (see Halperin 2004: Chapter 3). As a result, Europe's economic expansion took place within, and was crucially shaped by, an increasingly interdependent industrial system. Since interdependent parts must grow in some sort of balance if profitability is to be maintained, for much of the nineteenth century, the 'advanced sectors' of European and other economies developed less through direct competition with each than by means of a mutually reinforcing circuit of investment and exchange (see Halperin 2004: Chapter 3). Europe's ruling classes were not separate-but-similar classes. They formed a single, trans-regional elite, with broadly similar characteristics, interests and capabilities. While the properties of dominant groups in different parts of Europe may have varied, the connections and interactions among them were rich and concrete and, within the constraints and opportunities present in different contexts, produced a set of common solutions to the problems of organizing production along new lines. The late-eighteenth-century 'industrial revolution' in Europe did not involve any fundamental change in this trans-European social system. In fact, the reorganization of social relations of production in Europe as a result of the 'industrial revolution' brought different groups across states into closer relations of interdependence.

Europe emerged into its first century of industrial capitalism from the crucible of the 'Great War' (the Napoleonic Wars). A quarter of a century of war and revolutionary turmoil had made clear the central dilemma for dominant groups tempted by the possibilities of great profits to reorganize production along the lines of industrial capitalism: how to mobilize – train, educate and, in other ways, empower – labour while maintaining the basic relation of capitalism, i.e., the subordination of labour to capital.[6] The Great War had revealed the dangers of a trained and compact mass army: many analogies, in fact, were drawn between the mass army of soldiers created in the Great War and the mass industrial army of workers needed for industrial capitalist production.[7] This was the context within which elites throughout Europe undertook to mobilize labour for industrial production.

Elites were cohesive, had much to gain, controlled immense resources and were free to deploy these resources in a sustained pursuit of their aims. They

---

6 Ernest Gellner argued that 'a mobile, literate, culturally standardized, interchangeable population' is needed for industrialization, and that nationalism and nation-building emerged as a reflection of and means of meeting this need (1983: 20, 46).

7 Employers called into use the language and protocols of military operations. They saw themselves as 'captains' of industry and their task as one of 'conscripting, training and commanding' an industrial 'army' that they housed in large-scale, multi-family tenements or rental 'barracks'. In Prussia, miners wore uniforms and saluted their supervisors (Gillis 1983: 154).

either controlled the apparatus of the state directly or had access to political leaders and could trade their political support, or the withdrawal of political opposition, for concessions from them. They were therefore able to carry on a class struggle through the nineteenth century by means of a purposive, determined and essentially coherent legislative, legal, military and political assault on artisans, labourers and peasants.

The 'European Model' of Industrial Capitalist Expansion: A Reinterpretation
Foreign trade was the primary engine of economic growth in England in the nineteenth century; but it was the home market that initially gave the impetus to industrial growth in England between 1750 and 1780 (Eversley 1967: 221; see also Mathias 1983: 16, 94). Britain's industrial output quadrupled during the eighteenth century and the bulk of this output consisted of mass consumption goods. Thus, during the century, England's breakthrough in production was accompanied by a 'democratization of consumption' at home.[8] In the nineteenth century, however, and long before it had been exhausted as a market for goods and capital, Britain's domestic economy ceased to expand – so much so that by 1914 it had become under-mechanized and a poorly integrated relative of the domestic economies of other advanced countries.

Numerous scholars have pointed out that British investors under-invested in the domestic economy and, instead, massively exported capital. They point out that funds used for British foreign investment could have been used to improve the technical performance of British industry (Lewis 1972: 27–58; 1978a: 176–77; see also Trebilcock 1981); they could have 'helped to augment the stock of domestic housing and other urban social overhead projects and, thus, expand the domestic market for the expanded output of the British economy'.[9] Not only was investment needed at home, but also between 1880 and 1914 returns from overseas investment were 'far below what presumably could have been earned by devoting the same resources to the expansion of domestic industry' (Davis

8 In the course of the century, there was a marked improvement in the variety and quality of household furnishings, decorations and 'luxury' items among artisans and farmers. In fact, in Britain 'a greater proportion of the population than in any previous society in human history' was able 'to enjoy the pleasures of buying consumer goods' and 'not only necessities, but decencies, and even luxuries'. By 1801 the home market accounted for about £90 million per annum, or about £40 per household. Even allowing for inflation, this suggests a significant increase in per capita consumption of home products, and, although obviously not all householders reached this average, McKendrick et al. have argued that it is 'extremely improbable' that all the extra domestic consumption could have been 'absorbed by the top layers of income' (1982: 29).

9 Barratt Brown, 1970: x. See also Davis and Huttenback 1988. For similar arguments concerning Germany, see Wehler 1969; for France, see Langer 1931; Wesseling 1997.

and Huttenback 1988). Moreover, these investments were generally exposed to more risk than domestic investments.

Why, then, did investors neglect opportunities for profitable home investment and, instead, pursue investments overseas that were riskier, more difficult and costly to acquire and, in some cases, not as lucrative? The usual explanation is that the domestic market was not yet developed enough to absorb the output of expanded production and to provide profitable investment opportunities for surplus capital, and that, as a result, capitalists were forced to seek larger markets and more profitable fields of investment abroad. But capital exporters did not then, and even now tend not to have capital-saturated domestic economies. Britain and other European economies did not, as is usually assumed, develop initially on the basis of the expansion of the internal market and subsequently expand into the foreign, colonial and world markets: they expanded production first and foremost for foreign markets, long before the opportunities for profitable investment had been exhausted at home (Trebilcock 1981; Lewis 1972: 27–58; Cameron 1961: 123, 152; Cairncross 1953: 225; Lévy 1951–52: 228; Sée 1942: 360).

In fact, the market that was 'saturated' in Britain in 1902 and before was, as John Hobson made clear, the one constituted solely by the wealthy classes. Thus, to speak of 'saturation' assumes that the mass of the population had no demand for any goods other than those necessary for their own physical reproduction. 'It is not industrial progress that demands the opening up of new markets and areas of investment', Hobson argued, 'but mal-distribution of consuming power which prevents the absorption of commodities and capital within the country' (1902: 85). This, he observed, was a typical consequence of capitalism, but not a necessary one. He argued that whatever was produced in England could be consumed in England, provided that there was a proper distribution of 'the "income" or power to demand commodities' (1902: 88). But, as Hobson noted, more than a quarter of the population of British towns was living at that time at a standard 'below bare physical efficiency' (1902: 86).

Some theorists argue that while capital exports may not have been necessary as a means of securing markets for surplus goods, they were necessary to Europe's industrialization as a means of acquiring raw materials and accumulating capital (see, e.g., Wallerstein 1974: 38, 51, 93–95, 237, 269, 349). However, Paul Bairoch has argued that the 'core' countries had an abundance of the minerals of the Industrial Revolution (iron ore and coal); they were almost totally self-sufficient in raw materials and, in fact, exported energy to the 'Third World'.[10] Colonialism, Bairoch argues, was therefore not necessary for industrial

---

10 Bairoch 1993: 172. The minerals prominent in tropical trade today did not come to the fore until

growth in Europe. In fact, he argues that, 'If one compares the rate of growth during the nineteenth century it appears that non-colonial countries had, as a rule, a more rapid economic development than colonial ones' (1993: 77).

Given the difficulties with standard interpretations of British investment, it seems reasonable to look elsewhere for an explanation.

Production processes, as Alfred Sohn-Rethel has pointed out, are structured in ways that enable capital to retain its control over the class struggle (1978: 163). Decisions about whether and how to increase or restructure production are based on calculations about the conditions necessary for the realization of profit. Disadvantageous social externalities created by the introduction of new production methods and by an expansion of output would be part of those calculations. Had the 'democratization of consumption' of the eighteenth century continued, and had a broad-based industrial growth developed, along with the mass purchasing power and internal market needed to support it, the class, land and income structures on which the existing structure of social power in Britain rested would have been destroyed.

Britain's consumer revolution in the eighteenth century had important implications for the structure of British society.[11] The consumer revolution and the emergence of a domestic market for mass-produced consumer goods was politically threatening because it worked to undermine class distinctions and increase social mobility; thus, it was not encouraged. A fully industrialized economy requires mass mobilization. Mass mobilization for industry (as for war) creates, out of the relatively disadvantaged majority of the population, a compact and potentially dangerous force; thus, elites showed little interest in the expansion of industry at home.

It might be argued that owners of wealth were not conscious of the social externalities associated with the application of large masses of labour to production. This seems hardly plausible. The problems of setting to work and controlling masses of labour are not so substantially different in capitalist

---

the end of the nineteenth century. In 1913, minerals were prominent in the exports only of Peru and Mexico (Lewis 1978a: 201). Moreover, through the nineteenth and early twentieth centuries (until around 1920), terms of trade were unfavourable for Britain (see Strachey 1959: 149–51) and improved for the less developed countries. It was only after the Second World War (in the 1950s and again in the 1980s) that terms of trade in primary goods deteriorated (Bairoch 1993: 113–14). The exception – and, as Arthur Lewis points out, it is an important one for Latin America – is sugar.

11 That this was widely recognized is evident in the sumptuary laws restricting the personal consumption of goods based on class and income. Sumptuary laws were enacted in Europe between the fifteenth and eighteenth centuries and were retained by many states well into the nineteenth century. See, e.g., Dorwart 1971: 45, 50; see also Hunt 1996; Vincent 1969; Baldwin 1926; Greenfield 1918.

production as to have made all prior problems and their solutions irrelevant. For centuries landlords had been confronted with the 'great fear' of mass peasant uprisings and had organized production in ways that reinforced the existing relations of power and authority. The difference in capitalist production, and it is crucial, is not the strategic power that workers have – peasants had that too – but that for industry to grow and remain competitive a sizeable portion of the labour force must be educated, skilled and mobile. If property owners were not conscious of the dangers of mass mobilization for industry, would they not have been after Marx spelled it out for them in the widely read and cited *Communist Manifesto*?

The development of exogenous demand and consumption through the export of capital and goods limited the distribution of the benefits of expanded production. In 1914, British industrialization was as sectorally and geographically limited as dualistic colonial economies. Mechanization, skilled labour and rising productivity and real wages were found only in sectors producing for export. These sectors had only a limited impact on the rest of the economy. Little attempt was made to expand or mechanize industries producing goods for domestic household consumption. Consequently, the building industries grew by expanding employment, rather than by introducing innovations either in organization or technology.[12] New techniques were introduced 'slowly and with considerable reluctance'. In the 1930s, half the industry's workforce still practised 'their traditional handicrafts, especially in house-building, largely untouched by mechanization' (Benson 1989: 20). Although Britain had pioneered electro-technics, by 1913 the output of the British electrical industry was little more than one-third of Germany's (Hobsbawm 1968: 180). Before the Second World War, less than one-third of those employed in the transport sector were employed by the railways (28 per

---

12 Profit is increased by producing goods with fewer or cheaper workers (i.e., by reducing the cost of labour). One way of doing this is to use machines to increase productivity, so that fewer workers are needed to produce the same number of articles. This means that each article costs less labour to produce. However, these machines require skilled and relatively valuable (higher cost), workers. Rather than use fewer workers, you can increase profit by cheapening the cost of workers. This can be done by reducing the price of food and other wage goods sectors and, consequently, the cost of labour (the cost of reproducing labour physically). However, this entails the reform of land tenure and agricultural systems and also increases the value of agricultural workers (eventually, Britain was able to develop cash crops abroad in order to import cheap food). Another means of increasing profits reduces the cost of labour by applying large quantities of unskilled or semi-skilled labour to production. This is typical of primary export production in the contemporary 'Third World'. In Britain, whole families (women and children) were put to work to earn, together, the same wage once paid to a single 'head of household'. When the whole family contributes to its reproduction rather than a single 'head of household', the employer gets more workers for no additional cost.

142

cent in 1931). A majority of those engaged in transport worked for a small employer or were self-employed (Benson 1989: 22–23). Despite the British origins of the machines and machine tools industries, it was not until the 1890s that automatic machine-tools production was introduced in Britain. The impetus came from the US and the desire on the part of employers 'to break down the hold of the skilled craftsmen in the industry' (Hobsbawm 1968: 181). Gas manufacture was mechanized late and as a result of pressure from trade unions.

Even Britain's export industries were slow to adopt new techniques or improvements, not only in textiles but also in coal, iron, steel, railways and shipbuilding. The supply of coal increased, not by introducing labour-saving techniques but by increasing the numbers of coal miners. In the 1930s, 'more than 40% of British coal was cut and practically 50% conveyed without the aid of machinery' (Benson 1989: 16). Although Britain was pre-eminent in steel production and had pioneered major innovations in its manufacture, with the exception of the Bessemer converter (1856), Britain was slow to apply the new methods and failed to keep up with subsequent improvements. By the early 1890s, Britain's steel industry had fallen behind that of Germany and the US. American shipbuilding expanded at a faster rate than British and, by 1860, had almost caught up. Although British industrialization was based on the expansion of capital goods production for railway-building, rapid technical improvement came, even here, only when compelled by military competition and the modernizing armaments industry.[13]

The Circuit of Capital: the Nineteenth-Century Origins of Contemporary Global Governance

Europe's economy before the Second World War[14] was based on the development of external markets for heavy industry and high-cost consumption goods. By expanding its shipbuilding, boiler-making, gun and ammunitions industries, Britain was able to penetrate and defend markets overseas. This, in

13 See Mathias, who contends that arguments about earlier and later industrializing countries do not explain the 'failure in innovation and development, widespread in the British economy' (1983: 375).
14 Although the structure of European society was profoundly affected by the First World War, forces of resistance during the interwar years prevented its breakdown. As a result, the essential contours of Europe's nineteenth-century socioeconomic and political system were preserved after the First World War. As Karl Polanyi rightfully points out, the First World War was part of the old nineteenth-century system, 'a simple conflict of powers unleashed by the lapse of the balance-of-power system'. It did not, as would the Second World War, form 'part of the world upheaval' that marked the great transformation (1944: 30).

turn, provided opportunities for Britain to build foreign railways, canals and other public works, including banks, telegraphs and other public services owned or dependent upon governments. British exports of capital provided purchasing power among foreign governments and elites for these goods and services, and funded the development and transport of food and raw materials exports to Europe, thus creating additional foreign purchasing power and demand for British goods, as well as decreasing the price of food and, thereby, the value of labour in relation to the value of what it produced.[15] At the centre of this circuit was the City of London, which, like the advanced sector of a 'dependent' economy, depended 'only slightly' on Britain's economic performance (Boyce 1987: 18–19).

The bulk of Britain's capital exports between 1880 and 1913 went to the Dominions, Europe and the US. Almost 70 per cent of it went into docks, tramways, telegraphs and telephones, gas and electricity works and, in particular, the enormously capital-absorbing railways.[16] Only the production of modern armaments is more capital-absorbing (the mass production of armaments in the US and their export to Europe's great and small powers began in the 1860s).[17] Increasing blocs of territory throughout the world became

15 Britain's industrial wage-earners realized 55–60 per cent of their wage in the form of food; the steady fall in prices of staple food imports after 1874 (grain, tea, sugar, lard, cheese, ham and bacon; Mathias 1983: 345) allowed real wages in Britain to rise until the First World War. The real wages of industrial workers are made up of: (1) the productivity of labour (output per worker in each industry expressed in units of that industry's product); (2) the share of that industry's product that goes to the wage-earner (e.g., the bootmaker's wage in boots); (3) the barter terms on which these units of the worker's own product can be exchanged for objects of his own consumption.

In Britain, the real wage per head was raised as the product per worker was, for the most part, progressively raised. However, *'the share of this product handed over to the worker himself as his wage did not rise or fall much'* (Brown 1968: 31; my emphasis). If the product increases while wages as a share of the product decline, workers are worse off, not in absolute terms but in relation to the value of what they produce. The *standard of consumption* of labour (the mass of the population) bears no relation to its productivity, to its increased power of production. Wage-earners cannot buy back what, as workers, they produce. A rise in real wages does not necessarily mean that there is an increase in purchasing power or the standard of consumption.

16 As did the bulk of French and Belgian foreign investment. Twelve per cent of British investment went into extractive industries (agriculture and mining); only 4 per cent went into manufacturing (Edelstein 1981: 73).

17 Dobb 1963: 296. Hobsbawm argues that, at least in the short run, railway-building in Britain had little to do with developing the domestic market. All industrial areas were within easy access of water transport by sea, river or canal, and water transport was and is by far the cheapest for bulk goods (coal mined in the north had been shipped inexpensively by sea to London for centuries). He argues that investors were looking 'for any investment likely to yield more than the 3.4 per cent of public stocks'. Railway returns eventually settled down at an average of about 4 per cent (Hobsbawm 1968: 111; see also pp. 113–18).

covered with networks of British-built and financed railways, provisioned by British steamships and defended by British warships.

Throughout the circuit, within and outside Europe, the same overall pattern of dualistic growth emerged, though with variations according to each country's place in the circuit and the types of goods it produced for sale. France, whose empire, export earnings and foreign investment were second only to Britain's, exported high-cost textiles and luxury goods (e.g., silks, laces, wines, delicacies) and built railways in Russia with French equipment and capital. Germany's dualistic industrial expansion took off with its 'marriage', not of 'iron and finance', as in Britain, but of 'iron and rye', celebrated, in 1879, along with the enactment of an Anti-Socialist Law and state legal enforcement of cartel agreements to limit production. In Italy and Austria-Hungary, industrial development focused on expanding heavy industry and gaining railway concessions in the Balkans.

Other states – Russia, the United States, Canada and Australia – were incorporated into the circuit as raw-materials producers. These increased their production of agricultural and other raw-materials exports to pay for railways, iron and steel, armaments and other foreign manufactures. Russia paid for these imports and the interest on its enormous foreign debt by steadily increasing agricultural exports, even during famines (Munting 1982: 31). Colonial territories that became independent states – for instance, states in Latin America and in the Balkans – remained within the circuit. Local elites in colonies, former colonies, or states that had never been colonies, imported British capital and goods, developed mines and raw materials exports and built railways and ports, in order to extend, consolidate and maintain their power and become wealthy.[18]

This circuit and the overall pattern of dualism that it produced made it possible for elites to expand production without the redistribution and reform necessary for the further development of the home market. However, by the eve of the First World War, the extremes of wealth and poverty created by dualistic economic expansion were generating more or less continual conflicts (see Halperin 2004: chapters 4 and 5). By 1914, tensions were rising not only within European states but also among them. As more and more countries began pursuing dualistic, externally oriented economic expansion, conflict over

18 Some former colonies did not develop the sharp dualism that characterized industrial expansion in Europe. In Australia, Canada and New Zealand there was no pre-existing landed elite and the colonists displaced, overwhelmed or destroyed prior inhabitants. In these countries, revenues were not used solely to enrich a traditional landowning class and its allies as they were in Europe. In the US, where a strong landowning class developed in the south, a struggle between landowners and industrialists culminated in civil war and the victory of the industrial capitalist bourgeoisie.

territories in Africa and Asia increasingly threatened to lead to war. At the same time, expansionist aims began more and more to focus on Europe itself and, as they did, Europe's balance of power and imperialist regimes began to dissolve.

The First World War succeeded in bringing into conflict the two central features of Europe's industrial development – internal restriction and external expansion.

In the eighteenth century, governments had relied on the social elite to pay for mercenary troops and to provide military leaders to fight professional wars. These wars tended to reinforce the status quo by heightening existing social inequalities. However, the wars fought by Napoleon's mass 'citizen' armies and the mass armies mobilized to fight against them had very different consequences. The participation of the lower classes in the war effort and in areas of work and social life usually barred to them worked to enhance the power of labour and to strengthen its market position. It also compelled governments to ensure their loyalty by extending to them various rights. Thus, after the end of the Napoleonic Wars, and despite the difficulty of raising and maintaining large mercenary forces, Europe's use of citizen armies largely ended. The new weapon introduced by Napoleon was used in 1870 by France and Germany, also with frightening consequences (the rising of the Paris commune), and then not again until 1914.[19]

In 1914, aggressive imperialist threats on their frontiers forced European states, once again, to use what was then still the most powerful weapon of mass destruction: the *lévee en masse*. The mass mobilizations for the First World War set in motion a social revolution that, between 1917 and 1939, swept through all of Europe. The efforts of Western governments and ruling elites to prevent its further spread and escalation led directly to the Second World War.[20] At its end, the region was wholly transformed. While previous regional conflagrations had been followed by restorations (e.g., the Napoleonic Wars, the revolutions of 1830 and 1848 and the First World War), the Second World War, by shifting the balance of class power throughout Europe, made restoration impossible. The vastly increased organizational strength and power of working classes and peasant masses, and the decline of the aristocracy as a result of wartime changes, created the conditions for a historic class compromise and for the achievement

19 See, for an overview of this issue, Howard 1961: 8–39. Russia conscripted large numbers of men for the Crimean War; but contrast a description of this (Royle 1999: 91–92) with the account of the French mobilization in 1870–71 in Taithe 2001: 6–13, 22–28, 38–47.

20 The overriding concern of European statesmen, from the beginning of the interwar period until the outbreak of the Second World War, was the rise of the left in Europe and the westward spread of Bolshevism from the Soviet Union. It was this concern that led Britain and France to ally with the Fascist powers (Germany, Italy) in the Four Power Pact and to encourage and aid in the revival and expansion of German power. For an extended discussion of the politics of the interwar period in Europe, see Halperin 2004: Chapter 7.

in Western Europe of universal suffrage, a relatively more nationally embedded capitalism (i.e., a more balanced and internally oriented development) and, for a time, unprecedented growth and relative peace and stability.

The Reconfigured Circuit

The adoption of social democratic policies effectively ended the dualism that once had characterized European economies. As a result, European economies expanded in ways that after the Second World War became associated with 'First World' and 'Second World' development. However, the circuit of exchange that had produced dualism in Europe endured and continued to reproduce it elsewhere in the world. The survival of this pattern of development was the result of a massive and coordinated campaign by Western, newly independent, 'developing' states to eradicate social democracy and consolidate dualistic structures throughout what became, as a result of their efforts, the vast, global 'Third World'. Once socialism had been destroyed in the 'Third World' and the 'Second World', Western states began a campaign to reverse their own post-Second World War social settlements. The emerging trend, therefore, is of reintegration, of the 'Second World' and, eventually, the 'First World' into a system of local and trans-local relations similar to the one that in those areas of the world pre-dated the crisis of the World Wars and the Great Depression.

Within the circuit of exchange that linked dualistic economies around the world in the nineteenth century, there emerged a struggle for power among European ruling groups that culminated and came to a conclusion in the two-phased war in Europe at the beginning of the twentieth century. The crisis in Europe provided an opportunity for elites in states and territories in other parts of the world to better their position within the circuit. Restricted in their access to benefits enjoyed by European elites and not fully accepted by them, these elites sought to wrest a larger share of political power for themselves. As had been the case with similar intra-elite struggles in Europe, nationalism was used by these contending elites to articulate their demands, win the support of the lower classes and gain state power. And as had been the case in Europe, in the newly 'independent' states established after the Second World War, these nationalist movements became fused with a programme of capitalist expansion that consolidated dualism.[21]

21 The elites that led movements for decolonization and national independence were part of a transnational elite. Their concern was with their role in the overall system – rather than with vertical inequality (exploitation). As in Europe, in the 'developing world', elites legitimized their claim to represent the people/nation by asserting that the nation as a whole is locked into a vertical/exploitative relationship with other nations.

Thus decolonization and nationalism did not mark the end of the circuit, but rather the emergence of a modernized, more efficient form of it. The nationalist elites who had won 'independence' from the imperialist powers were able to police more effectively local labour and consolidate different systems for transnational and local interests and actors. Once in control of state power, nationalist elites continued to build up export industries[22] and continued, within restricted foreign-oriented enclaves, to accumulate wealth and enjoy Western standards and styles of living without transforming their largely traditional and non-industrial economies and societies.[23] They purchased masses of weapons from Britain and the US to protect these enclaves so that local elites could continue to accumulate wealth safe from the mass misery growing up around them. Eventually, in Britain and America, after they had become the world's two largest weapons exporters, expanding military-industrial complexes began to draw industrial capital from the mass-consumption goods sector and to free it from the need to maintain mass purchasing power. As a result, wage levels and work conditions began to erode, along with other gains that labour had made in those and other Western countries as a result of the post-war social settlements.

A global crusade to contain the spread of socialism was launched after the Second World War by a US-led coalition of anti-communist ruling groups in Europe, Asia, the Middle East, Africa and Latin America. By the late 1970s, this crusade had succeeded to a phenomenal degree. Western states then began a forceful campaign to reverse the social settlements that had tied capital to the development of their own national communities.[24] By the mid-1980s and in the

22 Between 1945 and 1971, import-substitution industrialization (ISI) was pursued as an engine of growth in Latin America by a 'triple alliance' of state-owned firms, national private enterprises and transnational corporations. This strategy was eventually seen as producing another form of colonial dependency. Though ISI in Latin America emphasized production for the domestic market, and higher wages and levels of domestic consumption, it did not lead to the expansion and integration of domestic markets (by 1969 Brazil's market was about half as large as that of the Netherlands, although her population is nearly six times as large; Merhav 1969: 27–28). At the end of the 1960s, with national private enterprises increasingly losing ground to public enterprises and transnational corporations, analysts from Chile, Argentina, Brazil and Peru elaborated a critique of the triple alliance and its production of 'dependent' industrialization in Latin America. This marked the start of a move away from ISI.
23 The result, in the Middle East, is that the share of manufacturing in production in 1990 – 13 per cent – was precisely what it was in the mid-1950s.
24 The crusade had started with Western Europe immediately after the Second World War. As has been frequently pointed out, 'One of the motives for the Marshall Plan was to forestall the advent of a 'socialist' Europe.' Likewise, US efforts to encourage European integration were aimed at averting any possibility of Germany joining the Soviet camp (Heilbroner and Milberg 1969: 49). Block (1977) provides a detailed discussion of US policies towards, and relations with, Western European countries following the Second World War.

context of a new opportunity structure (the combination of the decreased threat of socialism and increased international competition), the US and West European states had begun to dismantle restrictions on capital mobility and to restructure or eliminate regulatory agencies and social welfare programmes. The result of these measures has been an expansion of the export-oriented growth that characterized the pre-World War international political economy.

US capital exports since the late 1970s differ in a number of ways from those that had characterized the outflow of US 'productive' capital to Europe and elsewhere after the Second World War. Before the 1970s, US capital exports were relatively small (British capital exports in the nineteenth century had amounted to 10 per cent of GDP; at their peak, those of the US had been around 2 per cent of GDP). US firms had invested in Europe because it was the only way to access European markets given '[t]he sharp drop in the trade share of GDP that occurred in Europe subsequent to the depression, the persistence of capital and currency controls, and the presence of substantial non-tariff barriers...' Moreover, these investments had supported an overall system of welfare, income equality and higher wages at home. 'While firms fought for market share overseas, they did so in ways that boosted workers' incomes and domestic demand rather than suppressing those incomes' (Schwartz 2002–03: 340–41).

The US capital exports that began in the late 1970s are, however, part of an overall shift that involves downsizing workforces and resetting corporate activity 'at ever lower levels of output and employment' (Williams et al. 1989: 292). In fact, despite the tendency to refer to current trends collectively as *'neo-liberal'* globalization, the expansion underpinning 'globalization' has been – like Europe's nineteenth-century expansion – essentially *anti-liberal* in nature. It is characterized by increasing concentration and monopoly, by the increasing tendency of large firms to buy existing assets through mergers and acquisitions rather than to build new ones (Schwartz 2002–03: 241).

With the increase in capital mobility and foreign investment has come the ability to move production to low-wage areas. This has reduced the bargaining power of labour relative to capital in negotiations that determined wages and working conditions, not only in industries experiencing capital outflow but also in related industries (Crotty and Epstein 1996: 131). As a result, methods of absolute surplus value production have returned: intensifying work regimes, reducing real wages, cutting health, pension and social safety-net protections and restructuring employment away from full-time and secure employment into part-time and insecure work.

The overall trend to which all this points is a reconfiguration of the circuit of capital, once again. It was reconfigured after the Second World War to accommodate social democratic concessions in the West. Now it may be in the process of a reconfiguration involving the reintegration of the 'Second World' and much of the 'First World' into the circuit on the basis of the dualistic growth that characterized their development previously and which, throughout the post-Second World War era, has continued to characterize the 'development' of the 'Third World'.

References

Abu-Lughod, J., 1989, *Before European Hegemony: The World System AD1250–1350*, New York, Oxford University Press.

Bairoch, P., 1993, *Economics and World History: Myths and Paradoxes*, London, Harvester.

Balch, R., 1978, 'The Resigning of Quarrels: Conflict Resolution in the Thirteenth Century', *Peace and Change*, 5, 33–38.

Baldwin, F. E., 1926, *Sumptuary Legislation and Personal Regulation in England*, Baltimore, MD, Johns Hopkins University Press.

Barratt Brown, M., 1970, *After Imperialism*, rev. edn, London, Merlin Press.

Benson, L., 1989, *The Working Class in Britain, 1850–1939*, London, Longman.

Blaut, J., 1993, *The Colonizer's Model of the World: Geographical Diffusionism and Eurocentric History*, London, The Guilford Press.

Block, F., 1977, *The Origins of International Economic Disorder*, Berkeley, University of California Press.

Boyce, R. W. D., 1987, *British Capitalism at the Crossroads, 1919–1932*, Cambridge, Cambridge University Press.

Brown, P., 1968, *A Century of Pay*, London, Macmillan.

Cairncross, A. K., 1953, *Home and Foreign Investment, 1870–1914*, Cambridge, Cambridge University Press.

Cameron, R., 1961, *France and the Economic Development of Europe*, Princeton, NJ, Princeton University Press.

Coates, D., 2000, *Models of Capitalism: Growth and Stagnation in the Modern Era*, Cambridge, Polity.

Crotty, J., and G. Epstein, 1996, 'In Defence of Capital Controls', in L. Panitch (ed.), *Are There Alternatives? Socialist Register 1996*, London, Merlin Press.

Davis, L. E,. and R. A. Huttenback, 1988, *Mammon and the Pursuit of Empire*, New York, Cambridge University Press.

Dobb, M., 1963, *Studies in the Development of Capitalism*, rev. edn, New York, International Publishers.

Dorwart, R. A., 1971, *The Prussian Welfare State before 1740*, Cambridge, MA, Harvard University Press.

Edelstein, M., 1981, 'Foreign Investment and Accumulation, 1860–1914', in R. C. Floud and D. N. McCloskey (eds), *The Economic History of Britain Since 1700*, II, Cambridge, Cambridge University Press.

Eversley, D. E. C., 1967, 'The Home Market and Economic Growth in England, 1750–1780', in E. L. Jones and G. E. Mingay (eds), *Land, Labour, and Population in the Industrial Revolution*, London, Arnold.

Gagliardo, J. G., 1967, *Enlightened Despotism*, New York, Thomas Y. Crowell.

Gerschenkron, A., 1962, *Economic Backwardness in Historical Perspective*, Cambridge, MA, Harvard University Press.

Gellner, E., 1983, *Nations and Nationalism*, Ithaca, NY, and London, Cornell University Press.

Gillis, J. R., 1983, *The Development of European Society, 1770–1870*, Boston, Houghton Mifflin.

Goodman, N., 1978, *Ways of Worldmaking*, Indianapolis, Hackett Publishing Company.

Granshof, F., 1970, *The Middle Ages: A History of International Relations*, New York, Harper and Row.

Greenfield, K .E., 1918, *Sumptuary Law in Nürnberg: A Study in Paternal Government*, Baltimore, MD, The Johns Hopkins University Press.

Halperin, S., 1994, 'State Autonomy Versus Nationalism, Historical Reconsiderations of the Evolution of State Power', in Ronen Palan and Barry K. Gills (eds), *Transcending the State–Global Divide: the Neo-Structuralist Agenda in International Relations*, Boulder, CO, Lynne Rienner Publishing Co.

— 1997, *In the Mirror of the Third World: Industrial Capitalist Development in Modern Europe*, Ithaca, NY, Cornell University Press.

— 2004, *War and Social Change in Modern Europe: The Great Transformation Revisited*, Cambridge, Cambridge University Press.

Heilbroner, R., and W. Milberg, 1969, *The Crisis of Vision in Modern Economic Thought*, Cambridge, Cambridge University Press.

Hobsbawm, E., 1968, *Industry and Empire*, London, Weidenfeld and Nicolson.

Hobson, J. A., 1902, *Imperialism: A Study*, London, Allen and Unwin.

Howard, M., 1961, *The Franco-Prussian War*, London, Rupert Hart-Davis.

Hunt, A., 1996, *Governance of the Consuming Passions: A History of Sumptuary Law*, Basingstoke, Macmillan.

Johnson, A. A., 1979, *The Disappearance of the Small Landowner*, Fairfield, NY, A. M. Kelly.

Johnson, P., 1994, 'The Welfare State', in R. C. Floud and D. N. McCloskey (eds), *The Economic History of Britain Since 1700, Vol. 3, 1939–92*, Cambridge, Cambridge University Press, 284–317.

Kindleberger, C., 1964, *Economic Growth in France and Britain, 1851–1950*, Cambridge, MA, Harvard University Press.

Langer, W. L., 1931, *European Alliances and Alignments, 1871–1890*, New York, Alfred A. Knopf.

Lévy, M., 1951–52, *Historie économique et sociale de la France depuis 1848*, Paris, les Cours de Droit, Institut d'Etudes Politiques.

Lewis, A., 1972, 'The Historical Record of International Capital Movements to 1913', in J. H. Dunning (ed.), *International Investment: Selected Readings*, Harmondsworth, Penguin.

— 1978a, *Growth and Fluctuation, 1870–1913*, London, George Allen & Unwin.

— 1978b, *The Evolution of the International Economic Order*, Princeton, NJ, Princeton University Press.

Lie, J., 1993, 'Visualizing the Invisible Hand', *Politics & Society*, 21, 275–306.

Luxemburg, R., 1976, *The National Question*, New York, Monthly Review Press.

Mann, M., 1988, 'European Development: Approaching a Historical Explanation', in J.

Baechler, A. Hall and M. Mann (eds), *Europe and the Rise of Capitalism*, Oxford, Basil Blackwell.

Mathias, P., 1983, *The First Industrial Nation*, 2nd edn, New York, Methuen.

Mattingly, G., 1955, *Renaissance Diplomacy*, Baltimore, Penguin Books.

McKendrick, N., J. Brewer and J. H. Plumb, 1982, *The Birth of a Consumer Society*, London, Europa.

Merhav, M., 1969, *Technological Dependency, Monopoly and Growth*, Oxford, Oxford University Press.

Meynial, E., 1926, 'Roman Law', in G. C. Crump and E. F. Jacob (eds), *The Legacy of the Middle Ages*, Oxford, Oxford University Press.

Moore, B., 1966, *Social Origins of Democracy and Dictatorship*, Boston, Beacon.

Munting, R., 1982, *The Economic Development of the USSR*, London, Croom Helm.

Nitzan, J., 2002, 'Regimes of Differential Accumulation, Mergers, Stagflation and the Logic of Globalization', *Review of International Political Economy*, 8(2), 226–74.

Pirenne, H., 1958, *A History of Europe*, Garden City, NY, Doubleday.

— 1969, *Economic and Social History of Medieval Europe*, New York, Harcourt, Brace and Co.

Polanyi, K., 1944, *The Great Transformation: The Political and Economic Origins of Our Time*, New York, Farrar and Rinehart.

Royle, T., 1999, *Crimea: The Great Crimean War, 1854–1856*, Boston, Little Brown and Company.

Schumpeter, J. A., 1976, *Capitalism, Socialism and Democracy*, London, Routledge.

Schwartz, H., 2002–03, 'Hobson's Voice: American Internationalism, Asian Development, and Global Macro-economic Imbalances', *Journal of Post-Keynesian Economics*, 25(2), 331–51.

Sée, H., 1942, *Histoire économique de la France II: Les temps modernes, 1789–1914*, Paris, Colin.

Sohn-Rethel, A., 1978, *Intellectual and Manual Labour*, London, Macmillan.

Sorokin, P., 1927, *Social Mobility*, London, Harper.

— 1969, *Society, Culture, and Personality: Their Structure and Dynamics*, New York, Cooper.

Strachey, J., 1959, *The End of Empire*, New York, Praeger.

Strayer, J., 1970, *On the Medieval Origins of the Modern State*, Princeton, NJ, Princeton University Press.

Strikwerda, K., 1993, 'The Troubled Origins of European Economic Integration: International Iron and Steel Migration in the Era of World War I', *American Historical Review*, 98, October, 1106–29.

Stubbs, W., 1967, *Seventeen Lectures on the Study of Medieval and Modern History and Kindred Subjects*, New York, Fertig.

Taithe, B., 2001, *Citizenship and Wars: France in Turmoil, 1870–1871*, London, Routledge.

Thirsk, J., 1978, *Economic Policy and Projects: The Development of a Consumer Society in Early Modern England*, Oxford, Clarendon Press.

Tocqueville, A. de, 1955, *The Old Regime and the French Revolution*, Garden City, NY, Doubleday.

Trebilcock, C., 1981, *Industrialization of the Continental Powers 1780–1914*, London, Longmans.

Van Der Pijl, K., 1998, *Transnational Classes and International Relations*, London, Routledge.

Vincent, J., 1969, *Costume and Conduct in the Laws of Basel, Bern, and Zurich, 1370–1800*, New York, Greenwood Press.

Wallerstein, I., 1974, *The Modern World System*, I, New York, Academic Press.

— 1991, *Unthinking Social Science: The Limits of Nineteenth-Century Paradigms*, Cambridge, Polity Press.

— 1996, *Historical Capitalism*, 2nd edn, New York, W. W. Norton.

Wehler, H.-U., 1969, *Bismarck und der Imperialismus*, Cologne, Kiepenheuer.

Wesseling, H. L., 1997, *Imperialism and Colonialism*, Westport, CT, Greenwood Press.

Williams, K. et al., 1989, 'Do Labor Costs Really Matter?', *Work, Employment, and Society*, 3, 281–305.

CHAPTER 8

Multiple Solidarities:
Autonomy and Resistance

Nathalie Karagiannis

This chapter looks at world-making from the viewpoint of one of its constitutive ingredients: solidarity. Solidarity is the substance of a successful world-making, if world-making is defined as the creation of a common universe. It makes sense to think that in order for this common universe to exist, there must be something that holds it together. Here, I will argue that solidarity should not be conceptualized as the 'something that holds the common universe together' but rather as the 'there must be something that holds the common universe together'. The distinction here lies in a step I think worth taking, which sees in the ambiguous nature of the concept an (often a posteriori) description of a certain *social* reality at a certain time, and an (often a priori) *political* project, the two aspects being inseparable. That they coexist historically in such an intimate way is mirrored by the flexibility of the concept.[1] For the imagery of the massive

---

1 Solidarity is as flexible as modernity in its possible characterizations: social solidarity is referred to most frequently (Outhwaite and Ray 2005), but there is also national solidarity (Donzelot 1986; Esping-Andersen 2000), class solidarity (Esping-Andersen 2000), political solidarity (as in Poland), even human solidarity (Rorty 1989) and, lately, European solidarity (Habermas 2001), not to mention 'cultural solidarity', a solidarity that is never really explicitly defined, but that serves to remind a people of their historical bonds. Clearly, each adjective carries with it connotations of disciplinary vantage points and often more or less conservative political preferences. In this chapter, concern about 'human' solidarity will not be discussed, neither will any conception of solidarity based on ethical grounds. Class solidarity will only make a brief appearance in historical terms in the discussion of the welfare state. This chapter also rejects the implicit, current understanding of solidarity as a cultural phenomenon. Instead, it views political and social modes of solidarity as the crucial aspects of the concept. The assumption, detailed elsewhere (Karagiannis and Wagner 2005), is that the political and the social must be more closely theorized – that is, in close relation to each other – than they have been in the past. I will just note here that historically a strict division of the political and the social may have indeed

solidity of a people – painted abstractly – we must substitute the idea of a *recurrent specification of social bonds with a political view*.

This idea, the guiding thread for the following thoughts, unveils the fact that three of the characteristics that have been ascribed to solidarity – reason, abstraction and equality – are more problematic than they would seem to be at first sight. Hannah Arendt, writing on the end of the eighteenth century, expresses with exemplary clarity what we can now call the received twentieth-century view of the concept. 'It is out of pity that men are "attracted toward *les hommes faibles*" ', Arendt tells us, 'but it is out of solidarity that they establish deliberately and, as it were, dispassionately a community of interest with the oppressed and the exploited'.[2] 'For solidarity', she adds, 'because it partakes of reason, and hence of generality, is able to comprehend a multitude conceptually, not only the multitude of a class or a nation or a people, but eventually all mankind.'

Thus, first, solidarity 'partakes of reason'; it is beyond the realm of petty emotions or grand passions. The immediate objection to this sidestepping of emotions/passions as a component of solidarity is the historical difficulty one encounters in distinguishing several stages of nationalism (whose reasonableness *laisse à désirer*) from solidarity. Additionally, it is doubtful whether the normative exclusion of passions from debates on the social bond is fruitful in the context of a demand for the real possibility of dissent.[3]

Second, intimately related to solidarity's reason is its universalization, since the extension of solidarity over class and nation to humanity ('mankind') pertains to the same characteristic, since the greatest possible 'generality' is achieved through reason. In contemporary thought, we can recognize the same idea in Jürgen Habermas's 'solidarity among strangers', and in 'the process of *abstraction*' (emphasis added) that allows him to view the passage from the European nation states to the European polity as describing a contemporary need for an effort of strictly the same nature as that which had been made in the nineteenth century (Habermas 2001). Were such a contestable reading of history not accompanied by a substantive appeal for the politicization of the

reinforced some types of solidarity. For example, it is interesting to note that the colonial state in India effected just such a separation in order to ensure better control over the population: 'A new ontology, based on the distinction between economy, polity and society as three separated domains that had internally specific features, appropriate to the intrinsic nature of each sphere, was introduced by the self-limiting impulses of the colonial state justifying its claims that it could not be responsible for intervening in that vast and complex society ... Indians, on their part, viewed this distinction as an extension of a traditional conceptual dichotomy between an 'inside' and an 'outside', and claimed that religious activities or social reforms fell within the internal affairs of Hindu society' (Kaviraj 2000: 148).

2 All the quotes are from the same passage of Arendt 1963: 84.

3 For an 'agonistic' inclusion of passions in the political and the conclusion that this necessarily leads to the exclusion of some, see Mouffe 2000; Rancière 1999.

European project, it would be as practically inoperative as Richard Rorty's 'human solidarity' (Rorty 1989).

Arendt continues by comparing solidarity, pity and compassion:

> But this solidarity, though it may be aroused by suffering, is not guided by it, and it *comprehends the strong and the rich no less than the weak and the poor;* compared with the *sentiment* of pity, it may appear cold and abstract, for it remains committed to 'ideas' – to greatness, or honor, or dignity – rather than to any 'love' of men ... But pity, in contrast to solidarity, does not look upon both fortune and misfortune, the strong and the weak with an equal eye ... Terminologically speaking, *solidarity is a principle that can inspire and guide action,* compassion is one of the *passions,* and pity a sentiment.

The third characteristic of solidarity that this conceptualization proposes is the inclusion in the same community of the oppressed and the non-oppressed, the exploited and (one must surmise) the exploiting, the wealthy and the poor. Although there is no direct objection to be formulated here, it is worth noting that Arendt glosses over the one fundamental ambiguity of solidarity that becomes clear in her text: that solidarity may well aim at overcoming inequality (as she wishes) but solidarity can exist only if there is inequality. Only if there are rich and poor can solidarity be inclusive; only if there are oppressed and their oppressors can there be a dispassionate community; only if there are less powerful and more powerful classes can there be class solidarity.

The three features that are ascribed by the received view of solidarity recognizably place the concept in the context of modernity. First, however, the 'context of modernity' seems to be defined rather restrictively. If we adopt a broader understanding of modernity as a condition under which bonds are repetitively broken and made anew, but with no strong substantive content, we can bring our initial definition of solidarity close to this understanding. This also brings us to the idea of world-making, which, regardless of the world that is referred to, insists on its creation and, consequently, on the possibility of changing it.

But, second, the rapprochement between modernity and solidarity does not seem inevitable and it will remain open in this chapter. The levels of ambiguity involved, for instance, in the relationship between solidarity and equality and between solidarity and dissent are witnesses to this lack of inevitability. Thus, the paradox of inequality is inescapably present when solidarity is considered to be a description of the present (which always relies on a concept of the 'traditional' past), and when it is considered a project of modernity. In the same way, while calls for solidarity often insist on the existing present or past, and so again on an *'acquis',* or tradition, of solidarity, they fail to acknowledge that any normative call for solidarity must accept that it tends towards the overcoming of strife and thus acknowledge existing discord or inequality.[4] While in both examples several distinct layers separate the two sides of the 'paradoxes' (analytic vs normative, descriptive vs ascriptive, past vs present), I think they convincingly illustrate the central quality of solidarity as the recurrent specification of a certain type of bond.

For the purposes of this contribution, I first explore solidarity as something that creates a particular modality and space in which human beings are tied together by a commonness. Second, I look at solidarity as the institutionalization of that commonness and as that which, in contrast, aspires to the breaking of that commonness. Indeed, the concept has been paramount in the historical creation of the socio-political common, that is, in specifying social relations in ways such that world-making was, consequently, taking place. With the emergence of alternative worlds (here, I take the Christian example), solidarity has at some historical moments abandoned the political direction – without necessarily renouncing its social dimension[5] (see below, under the heading, 'Solidarity's Space'). At other historical moments it is precisely alternative world-making that has infused social solidarity with a strong political view, such as that which becomes evident when one looks at the passage from the organized, institutionalized solidarity of the twentieth century to the solidarity of resistance, to which I subsequently turn (see below, under 'Institutionalizing and Resisting "The Social"').

Solidarity's Space, In and Out of This World

The approach here is quasi-genealogical, seeking as it does the conceptual and 'empirical' ancestors of solidarity. Such an exploration reveals that the concept has been present in different guises in a number of historical experiences, to which particular interpretations are attached and which signal a passage from solidarity as first creating a 'modern' social space, to solidarity creating, second, a worldless, and third, a worldly, body.[6] If this retrieval is set in the context of

---

4   See, for instance, the shift between considering solidarity as a heritage, as a future project and as a present reality in passages by Habermas in 'Why Europe needs a Constitution' (2001). For a reading of Habermas's position, see Karagiannis 2006. Discord may be due to economic inequality, but it may also be due to political or other forms of discrimination.

5   This does not hold for every 'alternative world-making'; such world-makings may, in other cases, retain their political characteristics.

6   What makes solidarity modern would be its worldliness, in Arendtian terms. Worldliness, that is, being-in-the-world, at once brings close and separates (it can be seen as the equivalent of Kant's friendship in *Metaphysics of Morals*). Here, this would be about the (degree of) closeness of experience and interpretation, in opposition to worldlessness, which creates the greatest gap between the two.

157

modernity, two main interactions between solidarity and modernity can be observed. First, the space of solidarity involves issues of *autonomy* of that space; although that space is characterized by autonomy with regard to other spaces or bodies – that is, collective autonomy – the autonomy *within* may vary from space to space, or body. Second, if the characteristic of autonomy in modernity can also be translated into some process of *distancing*, as a gap that is opened in modernity between experience and interpretation, then solidarity is that which strives to bridge that gap.

Before becoming explicitly associated with biological metaphors of the body and the organism, in the eighteenth and nineteenth centuries, solidarity had contributed to creating and keeping the space of the city together. It is anachronistic to use the word 'solidarity' in the broad sense I use it here for any period before the nineteenth century, but the example of ancient Athens shows that a concept very close to 'solidarity' was then in use. Following Castoriadis (1986), it is possible to view in the Athens of the eighth to the fourth century BCE the first expression of modernity, as broadly understood self-reflection, that is, the combined pursuit of autonomy and mastery (rationality). Castoriadis locates the second such expression in a period that commences in nineteenth-century Europe, which, in the perspective of the question this chapter poses, is too quick a historical jump. Indeed, different forms of solidarity appear at times not belonging to modernity as it is defined by Castoriadis, such as the Middle Ages. What sort of solidarity is that solidarity? Would we have to challenge the inherited view of the Middle Ages as a non-reflexive epoch in order to find a *modern* solidarity? Or, would we have to admit that some forms of solidarity are not modern, a conclusion that is closer to the sociological tradition?[7] In any case, stretching the boundaries of modernity back to ancient Athens is an important step towards a concrete 'multiplication' of examples of modernity.

The idea of solidarity that existed in ancient Athens was that of *filia*, or friendship, later called *civic* friendship by the Romans. In practice, *filia* was closely tied to *eros*, or love. In socio-political terms, love signified the preparation of younger men for the duties and the manners of full manhood and citizenship. As a consequence, it was as much a preparation for collective autonomy or external political liberty, in the sense that it was a training for war, as it was a preparation for personal autonomy or internal excellence, since it formed young men for the athletic games, or the battles of art. And at the same time, love was

---

7　The broader question here is evidently whether sociology needs artificially to label what it studies as modernity, in other words, whether it is possible to approach broader spans of time without resorting to pure history. Interestingly, this question is posed mainly with regard to postmodernity; historical sociology only claims to historicize modernity.

most evidently linked to the need for and the praise of internal concord and friendship at the level of the city (see, for instance, Rahe 1994: 118–19): significantly, after having been the appanage of the Athenian aristocracy, by the fifth century BCE pederasty (*pais*: young boy, *eros*) came to be democratized and practised on a much larger scale. It was subordinated to the goal of friendship in the city.

Although it is not possible here to go into detail regarding the Greek *conceptualization* of civic friendship, it must be noted that Plato and Aristotle underlined its normative necessity as a binding element for the people of the polis (Ludwig 2002). Later on, Romans such as Augustine or Seneca read the Athenian experience as an idealized civic concord – not only praising it normatively but also affirming its empirical existence. In fact, however, *agon*, or strife – also regulated, as in the above example – was as much a part of the Greek city as was *filia*: one was also accompanied by the other. The major legal reforms in ancient Athens, those of Solon and of Kleisthenes, underline this: Athens valued solidarity but acknowledged that the opposite of solidarity (discord, strife, inequality) existed in the city. Solon, for instance, introduced the *stasis* law, which is of paramount importance for the illustration of my argument: the law stated that in civil strife any citizen who did not side with one of the opposing parties would be considered *atimos*, that is, without rights (Meier 1990: 263–64).[8] The intention behind this law was to enable the constitution of a majority that could counter the minority's *stasis*. The reform of Kleisthenes was more ambitious, since it aimed at the institutionalization of 'civic presence'.[9] Its most salient features were the reorganization of the administrative space of Attica into new administrative units (though the old ones continued to exist): the *phylai*; the concentration of decision-making and deliberations in Athens; and the bringing of the nobility and other social classes into closer contact. In the combination of these features we identify the first self-understandings of a relation between citizens qua citizens, irrespective of their other attributes. What is most relevant here is that it enables us to identify the first self-reflective institution of such an understanding: indeed, nowhere other than in the increasing demands for participation by the people did Kleisthenes find his inspiration (Meier 1990: 263–64).

However, if Athens is 'modern' in that particular self-reflective, simultaneous pursuit of personal and collective autonomy, Sparta, by contrast, cannot be similarly characterized, for various reasons related to its social composition (the

---

8 For a view of this measure as a combination of ethos and polis, see Castoriadis 1986.
9 Here, I follow Meier, whose expression this is (1990: 61).

proportionately overwhelming numbers of *eilotes*, or slaves), and to its political regime (the fundamental lack of auto-determination of the people and the existence of the *bassileis*, or kings). Nevertheless, despite such traits, Sparta was also characterized by a very strong sense of solidarity in its relation to the outside, stronger, indeed, than that which was to be found in Athens. Castoriadis gives the example of the Spartan fighters, whose collective way of fighting is indicative of the solidarity of the city (Castoriadis 2004: 121–22).

Similarly, if solidarity is broadly about redistribution within the space it creates (also through material redistribution), then the communal provisions instituted in ancient Athens through various means (subsidies drawn on the rich for theatrical and athletic competitions, or special taxes in case of war, or through the possibility of subsidizing people who declared themselves unable to work) were not very different – in their effects – from the more egalitarian-communitarian understanding of distribution of goods within Sparta.

The passage to Christianity takes this *filia* out of a confined space: solidarity, in the guise of charity, or *caritas*, embraces all Christians and, in its aspirations, all humankind. Augustine, following Arendt's reading, is particularly illuminating in this respect, as he opposes *caritas* to *cupiditas*. *Caritas* – the love of God and the highest good, life itself (Arendt 1996: 27) – leads to an alternative world based on shared values, while *cupiditas* – greed, love of money – reinforces the existing world of materialism and force (Arendt, 1996: 23, 144). *Caritas* is, therefore, a drive out of this world at the same time as it is an honouring of God through love for his creatures.[10] What is important for our purposes is the essential worldlessness of *caritas*, as it makes 'a desert' of this world and inaugurates a different understanding of relations of solidarity between human beings, who are brothers in God.[11] Here, solidarity is a point of passage from the singular human being to God, or, in other words, the love shown to the other for *the sake of* God. The consequences of the Christian view are radical: it takes solidarity and giving out of the public realm a confined space, and it postpones practical equality or symmetry until the world to come.

Brotherhood or fraternity, brotherly or fraternal solidarity, though it had never entirely disappeared, re-entered the world through specific spaces and

10 In *caritas*, whose object is eternity, man transforms himself into an eternal, imperishable being (Arendt 1996: 19). Clearly, eternity is another world, the world to come; both worlds must involve some world-making, since they are two.

11 Augustine's theory held that there was a twofold origin of one's relation to the neighbour or the social question: one – referred to above – is that of man coming *post mundum* into a desert world and, in isolation, facing God; and the other is of man as part of humankind and originating from Adam (Arendt 1996: 93). 'Self-denying love [of the neighbour] means to love all people so completely without distinction that the world becomes a desert to the lover' (95).

bodies, more decisively in the Middle Ages in Europe but also in Asia – for instance, in Islam.[12] Medieval merchant and craft guilds, first rejected and then strongly influenced by the Church, aimed at securing monopolies in their town markets through several measures, such as the establishment of equality between the members of each guild, the introduction of industrial education and the uniformity of the goods produced (Black 1984: 8). Mutual aid and providing for all the members of a guild were other objectives aimed at in yet another expression of solidarity vis-à-vis the outside (1984: 8). The fact of large differences in taxes paid by outsiders and guild insiders (who were, usually, exempt from taxes) is analogous to contemporary measures of protectionism of a solidary space (whether this is a nation state or an integrated region such as Europe). While there is collective autonomy here, it is an autonomy that is oddly only directed to the guilds' peers – the other guilds in other towns – and not to bodies of a different status such as the Church (formulated in terms of the similarity of ethos between guilds and the Church [Black 1984: 59; Chapter 9]).[13] The pervasive influence of the Church may then ultimately prevent us from considering this a modern solidarity – despite the explicit artificiality of the guild bond and the acknowledgement of the making of the world. While Michael Walzer could well call this slipping of one sphere of justice (the ecclesiastical) into another (the market) tyrannical, there is no guarantee against such tyranny in modernity, as Arendt's or Lefort's writings have shown with regard to the origins of totalitarianism.

This language of fraternity-in-the-world was again not lost in the subsequent centuries.[14] In 1841, a pre-socialist, Pierre Leroux, writes: 'J'ai le premier emprunté aux légistes le terme de solidarité pour l'introduire dans la philosophie, c'est à dire selon moi, dans la religion. J'ai voulu remplacer la charité chrétienne par la solidarité humaine' (Fiegle 2005). William Sewell has shown that the discourse of the revolutionary workers' movement of the period around 1848 bore the imprint of the old regime's corporate language – a language that enhanced moral solidarity between members of one 'corps de

---

12 See Arendt 1996: 108 for early Christian uses of the metaphors of brotherhood and the body; and Black 1984, for early, Greek, Roman and Germanic guilds; however, it is not possible to know whether they had the same values as Christian, medieval guilds (Arendt 1996: 5).

13 Could one distinguish between a horizontal and a vertical autonomy? Can 'giving oneself one's own laws' (once it is separated from the Kantian absolute) exist in one direction but not in the other? And it may not be their 'nature' that distinguishes guilds and the Church (for instance, they are a priori both apolitical).

14 Tu Weiming says: 'Fraternity, the functional equivalent of community, has attracted scant attention in modern political thought among the Enlightenment values advocated in the French Revolution' (Weiming 2000: 199).

metier' (Sewell 1980). The extraordinary evolution that took place in the years preceding the revolution is that this solidarity came to be seen not only as something uniting the members within one group but also as a bond uniting people *across* professions: a horizontal or enlarged solidarity.

In *L'invention du social*, a major contribution to the conceptual origins of the notion of solidarity, Jacques Donzelot has shown how solidarity was devised as an answer to the fears about sovereignty of revolutionaries and conservatives in the French Third Republic (Donzelot 1984). On the one hand, because sovereignty was the sovereignty of all and pointed to an absolute fraternity, the revolutionary fear was always directed to the possibility of a *complot de réaction*, which would limit the unlimited conception of the state that was wished for. On the other hand, it is the exact possibility of unlimited state power, the 'haunting of state socialism', that made the well-off classes feel threatened. In this setting, solidarity was a 'strategic invention' mediating between the individual as principle of intelligibility of social reality and the class struggle as motor of history. In other words, solidarity intervenes between Marxism and liberalism, borrowing elements of both.

The 'strategic invention' is Durkheim's, although the use of the word can be traced back to earlier periods, as we have seen. In Durkheim's well-known 1893 conceptualization, society's founding principle was transformed from 'mechanic solidarity', based on the similarity of conditions, to 'organic solidarity', based on the division of labour, which increased interdependence by increasing the specificity of tasks. This theory of solidarity serves a threefold purpose: first, that of a 'scientific foundation' for the republican position, according to which society lives according to laws that are proper to it: as such it cannot be maintained in its archaic order and it cannot be altered through political will. The second purpose is a legitimate opening for and towards the republican position: it is neither society's structure nor the individual's nature that is crucial, but the loss – and the re-establishment – of the perception of the link of solidarity between members of society. Finally, this theory serves the definition of the republican state, which is perceived to be at the service of society (Donzelot 1984).

Durkheim's theory of solidarity was then refined and worked in different directions – most significantly in law, with the creation of the concepts of 'public service' and 'institution' that are still central to the French understanding of the role of the state. The solidarism of Leon Bourgeois charts the most significant direction here: according to him, there is a 'social debt' of the living vis-à-vis their predecessors and also their successors. By virtue of the fact that it precedes the law, the levy of this 'social debt' – through taxes, for instance – comes before its bestowal, which takes place according to situations of fact, not law. This will, in fact, be a reparation of society and provide assurance for its members against the risks they suffer precisely because of their interdependence. Such a solidarity works for social progress because it perceives that all members of society work to pay the debt – and thus access (dispose of) the social *acquis*.[15]

The passage of solidarity from its position in the world (in Athens, Sparta) to a position out of it (in Christianity), and its return (through guilds, the society of a nation), supports the view that solidarity corresponds to the recurrent specification of bonds, rather than being thought of as a fixed solidifier, on the one hand, or as a component of the Habermasian 'painful process of abstraction' (Habermas 2001), on the other. Depending on the container – the substance of the project – for which solidarity is a medium, and also on the political end it sets out to achieve, it organizes, deletes and supplements social bonds: the same operations that Goodman mentions as being characteristic of epistemic world-making (Goodman 1978).

Institutionalizing and Resisting 'The Social'

The ambiguity of solidarity (concerning the necessary inclusion of inequality, as it were) can also be translated in terms of generality and particularity – solidarity aims at generality while unavoidably enhancing particularities; and, in terms of order and disorder – solidarity enhances the established order and produces resistance of its own to the existing order.[16]

Briefly, the generality/particularity issue is none other than the problem of autonomy – of the creation and breaking of bonds. Thus, in a welfare state scheme, if the main objective is to generalize insurance, this objective is nevertheless unavoidably set against differences in existing social situations. 'Unavoidably' means that this is the very raison d'être of the welfare state: as the right and the socialist left have pointed out indirectly, the end of inequality would entail the end of the welfare state (Offe 2000). This does not only apply to European welfare states. This dialogue between generality and particularity

15 Donzelot: 'le recours à la notion de solidarité permet de substituer, à l'exigence de souveraineté, la croyance dans le progrès' (1984).
16 A related idea can be found in Outhwaite and Ray (2005: 44): 'The symptoms of social disorganization – class conflict, abnormally fluctuating rates of crime and societal conflicts – are not the work of atomized individuals with disordered desires but, like any other collective activity, require organization, networks and a common purpose. Thus we reach the important if paradoxical conclusion that social disorganization is compatible with social solidarity. It all depends on the level of designation of 'society' at which solidarity is articulated and raises the question of negative consequences of social solidarity rooted in parochial sentiments creating exclusion as well as inclusion.' In order to lose neither the important change of the received picture that this observation effects, nor some stable definition of solidarity, parameters such as space, body, ground, etc., have to be taken together.

varies across welfare states and, after the attacks on the dependence created by the welfare state coming from the left and the right, deciding on what the balance should be between what ought to be general and which particularities should be acknowledged is no easy matter.

I now turn to discuss the issue of order and disorder in more length: historical accounts of modernity have regularly characterized it as being originally 'organized' and lately 'disorganized'. However, a cursory view of post-colonial modernities is enough to show that it was apparent 'disorganization' – so described when set against the frame of the imperial, colonial state – that led to a new 'order'. More subtly, it can be advanced that tactics of resistance or subversion, or those that involved the bypassing of the colonial order, ambiguously coexisted with the colonial order, in that such tactics were part of it, or it was part of them. Today, the concept of solidarity is most frequently used in the discourse of social movements that operate at local and global levels, which resist the existing order in 'reformist' or self-proclaimed 'radical' ways. The solidarity these movements claim is foremost an oppositional solidarity. By contrast, the welfare state is commonly understood to be the institutional expression of solidarity (or one of its expressions), that is, a solidarity that consolidates the existing order through giving.

Sociologists and anthropologists have often linked giving to the creation of the common (Karagiannis 2005); and the results of these investigations exude an ambiguity of the same nature as that of solidarity, for if presenting gifts has a function of initiation and consolidation of social exchange, it also notoriously serves to establish and reinforce hierarchical power positions. It is in both these ways that solidarity enhances order. By looking at the three major historical changes in the disciplining practices of giving and at their interpretations, this order-enhancing aspect of solidarity in the welfare state is revealed in a way that underlines the division between domains: first, the entrance of giving into the political domain (the political); second, its reappropriation by a newly invented 'social economy' (and thus, a conceptualization in terms of the social); and third, its return to political economy (the economic).

So the *first* change to be noted is that *caritas*, or charity, which we have previously encountered, slipped into the political domain only in the eighteenth century. Before then, it had escaped even the Church hierarchy, as we saw with regard to guilds (Black 1984; Donzelot 1991). A century after having entered the public realm, charity became contestable: nineteenth-century liberals spoke out against the inefficiency of the legal 'codification' of charity, since the attribution of rights to the poor legalized the obligation of the wealthy and thus encouraged the institutionalization of the poor.

The *second* important historical change that took place in the welfare discourse with regard to giving is, according to Giovanna Procacci (1991), 'the new philanthropy' of the industrial era, which brought to the fore a new *savoir*: social economy, that is, a critique of and to a large extent a substitute for classical political economy. While political economy was a science, which invented its own scientific object by abstraction from the real (the economic), social economy as a *savoir* was defined by its use of the previously invented scientific object for interventions in the real world. Thus, the object of political economy – to *eliminate* the poor – was transformed into the aim of *administrating* the poor.

The *third* big historical change was the reintroduction of political economy as a remedy for ignorance among the poor of their duties, as these were understood by the wealthy, a similar process to the edification of the colonized. Its purpose is the inclusion of the poor in the existing order, as a means of enlarging the middle classes. The accent is put on giving education (training) and offering participation (legitimacy).[17]

On the other hand, if we translate this disciplinary evolution in the way poverty was being tackled into a more precise questioning of the origins of the welfare state, we inevitably stumble on observations reminding us that the welfare state grew under conditions of industrialization, that it was a balancing device vis-à-vis market capitalism (Polanyi 1944) despite what the liberals and Marx had thought (Pierson 1991), and that social citizenship constituted its core idea.

This last idea, famously advanced by Marshall in an assessment of the British experience in 1963, depicted social rights of the twentieth century as the outcome of an evolution that had started in the eighteenth century with civil rights based on the principle of individual freedom, and developed in the nineteenth century with political rights based on political freedom. Clearly, in the twentieth century, the underlying notion was modernization, a theory that was later to become fashionable on the western side of the Atlantic, where it was used to explain the delay in the development of 'Third World' countries in the context of the Cold War.[18] Thus, the twentieth-century welfare state was seen as one aspect of a more widespread process of modernization. However, seeing in the welfare state only the felicitous result of a struggle over needs and rights

---

17 The creation of community through giving brings to mind Walzer's conceptualization of the community as a good that can be distributed. Although its distribution depends on those who are already in it, community also entails giving mutual aid, or, when the inequalities in economic terms are significant, redistributing income. In such a context, it would be scandalous not to give, which amounts to saying, as Walzer does, 'that every political community is in principle a "welfare state" '. In this context, questions of merit or deserving are better left unasked and giving is a regular communal provision (Walzer 1983).

18 For one of the best critical accounts, see Gendzier 1985.

has recently elicited a few critiques, of which two seem to strike rather direct blows.

The first is epitomized by Esping-Andersen's now famous portrayal of the 'three worlds of welfare capitalism', in which he outlines the necessary differentiation among the 'stratifications' operated by the various forms of welfare state. (Esping-Andersen 2000).[19] Crucially, the argument is based on a view of the welfare state as 'an active force in the ordering of the social world'. There are three main forms of welfare state. The first, the 'liberal' type, which operates in the United States, Canada and Australia, is based on means-tested social insurance. Interestingly, this type is exemplified by Bismarckian policy, which also created status differentiation in a *corporatist* lineage. It stigmatizes recipients, offers low benefits and, consequently, encourages the market. The second type is the 'corporatist' welfare state of Austria, France, Germany and Italy, which also originates in Bismarckian status differentiation in a *corporatist* lineage. This type displaces the market as welfare provider, but is not highly redistributive because of the status differentiation inherent in it. The third type is the 'social democratic' welfare state of the Scandinavian countries. The market is to a very large extent substituted by the state, so this type of welfare state provides high benefits, but is also committed to full employment.

If we translate this typology in terms of solidarity, we immediately see solidarity widening from countries of the first type to the last. However, a glance at the historical predecessor of each welfare state renders such an immediate judgment more complicated, or, rather, the notion of solidarity is seen to be less straightforward. If we take the example of the Beveridge model, where class or market positions are irrelevant to benefits, which are distributed on a universal basis, we see a cross-class, national solidarity emerging. This system works as long as most of the population is content with low benefits. In fact, the middle classes can also veto themselves out of universal benefits. When, as happened in Britain, the middle classes emerge, expectations rise, with the result that the poor rely for welfare on the state and the rich on the market. The same complications relative to what solidarity means are encountered in the other two types of welfare state: in the 'corporatist' tradition, the *esprit de corps* may have difficulty transforming itself into national solidarity. Consequently, redistribution – one of the key defining expressions of solidarity – may be rather low at the national level, while intra-*corps* – or status solidarity, as it is now called – and family solidarity are high (Esping-Andersen 2000: 162). Regarding the

---

19 Other such typologies include the one of social policy (not welfare state) by Titmuss (residual welfare model, industrial achievement-performance model, institutional redistributive model) and Therborn's (strong interventionist, soft compensatory, full-employment-oriented, small, market-oriented). For overviews, see Pierson 1991.

third type, Esping-Andersen speaks of 'an essentially universal solidarity in favour of the welfare state' (2000: 163), but the very large extent to which the welfare state has been instrumental in the consolidation and enhancement of the middle classes who support it raises the same questions as notions such as membership and participation. Is order not the ultimate aim of a carefully infused feeling of solidarity, rather than society?

Closely related to the above analysis of the disciplinary evolution of giving, poverty and solidarity, the second type of critique of Marshall's typology asks specifically whether a concern with order has not taken over the concern with society in the context of the debate on the 'crisis' of the welfare state. This corresponds to the issue of the exclusion of the poor from social citizenship, in a process that has increasingly dissociated poverty from the 'socialization of risk' and the responsibility that ensues from this (Ewald 1986). By viewing social citizenship as the endpoint of the emergence of rights, Marshall's approach undermines the political nature of social citizenship (that is, the fact that it can be talked about, chosen and changed – that it can be *made*, for our specific purposes) and disregards its uniqueness.

Marshall's depiction of the evolution towards the welfare state reaches its limits – in so far as it relates to solidarity – with the shift of analytical focus first from Western Europe and second from the European continent. Thus, the 'communist' welfare states had a very different outlook on solidarity from the Western European ones and evolved in a very different way from the periods preceding the communist regimes and through the so-called post-communist transition. Overall, state socialism was characterized by a free and universal system of health, education and training, subsidized housing, no formal unemployment, generous childcare and low income inequality (Offe 1996, cited in Outhwaite and Ray 2005). Therefore, the state was the sole provider of welfare, and solidarity – at the national level – was highly institutionalized, with informal solidarity being marginal, limited to mutual aid between consumers at times of shortage (Outhwaite and Ray 2005: 49). Most 'communist' welfare states emerged from authoritarian, class-dividing welfare states. Their demise in the post-communist transition is normally depicted in the bleakest way, stressing the rapidity and brutality of the rise of unemployment and poverty. Even though these differences reveal a profound problem of sociological analysis, they do not answer the question of the modernity of the communist welfare state in the expected way. As Johann Arnason shows, 'communism was a distinctive but ultimately self-destructive version of modernity rather than a sustained deviation from the modernising mainstream' (Arnason: 2000: 61).

On the other hand, examples of non-European welfare states speak of totally different ties of solidarity, no matter whether these are institutionalized in the welfare state. East Asia's modern social vision, for instance, is generally influenced by the Confucian tradition, and thus government leadership in the market economy is not only unavoidable but also desirable (Weiming 2000: 205–06). Nonetheless, there are big differences between, say, the Japanese welfare state (which is characterized by institutional commitment to full employment but with low social entitlements), Singapore's interventionism and China's particular policy mix. To the extent that it strongly relies on family and group membership in an organic way, on ritualistic interaction and on a civil society that aims at attaining, at the level of the state, the cohesion of the family level (Weiming 2000), the forms of solidarity corresponding to each of these organized expressions of welfare care have certain commonalities in these spaces, but social individuation is certainly stronger in Japan than in China.

The crisis of the welfare state has shown, perhaps more saliently in the post-communist countries, that the welfare state enhanced some types of order – such as balancing the functioning and effects of the capitalistic market, or providing the basic requirements for massive socialist mobilization for production. This does not mean, of course, that absolute disorder in the individualist guise (close to Durkheim's *anomie*) reigns in the disappearance of the welfare state, since, as has been demonstrated by David Lockwood (1992), class or other types of societal conflict also require organization and a common sense of purpose and, thus, some type of order. But the welfare state clearly ordered what we call 'the social'. That is the order the new social movements resisted.

'Solidarity' has been the rallying word for the emergence of the 'new social movements' – for the historical predecessors and the current contributors to and participants in the 'no-global' movement. However, contrary to the universalizing tendency of the nation state's solidarity and the potential for international solidarity (i.e., between nation states – if such a thing could ever exist),[20] the solidarity of a social movement 'starts from a sense of particularity' (Gilroy 1995). Although it might be thought that the same sense of particularity served as an objective for 'national' solidarity, this is not true: 'national' solidarity never aimed at the nation, but always at society (Donzelot 1984). Solidarity created 'the social' when the 'nation' was already there. This can be accounted for by its having picked up elements from Marxism and liberalism – both universalizing discourses. The solidarity of social movements presents the specificity of resisting this kind of 'social', since it addresses categories that were ignored by 'the social' as it was constructed – in other words, it has been twisted from its original meaning – put another way, this solidarity places an ever-

---

20 Looking at development discourse shows that 'solidarity' has rarely been part of its rhetorical apparatus. In contrast, solidarity is at the justificatory centre of humanitarian discourse.

stronger accent on recognition, while aiming at redistribution (Honneth 1995).

'The creation of solidarity from a sense of particularity is an objective for these groups and their political behaviour is not exclusively directed towards the outside,' says Paul Gilroy (1995). There exists, therefore, a solidarity turned towards the inside, which seeks to establish/strengthen the 'social' link of the members of the 'group'. If this 'social' link that is being strengthened has any genealogical relation to the older 'social' that is being resisted, it insists on the multiplicity of its components and claims in such a way that it may to a certain degree be distinguished from the former 'social'. In other words, the new 'social' link advocates the inclusion of economic and political issues in different constellations of themes, while the older 'social' was there to separate 'the social' from 'the political' and the 'economic' (Kaviraj 2000: 150). To distinguish the two 'socials' in this way is not equivalent to saying that there is no more 'real' society (because it would have melted into a variety of economic strategies or personal experiences), or that there is no continuity between them.

With the emergence of the new 'global social movement', solidarity is increasingly addressed to the outside of each of the movements that comprise it. Added to the 'creation of solidarity through a sense of particularity', the new solidarity extends to all those who protest against the current world order: it has a clear, universalizing tendency, extending well beyond the nation state. The main problem that arises concerns the double nature of this solidarity – one that looks inside and outside, that is at once about redistribution and recognition and, most crucially, that is particularistic and universalistic at the same time (the *problematique* of exclusion–inclusion). To answer that such a duality is the consequence of globalization postpones thinking on the possibility of solidarity and recasts the problem in unhelpful terms – not least because whatever emancipatory promise there might be in solidarity is overshadowed by an impression of inevitability. Thus, it is clear that this solidarity is not about a pre-given, factual, objective interdependence between members of a community, but about a link between people belonging to communities they have fought for and sometimes created (and which are, at that level, characterized by solidarity as an objective).

A clue to starting to think about these issues is given by Gilroy's phrase: at the level of the plurality of social movements, solidarity is an objective. This is very different from the accusation levelled at the Durkheimian understanding of solidarity, which sees it as a legitimizing device, an a posteriori 'rationalization of social practices' founded on the principle that the 'true' link of solidarity had been forgotten, misperceived or buried, but that it was always there. The solidarity of social movements is an a priori creation: as the movement is created, so is its solidarity. In the first instance, solidarity is a pre-existing foundation that sanctions the group; in the second, solidarity is projected into the future as a common aim of a group that will become a group through pursuing it. It is possible to see a link between this solidarity and the solidarity of the nineteenth-century French fraternity, as given in Sewell's account, in so far as its direction is bottom-up, rather than the top-down approach of social policy. But this would be ignoring the multitude of problems that have been unearthed by post-colonial thought concerning the possibility of representation (and, as in Marx, between class consciousness and class in itself). More practically, it would also mean ignoring the problem of the 'fallacy of the grass roots' (Karagiannis 2004), that is, the assumption that such groups are entirely self-created, instead of being encouraged to 'solidify' themselves from the top.

Clearly, in late modernity solidarity exists without stringently relating attachment to the group to regulation or discipline, or, if there is a relation, it is situated outside the established 'social' order. In so far as it works against regulation – that is, as long as it positions itself to resist the predominant order; in so far as it enhances collective autonomy by holding the group together as an effect of attachment to the group (this is Gilroy's 'sense of particularity'); and in so far as the human need for recognition is fulfilled through the group, solidarity can be cautiously said to partake of the emancipatory project of modernity. However, it is equally clear that not all expressions of modernity – not all modernities in their multitude – create a space for an emancipatory solidarity or include the possibility of the emergence of a solidarity against the established order. Between liberty and discipline (Wagner 1986) – between order and the possibility to exit the order – the balance of different expressions of modernity shows different compromises; and solidarity corresponds to both liberty and discipline.[21]

At the provisional end of this brief overview, it should be noted that a variety of conceptualizations and their accompanying *problematiques* have been raised. From the images of solidarity as creating and delimiting the space, to solidarity as organizing and institutionalizing the social or, on the contrary, as resisting the social, it appears that the concept has contributed to various world-makings, even multiple and opposing world-makings at the same time. The *problematiques* that accompanied such conceptualizations (and the consequent world-makings) express tensions in the concept, such as the inevitable incorporation of inequality; particularity versus universality; order versus disorder. At this point, two elements that seem to be of greater programmatic significance and which are intertwined should be highlighted.

21 Another example is how the dominance of caste politics is a direct consequence of modern Indian politics, as Kaviraj writes (2000: 156).

First, the idea and the practice of dissent must be taken in the concept. Seeing in solidarity the opposite of dissent belittles the concept in a way that is socially inaccurate and politically undesirable. Exclusion – resulting from dissent – is not the necessary consequence of 'solidaristic' practice. Inclusion, on the other hand, does not mean uniformity and homogeneity; it does not even necessarily entail permanent consensus. Parallels can be found in theorizations of modernity: Arnason says that, with the emergence of cultural pluralism, conflict is recognized as inherent and essential to modernity, which is another way of saying that modernity contains its self-critical alternatives and its utopian projections (Arnason 2000: 65).

Second, solidarity must be seen as a self-reflexive re-specification of social bonds in a *political* view. Rather than an unwit 'painful process of abstraction', solidarity has now become the wilful political process of understanding social bonds as belonging to particular social constellations that can be amended or changed. The multiplicity of solidarities is witness to a healthy multiplication of self-definitions.

References

Arendt, Hannah, 1963, 'The Social Question', in Hannah Arendt, *On Revolution*, New York, The Viking Press.
— 1996, *Love and Saint Augustine*, Chicago, University of Chicago Press.
Arnason, Johann, 2000, 'Communism and Modernity', *Daedalus*, 129(1), 61.
Black, Anthony, 1984, *Guilds and Civil Society in European Political Thought from the Twelfth Century to the Present*, London, Methuen.
Castoriadis, Cornelius, 1986, 'La *polis* grecque et la création de la démocratie', in Cornelius Castoriadis, *Les carrefours du labyrinthe*, Paris, Seuil.
— 2004, *Ce qui fait la Grèce*, Paris, Seuil.
Donzelot, Jacques, 1986, *L'invention du social. Essai sur le déclin des passions politiques*, Paris, Fayard.
— 1991, 'The Mobilization of Society', in Graham Burchell, Colin Gordon and Peter Miller (eds), *The Foucault Effect: Studies in Governmentality*, Chicago, University of Chicago Press.
Esping-Andersen, Gosta, 2000, 'Three Worlds of Welfare Capitalism', in Christopher Pierson and Francis G. Castles (eds), *The Welfare State Reader*, Cambridge, Polity Press.
Ewald, François, 1986, *Histoire de l'Etat providence. Les origines de la solidarité*, Paris, Grasset.
Fiegle, Thomas, 2005, 'The "Law" of Solidarity: From French Counter-revolution to Modern Social Sciences', paper on Social and Political Thought, presented at the University of Sussex.
Gendzier, Irene, 1985, *Managing Political Change: Social Scientists and the Third World*, Boulder, CO, Westview Press.
Gilroy, Paul, 1995, 'Urban Social Movements, "Race" and Community', in Patrick

Williams and Laura Chrisman (eds), *Colonial Discourse and Postcolonial Theory*, New York, Harvester Wheatsheaf.

Goodman, Nelson, 1978, *Ways of Worldmaking*, Indianapolis, Hackett Publishing Company.

Habermas, Jürgen, 2001, 'Why Europe needs a Constitution', *New Left Review*, 11, September–October.

Honneth, Axel, 1995, *The Struggle for Recognition*, Cambridge, Polity Press.

Karagiannis, Nathalie, 2004, *Avoiding Responsibility*, London, Pluto.

— 2005, 'Die Gabe der Entwicklung', in Frank Adloff and Steffen Mau (eds), *Von Geben und Nehmen*, Frankfurt, Campus.

— 2006, 'Solidarity within Europe, Solidarity without Europe', *European Societies*, 8.

Karagiannis, Nathalie, and Peter Wagner, 2005, 'Towards a Theory of Synagonism', *Journal of Political Philosophy*, 13(3).

Kaviraj, Sudipta, 2000, 'Modernity and Politics in India', *Daedalus*, 129(1).

Lockwood, David, 1992, *Solidarity and Schism. The Problem of Disorder in Durkheimian and Marxist Sociology*, Oxford, Clarendon Press.

Ludwig, Paul W., 2002, *Eros and Polis, Desire and Community in Greek Political Theory*, Cambridge, Cambridge University Press.

Meier, Christian, 1990, *The Greek Discovery of Politics*, Cambridge, MA, Harvard University Press.

Mouffe, Chantal, 2000, *Deliberative Democracy or Agonistic Pluralism*, Vienna, Institut für höhere Studien (Political Science series 72).

Offe, Claus, 2000, 'Some Contradictions of the Modern Welfare State', in Christopher Pierson and Francis G. Castles (eds), *The Welfare State Reader*, Cambridge, Polity Press.

Outhwaite, William, and Larry Ray, 2005, *Social Theory and Postcommunism*, Oxford, Blackwell.

Pierson, Christopher, 1991, *Beyond the Welfare State*, Cambridge, Polity Press.

Polanyi, Karl, 1944, *The Great Transformation*, Boston, Beacon Press.

Procacci, Giovanna, 1991, 'Social Economy and the Development of Poverty', in Graham Burchell, Colin Gordon and Peter Miller (eds), *The Foucault Effect: Studies in Governmental Rationality*, London, Harvester Wheatsheaf.

Rahe, Paul A., 1994, *Republics Ancient and Modern*, Chapel Hill, NC, University of North Carolina Press.

Rancière, Jacques, 1999, *Disagreement: Politics and Philosophy*, Minneapolis, MN, University of Minnesota Press.

Rorty, Richard, 1989, *Contingency, Irony and Solidarity*, Cambridge, Cambridge University Press.

Sewell, William, 1980, *Work and Revolution in France: The Language of Labor from the Old Regime to 1848*, Cambridge, Cambridge University Press.

Wagner, Peter, 1986, *A Sociology of Modernity: Liberty and Discipline*, London, Routledge.

Walzer, Michael, 1983, *Spheres of Justice*, Oxford, Martin Robertson.

Weiming, Tu, 2000, 'Implications of the Rise of "Confucian" East Asia', *Daedalus*, 129(1).

CHAPTER 9

The Making and the Unmaking of Europe in its Encounter with Islam: Negotiating French Republicanism and European Islam

Nilüfer Göle

The point of departure for this chapter is that Islam is an active agent in the alteration of European space, necessitating a new frame for thinking about the relationship between the political and the religious bond, and the ways in which this relationship reinforces or transforms the meaning of a polity such as the French Republic or a religious community such as European Islam. Rethinking the relations between Islam and Europe requires a new conceptual space, a new frame that introduces an intercultural perspective to our readings of European modernity. It requires a sensitivity to the duality of certain key processes: how religious and secular causes become entwined with one another, and how Islam translates and is translated into European modernity.

In this chapter I argue for a new conceptual frame that will enable us to understand the nature of the encounter between Islam and Europe as a novel experience of modernity. This calls for an opening up of our readings of modernity to Muslim experiences that are neither shaped exclusively by Western liberalism and secularism, nor identifiable as the reproduction and transmission of religious traditions. Islam takes on new discursive meanings through its interaction with modernity. It achieves a performative visibility. Through this, and with the aid of various religious agencies and discursive practices, Muslim actors distance themselves from the traditional interpretations and prescripts of Islam, as well as rejecting the notion of assimilative modernity.

Instead of relegating the study of Islam merely to the problems of immigration and the politics of integration, which supposes a vertical representation of the relations between Muslim populations and nation states, I suggest a transversal reading of the encounter between the two. Framing the problem in terms of the integration of Muslims and the accommodation of Islam with European values supposes the pre-existence of a system (of nation states or of a wider European project) in which Muslims are expected to take part. However, the presence of Muslims questions the very principles on which the system is framed and instituted. Hence a two-way mutual transformation is taking place, and the advent of the Islamic presence in European contexts means both a refashioning of Muslim identities and a change in European self-presentation. It is by studying the zones of contact, interaction and interpenetration that we can grasp the two-way changes and the nature of this encounter (Göle 2005). It is in the public sphere that this encounter is taking shape; problems are brought into public consciousness and debated publicly. It is the notion of the public sphere more than the political realm or civil societal associations that enables us to observe the making or the unmaking of a bond. The main hypothesis that underlies this chapter is that there is a structural process that produces 'commonness', which brings Muslims and Europeans into closer contact with one another. This commonness can be conceptualized in terms of space (public space and European territorial space) and in terms of temporality (Islam as part of Europe's present). Immediate proximity characterizes both of these. In spite of the idea, which is widespread in Western public debate, that public religion is an anachronism in modern society, Islam enters into the public arena and shapes contemporary issues and consciousness.

Another suggestion I wish to make is that the advent of Islam in European contexts challenges the secularist, liberal and universalist claims on which – many versions of – Western citizenship and its publics are founded. How to deal with cultural and religious difference becomes a major problem for European pluralistic democracies. Disputes over the meanings of religious symbols become crucial in various European populations. Is veiling a symbol of religious faith? Does it stand for fundamentalism, cultural identity or gender body politics? Similarly, is the crucifix in school classes a religious symbol of Christianity, of collective European cultural identity, or a symbol of majority – Western hegemony in a multi-cultural society? Symbols do not have fixed meanings, of course, or meanings independent of the subjectivities and inter-subjectivities that give sense to them. Symbols are transformed by those who adopt them, as well as by those who observe them and attach meaning to them. The public sphere is the site of the communication and presentation as well as the perception and misconception of symbols.

Rethinking the frames of modernity from the vantage point of Islam necessitates a new *intellectual* agenda. However, the latter is closely related with a *political* question that raises the issue of diversity and pluralism in Europe. And, last but not least, in addition to the intellectual and political aspects of this encounter, there is an *emotional* dimension, which is ever-present. An emotional charge seems to intervene in the unfolding of private passions into public opinion and seems to take hold of public reasoning. It is the very proximity and commonness of Islam and Europe that generates emotional anxiety about the loss of markers and invites calls for boundary maintenance.

Having tried to introduce the frame of analysis for understanding the making of Europe in its encounter with Islam, let me turn now to the central protagonists and to Islam in particular. By 'Islam' I do not imply a homogeneous religious entity inured to historical change, nor do I seek to reduce it to infinite multiplicities (as many 'little Islams' as there are Muslims). Instead, I refer mainly to Muslim actors who appropriate Islam (discursively and perform-atively) as a means of self-empowerment and criticism with regard to Western values and forms of modernity. In that respect, 'Islamism' is more accurate, as long as we do not reduce its meaning to the political and ideological dimensions of the movement, nor conflate it with terrorism, but use it to distinguish from the Islamic religion as such and to put the accent on socially interpreted forms of religion by means of personal and political actors. Meanwhile, the vocabulary that we use naturally has its own lifetime and evolution. 'Islamism' has been widely used in political science approaches that have privileged the ideological and political dimensions of action, oriented towards state power and confined to nation-state scales of analysis. However, in the last two decades, con-temporary Islamism has been undergoing a change, circulating at a global scale, settling in European political contexts, and reacting to different kinds of cultural exposure. Notions such as post-Islamist (referring, basically, to the Iranian post-revolutionary period) or ex-Islamist (more appropriate for the Turkish case) try to capture the new stage of Islamism during which Muslim youth, women, cultural mediators, entrepreneurs and middle classes emerge and make their way in secular publics and the liberal market and develop new self-presentations, consumption patterns and forms of piety. In this second stage, Islamic intellectuals or public spokespersons circulate and communicate between local, national and global publics, intermingling secular and religious idioms, trying to maintain a bond between the several publics through which they constitute their life strategies. 'Islam becomes public' (Göle and Amman 2004) is a term intended to mean that Muslims are communicating, as well as disputing, their religious claims and presence in secular pluralistic European publics, defying thereby the private–public boundaries, gender equality, freedom of expression and the citizenship definitions of those publics.

European countries are the main arena in which this encounter is taking place and is politically shaped and publicly debated. The European Union project has intensified and accelerated the ways in which relations with Islam are debated in various publics at the national and cross-national levels. Issues related to the

175

Muslim immigrant population and to Turkish candidacy for membership of the EU have become a subject of major public debate and controversy in the majority of European countries. By means of discussions on the problems of integration, accommodation and cultural dissension, Islam has become an active ingredient in the making of Europe. However confrontational this process is, new patterns of interaction, perceptions of difference and presentations of the self are under way, leading to a major debate concerning European values and modernity.

Critiques of Western modernity are not new, and Europe's intellectual legacy is shaped by such critiques. The anti-modernist tradition is an intrinsic part of modernity, and it has contributed considerably to the modern sense of liberty (Compagnon 2005). Perspectives that were open to experiences outside Europe have also shaped the ways we think of modernity as an interdependent phenomenon creating a single 'world system'. The nature of relations between the West and the rest, the impact of the West on different historical and cultural contexts, the interdependence between the centre and the periphery, the inter-connectedness of historical experience, the experiences of colonialism – all have shaped, our language of the social sciences in different ways. Latin American 'dependence theory', critiques of 'Orientalism', Indian 'post-colonial studies', the historiography of the 'subaltern' and more recent approaches that stress 'multiple modernities' or 'alternative modernities' have deeply transformed the Eurocentric and standardized ways of narrating modernity. But Islamic criticisms of modernity cannot be rendered fully by criticisms along the lines of Orientalism, theories of globalism, or post-colonial readings. A sense of geographical and temporal remoteness is implicit in all these theories, as well as a preference for the *longue-durée* perspective. Islamic actors and critiques, by contrast, enter European space in the present time, involve face-to-face conversation and confrontation, and bring forth a new repertoire of politics in the populations of Europe, challenging thereby our readings of modernity.

In that respect, Europe provides more than anywhere else a privileged site to observe the ways in which the orientations of modernity become a battleground between religious and secular actors. Islamic discourse speaks from a vantage point that is 'external' to the Western Enlightenment tradition. But, at the same time, Islam becomes a source of self-guidance and political contestation for those Muslims who are already deterritorialized, adulterated and situated 'within' the life experiences of European modernity. The significance of contemporary Islam rises from this double conversation and entwining of modernity with religion. Religious actors address a criticism to the cultural realm of modernity; liberal definitions of the self, gendered equality, private–public boundaries and secularism. Hence a new repertoire of conflict arises, ranging from conceptions of self, gender and everyday morals to the realm of the polity.

176

Islam is used as a source with which to dispute the cultural orientations of modernity; but this is possible because Muslim actors enter into the spaces, experiences and temporalities of modernity. Islam, far from remaining unaltered as a distinct civilization, enters into the world-making scene, becomes part of these modern arenas and challenges in turn the Western claims of civilizational ownership of modernity.

The impact of Western European modernity on the Muslim mind and Muslim societies is not a recent phenomenon. Various political trajectories and social processes such as colonialism, the civilizing mission, voluntary Westernization, authoritarian secularism and waves of immigration have shaped Muslim societies' acquaintance with modernity. Muslims have seen themselves in the mirror of Western values, have interiorized selectively some of the universalist claims of Western civilization, while rejecting others, have evaluated their societies in comparison with Western hegemony, and have engaged in diverse conversations with modernity in different periods, ranging from mimetic Westernism to post-colonial criticism and the affirmation of authenticity. Overall, the histories of non-Western societies have by and large been shaped by their interpretations of Western modernity. What is novel in the contemporary global context is the increasing role and visibility of different forms of Islam in European contexts and in the world-making process in general. As Islam and Western societies come into closer contact and start to share the same European spaces and temporality, the nature of their relation changes from a one-sided hegemonic domination by the West to a more horizontal two-way interaction. The interaction between the two means a process of transformation for both parties, however asymmetrical the power relations are. Consequently, one can no longer preserve a geographical separation and a historical time lag in thinking about the relation between Islam and the West. Islam also becomes an intrinsic part of the West and acts as its mirror. However, reading the European project in the mirror of Islam is not an easy task. Islam, in different ways, destabilizes European people's lives and perceptions. Muslim actors use religious difference for their self-presentation, while in the eyes of European citizens Islam becomes too visibly different (by means of religious signs), too physically preponderant (in terms of sheer numbers), and too physically close (in terms of sharing the same space). In the eyes of many, a threshold of tolerance is surpassed, and in that sense the Muslim presence in Europe disturbs and creates fear and resentment.

Thinking about the relations between Europe and Islam is no simple task, therefore. As I have already mentioned, an emotional charge blurs the appropriate perceptions of the self and the other. One can also speak of an intellectual deficit in covering Islam in our readings of modernity, and the absence of a political vision for providing a frame. Both 'republican' and 'multiculturalist' politics seem to fall short of providing a frame for incorporating the advent of Islam in European contexts. Multiculturalism speaks for the recognition of difference, but does not provide any key for understanding commonness. Republicanism, on the other hand, claims to offer a discourse of equality and individual integration which is, in fact, largely specious; educational failure, economic poverty, social segregation and the ghettoization of immigrant populations are recognized facts. In different ways, French republicanism and Dutch multiculturalism face tensions in relation to Islam and to the European project.

The European project can be thought of as a means of world-making, instituting a novel political form, a window of opportunity for rethinking the question of difference and commonness with Islam. But the interaction between Europe and Islam is not only structured by the democratic means of politics or public debating. Terrorist acts are part of the process, something that reveals the confrontational ways in which Islam enters into the world-making scene. On the one hand, terrorist acts testify to the 'commonness', the common grounds, that bring together terrorists and their victims; on the other, these terrorist acts aim to destroy and negate the bond between Muslims and Europeans. Terrorism aims to intimidate Muslim conversations with modernity and to trigger collective fear, threatening and shrinking thereby the very existence of the political realm and its potential for negotiation and inclusion. Since the Al Qaeda terrorist attacks on September 11 2001 in New York, the cleavages between Islam and the Western world seem to have deepened and expanded into new domains. The Al Qaeda bombings that took place in Istanbul (November 15 and 20 2003) and in Madrid (March 11 2004) were among other indications that terrorism seeks to impose its own agenda and position itself at the centre of relations between Islam and Europe.

In Holland, the November 2004 assassination by a Moroccan immigrant of the Dutch intellectual Theo Van Gogh, a well-known public figure who personified the Dutch sense of freedom of speech, crystallized and intensified the ways in which issues surrounding migration and Islam take new twists in European contexts. Van Gogh had made a film called *Submission*, the author of which was Hirsi Ali, a well-known public figure herself. Ali is a member of the Dutch parliament, a Somali-born Muslim refugee, known for her outspoken criticisms of Islam. The production of the film by these two public figures, with quite different personal histories, cultural backgrounds and gender con-sciousness, exemplified the connection between these two worlds: it suggested a close encounter between the two, but one that could not avoid violence. The author of the film herself underwent religious oppression, but succeeded in transgressing the boundaries of an Islamic community in order to become a spokesperson for the emancipation of Muslim women. The film was meant to be a critique of Muslim women's oppression by religious interdictions, although the representation of Muslim women and the Quranic verses in the film were oversimplified and caricatured, perhaps to the extent of contributing to the debasing of Muslim women (Moors 2005).

In European contexts, Muslims are having to deal with the requirements of European gender definitions, as well as with relations with non-Muslims. One observes that gender issues and interfaith issues are becoming more and more central in shaping the dissension between different publics. The assassination of the film's producer brought forth a political repertoire that has shown the difficulties of negotiation between two distinct sets of values. While European citizenship is defined, as it is recalled in this case, around the principles of tolerance for individual freedoms of public expression and women's emancipation, Islamic publics raised the issue of religious blasphemy and conservative prescriptions of gender. One also observes the ways in which these issues have become part of a Dutch public controversy, grounded in Dutch public memory and in the public arena (literally so on the streets of Amsterdam by a terrorist who left a message addressed to Dutch citizens in Dutch). This incident shows the extent to which Islam is not confined to a given geographical region (labelled the 'Middle East'), nor a concern only for Muslim populations, but has been reterritorialized within European nation states, itself becoming a subject matter for European publics and not always by means of peaceful and rational debate. Islam circulates and is carried to different publics in different ways. The incident exposed the limits of Holland's multiculturalist discourse in facing these issues. As Paul Scheffer, one of the leading public intellectuals of the Dutch debate on the failure of multiculturalism, argues, the incident has shown that 'cultural avoidance' is no longer a possibility. The encounter between Muslims and Europeans is taking place, and it is becoming not only difficult but also undesirable to contain and draw boundaries between different, multiple cultural communities. Yet it is the growing anxiety about a breakdown of boundaries and a loss of identity that accompanies the dynamics of this encounter, from the perspective of Muslims and Europeans, leading to the reinforcement of national and religious identities and, consequently, to the weakening of the European project.

Islam Setting a New European Agenda in National Contexts

It is especially in France that the idea of maintaining boundaries and defending national identity has become particularly pronounced in relation to a series of public debates that have taken place during the last decade. The opposition to the Iraq war and criticisms made of American politics, the Islamic headscarf in state schools and the possibility of Turkish membership of the European Union have all triggered a shift in the presentation of Europe, as well as in the representation of the 'other'. The disagreement surrounding the Iraq war (March 2003) led to a fracture in the West, enhancing a definition of European values and politics in counter-distinction to the American search for hegemony. An anti-American attitude in the self-presentation of the French public gave impetus to the mobilization of pro-peace movements and the perception of their having a distinctively European character.

Maybe no other social issue has provoked in France more passion and debate than the Islamic headscarf in state schools, followed by the debate on Turkish membership of the European Union. Two distinct questions, whether young Muslim migrant girls have the right to wear a headscarf in secular state schools and whether Turkey can become a member of the European Union, provoked a debate on the definition of French republicanism as well as that of European identity. Two distinct claims made by Muslims – the right to wear the headscarf in French state schools and the right of Turkish membership of the European Union – both touched deep-rooted anxiety and triggered a larger debate on the values of secularism on the one hand and that of Europeanism on the other.

The headscarf debate is related to issues of immigration, the education system and criteria of citizenship. It concerns the politics of integration and, hence, domestic politics – yet the scope of Islamic claims extends beyond the national arena. Turkish membership is a question that can neither be equated with problems of migration (even less so in France than in Germany) nor identified with 'Islam' (Turkey is a secular state). Yet by means of a public debate over the course of two years, one can observe the ways in which the theme of Turkish candidacy moved from the realm of foreign affairs to the realm of internal politics, to the extent that it came to be decisive for the referendum on the European constitutional treaty (May 29 2005). The opponents of the constitutional treaty (a coalition of socialists and the nationalist right) used the Turkish candidacy question in their campaign, establishing a link between the two and implying that a rejection of the treaty would guarantee the non-entrance of Turkey into Europe. The rejection of the European constitutional treaty by 56 per cent of the French population can be read as an indicator of the rise of nationalism and particularism, whether defined by French exceptionalism with regard to the notion of *laïcité* in a multicultural world, with regard to social rights in a global liberal economy, or French sovereignty against European solidarity.

These debates are obviously of a fundamentally different nature. But it is the way that they are 'issuetized' and problematized that is interesting: the way in which Turkish membership becomes an agenda-setting issue for French identity-politics, and the way *l'affaire du foulard* (the headscarf issue) provokes a larger debate on secularism. This can stand as a point of departure for understanding the making of Europe in its encounter with Islam. It is in these micro-level practices that we can pursue the hidden dynamics of the process. These public debates contributed, in different ways, to the problematization of the bond between European and Muslim identities. In relation to the headscarf issue, the principle of republican secularism (*laïcité*) was mobilized as French exceptionalism. In relation to Turkish membership of the EU, a different set of values was mobilized (and, interestingly, not secularism). The definition and the defence of Europe as a distinct civilization became a key theme; whether or not Turkey was part of European geography, history and religion became a major question of debate. In these debates, one can observe the ways in which Turkey came to represent the 'other' against whom European 'identity' was reinforced and reconstructed, while the Islamic headscarf was equated with the 'oppressed gender', against which the emancipatory principles of feminism and secularism were interlaced as prerequisites of European citizenship. Both cases brought in the question of 'territory'. Turkey represents a territorial Islam, but by her possible membership implies an enlargement of European territory. Third-generation Muslim migrants are distant from their countries of origin and bring to public awareness their experiences of a denationalized Islam. The question of territory is also raised by their visibility and presence as Muslims – and the claim of the right to do so – on the European Continent in public spaces, cities, schools, hospitals and prisons. In relation both to the Turkey and the headscarf debates, we witness a slide from a political to a religious over-determination of the issue.

In different ways in both debates, anti-Americanism provided an anchor for the elaboration of a collective French and European self-presentation. In the headscarf debate, communitarianism and multicultural liberalism, identified with Anglo-Saxon ways of dealing with difference, served as an ideal-type in opposition to the republican French universalism that is praised for enhancing individualism and public neutrality through *laïcité*. As to the membership of Turkey, the 'forcing' of the issue by the US was considered not only diplomatically unacceptable but, furthermore, as an attempt to subvert the European project. One can see in these debates a struggle for ways of thinking about Europeanness and self-presentation in counter-distinction to America. (One should add, however, that new political configurations between the populist right and religious conservative movements are rising both in Europe and the United States, indicating that the two continents are becoming closer and more similar than some might wish to think.)

Definitions of European values and identity are therefore undergoing an examination. The foundational principles are being revisited. It is the encounter with Islam that is the instigator of this process. The question that remains to be answered is the one about the impact of this identity-recalling process on the making of Europe. What does it do in terms of the European claim to institute a common that is inherently pluralistic? It is not by chance that the two countries that rejected the European constitutional treaty, France and the Netherlands, are the two countries where Islam has been most publicly debated, giving rise to a defence of national values, to French and Dutch 'exceptionalism'. How are these identity-raising processes to be thought of in relation to the multicultural reality of Europe (Kastoryano 2005)? Is the sense of Europe as a project, as a means of creating a mutual bond providing social solidarity – in short, the making of a European polity – weakened by this, or rather revitalized? Let me turn to the debates and examine in more detail what kinds of shifts and changes they indicate in the framing of relations between Europe and Islam.

French *laïcité* and the Islamic Headscarf

The debate on the Islamic headscarf started fifteen years ago in 1989, when in Creil (a little town close to Paris), three young female students came to school wearing a scarf and were refused entry by the school authorities (Gaspard and Khosrokhavar 1995). In September 1994 a regulation was issued by the Minister of Education, François Bayrou (the *circulaire Bayrou*), that banned students from wearing 'ostentatious' religious signs in state schools, including crosses, kippas and headscarves. (The word 'ostentatious' was to reappear ten years later, in the autumn 2003 debate.) But the decision as to whether to exclude the girls was then left to the school authorities. A deeper and more passionate public debate on the same issue began in autumn 2003, ending with new legislation in March 2004 to ban the Islamic headscarf, alongside other religious signs, from state schools.

Leading political figures, well-known public intellectuals, historians, feminists, experts on Islam, spokespersons for Muslim women and the immigrant population all participated in the debate. It was conducted in all sorts of media, ranging from daily newspapers, weekly magazines, television channels, Internet sites and academic conferences to discussions in market places, coffee houses and at dinner tables. As well as the high publicity the debate attracted, a commission was created at the request of President Chirac on July 3 2003. The twenty-member commission was to examine the application of the principle of secularism in the Republic. The status of the commission and the role it played in the public debate demand particular attention. An 'enlightened public' was created, the members of which were called *les sages* ('the wise people'). Among the members were public servants, public intellectuals, academics, businessmen, representatives of non-governmental organizations and personalities with interfaith credentials.

After five months of intensive work and a series of semi-private hearings, the commission published a report, 'Laïcité et République' (December 11 2003) and presented its recommendations with near-unanimity (the single dissenting voice was that of the historian and specialist in French secularism, Jean Bobérot). The public was presented with an alarming diagnosis. The situation, it was argued, was more serious than had previously been thought and secularism was threatened. According to the report, organized groups were testing the secular state by formulating demands for religious rights and forcing Muslims to identify themselves primarily with their religious faith rather than with their French citizenship. The theme of communitarian oppression that was predominant in the public debate was also taken up in the commission's report. The persistence of inward-looking communities confirmed, according to them, the failure to integrate the Muslim immigrant population and was seen as fertile terrain for Islamist groups wanting to exercise control over those who did not wish to live in accordance with religious prescripts. Young Muslim girls and women were designated as the first target of oppression and manipulation for the communitarian politics of Islam. Secondly, state schools were supposedly afraid of becoming a battleground for religious politics and hostility among youth. The rise of anti-Semitism among Muslim youth caused a series of violent incidents and threats to Jewish students, and rejections, in some schools, of the teaching of Jewish history and the Holocaust. Furthermore, an escalation of demands for special religious privileges, from schools to other sectors of public life, was feared. The separation of swimming times for men and women in state swimming schools, the treatment of female patients exclusively by female doctors, and pressure brought by some Muslim prison inmates on other prisoners demanding strict religious observance, were among the examples that were quoted in the report and that alarmed the commission members.

But, apart from this diagnosis, according to which French *laïcité* was threatened by the advent of Islamist groups and the Muslim immigrant population was enclosed in an oppressive form of communitarianism, the report also pointed to the necessity of opening up the principle of secularism to embrace the multicultural reality of present-day French society. The commission made the observation that a 1905 law codifying the separation of church and state was no longer adequate, given the multicultural and religious composition of present-day French society. The report acknowledged that, due to the process of immigration, French society had become more diverse in terms of its spiritual and religious composition, and the challenge was to give space to new religions, namely Islam, which, with 4,200,000 Muslims, the country's largest minority, had become the second religion of France. So the crucial question of how to accommodate French *laïcité* in a multicultural context was directly addressed in the report. One can observe, following Immanuel Wallerstein, that the report proposed a pluralistic interpretation of French *laïcité* (Wallerstein 2005). A balanced revision of the regulations and practices was recommended, in order to respond to the new needs of a multicultural, multifaith society, such as attention to dietary requirements or the reorganization of graveyards and religious rituals. Among the recommendations was the suggestion that a Jewish and a Muslim holiday be made national holidays, alongside Christmas and Easter. Yet such propositions were viewed as far-fetched fantasies, or were simply ignored. Later, some of the commission members expressed their disappointment that their recommendations had not been taken into consideration and that the only provision that had been implemented was the forbidding of the headscarf.

One should recall that the debate was initiated by those who argued that the 'liberal' hypothesis – in practice: tolerating few incidents of scarf-wearing as private occurrences – had failed because the increase in the frequency of students asserting their religious rights had made it impossible to leave decisions on individual cases to the school authorities. Initially, a strong call for state legislation was therefore at the core of the debate. Multicultural discourse has never been very popular in republican France (Wieviorka 2001): it has been seen as leading to communitarian politics, an anti-French model identified negatively with Anglo-Saxon politics. In spite of the commission's attempt to formulate the ban within a pluralistic frame, to avoid the stigmatization of Islam and foster a careful definition of *laïcité* and tolerance for all religions, and hence take into account the multicultural reality of French society, it is not an overstatement to say that, overall, the debate and the legislation that followed ruled out, at least for some time, any possibility of introducing a multiculturalist approach to the problem.

The debate, rather than engage different voices, mobilized collective opinion in one direction, in favour of legislation to ban from state schools religious symbols that were considered to be *ostensible*. There was a discussion over the meaning of the French adjectives, *ostensible* (apparent) and *ostentatoire* (ostentatious). The distinctions were not evident and were subject to interpretation; small crosses, stars of David, hands of Fatima and small Qurans were considered discreet and acceptable. The headscarf remained the central concern for the legislation. Although at the beginning of the debate one frequently heard that the principle of *laïcité* was not to be discussed in relation to a 'piece of cloth', that is exactly what happened in the end. Emmanuel Terray has described the debate as 'collective hysteria', to the extent that it became contagious: all positions pulled in the same direction in favour of legislation to ban the headscarf (Terray 2004). Public opinion, the commission and the legislation all followed the same line of argument. Obviously there was no single argument, but a constellation of themes that mobilized public consciousness: the importance of a uniform education system for the formation of citizens and as an opportunity to distance oneself from one's origins; the republican model that encourages integration at an individual level rather than the community level; the incompatibility of the secular foundations of the public sphere with the multiculturalist recognition of difference; and, last but not least, the equality of the sexes as the basis of citizenship.

The law, as Seyla Benhabib argues, is a means for repositioning and rearticulating rights in the public spheres of liberal democracies. The law can sometimes guide this process, legal reform may run ahead of popular consciousness and may raise popular consciousness to the level of the constitution – but the law may also lag behind popular consciousness. According to Benhabib, 'to ban the wearing of the veil in state schools seemed at first the attempt of a progressive state bureaucracy to modernize the "backward-looking" customs of a particular group'. However, this intervention 'cascaded into a series of democratic iterations' (in the sense used by Derrida, referring to how the repetition of a term or concept never simply produces a replica of the original usage, but rather transforms in meaning with every iteration) 'leading to public self-reflexivity as well as to public defensiveness' (Benhabib 2006: 13).

The debate instigated, albeit unintentionally, various shifts in the definition of the problems at stake. First, almost paradoxically, the ban imprinted the Islamic headscarf in the French collective consciousness. The headscarf, identified with a non-European population thought to be confined to the Middle East region, became a French possession (Barkat 2004).

Second, a gradual shift of language occurred and the use of the word 'headscarf' was replaced by 'veil', the latter indicating more forcefully the link to the Islamic religion. Over the course of twenty years, Islam has become a salient feature in French discourses of Frenchness and immigration, to the extent that other issues have become entwined. Third, it is through the image of 'veiled girls' that a kind of 'feminization' of the immigrant population has occurred. The ban was justified on the basis that veiling was not an individual choice but an expression of Islamist or communitarian oppression. There was therefore a collective denial of 'agency' to Muslim girls who were serious about their religion. Yet the Islamic veiling brought religious visibility, as well as gender visibility. The first generation of immigrants was symbolized by the single adult working male (*travailleur immigré*); the second-generation young male Arabs, the *beurs* generation, revealed the problems of integration, education and unemployment; and in the youngest generation, the veiling of young girls introduced the aspect of gender difference and religion into the immigrant population. But at the same time they embodied a form of integration into French society. The previous generations of immigrants were defined with reference to their industry or idleness, and especially to their lack of education and language skills. It was in the state schools that the issue of veiling appeared, as this generation of young girls made their entrance into French education and language. Their French citizenship was foregrounded in various ways. For instance, during the demonstrations veiled girls displayed their French identity cards.

Fourth, a new archetype emerged: the movement *ni putes ni soumises* ('neither prostitute nor docile') gave voice to secular Muslim women who felt stigmatized both by Islamic perceptions and French non-recognition, and who searched for a space of existence and autonomy.

And fifth, the feminist movement in France has been transformed in relation to the veiling issue. A new kind of republican feminist discourse emerged in the public debate with which the spokespersons of the movement *ni putes ni soumises* aligned themselves and thereby gave their secular Muslim women support (Guenif 2004). But well-known public female figures also intervened in favour of republicanism; a collective letter signed by writers, actresses and feminists was addressed to the President of the Republic and published in the weekly women's fashion magazine, *Elle*, expressing indignation and fear vis-à-vis the Islamic threat to feminist rights and arguing for legislation. From the point of view of the radical feminism of the 1970s, the addressee of this letter – male republican power – and the public medium in which it was published – a magazine in which the female body is represented in conformity with commercial market values – would have been a matter of feminist criticism. This seemed to indicate the ways in which the secularist discourse had overtaken feminist priorities. Another reorientation of feminist discourse and its alignment with secularism carried overtones that were much more affirmative and combative (Fourrest and Venner 2003). The expression *laicards, puisque féministes* made its way into the public debate and encapsulated well the new alliance between feminism and secularism. The new republican feminism expressed itself combatively in endorsing *laïcité* politically (the term *laicard* referred critically to those who transformed secularism into an authoritarian ideology). The republican brand of anti-Islamist feminism distinguished itself from the other feminist movements (which were against both the law and the veil), accusing them of being insufficiently ardent in their defence of secularism.

186

A fracture in the feminist movement became apparent and in 2005, the participation of veiled Muslim women in the annual women's demonstration on March 8 became a battleground between feminist organizations. Contrary to republican feminism, 'feminists for equality' (including the well-known feminist, Christine Delphy) defended 'schooling for everybody', criticized the protagonists of secularism for their exclusionary politics, and entered into dialogue with Muslim women, questioning thereby the limits of Western feminist discourse underpinned by civilizational and colonial claims.

European Identity and Turkish *alterité*

Turkish secularism mirrors in many ways French *laïcité*. Not only does the Turkish *laiklik* (the term itself is borrowed from the French) imply the exclusion of religious signs from the public sphere, but also the headscarf debate was at the centre of public controversies and shaped political life in Turkey from the beginning of the 1980s. The ban on wearing the headscarf in universities is a major political issue that has continued to divide profoundly the secular and Muslim publics for more than two decades. While legal attempts to ban the Islamic headscarf from state schools were discussed in France, in Turkey the official ceremony for the annual celebration of the Turkish Republic (October 29 2003) turned into a public controversy. The spouses of the deputies of the AK Party, the Turkish moderate Islamist party, which had been in government since the general elections on November 3 2002, were not invited to the official ceremony to celebrate the Turkish Republic, held each year on October 29. The president, Ahmet Necdet Sezer, an intransigent secularist, wanted to avoid the presence of the 'covered' spouses of AKP deputies, while the spouses of the deputies of the Republican People's Party (all uncovered) were welcomed and treated as the natural representatives of the republic. His attitude was considered discriminatory not only by AKP politicians and Islamist intellectuals but also by some liberal secularist columnists and public figures. This was more than just a single incident: tensions between those holding to the secularist principles of the republic and those claiming their right to carry religious signs in public life are recurrent on various public stages, including schools, universities and official ceremonies, defying the implicit secularist foundations and regulations of public life in Turkey. Hence, the reconciliation of secularism with the expansion of democratic rights becomes a major challenge for participatory democracy in Turkey.

The historical trajectories and cultural composition of the two countries are obviously very different. France's colonial past and the dismantling of the multi-religious Ottoman Empire shaped the ways in which contemporary cleavages

187

between secularists and Muslims are framed in the two countries. We speak in the French case of a migration-related, minority Muslim population, whereas in the case of Turkey the politics of *laïcité* are addressed to a majority Muslim population in which authoritarian political power has backed up the process of secular modernization. But, in spite of these differences, and in asymmetrical ways, what is at stake in both countries is the encounter of the republic with Islam. We can speak of commonness between Turkey and France, to the extent that in both countries there is felt to be an opposition between the republic and Islam, and the relation between the two is framed by state secularism. Turkish *laiklik* has been criticized for not being in conformity with its French ideal-type, and instead of respecting, for instance, the autonomy of religion, it has been rightly pointed out that the state attempts to control religion (for instance, imams are educated in state schools and are salaried public servants). Today, the French Republic, in its endeavour to create French Islam (i.e., public recognition of Islam's presence while separating it from its national origins and influences), fosters a new institution to 'represent' Islam, namely le Conseil Français du Culte Musulman, through which the state aims to control and shape the Muslim interlocutor. The comparison between French and Turkish secularisms becomes meaningful from the perspective of the encounter of the republic with Islam. Secondly, in both cases, Islamic claims are addressed in the context of secular publics, in a pluralistic political context and in interaction with non-religious lifestyles. And thirdly, the European project intervenes as a central player in this game and enacts a shift of scale, adding a new dimension to ways of considering the bond between the republic and Islam. In that respect, decentring – even in literally spatial terms – our readings of Europe by means of a dislocation of the focus on Turkey brings to our attention the tensions between republicanism and the European project.

In the minds of the French public there is no evident hiatus between republicanism and the European project. For many, on the contrary, Europe should be constructed without giving up French republicanism. Europe should be French republicanism writ large. But the picture appears quite differently seen from the perspective of the Turkish experience. European influence forced Turkey to introduce a reformation of the republican definitions of citizenship in order to be in harmony with democratic and pluralistic definitions of ethnic, political, religious and individual rights. Turkish republicanism, as the nation state ideology, has been founded on two pillars: secularism and nationalism, called 'Kemalism' after the founding father of the Republic, Kemal Atatürk. But these principles were also coupled with monocultural definitions of society, giving rise to anti-democratic versions of these principles, namely authoritarian secularism and assimilative nationalism. The working of the European project in Turkey meant the dismantling of the authoritarian and assimilative nature of republicanism. In the eyes of many hard-line nationalists and secularists (*laicards*), the European project is leading Turkey in the direction of democratization and demilitarization, and this constitutes a danger to the stability of the country, opening the gate to escalating demands from Kurdish nationalists and religious fundamentalists. In spite of deeply rooted resistance among republican nationalists, a Muslim-background AK Party government (The Party of Justice and Development) passed during the course of 2002–03 a series of legislative reforms to reconcile Turkish law with the Copenhagen criteria, supported by pro-European public opinion and a civil society in favour of democratization.

In France, a debate on the legitimacy of Turkish membership started the moment Turkey accomplished the bulk of its requirements for accession. Once again, one should note that it is the proximity, the encounter between the two, that is the source of conflict and controversy. Turkish membership triggered anxiety in French public opinion: a desire for boundary maintenance shaped public debate. The question of geographical frontiers, civilizational belonging, religious difference and past memories all entered into the debate as a constellation of seemingly insurmountable differences. Europe, until then an affair left in the hands of Eurocrats, made its way into public debate, recomposing the political and intellectual arena independent of left–right, secular–religious, liberal–republican, feminist–conservative divisions. Identifying Europe meant 'othering' Turkey. Europeanism appeared as an identity defined by shared history and common cultural values rather than as a project for a new kind of world-making, a pluralistic way of thinking through the political bond. Once again, it is in contexts outside the core of Europe that Europe appears as a project and has the power to induce democratization. In Turkey, where Europeanness is not part of a 'natural' identity, it has been appropriated voluntarily as a political project promising a democratic frame for rethinking commonness and difference.

The Turkish candidacy revealed, unintentionally, the tacit equation between the European project and European identity on the one hand, and the tensions between universalist claims and the Judaeo-Christian legacy on the other. European claims for universalism and its limits are tested by Turkish membership. The possibility is raised of surpassing a mono-civilizational definition of Europe, and thereby opening it to new ways of rethinking the European polity. European Islam becomes a possibility only if the European project undergoes a process of self-examination in the mirror of Islam.

The encounter between Muslims and Europeans can be thought of as the creation of a common bond through hyphenated identities such as European-

Islam, French-Muslims and Euro-Turks. Today the problem is not the recognition of diversity but, on the contrary, the recognition of commonness. The comfort of distance and difference is challenged by Muslim proximity. Furthermore, Muslims force this proximity, expressing their 'desire' (as in the case of Turkish membership) to be part of the project and making themselves visible (as in the case of veiling and the activities of various religious actors). Europe, as a project, offers the possibility of surpassing the fixity and purity of identities in favour of an intersubjective social experience and intercultural world-making. Will the European project seize this opportunity and offer a new kind of world-making, or will it replicate the lines of global cleavages? It is an open, two-way question, the answer to which will define the making or the unmaking of Europe.

References

Barkat, Sidi Mohammed, 2004, 'La loi contre le droit', in C. Nordmann (ed.), *Le Foulard islamique en questions*, Paris, éditions Amsterdam, 28–37.

Benhabib, Seyla, 2002, *The Claims of Culture: Equality and Diversity in the Global Era*, Princeton, NJ, Princeton University Press.

— 2006, 'Democratic Iterations, The Local, the National and the Global', in *Another Cosmopolitanism: Hospitality, Sovereignty and Democratic Iterations*, Oxford, Oxford University Press.

Compagnon, Antoine, 2005, *Les antimodernes, de Joseph de Maistre à Roland Barthes*, Paris, Gallimard.

Fourrest, Carlonie, and Fiammetta Venner, 2003, *Tirs croisés, la laïcité à l'épreuve des intégrismes juifs, chrétiens et musulmans*, Paris, Editions Calmann-Lévy.

Gaspard, Françoise, and Farhad Khosrokhavar, 1995, *Le foulard et la République*, Paris, La Découverte.

Göle, Nilüfer, 2005, *Interpénétrations; L'Islam et l'Europe*, Paris, Galaade éditions.

Göle, Nilüfer, and Ludwig Amman (eds), 2004, *Islam in Sicht. Der Auftritt von Muslimen im öffentlichen Raum*, Bielefeld, Transcript (English edn: *Islam in Public*, Istanbul, Bilgi University Press, 2006).

Guenif, Nacira, 2004, 'Ni pute, ni soumise, ou très pute, très voilée', in C. Nordmann (ed.), *Le Foulard islamique en questions*, Paris, éditions Amsterdam, 81–89.

Kastoryano, Riva (ed.), 2005, *Quelle identité pour l'Europe? Le multiculturalisme à l'épreuve*, 2nd edn, Paris, Sciences Po.

Moors, Annelies, 2005, 'Submission', Debates on Islam in Europe, *ISIM Review*, 15.

Terray, Emmanuel, 2004, 'L'hystérie politique', in C. Nordmann (ed.), *Le Foulard islamique en questions*, Paris, éditions Amsterdam, 103–18.

Wallerstein, Immanuel, 2005, 'Render unto Caesar? The Dilemmas of a Multicultural World', *Sociology of Religion*, XLVI(2), 121–33.

Wieviorka, Michel, 2001, *La Différence*, Paris, Balland.

Wieviorka, Michel (ed.), 2001, *L'Avenir de l'Islam en France et en Europe*, Actes des entretiens d'Auxerre, Paris, Balland.

PART 3

FRAMING A WORLD

CHAPTER 10

Democratic Justice in a Globalizing Age: Thematizing the Problem of the Frame

Nancy Fraser

Globalization is changing the way we argue about justice. Not so long ago, in the heyday of social democracy, disputes about justice presumed what I shall call a 'Keynesian–Westphalian frame'. Typically played out within modern territorial states, arguments about justice were assumed to concern relations among fellow citizens, to be subject to debate within national publics, and to contemplate redress by national states. This was true for each of two major families of justice claims: claims for socioeconomic redistribution and claims for legal or cultural recognition. At a time when the Bretton Woods system of international capital controls facilitated Keynesian economic steering at the national level, claims for redistribution usually focused on economic inequities within territorial states. Appealing to national public opinion for a fair share of the national pie, claimants sought intervention by national states in national economies. Likewise, in an era still gripped by a Westphalian political imaginary, which sharply distinguished 'domestic' from 'international' space, claims for recognition generally concerned internal status hierarchies. Appealing to the national conscience for an end to nationally institutionalized disrespect, claimants pressed national governments to outlaw discrimination and accommodate differences among citizens. In both cases, the Keynesian–Westphalian frame was assumed. Whether the matter concerned redistribution or recognition, class differentials or status hierarchies, it went without saying that the unit within which justice applied was the modern territorial state.[1]

---

1 The phrase 'Keynesian–Westphalian frame' is meant to signal the national-territorial underpinnings of justice disputes in the heyday of the post-war democratic welfare state. The idea is that during the period from roughly 1945 through to the 1970s, struggles over distribution in North America and Western Europe were premised on the assumption of state steering of

To be sure, there were always exceptions. Occasionally, famines and genocides galvanized public opinion across borders. And some cosmopolitans and anti-imperialists sought to promulgate globalist views.[2] But these were exceptions that proved the rule. Relegated to the sphere of 'the international', they were subsumed within a problematic that was focused primarily on matters of security, as opposed to justice. The effect was to reinforce, rather than to challenge, the Keynesian–Westphalian frame. That framing of disputes about justice generally prevailed by default from the end of the Second World War through to the 1970s.

Although it went unnoticed at the time, the Keynesian–Westphalian frame gave a distinctive shape to arguments about social justice. Taking for granted the modern territorial state as the appropriate unit, and its citizens as the pertinent subjects, such arguments turned on *what* precisely those citizens owed each other. In the eyes of some, it sufficed that citizens be formally equal before the law; for others, equality of opportunity was also required; for still others, justice demanded that all citizens gain access to the resources and respect they needed in order to be able to participate on a par with others, as full members of the political community. The argument focused, in other words, on *what* should count as a just ordering of social relations within a society. Engrossed in disputing the 'what' of justice, the contestants apparently felt no necessity to dispute the 'who'. With the Keynesian–Westphalian frame securely in place, it went without saying that the 'who' was the national citizenry.

Today, however, the Keynesian–Westphalian frame is losing its aura of self-evidence. Thanks to heightened awareness of globalization and post-Cold War geopolitical instabilities, many observe that the social processes shaping their lives routinely overflow territorial borders. They note, for example, that

---

national economies. And national Keynesianism, in turn, was premised on the ideal of an international state system that recognized territorial state sovereignty over domestic affairs, which included responsibility for the citizenry's welfare. Analogous assumptions also governed disputes about recognition in this period. The term 'Westphalian' refers to the Treaty of 1648, which established some key features of the international state system in question. However, I am concerned neither with the actual achievements of the Treaty nor with the centuries-long process by which the system it inaugurated evolved. Rather, I invoke 'Westphalia' as a political imaginary that mapped the world as a system of mutually recognizing, sovereign territorial states, an imaginary that underpinned the post-war framing of debates about justice in the 'First World'. For the distinction between Westphalia as 'event', as 'idea/ideal', as 'process of evolution' and as 'normative score sheet', see Falk 2002.

2   It might be assumed that from the perspective of the 'Third World', Westphalian premises would have appeared patently counterfactual. Yet it is worth recalling that the great majority of anti-imperialists sought to achieve independent Westphalian states of their own. By contrast, only a small minority consistently championed justice within a global frame – for reasons that are entirely understandable.

decisions taken in one territorial state often impact on the lives of those outside it, as do the actions of transnational corporations, international currency speculators and large institutional investors. Many also note the growing salience of supranational and international organizations, both governmental and non-governmental, and of transnational public opinion, which flows with supreme disregard for borders through global mass media and cybertechnology. The result is a new sense of vulnerability to transnational forces. Faced with global warming, the spread of AIDS, international terrorism and superpower unilateralism, many believe that their chances for living good lives depend at least as much on processes that trespass the borders of territorial states as on those contained within them.[3]

Under these conditions, the Keynesian–Westphalian frame no longer goes without saying. For many, it is no longer axiomatic that the modern territorial state is the appropriate unit for thinking about issues of justice; nor that the citizens of such states are the pertinent subjects. The effect is to destabilize the structure of political claims-making that prevailed in the social-democratic era – and so to change the way we argue about social justice.

This is true for both major families of justice claims. In today's world, claims for redistribution increasingly eschew the assumptions of national economies. Faced with transnationalized production, the outsourcing of jobs and the associated pressures of the 'race to the bottom', once nationally focused labour unions look increasingly for allies abroad (Hathaway 2000; Moody 1997; Munck and Waterman 1999). Inspired by the Zapatistas, meanwhile, impoverished peasants and indigenous peoples link their struggles against despotic local and national authorities to critiques of transnational corporate predation and global neo-liberalism (La Botz 1995; Nash 2001; Niezen 2003). Finally, WTO protestors directly target the new governance structures of the global economy, which have vastly strengthened the ability of large corporations and investors to escape the regulatory and taxation powers of territorial states (O'Brien et al. 2000).

In such cases, disputes about distribution are exploding the Keynesian–Westphalian frame. No longer premised on national economies, claims for redistribution are no longer addressed exclusively to national states or debated exclusively by national publics. And they no longer focus solely on relations among fellow citizens. As a result, the grammar of distributive arguments has radically altered. Now, the issue is not just *how much* economic

---

3 Among the vast literature on this point, see: Basch et al. 1994; Castles and Davidson 2000, pp. 1–25, 156–83; Guidry et al. 2001; Held 2002; Kaldor 1999; Keck and Sikkink 1998; Khagram et al. 2002; Ong 1999; Zacher, 1992.

inequality justice permits but how much inequality *among whom*.

The same is true for disputes about recognition. In an era of transnational violence and imperial interventions, movements struggling against status hierarchies increasingly look beyond the territorial state. Under the umbrella slogan 'women's rights are human rights', for example, feminists throughout the world are linking struggles against local patriarchal practices to campaigns to reform international law (Ackerly 2000; Basru 1995). Meanwhile, religious and ethnic minorities, who face discrimination in territorial states, are reconstituting themselves as diasporas and building transnational publics from which to mobilize international opinion (Brah 1997: 178–210; Fouron and Schiller 2001; Soysal 1995). Finally, transnational coalitions of human rights activists are seeking to build new cosmopolitan institutions, such as the International Criminal Court, which can punish state violations of human dignity (Clapham 2003; Cullen and Morrow 2001; Lauren 2003; Panganiban 1997).

In such cases, disputes about recognition are also upending the Keynesian–Westphalian frame. No longer addressed exclusively to national states or debated exclusively by national publics, claims for recognition no longer focus solely on relations among fellow citizens. Here, accordingly, the grammar of argument has altered. Now, the issue is not only *what* constitutes equal respect but also *who* belongs to the universe of those entitled to claim it.

In general, then, globalization is changing the way we argue about justice. Whether the issue is distribution or recognition, the overall effect is the same: disputes that used to focus exclusively on the question of *what* is owed as a matter of justice to community members now turn quickly into disputes about *who* should count as a member and *which* is the relevant community. Not just 'the what' but also 'the who' is up for grabs.

Today, in other words, arguments about justice assume a double guise. On the one hand, they concern first-order questions of substance, just as before: how much inequality is permissible, how much redistribution is required, and according to which principle of distributive justice? Which kinds of differences merit public recognition, and by which means? But, above and beyond such first-order questions, arguments about justice today also concern second-order, meta-level questions: what is the proper frame within which to consider first-order questions of justice? Who are the relevant subjects entitled to a just distribution or reciprocal recognition in the given case? Thus, it is not only the substance of justice, but also the frame, which is in dispute.

The effect is to infuse disputes about justice with a new, vertiginous quality. With both the 'what' and the 'who' up for grabs, there appears to be no firm ground on which to stand. In the absence of any secure footing, we must struggle like neophyte jugglers to keep two balls in the air at once.

The result is a major challenge to our thinking about social justice. How shall we frame questions of justice today, when the forces that determine one's chances to live a good life routinely overflow the territorial borders of modern states? How, for example, shall we frame issues of distributive justice, when the idea of a national economy is increasingly notional? How, likewise, shall we frame questions of recognition, when cultural and political flows regularly transgress national boundaries, fracturing older status hierarchies and creating new ones? What, in sum, is the pertinent frame for determining the requirements of justice in a globalizing world?

In this chapter, I propose to investigate the problem of the frame. To illuminate the parameters of this problem, I shall examine some leading efforts to establish the appropriate frame for thinking about social justice in a globalizing world, and I shall assess the strengths and weaknesses of each. The result, to anticipate the argument, will be to bring to light a new question, over and above 'the what' and 'the who'. Thus, I shall suggest that in seriously considering those questions one is led ineluctably to a third order, *meta*-meta level question, which I shall call the question of 'the how'. Here the issue is in essence procedural: *how*, in a given case, should one determine the pertinent frame for reflecting on justice? By which criteria or decision procedure should one decide? And who is the 'one' who should determine the relevant frame?

Two Dogmas of Egalitarianism: from the 'What' to the 'Who' to the 'How'

Let me begin by shifting the scene from public-sphere politics to political philosophy. Here, in the discourses of the academy, the grammar of arguments about justice is undergoing a parallel shift. Increasingly aware of transnational processes, political philosophers are also beginning to call into question the Keynesian–Westphalian frame, which they had also tacitly assumed in the preceding decades. As a result of this major new opening of philosophical discussion, they are overcoming the first of what I shall call, with apologies to W. V. O. Quine, 'two dogmas of egalitarianism' (Quine 1953). Let me explain.

Until recently, political philosophers were chiefly engrossed in debating their own specialized version of the question of the 'what', which Amartya Sen (1987) called 'equality of what?' In the analytical tradition, theorists of distributive justice argued mostly about *what* should be fairly distributed, disputing the relative merits of rights, resources, primary goods, opportunities, real freedoms and capabilities as alternative metrics for evaluating the justice of social relations (for overviews, see Anderson 1999; Cohen 1989). Analogously, in the Hegelian tradition, theorists of recognition argued about *what* should be reciprocally recognized: group identity, individual achievement, or autonomous personhood; cultural distinctiveness, common humanity, or the claimant's standing as a partner in social interaction (Taylor 1994; Fraser and Honneth 2003). Focused intently on 'equality of what', philosophers in both traditions tended to overlook a second key question, which Deborah Satz has called 'equality among whom?' (Satz 1999; Young 2001). Unwittingly replicating the grammar of public-sphere argument, they, too, simply assumed without critical reflection the Keynesian–Westphalian frame. Failing to justify that premise against possible alternatives, they succumbed to what I am calling the 'first dogma of egalitarianism': the unexamined presupposition of the national 'who' (for early and important exceptions, see Beitz 1999 [1979]; Shue 1980).

Today, in contrast, philosophers openly argue about 'equality-among-whom', even as they continue to debate 'equality-of-what'. Increasingly, the field is divided between cosmopolitans, internationalists and liberal nationalists. For those in the first camp, there are no morally compelling reasons to privilege concern for one's fellow nationals over others; thus, justice necessarily concerns relations among all human beings (Nussbaum 2002; Singer 2002). For those in the second camp, in contrast, the special character of bounded political communities justifies two distinct sets of justice requirements: one more demanding set holds within such communities, while another, less demanding set holds among them (Calhoun 2002; Tan, 2004; Hurley 1999; O'Neill 2000). For those in the third camp, finally, the requirements of justice apply only within communities possessing such morally relevant features as a common political constitution, a shared ethical horizon, or a historical self-identification as 'a community of fate'; in the absence of special features, binding obligations of justice do not apply (Miller 1995, 1998; Walzer, 1984).

That such disagreements are now explicit represents the overcoming of the first dogma of egalitarianism: the tacit presupposition of the national 'who' in the absence of considered debate. To be sure, many theorists of justice still subscribe to the Keynesian–Westphalian frame, but now they must argue for it openly, against the alternatives. Overtly disputing the relative merits of alternative frames, political philosophers have finally awakened from their dogmatic slumbers concerning the 'who'.

Before we celebrate the lifting of repression, however, we should look more closely at these debates. Upon inspection, we shall see that while many philosophers have succeeded in overcoming this first dogma of egalitarianism, most still succumb to a second.

Consider current debates about the 'who' among analytical theorists of distributive justice. Centred largely on John Rawls's book, *The Law of Peoples*, and on his earlier Amnesty Lecture of the same name, these debates pit egalitarian liberal nationalists against proponents of global and international distributive justice (Rawls 2001, 1994). On one side stands Rawls himself, who denied that norms of egalitarian distributive justice have any applicability at the global or international level. Drawing a sharp Westphalian distinction between the domestic and international spheres, he made the domestic sphere the sole and exclusive province of distributive justice, while conceiving international justice in a way that provided no basis for egalitarian economic claims.[4]

On the other side, opposite Rawls, stand two other groups of philosophers, both of whom reject the Keynesian–Westphalian 'who', in favour of larger, post-Westphalian alternatives. For the first group, which defends a cosmopolitan 'who', egalitarian distributive norms apply globally, among individuals, irrespective of nationality or citizenship; thus, impoverished individuals in, say, the Sudan, have moral standing qua persons to make transborder claims for economic justice upon their fellow inhabitants of the globe (Jones 1999; Nussbaum 2004). For the second group, which defends an internationalist 'who', egalitarian distributive norms apply internationally, among territorially bounded collectivities. Here, impoverished 'peoples', such as the Sudanese, have moral standing as corporate bodies to make transborder claims for economic justice upon other, more prosperous 'peoples', such as the Dutch and the Americans (Hinsch 2001; Hurrell 2001). For the cosmopolitans, accordingly, the 'who' of distributive justice is the global set of individual persons; for the internationalists, in contrast, the 'who' is the set of corporate political communities that possess territorial states.

The result is a three-way debate over the 'who' among liberal-nationalists, egalitarian-internationalists and cosmopolitans. Highly sophisticated and complex, this debate involves a major disagreement about the relation between justice and toleration in a liberal society (Beitz 2000; Jones 2004; Metz 2004; Miller 2004; Voice 2004). Here, however, I leave aside that issue in order to focus on something else: namely, *how* exactly the participants go about determining the appropriate frame for distributive justice. Looking as it were beneath their respective views of the 'who', I propose to examine their underlying

---

4 On the one hand, Rawls excluded social and economic rights from the class of 'urgent' human rights that international society was obliged to protect; thus, he denied impoverished individuals in the 'Third World' the standing to make claims for distributive justice across state borders. On the other hand, Rawls also limited the economic obligations of prosperous, 'well-ordered peoples' towards impoverished 'peoples' in 'burdened societies' to a non-egalitarian 'duty of assistance'; thus, he denied the latter societies, qua corporate political communities, any basis for making transborder egalitarian claims as a matter of justice. The result was a double exclusion: both qua individuals and qua corporate political communities and the global poor were excluded by territorial borders from any 'who' of distributive justice that included the rich.

assumptions about the 'how'. The issue here is one of procedure: how do the various disputants envision the process of deciding between the Keynesian–Westphalian 'who', on the one hand, and the global or internationalist 'who', on the other? By reference to which criteria or decision procedure does each choose? And whom exactly, as a consequence, does each philosopher effectively authorize to determine the frame?

Following Rawls, most participants in this debate justify their choice of a frame by invoking the device of the 'original position'. Although they differ in terms of how best to model and apply that device, they agree that principles of international justice are to be chosen by 'parties' who are ignorant of some particular features of their own situation, but who possess a general background knowledge of society and history.[5] They assume, specifically, that the parties choose in the light of an empirical social-scientific understanding of the nature and extent of the social structures that determine the relative life chances of different individuals, an understanding that is supposed to be uncontroversial. Yet these philosophers disagree sharply as to the substantive content of the parties' knowledge. For the liberal-nationalists, the parties are assumed to 'know' that a person's life prospects depend overwhelmingly on the domestic institutional framework of her own society (Rawls 2001: 29–30). For the cosmopolitans, in contrast, the parties 'know' that the principal determinant of individual well-being is the basic structure of the global economy (Brown 1998; Caney 2002: esp. 114–88; Kuper 2000: esp. 645–48; Wenar 2001). For the egalitarian-internationalists, finally, the parties 'know' that one's life prospects are co-determined by institutional arrangements at both the domestic and international levels (Beitz 2000; Pogge 2000: esp. 197–99).

These differences in the parties' social-scientific background knowledge have an important bearing on their choice of principles of international justice. When, with Rawls (2001: 111–20), they assume high levels of national self-sufficiency, the parties adopt a 'law of peoples' that includes no provision for transnational distributive justice. When, with the internationalists, they assume that both national and international structures co-determine individuals' life chances, the

---

5 Among the key differences are these: the cosmopolitans endorse a single, global, original position, in which the parties represent individuals whose primary concern is the equal autonomy of individuals; the liberal-nationalists endorse a two-step procedure, in which principles of international justice are selected in a second run of the original position, by parties representing previously constituted 'well-ordered peoples', whose primary concern is the justice of their own domestic societies; and the egalitarian-internationalists endorse a procedure that combines elements of both those designs. For the purposes of the present enquiry, however, these disagreements are less important than another one, which concerns what exactly the parties are held to know about the nature and workings of contemporary society.

parties adopt an alternative 'law of peoples' that authorizes redistribution across borders for the maximum benefit of the worst-off societies (Beitz 2000; Pogge 2000). When, with the cosmopolitans, the parties assume the primacy of global structures, they choose a global difference principle, mandating the restructuring of the global economy for the maximum benefit of the worst-off individuals in the world (Brown 1998; Caney 2002; Kuper 2000; Wenar 2001).

In this debate, therefore, the choice of the 'who' comes down, in large measure, to how each philosopher answers the following questions: does there exist a global economy with sufficient influence over the relative life chances of individuals to count as a global 'basic structure'? Or are the relative life chances of different people determined exclusively or primarily by the constitutional structures of their respective domestic societies? Or, finally, are life chances co-determined by domestic and international structures?[6]

In general, then, the choice of the 'who' comes down in the end to a question of causal primacy: what precisely is the primary factor that determines people's life chances in the current conjuncture? Yet this question is never adequately conceptualized in this debate. Far from engaging it directly, the disputants only broach it obliquely, as each philosopher presents what is actually a controversial view as if it were settled fact. Rawls, for example, justifies his choice of the Keynesian–Westphalian 'who' in part by appealing to a putative social-scientific

---

6   In the first case, the empirical postulate of a global basic structure is held to justify the choice of the global cosmopolitan frame. In the second case, the contrary empirical postulate of a world composed of highly self-sufficient societies, each autonomously regulated by its own domestic basic structure, is held to justify the choice of the Keynesian–Westphalian frame. In the third case, finally, the empirical postulate of a two-tiered basic structure, comprising domestic and international elements, is held to justify the choice of a split-level frame with two different tiers of distributive obligations. What decides the 'who', in other words, is the relative causal weight of social structures at the national, international and global levels. It is each philosopher's understanding of that issue that determines his or her view of the concept that all consider the proper focus for reflection on distributive justice: 'the basic structure'. For the internationalists and cosmopolitans, the centrality of the causal issue is explicit; associating the basic structure with an objective system of interdependence, they maintain that all that is needed to secure a post-Westphalian 'who' is to demonstrate the trans-territorial causal efficacy of the world economy. What may be less evident, however, is that the causal question is also decisive for the liberal nationalists. Granted, they equate the basic structure with the 'constitutional essentials' of a politically organized 'scheme of co-operation', a view that is not ostensibly causal; and granted, too, they draw the ostensibly non-causal inference that, in the absence of a global or international polity, there exists no basis for a post-Westphalian 'who'. But when pushed to explain *why* the political community should constitute the unit of distributive justice, the liberal nationalists invoke a causal rationale. For them, that structure is 'basic' because it, more than anything else, determines individuals' chances to live good lives. This causal postulate is as central for Rawls, who privileges the constitutional essentials of a bounded political community, as it is for his critics, who ascribe greater efficacy to the objective system mechanisms of global capitalism (see Benhabib 2004, to whom I am also grateful for raising this issue with me).

fact: that the principal cause of 'Third World' poverty lies not in international political economy but in the deficient internal constitution of 'burdened societies' (Rawls 2001: 105–13). In the same way, his critics justify their choice of a post-Westphalian 'who' by insisting on a contrary social-scientific fact: that global and/or international structures play a substantial role in causing and reproducing such poverty, as well as in deforming the internal political constitution of 'Third World' societies (Beitz 2000; Buchanan 2000; Caney 2002; Kuper 2000). In each case, the controversial character of the postulated 'fact' is disavowed, as is the latter's dependence on tacit social-theoretical assumptions and historical interpretations, which are themselves controversial. The effect is to posit an offstage 'elsewhere', in which social scientists have supposedly already settled such difficult questions.[7]

In this debate, therefore, all sides determine the 'who' in a similar way. All assume that the frame of distributive justice should match the reach of whatever structure proves to be 'basic' in the sense of wielding causal primacy over people's life chances. And all assume that the identity of that structure is an uncontroversial matter of empirical fact. As a result, all the philosophers in this debate effectively authorize the social scientist to determine the frame.

Here, accordingly, lies the second dogma of egalitarianism: the tacit, unargued assumption that normal social science can determine the 'who' of justice. In the next part of this chapter, I shall consider the relative merits of this assumption vis-à-vis an alternative. Here, in contrast, I wish only to draw attention to the unreflective way in which a particular view about the relation between normative theory and social science enters current debates. In so far as philosophers simply assume this view, they fail to subject the procedural question to critical reflection. They fail to ask, in a methodologically self-reflective way: *how* should one determine the pertinent frame for reflecting on social justice in a globalizing world? What criterion or decision procedure should one invoke? And who in the end is the 'one' who should decide?

In general, political philosophers have so far failed to reflect systematically on such questions. This is the case for the analytic theorists of distributive justice I have considered here. But it is equally true of their Hegelian counterparts, whose theories of recognition also tend to glide over the question of the 'how', even as they are now beginning in earnest to question the 'who'.[8] This situation

---

7 An exception is Thomas Pogge (2001; 2002: Chapter 5), who has developed a sophisticated conceptual argument against 'explanatory nationalism'.

8 Usually, philosophers in this tradition tacitly assume a hermeneutical approach to the 'how'. Thus, Charles Taylor (1994) assumes that the proper way to determine the 'who' is by explicating the collective self-understandings of the peoples in question; but he neglects to weigh the merits of this assumption against the alternatives. Another, more promising tack is that of Rainer Forst,

may strike some as ironic: at the very moment when they are overcoming the first dogma of egalitarianism, philosophers in both traditions are succumbing to the second.

The effect is to leave those of us who argue about justice today in an awkward position. On the one hand, having left behind our dogmatic attachment to the Keynesian–Westphalian frame, we now have access to a range of possible answers to the question of the 'who'. On the other hand, in the absence of considered reflection on the 'how', we lack a defensible procedure for deciding among them. Thus, we still await a convincing answer to the burning question of our day: what is the pertinent frame within which to reflect on the requirements of justice in a globalizing world?

Beyond the Second Dogma of Egalitarianism: from the Normal-Social-Scientific to the Critical-Democratic 'How'

If we are ever to arrive at a satisfactory answer to that question, we need to overcome the second dogma of egalitarianism by beginning a new round of reflective discussion about the 'how'. I want now to sketch some parameters for such a discussion. I shall begin by canvassing some strengths and weaknesses of the approach just discussed, which I shall henceforth call 'the normal-social-science approach' (cf. Kuhn 1970). Then, I shall sketch an alternative, 'critical-democratic', approach to the 'how'.

The normal-social-science approach finds at least initial support in three interrelated ideas. First, it appreciates the importance of situating arguments about justice in relation to the social circumstances in which they arise and the need to frame them in terms appropriate to those circumstances. Second, the versions of this approach that I have considered here posit a plausible conceptual link between one such circumstance, namely, the reach of the basic structure, and the 'who' of distributive justice: that is, they posit that what turns a collection of people into fellow subjects of distributive justice is their co-imbrication in a common framework, which sets the terms of their social interaction, distributing benefits and burdens among them and shaping their respective life chances. Third, what underlies that idea, and lends this approach further plausibility, is a version of the 'all-affected' principle, which holds that all those affected by a

---

which also derives from recognition-theoretical premises. In *Contexts of Justice*, Forst (2002, esp. pp. 230–41) usefully distinguishes between four different contexts of justice, which correspond to four different types of justification, and, in effect, to four different normative 'whos': moral, legal, political and ethical. But he neglects to tell us how we are to resolve disputes as to which of these contexts applies when. Here also, therefore, is a sophisticated account, which insightfully differentiates among various 'whos', but fails to grapple seriously with the 'how'.

given social structure have moral standing as subjects of justice in relation to it.

Together, these three ideas constitute a powerful conceptual constellation. They suggest that current disputes over the 'who' can only be satisfactorily resolved in the light of a well-founded understanding of our social and historical circumstances, which comprehends the forces that shape people's lives in a globalizing world. Stated thus, in the most general terms, this suggestion appears unimpeachable. Any acceptable approach to the question of the 'how' must incorporate defensible interpretations of the circumstances of justice, the major causal forces, and the all-affected principle – while also theorizing the relations among them.

Everything depends, however, on how precisely one conceptualizes those ideas. Those who rely on the normal-social-science approach construe them as settled matters of empirical fact, which do not depend on controversial assumptions. On their view, which is reminiscent of positivism, there is no need for those of us who argue about justice to embroil ourselves in social-theoretical disputes. Far from having to worry about the relation between fact and value, causal explanation and historical interpretation, we need only consult the established fruits of normal science.

In fact, however, none of the key concepts at issue can be elaborated in this way. Far from being reducible to settled matters of empirical fact, proposed accounts of the circumstances of justice are inherently theory-laden and value-laden, which is why they are controversial. We need only recall current disputes about the extent and reality of globalization to see that efforts to specify those circumstances rest on normatively suffused interpretations and political judgments (Hirst and Thompson 1996; Held et al. 1999). The task of adjudicating rival characterizations cannot, accordingly, be entrusted to a positivistically conceived social science. It must, rather, be handled dialogically, in a multifaceted practical discourse that canvasses alternative conceptions, unpacks their underlying assumptions and weighs their relative merits – all in full awareness of the internal relations between social knowledge and normative reflection. The upshot is that we cannot settle arguments about the 'who' by appealing to the 'circumstances of justice', as if that were simply a matter of uncontroversial, empirical fact. On the contrary, disagreements about what precisely should count as the relevant circumstances, and how exactly those circumstances should be characterized, should be opened up and made explicit, treated as part and parcel of broader political arguments about the 'who' of social justice in a globalizing world.

The same is true for the concept of the 'basic structure'. That idea was originally developed by Rawls in his book, *Theory of Justice*, for a 'closed society', which one entered only by birth and exited only by death (Rawls 1999). Having excluded all transborder movements, Rawls posited a self-sufficient society, whose members' life chances depended exclusively on their own internal institutional arrangements. Given those idealized assumptions, it made sense, perhaps, to imagine that those arrangements constituted a single structure with a uniform reach that determined the life chances of an identifiable bounded population – and of no one else. But, in the absence of such counterfactual assumptions, the idea of a single basic structure with a uniform reach is hard to sustain. As soon as we introduce transborder interactions, we admit the possibility of multiple non-isomorphic structures, some local, some national, some regional and some global, which mark out a variety of different 'whos' for different issues. In the same breath, we admit the likelihood that people's life chances are over-determined by multiple structures that partially overlap each other, but differ in reach. How precisely such structures interact is by no means well understood by social scientists, whose accounts are mutually contradictory and controversial. Under these conditions, attempts to determine the 'who' by appealing to bare social-scientific fact are highly implausible. To consider seriously what sense to make today of structural causation is to enter contested terrain, where rival social theories and historical interpretations must be assessed. Debates about these matters also need to be opened up and rendered explicit. No longer treated as external to the theory of justice, they should be brought into direct communication with normative reflection within broader arguments about the 'who'.

Analogous complexities surround the all-affected principle. It is intuitively plausible, to be sure, to hold that all those affected by a given structure should have moral standing as subjects of justice in relation to it. But it doesn't follow that we can operationalize that principle by appealing to uncontroversial social-scientific fact. The problem is that, given the so-called butterfly effect, one can adduce empirical evidence that just about everyone is affected by just about everything. What is needed, therefore, is a way of distinguishing those levels and kinds of effectivity that are deemed sufficient to confer moral standing from those that are not. Normal social science, however, cannot supply such criteria. On the contrary, to operationalize the all-affected principle requires complex political judgments, which combine empirically informed normative reflection with historical interpretation and social theorizing. Inherently dialogical, such judgment involves weighing the relative merits of alternative interpretations of the all-affected principle, which generate alternative accounts of the 'who'.

In general, then, the normal-social-science approach to the 'how' positivistically misconstrues its central concepts. As a result, this approach fails to recognize the performative dimension of framing decisions. Its adherents suppose that they can justify the choice of a 'who' by referring to states of affairs in the world concerning who is affected by what, which they take to be independent of framing decisions. In many cases, however, there is no fact of the matter about who is affected by a given structure that is independent of the decision to constitute that structure in a given way, with a given reach. In such cases, where structures have been designed expressly to mark out specific 'whos', they themselves create 'facts on the ground'. Thus, the 'empirical fact' of who is affected, far from being independent, is a performative artefact of prior design. To appeal to normal social science to determine the 'who' in such cases is not to introduce independent epistemic considerations. It is rather uncritically to ratify a previous framing decision.

Then, too, this approach misconstrues the subjects of justice. Those who would determine the 'who' by appealing to normal science tend to treat the subjects of justice as if they were objects. Focused on discovering the facts as to who is affected by what, they construe human beings primarily as passive objects under the sway of structural forces. Granted, their ultimate aim is to enhance the private autonomy of individual persons, their equal freedom to devise and pursue their own life plans. But the effect is to neglect the importance of public autonomy, the freedom of associated social actors to participate with each other in framing the norms that bind them. In so far as this approach confers the authority to determine the frame on social-scientific experts, it denies the public autonomy of those whom it subjects to those experts' determinations. Thus, it deprives decisions concerning the frame of democratic legitimacy.

Taken together, these shortcomings of the normal social-scientific approach suggest the need to rethink the question of 'how' we should determine the 'who' in a globalizing world. A viable approach requires new conceptualizations of the circumstances of justice, structural causation and the all-affected principle. The task is to reconstruct each of those concepts in the light of a post-positivist understanding of social knowledge.

The starting point must be a frank acknowledgment that we currently lack a settled, uncontroversial account of these crucial concepts. This meta-premise differs in kind from the sort of first-order premises assumed by the philosophers discussed in the previous section of this chapter. Whereas they began by assuming the settled truth of one or another substantive claim about causal primacy, I propose to begin by assuming the contested character of all such claims. [9] The effect is to suggest another, more complex, view of the process by which disputes about the 'who' should be resolved.

On this view, which I shall call the 'critical-democratic' approach to the 'how',

---

9 I am grateful to David Peritz for enlightening discussions of this issue and for letting me benefit from reading his unpublished manuscripts (see Peritz n.d.).

arguments over the 'who' have a double character, simultaneously epistemic and political. In their epistemic aspect, these arguments deploy knowledge claims about the nature of vulnerability and the extent of interdependence in a globalizing world, which cannot, however, be vindicated by normal science. To adjudicate them, rather, requires a wide-ranging, open-ended mode of reasoning, in which the argument shifts back and forth among different levels and kinds of questions, some evidentiary, some interpretative, some normative, some historical and some conceptual. At each level, the disputants offer reasons and counter-reasons, although they lack any settled consensus about what counts as a good reason. Often, accordingly, their arguments become reflexive, scrutinizing previously taken-for-granted aspects of their own processes. In this approach, therefore, arguments over the frame exhibit the sort of dialogic, communicative rationality that goes with a post-positivist understanding of social knowledge. Far from appealing to normal science, then, the critical-democratic approach to the 'how' incorporates modes of reasoning that are associated with Critical Theory.

But the epistemic dimension does not exhaust the nature of disputes over the 'who'. On the critical-democratic view, rather, these disputes also have a political dimension. Fraught with controversy on multiple levels, the arguments implicate the evaluative and interpretative commitments of the disputants. Far from concealing this political aspect by appealing to normal science, this approach proposes to bring it into the open, encouraging interlocutors to disclose publicly, and frankly contest, the interests and value commitments suffusing their claims. At present, however, the disputants do not participate on terms of parity in arguments about the frame. Situated in unequally favourable social locations, they find their contests shot through with disparities of power. These, too, should be rendered explicit. Drawing once more on the reflexive capacity of communicative reason, the critical-democratic approach encourages participants to problematize the power disparities that taint their disputes. The aim, in other words, is to make a virtue of necessity. Recognizing their irreducible political aspect, this approach seeks in so far as is possible to democratize arguments over the 'who'.[10]

In general, then, the critical-democratic approach to the 'how' combines two fundamental ideas: on the one hand, a critical-theoretical conception of the relation between social knowledge and normative reflection; on the other, a democratic political interest in fair public contestation. Thanks to this combination of epistemic and political commitments, this approach should be

10 I am grateful to Bert van den Brink for very helpful discussions of this issue.

able to remedy the deficits of the normal-scientific approach – without throwing out the baby with the bathwater. Important notions, such as 'the circumstances of justice', 'structural determination', and the 'all-affected', principle, are not discarded but rather dialogized, opened up to critical reflection through democratic debate. Far from excluding social knowledge of our globalizing world, the effect is to reclaim it from the experts and to resituate it within a wide-ranging democratic debate about the 'who'. Acknowledging the irreducibly performative dimension of every determination of the frame, this approach construes the subjects of justice not only as causal objects but also as social and political actors. Appreciating the importance of public autonomy, it aims to foster procedures for deciding the 'who' of justice that can claim democratic legitimacy.

Democratizing Disputes Over the 'Who': Institutional and Conceptual Issues

In several respects, then, the critical-democratic approach to the 'how' improves on the normal-social-science alternative. But its full implications still need to be worked out. Institutionally, this approach points to the need to create new transnational arenas for democratically mooting, and resolving, arguments about 'the who'. Such arenas would be discursive spaces for hearing the claims of those who contend that existing territorially based frames unjustly exclude them. The point, however, is not to replace the Keynesian–Westphalian frame with a single, all-encompassing global frame. In so far as globalization involves the interpenetration of multiple structures of injustice, the point is rather to generate, through democratic debate of the claims of the excluded, a more adequate, intersubjectively defensible understanding of who is entitled to consideration in a given case. The probable result would be a set of multiple, functionally defined frames, corresponding to the multiple, functionally defined 'whos' that emerge through such debates and are judged entitled to consideration with respect to various issues. Nevertheless, the critical-democratic approach to the 'how' does not envision the abolition of territorially defined frames, nor their wholesale replacement by functionally defined alternatives. It is likely, rather, that territorially defined frames and 'whos' will remain important for many purposes, and that they will continue to exist alongside functionally defined frames and 'whos'.

The key point, in any case, is this: whatever configuration of frames emerges as provisionally justified must itself be open to future revision, as new claims of exclusion emerge to challenge that configuration. Assuming that disputes over the frame will not be susceptible to any definitive, final resolution, the critical-democratic approach to the 'how' views them as an enduring feature of political life in a globalizing world. Thus, it proposes new, permanent institutions for staging and provisionally resolving such disputes democratically.

Certainly, there remain many difficult, unanswered questions about how to institutionalize this approach. One issue is how to ensure adequate representation and equal voice for those who claim standing vis-à-vis a given issue but who are excluded by existing, territorially based frames. Another issue is how to envision an appropriate division of labour between weak publics, which merely debate alternative frames, and strong publics, which provisionally resolve such debates by taking binding decisions (Fraser 1991; see also Habermas 1996: 207ff.). Yet another issue concerns the possible role of impartial, third-party judges or arbitrators in hearing and resolving disputes about the frame (Archibugi 2003). A further issue is how to deal with knee-jerk, ideological nationalism, which refuses to enter into good-faith dialogue with those who plead for a post-Westphalian 'who'. To handle these and related issues requires institutional imagination in the spirit of realistic utopianism.

In addition, the critical-democratic approach faces at least three strong conceptual challenges. One such challenge is the spectre of an infinite regress, given that this approach introduces a new, meta-meta-level question: *who* should participate in the democratic process of determining the frame? In so far as the critical-democratic approach requires a second-order democratic 'who' or meta-*Demos*, it seems to court a version of 'the democratic paradox', which holds that boundaries and frames cannot be determined democratically, as the *Demos* cannot determine the *Demos* (Whelan 1983; see also Connolly 2002; Mouffe 1996). Although it is sometimes considered a knockdown argument, I do not find this objection convincing. Whatever force it may have had in the Keynesian–Westphalian era, when the need for a non-democratically determined (national) 'who' was widely accepted, seems to me to have dissipated today, when democratic expectations are higher, territorially bounded 'whos' are contested, and many are demanding a say in the reframing of questions of justice. Because disputes about the frame are unlikely to go away any time soon, we should treat them not only as a challenge but also as an opportunity – a spur to creative institutional thinking. Thus, instead of throwing up our hands in the face of a logical paradox, we should try to envision ways to finesse it, by imagining institutional arrangements for resolving such arguments democratically (see, e.g., Pogge 1997).

A second conceptual challenge to the critical-democratic approach to the 'how' arises from the circularity of the relations between justice and democracy. In so far as this approach seeks to resolve arguments about the frame democratically, it seems to presuppose as a prior background condition the very outcome it seeks to promote: namely, social arrangements that are sufficiently just to permit all to participate as peers in democratic discussion and decision-making. This objection rightly notes the internal conceptual links between democracy and justice, not to mention the real-world disparities in resources and status that taint existing deliberations that are claimed to be democratic. Nevertheless, the objection applies quite generally to all democratic processes, including those at the level of territorial states. Just as democrats do not cravenly bow down before this objection at that level, so should we not do so here. Rather, we should try to envision ways to transform what looks like a vicious circle into a virtuous spiral. The idea is to begin by establishing what could be called, with apologies to D. W. Winnicott, 'good-enough deliberation'.[11] Although such deliberation would fall considerably short of participatory parity, it would be good enough to legitimate some social reforms, however modest, which would, when institutionalized, ensure that the next round of deliberation would come closer to participatory parity, thereby improving its quality. This next round, accordingly, would be good enough to legitimate additional, slightly less modest reforms that would in turn improve the quality of the following round – and so on.[12] In the case of this challenge, then, as for one just discussed, the solution is to draw on democracy's reflexive capacity: its ability to problematize and revise aspects of its own procedures and frames that were previously taken for granted.

A third conceptual challenge concerns the distinction between the moral and the political. That distinction assumed a sharp guise within the Keynesian–Westphalian frame, which contrasted political obligations, owed to fellow citizens, with moral obligations, owed to human beings as such. The approach proposed here, in contrast, appears to collapse the distinction, and thus threatens to moralize politics, by suggesting that all questions of justice should become political in a globalizing world. Or so the argument goes. In fact, however, the objection is misplaced. Granted, the critical-democratic approach entails building new political institutions for handling trans-territorial problems

---

11 Thanks to Bert van den Brink for suggesting this expression.

12 Some political theorists appear to have in mind something like this idea of a virtuous spiral starting from 'good-enough deliberation'. One promising proposal, suggested by Rainer Forst (2002), is to institutionalize a 'basic justification procedure', within which arguments about global justice can be mooted, and which can itself be reconstructed on increasingly egalitarian and just terms, as a result of reforms that emerge from, and are validated through, such arguments. So far as I know, Forst has not (yet) envisioned the possibility of applying his idea of a basic justification procedure at the meta-level, to disputes about the frame, when not just the 'what' but also the 'who' is up for grabs; but I see no reason why this could not be done. A similar idea appears to inform Jürgen Habermas's proposal (1996) to institutionalize basic rights that point towards the fair value of political liberty, while also allowing that the content of those rights will be unfolded and enriched over time, as a result of ongoing (quasi-) democratic contestation.

of justice, which appeared to be 'merely' moral from the older perspective. But it does not entail that every question of justice becomes political in exactly the same way. A more likely outcome is that the sharp Westphalian contrast between the moral and the political will give way to a continuum encompassing 'thicker', territorially framed political questions at one end, and 'thinner', non-territorially framed political questions at the other. In that case, the result will not be to moralize politics, but rather to nuance it, disclosing a range of different forms of the political. From this perspective, moreover, the sharp distinction between the political and the moral is revealed to be an artefact of the Keynesian–Westphalian frame, which wrongly denied the possibility of transnational political institutions. But it does not on that account follow that that distinction can no longer be drawn. What does follow is that the distinction must henceforth be drawn in a different way. Treated as contestable and subject to revision, it, too, must be adjudicated dialogically. Thus, the question of where and when to distinguish the political from the moral now appears a political question, subject to democratic debate (Ferrara 2003).

In general, then, the critical-democratic approach to the 'how' need not in principle be stymied by conceptual objections. I would like to conclude, accordingly, by suggesting that it is well worth the effort to develop this approach in a form that can satisfactorily resolve the outstanding institutional and conceptual problems. Three considerations in particular are worth stressing.

First, by developing this approach we can make significant strides in overcoming the second dogma of egalitarianism. By articulating a plausible and attractive critical-democratic alternative, we can help dissolve the unjustified aura of self-evidence that currently insulates the normal-social-science approach to the 'how' from critical reflection.

Second, by developing this approach we can deepen the connections between justice and democracy. At present, our most robust egalitarian theories of post-Westphalian justice proceed largely in isolation from democratic theory, while our most ambitious theories of post-Westphalian democracy have yet to develop the strongly egalitarian conceptions of social justice that they require as a necessary complement. The critical-democratic approach to the 'how' promises to connect these two bodies of political-theoretical reflection, while opposing the current de facto alliance of egalitarianism with technocracy on the one hand, and that of democracy with nationalism on the other.

Finally, and most importantly, unless we develop a defensible critical-democratic approach to the 'how', we will never arrive at a defensible answer to the question of the 'who'. And that means we will still be in no position to answer the burning question of our day: how shall we frame questions of justice in a globalizing world?

Acknowledgments

First delivered as the 2004 Spinoza Lecture at the University of Amsterdam, this text was revised at the Wissenschaftskolleg zu Berlin in 2004–05. Thanks to both institutions for their support of this work, to James Bohman for bibliographical advice, to Kristin Gissberg and Keith Haysom for research assistance, and to Amy Allen, Seyla Benhabib, Bert van den Brink, Andrew Chitty, Alessandro Ferrara, Rainer Forst, Charlotte Girard, Gary Hazeldine, Ted Koditschek, Maria Pia Lara, David Peritz and (especially) Eli Zaretsky for helpful comments and stimulating discussion..

References

Ackerly, Brooke A., 2000, *Political Theory and Feminist Social Criticism*, Cambridge, Cambridge University Press.

Anderson, Elizabeth, 1999, 'What is the Point of Equality?', *Ethics*, 109, 287–337.

Archibugi, Daniele, 2003, 'A Critical Analysis of the Self-Determination of Peoples: A Cosmopolitan Perspective', *Constellations*, 10(4), 488–505.

Basch, Linda, Nina Glick Schiller and Christina Szanton Blanc, 1994, *Nations Unbound: Transnational Projects, Postcolonial Predicaments, and De-territorialized Nation-States*, New York, Gordon and Breach.

Basru, Avtar (ed.), 1995, *The Challenge of Local Feminisms: Women's Movements in Global Perspective*, Boulder, CO, Westview Press.

Beitz, Charles R., 1999 [1979], *Political Theory and International Relations*, 2nd edn, Princeton, NJ, Princeton University Press.

— 2000, 'Rawls's *Law of Peoples*', *Ethics*, 110(4), 670–78.

Benhabib, Seyla, 2004, '*The Law of Peoples*, Distributive Justice and Migrations', *Fordham Law Review*, 72(5), 1761–87.

Brah, Avtar, 1997, *Cartographies of Diaspora: Contesting Identities*, London, Routledge.

Brown, Chris, 1998, 'International Social Justice', in David Boucher and Paul Kelly (eds), *Social Justice: From Hume to Walzer*, London, Routledge, 102–19.

Buchanan, Allen, 2000, 'Rawls's *Law of Peoples*: Rules for a Vanished Westphalian World', *Ethics*, 110(4), 697–721.

Calhoun, Craig, 2002, 'The Class Consciousness of Frequent Travelers: Toward a Critique of Actually Existing Cosmopolitanism', *South Atlantic Quarterly*, 101(4), 869–98.

Caney, Simon, 2002, 'Cosmopolitanism and *The Law of Peoples*', *Journal of Political Philosophy*, 10(1), 95–123.

Castles, Stephen, and Alastair Davidson, 2000, *Citizenship and Migration: Globalization and Politics of Belonging*, London, Routledge.

Clapham, Andrew, 2003, 'Issues of Complexity, Complicity and Complementarity: From the Nuremberg Trials to the Dawn of the New International Criminal Court', in Phillipe Sands (ed.), *From Nuremberg to The Hague: The Future of International Criminal Justice*, Cambridge, Cambridge University Press, 233–81.

Cohen, G. A., 1989, 'On the Currency of Egalitarian Justice', *Ethics*, 99, 906–44.

Connolly, William, 2002, *Identity/Difference: Democratic Negotiations of Political Paradox*, Minneapolis, MN, University of Minnesota Press.

Cook, Rebecca J. (ed.), 1994, *Human Rights of Women: National and International Perspectives*, Philadelphia, PA, University of Pennsylvania Press.

Cullen, Holly, and Karen Morrow, 2001, 'International Civil Society in International Law: The Growth of NGO Participation', *Non-State Actors & International Law*, 1(1), 7–39.

Falk, Richard, 2002, 'Revisiting Westphalia, Discovering Post-Westphalia', *Journal of Ethics*, 6(4), 311–52.

Ferrara, Alessandro, 2003, 'Two Notions of Humanity and the Judgment Argument for Human Rights', *Political Theory*, 31, June 3, 392–420.

Forst, Rainer, 2002, *Contexts of Justice*, Berkeley, CA, University of California Press.

Fouron, Georges Eugene, and Nina Glick Schiller, 2001, *Georges Woke Up Laughing: Long-Distance Nationalism and the Search for Home*, Durham, NC, Duke University Press.

Fraser, Nancy, 1991, 'Rethinking the Public Sphere: A Contribution to the Critique of Actually Existing Democracy', in Craig Calhoun (ed.), *Habermas and the Public Sphere*, Cambridge, MA, MIT Press, 109–42.

Fraser, Nancy, and Axel Honneth, 2003, *Redistribution or Recognition? A Political-Philosophical Exchange*, trans. Joel Golb, James Ingram and Christiane Wilke, London, Verso.

Guidry, John A., Michael D. Kennedy and Mayer N. Zald (eds), 2001, *Globalization and Social Movements: Culture, Power and the Transnational Public Sphere*, Ann Arbor, MI, University of Michigan Press.

Habermas, Jürgen, 1996, *Between Facts and Norms: Contributions to a Discourse Theory of Law and Democracy*, trans. William Rehg, Cambridge MA, MIT Press.

Hathaway, Dale, 2000, *Allies Across the Border: Mexico's 'Authentic Labor Front' and Global Solidarity*, Cambridge, MA, South End Press.

Held, David, 2002, 'Cosmopolitanism: Ideas, Realities and Deficits', in David Held and Anthony McGrew (eds), *Governing Globalization: Power, Authority, and Global Governance*, Cambridge, Polity Press.

Held, David, Anthony G. McGrew, David Goldblatt and Jonathan Perraton, 1999, *Global Transformations: Politics, Economics and Culture*, Stanford, CA, Stanford University Press.

Hinsch, Wilfried, 2001, 'Global Distributive Justice', *Metaphilosophy*, 32(1/2), 58–78.

Hirst, Paul, and Graham Thompson, 1996, *Globalization in Question: The International Economy and the Possibilities of Governance*, Cambridge, Blackwell.

Hurley, Susan L., 1999, 'Rationality, Democracy and Leaky Boundaries: Vertical vs. Horizontal Modularity', *Journal of Political Philosophy*, 7(2), 126–46.

Hurrell, Andrew, 2001, 'Global Inequality and International Institutions', *Metaphilosophy*, 32(1/2), 34–57.

Jones, Charles, 1999, *Global Justice: Defending Cosmopolitanism*, Oxford, Oxford University Press.

— 2004, 'Global Liberalism: Political or Comprehensive?', *University of Toronto Law Journal*, 54(2), 227–48.

Kaldor, Mary, 1999, *New and Old Wars: Organized Violence in a Global Era*, Cambridge, Polity Press.

Keck, Margaret E., and Kathryn Sikkink, 1998, *Activists Beyond Borders: Advocacy Networks in International Politics*, Ithaca, NY, Cornell University Press.

Khagram, Sanjeev, James V. Riker and Kathryn Sikkink (eds), 2002, *Restructuring World Politics: Transnational Social Movements, Networks, and Norms*, Minneapolis, MN,

University of Minnesota Press.

Kuhn, Thomas, 1970, *The Structure of Scientific Revolutions*, Chicago, University of Chicago Press.

Kuper, Andrew, 2000, 'Rawlsian Global Justice: Beyond *The Law of Peoples* to a Cosmopolitan Law of Persons', *Political Theory*, 28(5), 640–74.

La Botz, Dan, 1995, *Democracy in Mexico: Peasant Rebellion and Political Reform*, Cambridge, MA, South End Press.

Lauren, Paul Gordon, 2003, *The Evolution of International Human Rights: Visions Seen*, Philadelphia, PA, University of Pennsylvania Press.

Metz, Thaddeus, 2004, 'Open Perfectionism and Global Justice', *Theoria: A Journal of Social & Political Theory*, 114, 96–125.

Miller, David, 1988, 'The Ethical Significance of Nationality', *Ethics*, 98, 647–62.

— 1998, 'The Limits of Cosmopolitan Justice', in D. Maple and T. Nardin (eds), *International Society: Diverse Ethical Perspectives*, Princeton, NJ, Princeton University Press.

— 1995, *On Nationality*, Oxford, Oxford University Press.

Miller, Richard W., 2004, 'Cosmopolitanism and its Limits', *Theoria: A Journal of Social & Political Theory*, 114, 38–43.

Moody, Kim, 1997, *Workers in a Lean World: Unions in the International Economy*, London, Verso Books.

Mouffe, Chantal, 1996, 'Democracy, Power and the "Political"', in Seyla Benhabib (ed.), *Democracy and Difference: Contesting the Boundaries of the Political*, Princeton, NJ, Princeton University Press, 245–56.

Munck, Ronaldo, and Peter Waterman, 1999, *Labour Worldwide in the Era of Globalization: Alternative Union Models in the New World Order*, New York, Palgrave Macmillan.

Nash, June, 2001, *Mayan Visions: The Quest for Autonomy in an Age of Globalization*, London, Routledge.

Niezen, Ronald, 2003, *The Origins of Indigenism: Human Rights and the Politics of Identity*, Berkeley, CA, University of California Press.

Nussbaum, Martha, 2002, *For Love of Country*, Boston, Beacon Press.

— 2004, 'Beyond the Social Contract: Capabilities and Global Justice', *Oxford Development Studies*, 32(1), 1–15.

O'Brien, Robert, Anne Marie Goetz, Jan Art Scholte and Marc Williams, 2000, *Contesting Globalization: Multilateral Economic Institutions and Global Social Movements*, Cambridge, Cambridge University Press.

O'Neill, Onora, 2000, *Bounds of Justice*, Cambridge, Cambridge University Press.

Ong, Aihwa, 1999, *Flexible Citizenship: The Cultural Logics of Transnationality*, Durham, NC, Duke University Press.

Panganiban, Rik, 1997, 'The NGO Coalition for an International Criminal Court', *UN Chronicle*, 34(4), 36–39.

Peritz, David, n.d., 'The Complexities of Complexity: Habermas and the Hazards of Relying Directly on Social Theory', unpublished manuscript (on file with the author).

— n.d. 'A Diversity of Diversities: Liberalism's Implicit Social Theories', unpublished manuscript (on file with the author).

Pogge, Thomas, 1997, 'How to Create Supra-National Institutions Democratically: Some Reflections on the European Union's Democratic Deficit', *Journal of Political*

Philosophy, 5, 163–82.

— 2000, 'An Egalitarian Law of Peoples', *Philosophy and Public Affairs*, 23(5), 195–224.

— 2001, 'The Influence of the Global Order on the Prospects for Genuine Democracy in the Developing Countries', *Ratio-Juris*, 14(3), 326–43.

— 2002, *World Poverty and Human Rights: Cosmopolitan Responsibilities and Reforms*, Cambridge, Polity Press.

Quine, Willard Van Orman, 1953, 'Two Dogmas of Empiricism', in W. V. O. Quine, *From a Logical Point of View: 9 Logico-Philosophical Essays*, Cambridge, MA, Harvard University Press, 20–46.

Rawls, John, 1994, 'The Law of Peoples', in Stephen Shute and Susan Hurley (eds), *On Human Rights: The Oxford Amnesty Lectures*, New York, Basic Books, 41–84.

— 1999, *A Theory of Justice*, Cambridge, MA, Harvard University Press.

— 2001, *The Law of Peoples*, Cambridge, MA, Harvard University Press.

Satz, Deborah, 1999, 'Equality of What among Whom? Thoughts on Cosmopolitanism, Statism and Nationalism', in Ian Shapiro and Lea Brilmayer (eds), *Global Justice*, New York, New York University Press, 67–85.

Sen, Amartya, 1987, 'Equality of What?', in Sterling M. McMurrin (ed.), *Liberty, Equality, And Law*, Salt Lake City, UT, University of Utah Press, 137–62.

Shue, Henry, 1980, *Basic Rights*, Princeton, NJ, Princeton University Press.

Singer, Peter, 2002, *One World: The Ethics of Globalization*, New Haven, CT, Yale University Press.

Soysal, Yasemin, 1995, *Limits of Citizenship: Migrants and Postnational Membership in Europe*, Chicago, University of Chicago Press.

Tan, Kok-Chor, 2004, *Justice without Borders: Cosmopolitanism, Nationalism, and Patriotism*, Cambridge, Cambridge University Press.

Taylor, Charles, 1994, *Multiculturalism: Examining the Politics of Recognition*, ed. Amy Gutmann, Princeton, NJ, Princeton University Press.

Voice, Paul, 2004, 'Global Justice and the Challenge of Radical Pluralism', *Theoria: A Journal of Social & Political Theory*, 114, 15–37.

Walzer, Michael, 1984, *Spheres of Justice: A Defense of Pluralism and Equality*, New York, Basic Books.

Wenar, Leif, 2001, 'Contractualism and Global Economic Justice', *Metaphilosophy*, 32(1/2), 79–94.

Whelan, Frederick, 1983, 'Democratic Theory and the Boundary Problem', in J. R. Pennock and R. W. Chapman (eds), *Nomos XXV: Liberal Democracy*, New York and London, New York University Press, 13–47.

Young, Iris Marion, 2001, 'Equality of Whom? Social Groups and Judgments of Injustice', *Journal of Political Philosophy*, 9(1), 1–18.

Zacher, Mark W., 1992, 'The Decaying Pillars of the Westphalian Temple', in James N. Rosenau and Ernst-Otto Czempiel (eds), *Governance without Government*, Cambridge, Cambridge University Press, 58–101.

CHAPTER 11

Contracting and Founding
in Times of Conflict

Charlotte Girard

The question of the emergence of a common world out of a diverse set of founding assumptions – and the question of what sort of world it can be – are crucial in the context of pronounced regional varieties of world-making conceptions. Assuming that world-making possibly means that a society must be framed, then this frame entails rules – i.e., rules can be the frame. This call for rules answers Nancy Fraser's call (in Chapter 10) for a frame. But the frame she suggests should be of a special kind. She argues that framing refers to transformative politics and thus should reconsider not only the persons who build justice – as beneficiaries or as providers – but also the constitutive process, the 'process of frame-setting'. I would argue that frame-setting can be done through rules. In that sense, frame-setting could consist in making rules to achieve the social constitutive objective: this world to be made.

This preliminary remark on the adequacy of a normative tool to fulfil the objective of world-making leads to the question of the types of rules needed to achieve it. Legal rules appear prima facie relevant to a concept of world-making. This is so under two conditions imposed on the way in which the words used here are understood. First, in the perspective suggested in this chapter, world-making is about *how* to make a world. Indeed the *how* question asks what it means to make a world. And this issue leads to the question of the power to make the intended world. Second, law is often defined as an order implying the exercise of power, that is to say, as a coercive order designed to bring about a certain social conduct. Therefore, rules of law are considered as a procedural instrument, among others,[1] to frame social conduct. Thus, the perspective of

---

1 Some procedural instruments are to be distinguished from judicial procedures, even though they

law makes world-making possible, in Europe and elsewhere, and world-making appears as a legal *problématique*.

In this respect, the legal *problématique* will be best formulated through the *how* question instead of the *what* question. The *what* question refers more adequately to a domain where *contents* of the above-mentioned social conduct are discussed and choices are eventually made. Generally speaking, law as a group of rules and as a procedural tool is not supposed to help in choosing which conduct should be adopted. It should act as the language by which an already chosen conduct is interpreted, ordered and controlled. It is then conceived as the tool through which a world is chosen, not as the choice itself. In such a legal perspective, a world in the making can be seen as the procedure or the means through which this world is chosen. Once the world is made, law corresponds to the means by which it is ruled.

The distinction between the *how* and the *what* questions highlights the constituting moment, that is, the period of time during which a world is framed. It shows the difficulty of distinguishing between the framing and the object that is framed. As applied to the concepts of world-making and law, since they both appear as processes, one can hardly make a difference between world-making as a progressive organization and the rules of organization. This progressive organization is helpfully exemplified by the European case. It is an operating construction and a current constituting moment. The European case stands as a particularly efficient illustration of the relevance of law in world-making. From the perspective of law, the European constitutional process shows how indispensable the legal tool is in the framing and formatting of a space in many of its dimensions.

Moreover, it reveals that conflict is a characteristic of such a world-making. It is not only because of French and Dutch referenda that European world-making should be considered a conflict. But conflict is present to the extent that

---

are affected or regulated by law. For example, procedure of public debate can be devised to satisfy requirements of fairness or any other requirements without being undertaken in a courtroom, under the authority of a member of the judiciary or in a tribunal, submitted to regulations relating to fair, public and unbiased requirements (mostly administrative). This precision is a reminder that procedure or processing, including rules aimed at protecting fairness of ensuing decisions, is not limited to trials or administrative legal procedures such as individual notices imposing expropriation, allocating funds or attributing marks in an exam. A common denominator of these procedures lies in the search for approval of the following decision. Whatever the procedure, judicial or not, the ensuing decision has to be accepted, otherwise the procedure would not be called adjudicative (*décisionnelle*). These considerations amount to a rough question of efficiency. Since a decision is best empowered with the consent of its addressee, it should be subject to the least contest possible. Similar considerations apply to the procedure followed during a trial: 'Justice must not only be done, it must be seen to be done', *R. v. Sussex Justices ex parte McCarthy, Heward CJ (1924)*. See Galey and Girard 2003: 53.

Europe's constituting process aims at enabling diverse world representations to meet. Matching different, if not opposing, visions of the world stands as the audacious European objective. One may consider such an attempt – as Edouard Glissant does – as a genuine act of foundation. Edouard Glissant, a West Indian poet, finds illuminating words to describe the issue of the act of founding on the basis of diverse origins: 'The Same requires Being, the Diverse establishes the Relationship'; and therefore: 'The Same is the sublimed difference; the Diverse is the consented difference' (Glissant 1981: 190–91). This aphoristic, poetic thought brings together the ideas that intervene to explain how European world-making could work: sameness, diversity, relationship, consent. It also articulates two modes that, despite their opposition, are useful together to reflect on world-making: the static and the dynamic. Glissant's thought strives to elaborate the concept of *Tout-monde* aimed at inoculating the idea of Diversity as constructive and likely to build a *lieu commun*, even when it results from chaos and abyssal hardship. This optimistic view strikes the balance in favour of Diversity as a positive and necessary value. It leads Glissant to elaborate on a concept of 'Chaos-monde', from which it could be a good idea to start: 'I call *Chaos-monde* the current clash of so many cultures which ignite, repel each other, disappear, and yet survive, fall asleep or transform, slowly or with lightning speed …' (1997: 22). This interpretation helps to understand the European process as a founding process stemming from the endeavour to set commonality. Indeed, the founding effect of the meeting of differences comes from the underlying requirement to find this *lieu commun*, which is assumed to be a desirable, possible and indispensable objective.

Commonality is a necessary condition to unify and delineate a space. For a space to be defined and thereby separated from other spaces, it must first be internally justified as expressing a commonality, irrespective of the diversity from which it originates. In other words, such a space must show that something within its boundaries is common. The concept of the common or 'commonality' is more adequate for our purposes than 'community', because it conveys the idea of something being common to people without a specific representation of a pre-existing group. Commonality can then be distinguished from community, which refers not only to something being in common between people but also to a group defined as circumscribed community. Commonality will not be envisaged here as a value per se, but as *a necessary yet always fictional condition to achieve world-making* in legal terms. Commonality appears as a process and as a founding potential.

The founding phase of world-making can be usefully described if one uses legal theory as a tool. The use of legal theory is appropriate because it explores that which eventually turns a statement into a legal rule, i.e., something that is obligatory by law (by contrast to something that is morally required). Regarding specifically the founding activity, legal theory will help to unveil the complex function of a word aimed at creating a legal space.

Founding is aimed at creating a new legal area, which is often assimilated into a state.[2] The equivalence, argued for in some legal-theoretical discourses, between a legal area – also known as a legal order – and a state helps to understand that to define a space in legal terms is to define a state. This observation must be related to the extraordinary phenomenon of European Community law, whereby EC law precedes the emerging – not yet constituted – European State. The founding process operated by EC rules can best be depicted with the help of discourse analysis and, more precisely, by speech act theory.[3] Although I cannot, for lack of space, develop a sophisticated analysis of the words of the European Union Treaty and Drafts, I nevertheless propose, for the present purposes, an overall view of this issue which resorts to such theoretical assumptions. Thus, first, it must be assumed that not only does a legal statement have a meaning but it also implies a force, i.e., an efficacy without which it would lose its legal specificity. Second, the legal efficacy of a norm works like the communication of any statement: it depends on its being 'received' by its addressee, no matter her/his understanding of it, according to the author's will.[4]

Coming back to Glissant's thought, it seems to suggest that the static-dynamic distinction helps to expose the meaning assigned to the action of founding. The static and dynamic viewpoints will be adopted in order to analyse the founding phenomenon as a world-making process applied to the European legal space, namely the European constitutional process. Finally, a critical viewpoint will conclude this reflection, with some suggestions on the interpretative approach involved in the concept of founding.

2   In H. Kelsen's *Théorie générale du droit et de l'Etat* (1997), the perfect equivalence between law and state is beyond doubt. This equivalence between law and state is a kind of *acquis* of normativist theory of law, which is now assumed by a majority of positivist legal theorists (see Troper 1994 and 2001).

3   Initiated by philosophers of language and analytical philosophers such as J. R. Searle (1969) and J. L. Austin (1962). Implementation of such a theory into the field of jurisprudence opens up new perspectives on legal theory and allows for a refined understanding of legal normativity (see Amselek 1986; and Cayla 1992).

4   A legal philosopher who was a contemporary of Austin, and broadly influenced by his views, added an element that reincorporates Austinian discoveries into the realm of modern political philosophy, from the legal theory viewpoint. Indeed, H. L. A. Hart reintroduced the idea of acceptance of the rule to make it complete as a legal rule, i.e., effective. The concept of the rule of recognition achieved this by stating that the validity of a legal rule was submitted to recognition by all the social agents, including, firstly, the addressee of the rule in question. Legal validity depends on practical application, meaning social agreement. This core idea will be developed (see Hart 1997).

Founding from a Static Viewpoint

From a static viewpoint, the relevant issue is whether something common is sufficient to stand as the common law of a social group. This issue can be translated into two broader questions: 1) Is law necessarily 'something common'? 2) Does common law really found?

As If Law Were Common

It appears prima facie that what becomes law actually pre-exists law and is 'something common' (conceptions, expectations, interests, etc.). The loose aspect of this 'something' is a key condition for its adaptability.

Becoming law, that is, the process of legalization – the process thanks to which legal normativity is reached – is central to a work of legal theory. If a link between 'something common' and legality is shown, then one may have grasped one criterion of legality: what is legal is that which is common. However, becoming law is a much more complex and less systematic process. On the one hand, not all common conceptions are law. For example, although it might be a common expectation that poverty be banished from our so-called advanced society, poverty is not proscribed by law. Poverty is given a legal status that does not amount to interdiction; quite to the contrary. On the other hand, not all legal rules correspond to effectively shared conceptions: this is due to the mere mechanism of majority which impedes, or renders merely probable rather than certain, such an equivalence. The wider reason for this complexity is that 'commonality' does not correspond to a concrete reality. Commonality cannot correspond to any reality because it is a concept, that is, a representation of the abstract idea of what is common.

Commonality as a Fiction

Commonality is a necessary fiction in the sense that it is a preliminary justification for any order imposed by law. It functions as a preamble likely to allow future norms to apply with the force of law: the fact that it is commonly shared is a reason given to render the order acceptable to the person subject to such an order. We read, for instance, in the first articles of the European Treaty:

> The [European] Union is founded on the principles of liberty, democracy, respect for human rights and fundamental freedoms, and the rule of law, *principles which are common to the Member States*. The Union shall respect fundamental rights, as guaranteed by the European Convention for the Protection of Human Rights and Fundamental Freedoms signed in Rome on 4 November 1950 and as they result from the *constitutional traditions common to the Member States*, as general principles of Community law ....[5]

5 Paragraphs 1 and 2 of Article 6 of the current Treaty on the European Union (emphasis added).

Such a presupposed commonality can be found in any other international convention, which amounts to an agreement on that which is common. Hence, what is legal is what is *assumed* to be common, which confirms the majority hypothesis. Indeed, in the majority system, all are bound by the general will, through a metonymic phenomenon. We act *as if* everyone had agreed on elements such as liberty, for example – an element that the Union shall respect – and on its obligatory quality: it should be preserved and implemented as 'a principle common to the Member States', although such an element is hardly defined. We act *as if* it were effectively common and shared.

In the quote above, the insistence on the flourishing notion of fundamental rights and principles and their equation with a dimension of commonality suggests that the complex operation of founding consists in a convention, that is, a social contract.[6] The paramount contractual dimension lies in the presupposition that fundamental rights are shown to embody a general social agreement on values that is nevertheless subject to approval through a conventional political process. The argument is tricky because it reflects the mainstream idea that the social contract, however fictitious, legitimates the legal rules that supposedly ensue: general will purportedly founds the whole legal order. This is the politico-legal side of the argument. The approval is political because it is the result of a choice eventually preceded by a debate. It is legal for the same reason but from a procedural viewpoint whereby the choice is organized through a procedure that is acknowledged by law and in fine recognized as legal because it was previously warned that the result of the choice would be legal. There is a moral aspect of the argument, too: according to the moral dimension, fundamental rights can act as foundation because of, and are justified by, their being vested in anyone by reason of her/his being human. This moral belief is presented as unquestionable and, as such, contradicts the will-based logic of the political-legal aspect of the argument. In legal-theoretical terms the two aspects are, respectively, positivist and natural law.[7]

Let us now turn to the dynamic aspect of this analysis, which in fact underlies the static part: convention refers to a procedure, the steps of which are legally organized.

---

6 A number of legal theorists have tried to explain the way the foundation of law is chosen. These theories amount to political theories of justice. We can see, from the twentieth century's American realists to socio-legal theorists, legal theory still being dominated by Dworkinian impact, styled in terms of moral philosophy and normative jurisprudence. For an account of the American realist movement, see Millard and Jouanjan 2000).

7 This distinction is detailed in almost every treatise of legal theory, especially those that claim to be positivist (see Bobbio 1998; and the enriched French edition of Kelsen's *Théorie générale du droit et de l'Etat*: Kelsen 1997).

Founding from a Dynamic Viewpoint

Legal experience shows that commonality is systematically questioned. This corresponds to the very situation that gives its meaning to any legal rule: conflict. Indeed, the situation of conflict is one through which a legal rule finds its raison d'être. It can best be defined as the meeting of differences. Such differences are embodied and acknowledged by the European Union Treaty itself: 'The Union shall respect the national identities of its Member States.'[8] Here, the idea of variety shows that conflict relates to differences in opinions, traditions, conceptions, expectations and interests, which legal instruments tend to have met[9] and eventually tend to abolish through a newly created commonality. In this sense, conflict has a founding virtue. It founds commonality.

Conflict as a Founding Condition

In a legal perspective, conflict points a priori to a situation that has negative connotations. It refers to a state of war – not only from a geopolitical point of view – which is usually what law endeavours to prevent (see Chapter 4 in this volume). Hence, it asks for the restoration of a non-conflictual situation. Such a situation of peace is, however, ideal. It is only virtual, since there will always be antagonism. The term 'restoration' implies that an ideal non-conflictual situation either exists already there, needing to be revealed, or, should a conflictual situation already exist, that it should be banned and systematically replaced by a non-conflictual situation. Restoring peace means that the current situation is war. This therapeutic social logic insists on a unifying, not a diversifying, trend. The objective consisting in 'de-conflictualizing' a situation can only be reached by unification from the viewpoint of the European drafters.

The artificial quest for commonality becomes quite clear in references to 'common principles' or 'common constitutional traditions' in texts that are supposed to institute a new group. And the newly born group appears to be linked to the space where it is currently living. This is a relationship of belonging that is legally organized. This community of persons may become a legal community through the constitution of a state, that is, a territory, a space. The spatial manifestation of a community of persons is a 'state' in terms of international public law. According to the principles in this field, a territory is one of the constitutive elements of a state, and a population and recognized government are the two others. This definition explicitly ties together space and

---

8 Paragraph 3 of Article 6 of the Treaty on the European Union.
9 Of course to presuppose a chronological precedence of difference/conflict is as arbitrary as to presuppose the common – something rarely acknowledged by conflict theories broadly understood. It is very different to say that the two coexist.

community of persons. It helps us to understand that in legal discourse, commonality expressed in terms of the existence of a population and public institutions is a criterion of the state. Such a commonality in public international law appears to be artificial, although it is an important element of the determination of a physical space: the state.

The trait of artificiality is striking in the European case because the European instituting text (the European Union Treaty) refers to something common as if commonality already existed. Yet, at the same time, it conveys a commonality to come: a 'Union of States' and peoples ruled by common institutions. Thus, here we are confronted with one of the particular characteristics of a founding legal text, which is marked by a contradictory presence:[10] a *present or past* non-conflictual situation that must be either preserved or retrieved (two distinct modes of restoration) and a *new* non-conflictual horizon about which parties deliberate and agree by legal means. This double presence marks the text and each situation represents an idealized vision of both what is and what ought to be. This last feature is in opposition to Hume's imperative that consists in rigidly separating 'is' and 'ought' as two differing modes of perception and understanding (Hume 2000), but in accordance with the Kantian structure of knowledge. Indeed, not only do contemporary founding texts draw an explicit link between 'is' and 'ought', but also the commentators themselves of these texts do so.[11] Founding texts are a sign of the widespread influence of the Kantian structure of knowledge, according to which the empirical world is inescapably inspired by a priori ideas. Some among these ideas, such as liberty or equality, which are not derived from empirical observation, are rational principles concerning communal life.

To give an example of the technical devices that are used to organize and settle commonality in the European case, here is one provision on common foreign and security policy among others: 'The Union shall define and implement a common foreign and security policy covering all areas of foreign and security policy, the objectives of which shall be to safeguard the common values, fundamental interests, independence and integrity of the Union in conformity with the principles of the United Nations Charter ....'[12] Henceforth, commonality stands for the alpha and the omega, the goal and the means, the 'is' and the 'ought' of any legal undertaking of a common world. It is illustrated in the last paragraph of Article 6 of the present Treaty, which is devoted to

---

10 Some would refer to a performative contradiction. See Austin 1962.
11 In Girard (2004) a rhetorical apparatus is described, showing the extent to which the Kantian mode of argumentation pervades contemporary legal reasoning.
12 Article 11 § 1 of Title V of the Treaty on the European Union.

founding the European Union: 'The Union shall provide itself with the means necessary to attain its objectives and carry through its policies.'[13]

It is remarkable that the process in which confusion between present and future is maintained also characterizes a typical act of sovereignty.[14] An act of sovereignty is not only defined by the fact that nobody can question it – it is an act imposing the last say – but also by the fact that the author of the act is the one to which it applies. The European Union Treaty seems to be a good example of this circular type of act – as is any act that purports to be constitutive of itself.

Thus, the Draft Treaty establishing a Constitution for Europe shows a similar ambit and structure. First, regarding the ambit, the Draft Treaty aims not only at political and social integration but also at a new representation of Europe in international relations, which implies an autonomous – that is, self-framed and original – existence. This means that not only does it purport to 'bring citizens closer to European design and European institutions and to organize politics and the European political area in an enlarged Union', but also 'to develop the Union into a stabilizing factor and a model in the new world order'.[15] A common development requires constant efforts: 'Reflecting the will of the citizens and States of Europe to *build a common future*, this Constitution establishes the European Union, on which the Member States confer competences to attain *objectives they have in common*. The Union shall coordinate the policies ... and shall exercise in *the Community way* the competences they confer on it.'[16]

Second, regarding the structure, the Europe of the Draft mirrors a community of values in a much more explicit way than beforehand: 'The Union is founded on the values of respect for human dignity, freedom, democracy, equality, the rule of law and respect for human rights, including the rights of persons belonging to minorities. *These values are common to the Member States* in a society in which pluralism, non-discrimination, tolerance, justice, solidarity and equality between women and men prevail.[17] The main argument here contains two elements: 1) Values are affirmed in a declarative mode. They are said to exist. Grammatically, values in the European Treaty are prima facie presented as *being*. 2) Nonetheless, their origin is referred to as the fact that they have been

13 Paragraph 4 of Article 6 of the Treaty on the European Union.
14 Antonio Negri (1997) considers it is a revolutionary act, for it is essentially unqualified.
15 Preface of the Draft Treaty establishing a Constitution for Europe according to its first version (June 18 2003), CONV 850/03, p. 1.
16 Article I–1 (Establishment of the Union) of the Draft Treaty establishing a Constitution for Europe, CIG 87/04, p. 9 (emphasis added).
17 Article I–2 (The Union's values) of the Draft Treaty establishing a Constitution for Europe, CIG 87/04, p. 10 (emphasis added).

shared by the member states for a long period of time; this means that they amount to traditions. These values are presented as *belonging in common* to the members of the group and to the space about to be constituted. Commonality is therefore defined as past (a common history), present (a common experience) and future (a desired being in common).

Diversity as a Competing Value

The Draft Treaty also pays great attention to diversity as a competing value that must be reconciled with commonality. Thus, together, commonality and diversity seem to play a role of constant animation of the European engine. Article I–8 of the Draft Treaty states that: 'The motto of the Union shall be: "United in Diversity"'.[18] The tension between these opposite terms allows a potentially never-ending motion and continuously justifies legal devices, designed to achieve commonality or the Community. For if, on the one hand, pluralism must be preserved as a value and as a concrete reality, commonality must, on the other hand, always be achieved.

The attempt to achieve commonality is one of the tasks of constitutional legal texts which reunite diverse traditions by providing a common normative discourse: the constitution is one and the European Union is its creature. Meanwhile, though, the same text maintains and nourishes pluralism by defending respect for 'constitutional traditions' or 'cultural diversity'.[19] Consequently, the ambiguity of the constitutional options can be interpreted as a justification for legal norms to intervene on both contradictory occasions: one is to achieve commonality, the other is to maintain diversity. Subject to such requirements, legal norms are indefinitely needed because their justification lies in the tension between two antagonistic objectives. The legally organized apparatus of self-justification described above can be seen as a means for constituting a recognized space. It contributes to the determination of a space because the motto 'United in Diversity' can be interpreted as meaning that diversity is to be maintained internally, provided it does not undermine a sufficient level of coherence to be opposed to potential external assaults – especially cultural ones. This is emphasized by the reference to 'Europe's cultural heritage', which is to be 'safeguarded and enhanced'. The Union's obligation to protect European cultural unity is especially stressed, as it is

18 Article I–8 § 3 (The symbols of the Union) of the Draft Treaty establishing a Constitution for Europe, CIG 87/04, p. 13.

19 Article I–3 § 3 in fine (The Union's objectives): 'The Union shall respect its rich cultural and linguistic diversity ... '

expressly directed against the 'wider world'.[20] Therefore, recognition comes from both inside and outside. Internal recognition stems from the repeated and accepted application of the rules grounded on such values.[21] Each such application will stand for a renewed acceptance of the rule and, further, of its founding value. Internal recognition of European space entails the approval of common values and the simultaneous agreement to abide by the rules founded upon. Viewed in this manner, foundation is not a static and motionless moment, but rather a durable process of implementation of rules. By contrast, external recognition stems from the acknowledgment and the acceptance, by foreign states, of the existence of a group itself accepting to submit to a number of rules that differ from the rules applicable in foreign states. Thus, foundation is again constituted by a repetition of acts of approval. Both internal and external recognition is foundational, in the sense that they approve of the first or constituent act.

The approval of the European Union Treaty by the Member States, from 1992 (Maastricht) to 2002 (Nice), was a quite banal act of international law. While a new legal order was being created (consisting of Community legislation), Europe as an international organization could at the same time be undermined by the cession of Member States from the Union. Nevertheless, the political will was to establish a new entity that would ultimately be comparable to a state and, most likely, a federal state, that is, an entity where unity and diversity would coexist.

This is illustrated by the latest attempt to approve the constitution by ratification, although it was recently rejected by referenda. According to article IV–447 of the Draft Treaty, each state must approve the text according to its own domestic constitutional rules. Thus, the current procedure both maintains diversity and brings together the various state entities. However, since this procedure still corresponds to an international law technique, whereby states have precedence over peoples, it does not allow the future text to act as a genuine constitutional act. Instead, the future text will probably act as the renewed constitution of a highly integrated organization of states, that is, an international organization. The international act will not be turned into a domestic act standing for a European social contract. In the current European Union, therefore, commonality is still concerned with states' traditions, constitutional habits and legalized moral values but not peoples' traditions.

20 'In its relations with the wider world, the Union shall uphold and promote its values and interests ... ', Article I–3 § 4.

21 To be compared with the process through which solidarity emerges as a politico-social phenomenon: 'a recurrent specification of social bonds with a political view'; see Karagiannis: Chapter 8.

However, the notion of 'peoples' traditions' is not a legal but rather a sociological and ethnological issue. In no way could legal theory attempt to describe and explain the extent to which European peoples actually share traditions and values – or do not. From the legal viewpoint, therefore, shared matters are those that are legally recognized as being shared, those that are declared by legal texts to be common. Describing commonality is therefore a matter of textual interpretation.

Founding as Interpretation: A Critical Viewpoint

As a form of power, textual interpretation resides in the judge, the judiciary. What happens when the judges interpret the texts in a controversial way? In other words: what if, once it has been stated, commonality results in a new conflict over its interpretation? Once the so-called constituent moment has passed, such a conflict is the only opportunity to discuss anew the social contract. The debate then centres on the meaning of the common words of the founding text. This debate occurs in courtrooms; legal trials present opportunities to discuss the meaning of common words. There are two opposing discourses concerning the correct interpretation of the words of legal texts.

On the one hand, the first discourse – the realist theory of law – claims that the judges' interpretation *is* by definition the right one. Therefore this interpretation *is* law.[22] According to this approach, since the judges' interpretation is the only way to ascertain the meaning of the common words and thus to make them conclusively common, it should be considered the law and be applicable as such. The force associated with a court's interpretation can then not be ignored, notwithstanding any dissent over its interpretation, its rationality or the form of its presentation.[23] Interpretation by the competent judge, which is called 'authentic' (Kelsen 1996), emphasizing thus the role of the judge as an authority of law, puts a clear-cut end to any debate about interpretation.[24]

---

22 This is the basic formulation of the realist theory of law, whose leading authors can be found at the beginning of the twentieth century and are mostly American (see Gray 1990; and in a more emblematic manner, Holmes 1897: 457; Pound 1930: 697; to be followed by Llewellyn 1962).

23 R. Dworkin has articulated and theorized an extensive critique of judges' interpretation, including his own judgment grounded on the merits of the judicial decision, but also on its form, which taken together constitute the concept of the so-called 'best light' requirement (see Dworkin 1991 [1986]). Dworkin's argument undeniably amounts to a Kantian aesthetical judgment, which he confuses with a value judgment (see Allard 2001).

24 Troper 2003: 100. To approach the debate about the realist theory of interpretation in France, turning around the work of Troper, see the attack by Pfersmann (2002: 231); and the reply by Troper (2002: 335).

On the other hand, the second discourse claims that the judges' interpretation is right so long as it is consistent with the requirements of rationality. The court's interpretation is not free, since it must be rational. Ambiguously, however, there is here a blurring of the boundary between what is rational and what 'truly' conforms to common values or commonality. The ambiguous circularity of the argument becomes evident when it is reformulated: the interpretation of commonality must 'exactly' conform to commonality in order to stand as commonality; the interpretation of commonality must correspond to the essence and the ideal version of commonality. If this correspondence is not achieved, the judges' objective – that their interpretation be the *common law*[25] – is not fulfilled. This approach has its origins in the academic literature on law and it is directed against controversial judicial decisions,[26] on the grounds that its flawed interpretation of commonality could have catastrophic consequences for the community. This line of argument is close to the natural law rhetoric that uses conformity to Nature (otherwise called Logic, Rationality, Reason, Reality, Truth, etc.) as the only normativity applicable to a community.[27]

The above discussion shows that what is at stake in the legal sphere is the power to interpret what 'we, the People', more or less collectively, name. As in the discipline of social theory, interpretative matters are discussed as representations of the world (Weltanschauungen) and as available methods for representing it (see Chapter 13 in this volume). These investigations not only address the issue of content: *what* is represented? They also address the issue of *how* a world is represented, namely, the procedure by which the leading representation is expressed and enforced. The procedure involves institutional actors and administrative forms (time limits and formulas, for instance). This means that the *who* question – who will determine its content?[28] – depends on the *how* question.

---

25 Take it as a play on words or not, but as it happens that the common law not only stands as the law that is shared by every member of the community – the term 'common law' appears, in turn, a pleonasm (common law is the law that is common ...) – but also stands as the common law defined as judge-made law, well-known Anglo-American customary rules driven by the compulsory precedent system of legal reasoning (see Stone 1964, 1985).

26 This discourse is often mentioned in the mass media. See, for example, the Perruche case, Cass., Ass. Plén., 17 November 2000, *Bull. Ass. plén.* no.9, p. 15. It caused an uproar in the newspapers, consisting of a petition by academic jurists and its critique (also academic), which reached a climax in late autumn 2000. It triggered a huge controversy until the final judicial decision was taken and Parliament passed an extraordinary act, which did not completely put an end to the dispute (see Cayla and Thomas 2002).

27 The other side of the coin is that it shifts the interpretative authority from the judges to experts, academic or not, whose authority is not always explicitly stated.

28 N. Fraser (see Chapter 10) interestingly wonders 'how we shall determine the relevant "who" '. In my opinion, this question demands the consideration of a fourth dimension, beyond the

In conclusion, commonality as a legal issue raises the perennial difficulty of locating authority. Where do we want authority to lie? This should be the first and only question to ask in a constitutional referendum. It has the merit of each time setting afresh the institutional game, notwithstanding the risks incurred with regard to established rules (which in any case change). However, referenda usually do not pose this question, rather tending to fuse consent and dissent into a pre-consensual apparatus. Ultimately, therefore, consent is fictitious, not only because the starting point of the referendum is the assumption that agreement was already effectively given but also because any political consent emanates from a body that cannot directly or unanimously[29] give its consent. Dissent is also complex, since it only serves to confirm consent. Indeed, in the process of adopting a new set of rules, dissent plays a nuanced role in that it does not stop a process, but continues it. In this respect, it is worth noting that one of the arguments used by some of the French 'No' militants during the referendum campaign on the European constitutional treaty was to say 'No' today in order to say 'Yes' tomorrow. Such an argument was actualizing the role deemed constructive that dissent could play in the constitutive process. It was also expected to play a constitutional role, in that the dissent was aimed at revealing a people with a constitutional role. Saying 'No' (again for only a part of the 'No' group) was supposed to initiate a 'genuine' constituent process. In this perspective, dissent had a converging aspect, which confirmed the consensus mode of choosing rather than a violent, chaotic opposition that was used as an argument against the 'No'-choice.

This choice-system, whereby consensus is privileged, reveals the role played by legal rules. It involves reducing opposition between pros and cons, since it sets a frame for the political game to happen. However, when choice is about the frame itself, opposition manifests itself in a more acute manner. If no actual choice were left about the rules of the game, it would cast doubts on the game itself, since the latter presupposes choice as a feature of liberty.[30] Therefore, rules of law must at least be seen to be freely agreed on, that is, free from violence or constraint. In that, law contains the seeds of its own contradiction,[31] as it is

---

economic, cultural and political: the legal one. Indeed, from the legal viewpoint, which itself merely puts things in a procedural light, framing appears a central concern.

29 This is a dangerous understanding of consent.

30 Note that liberty also stands as one of the pre-shared values.

31 In that sense, I partly disagree with N. Chomsky, who develops the idea of the subtle and gentle manufacturing of consent: 'In the democratic system, the necessary illusions cannot be imposed by force. Rather, they must be instilled in the public mind by more subtle means' (Chomsky 1989: 48). On the contrary, I claim that, although it can be argued, from the viewpoint of a media analysis, that consent is not obtained under duress, the same cannot be the case from the viewpoint of legal analysis. Indeed, democracy is not only committed to the media illusion of the

depicted both as the result of a collective free choice and made real and concrete through coercion on individuals. In the perspective of the foundation of a European world, the legal, too, thus appears both efficient and perverse.

References

Allard, J., 2001, *Dworkin et Kant. Réflexions sur le jugement*, Brussels, Editions de l'Université Libre de Bruxelles.

Amselek, P. (ed.), 1986, *Théorie des actes de langage, éthique et droit*, Paris, PUF.

Austin, J. L., 1962, *How to Do Things with Words*, ed. J. O. Urmson and M. Sbisá, Cambridge, MA, Harvard University Press.

Bobbio, N., 1998, *Essais de théorie du droit*, Brussels, Bruylant, Paris, LGDJ.

Cayla, O., 1992, 'La notion de signification en droit, Contribution à la théorie du droit naturel de la communication', unpublished PhD thesis, University of Paris II.

Cayla, O., and Y. Thomas, 2002, *Du droit de ne pas naître. A propos de l'affaire Perruche*, Paris, Gallimard, coll. Le Débat.

Chomsky, N., 1989, *Necessary Illusions, Thought Control in Democratic Society*, London, Pluto Press.

Dworkin, R., 1991 [1986], *Law's Empire*, London, Fontana.

Galey, M., and C. Girard, 2003, 'Le procès équitable dans l'espace normatif anglo-saxon: l'éclairage du droit public anglais', in H. Ruiz Fabri (ed.), *Procès équitable et enchevêtrement des espaces normatifs*, Paris, Société de législation comparée.

Girard, C., 2004, 'Des droits fondamentaux au fondement du droit. Réflexions sur les discours théoriques relatifs au fondement du droit', unpublished PhD thesis, University of Paris I.

Glissant, E., 1981, *Le discours antillais*, Paris, Seuil.

— 1997, *Traité du Tout-monde*, Paris, Gallimard.

Gray, J. C., 1990 [1909], *The Nature and Sources of the Law*, New York, Peter Smith.

Hart, H. L. A., 1997, *The Concept of Law*, Oxford, Clarendon Press.

Holmes, O. W., 1897, 'The Path of the Law', *Harvard Law* Review, 10, 457.

Hume, D., 2000, *A Treatise of Human Nature: Being an Attempt to Introduce the Experimental Method of Reasoning into Moral Subjects*, ed. D. F. and M. J. Norton, Oxford, Oxford University Press.

Kelsen, H., 1996, *Théorie générale des normes*, trans. O. Beaud and F. Malkani, Paris, PUF.

— 1997, *Théorie générale du droit et de l'Etat, suivi de la doctrine du droit naturel et le positivisme juridique*, trans. B. Laroche and V. Faure, Paris, LGDJ, Brussels, Bruylant.

Llewellyn, K., 1962, *Jurisprudence: Realism in Theory and Practice*, Chicago, University of Chicago Press.

Millard, E. and O. Jouanjan (eds), 2000, *Les théories réalistes du droit*, Strasbourg, Presses Universitaires de Strasbourg.

'free market of ideas' but also to the social contract theory and the theory of the monopoly of violence, whereby law enforcement is always the end of the story, whether democratically stated or not.

Negri, A., 1997, *Le pouvoir constituant*, Paris, PUF.

Pfersmann, O., 2002, 'Contre le néo-réalisme juridique. Pour un débat sur l'interprétation', *Revue Française de Droit Constitutionnel*, 50, 231.

Pound, R., 1930, 'The Call for a Realistic Jurisprudence', *Harvard Law Review*, 44, 697.

Searle, J. R., 1969, *Speech Acts*, Cambridge, Cambridge University Press.

Stone, J., 1964, *Legal System and Lawyers' Reasonings*, London, Stevens.

— 1985, *Precedent and Law: Dynamics of Common Law Growth*, London, Butterworths.

Troper, M., 1994, *Pour une théorie juridique de l'Etat*, Paris, PUF.

— 2001, *La théorie du droit, le droit, l'Etat*, Paris, PUF.

— 2002, 'Réplique à Otto Pfersmann', *Revue Française de Droit Constitutionnel*, 50, 335.

— 2003, *La philosophie du droit*, Paris, PUF.

CHAPTER 12

Worlds Emerging: Approaches to the Creation and Constitution of the Common

Angelos Mouzakitis

Implicit in the idea of world-making are the assumptions that human beings are the makers of their own history and that in the incessant shaping of their socio-historical worlds they experience some sort of commonality. This dual presupposition entails the attribution of at least some sort of control to both individuals and emerging collectivities over the status and direction of socio-historical institutions and life-trajectories. The allegedly 'common' world, emerging and/or persisting in time, poses a number of theoretical problems, of which this chapter attempts to examine only those relating to its creation and constitution. However, a preliminary task that I would like to undertake here involves the clarification of the meaning and characteristics of this 'common world', or, to be more precise, a questioning of the very nature of a social-historical[1] world in general. While there are certainly a number of legitimate ways of pursuing theoretical insights into the issue, in this contribution I intend to draw primarily on Heidegger's early phenomenological-hermeneutic understanding of the 'worldhood of the world' and of historicity, as well as on Gadamer's concept of 'belonging to a tradition' while sharing a cultural-historical horizon. In both cases, an attempt is made to situate the authors' elaborations within the wider context of their works so as to give a clearer picture to the reader and to avoid the grave consequences of complete decon-textualization.

---

1 Following Castoriadis (1997: 376–77). I frequently use the term 'social-historical' in order to indicate the often unacknowledged but inextricable link between society and history.

The World Qua Disclosure as a Problem for Fundamental Ontology

Heidegger's (1962) attempt in *Being and Time* to conceive Being in a primordial manner through the alleged destruction of the tradition of Western philosophy is also heavily premised on the substitution of the notion of Dasein for that of the Cartesian subject,[2] in order to bring to the fore the particularity of human beings. With this decentring of the epistemological function of the ego Heidegger wishes to make thematically available this peculiar state of affairs where questioning and ego co-emerge. On the one hand, this co-emergence disrupts the self-certainty of the Cartesian subject, namely, the conception of the singular human being understood in terms of a unique thinking substance, distinct from the body and inalienable even in the case of the body's inexistence. At the same time, Heidegger's conception poses a strong challenge to the alleged constancy of the Kantian 'I', as well as to the consequent grounding of a realm of objects, which in the Kantian account is dependent on the continuous flow of experiences premised on the active participation of a self-same consciousness (see Ricoeur 1990: 119).

Dasein is for this reason more than a mere substitute for consciousness, as Heidegger emphatically maintains in his reflections on the term's reception in academic circles. Dasein's peculiarity is rather that it 'names that which is first of all to be experienced, and subsequently thought accordingly, as a place – namely as *the locality of the truth of Being*' (Heidegger 1998 [1949]: 283). It has been rightly suggested that this interconnection between the meaning of Being and the meaning of being-human underlines the close linkage between philosophy's alleged failure to conceptualize Being in general and its subsequent failure in the conceptualization of human being.[3] Dasein is in Heidegger's early hermeneutic phenomenology, the entity 'which must first be worked out in an ontologically adequate manner' and, since his whole project revolves around the question of Being, Dasein is in this context the entity that in its Being always already tends towards this question. This entails that the question of Being consists precisely in the *radicalization* 'of an essential tendency-of-Being which belongs to Dasein itself – the *pre*-ontological understanding of Being' (Heidegger 1962: 35), while the prefix 'pre' points to Dasein's temporality (Biemel 1993:

---

2 Despite the similarities with Husserl's attempt to radicalize the Cartesian quest for certainty, Heidegger – or what seems to be the most fruitful interpretation of his thought – mainly attempts to redeem the lack of clarity regarding '*the meaning of the Being of the sum*' in Descartes' most celebrated dictum, *cogito ergo sum* (Heidegger 1962: 46).

3 'We do not know (*wissen*) what Dasein and a fortiori Being itself mean; we lack a conceptual fix (*begrifflich fixieren*) on them. But we always and already move about within an *understanding* of them ... and the task of hermeneutic phenomenology is to raise this pre-understanding to the level of an ontological concept' (Caputo 1987: 67).

59). It is thus hardly surprising that Heidegger should perceive Dasein's everydayness – i.e., that being the essential and persistent structures possessed by factical Dasein, wherein Dasein could be shown as it is proximally and for the most part[4] (Biemel 1993: 38–39) – as a safe indicator of temporality qua Dasein's very *meaning of Being*.

More importantly, the fundamental datum that Heidegger's project wishes to make thematically available is nothing less than the 'main structures' of Dasein's 'constitutive state of being', viz. of *being-in-the-world* (Heidegger 1992: 156–57). Being-in-the-world is thus the fundamental characteristic of Dasein's existence, the presupposition of the concomitant disclosure of entities and of the faculty of understanding (Heidegger 1992: 168–70). In a similar manner to Husserl's concept of the *lifeworld*,[5] Heidegger's concept of Being-in-the-world signifies the attempt to grasp the world on a more primordial level than that of 'manipulative objects' (Ricoeur 1981b: 141). The very process whereby natural and historical worlds co-emerge is regarded as being premised on Dasein's specific ability to disclose – and live in – such environing worlds, a state of affairs Heidegger calls *the worldhood of the world*. This latter concept already entails a critique of the Cartesian conception of the world as *res extensa*, which in Heidegger's view follows – and is complementary to – the conception of Being in terms of 'substance'. As is widely known, Heidegger treats both Cartesian concepts as having resulted from an allegedly detrimental privileging of the ontical level of enquiry, which is guided and verified by mathematics, and which entails a detrimental obliteration of the ontological presuppositions of the emergence of a world in general (Heidegger 1962: 125–34).

Heidegger's reflections on the derivative character of the Cartesian-mathematical concept of nature, on the spatiality of the world and on 'in-being'

---

4 Thus, for Heidegger, the abandonment of terms connoting aims and ideals such as *homo* and humanity in our attempt to illuminate Dasein's being are correlative to the placement of everydayness in the centre of philosophical reflection in such a manner as to unveil the fundamental structures of Dasein (see Heidegger 1992: 154–56).

5 On the sociological plane, Berger and Luckmann (1966) develop a phenomenological understanding of the 'world' stemming from Husserl's concept of the lifeworld, which is highly compatible also with Heidegger's account. However, their reluctance to step outside what they see as the legitimate ground for the sociology of knowledge impedes the posing of ontological-philosophical questions. Irrespective of this, I see as especially important their insight that although 'worlds' are but crystallizations of interactions and practices, they are mostly experienced by human beings as alien objects (see, e.g., the discussion in the second part of the book entitled 'society as objective reality'). A confrontation of more sociologically oriented accounts with the philosophical positions of Heidegger and Gadamer would necessarily involve an extended discussion of Habermas's – often criticized – distinction between systems, lifeworlds and media (especially money and power), which, regrettably, cannot be undertaken in the context of this chapter.

in general are of utmost importance for his project of fundamental ontology, since they are intended to serve as a ground for the pivotal argument in *Being and Time*, concerning the one-sided interpretation of Being in Western thought. However, of crucial importance for our purposes here are his investigations into the directly historical aspect of the *worldhood* of the world, i.e., in its functioning as a precondition for collective life (*Mitsein* and *Mitdasein*) and for the emergence of the 'Self' from the undifferentiated collective being (*Das Man*).

It is clearer now how the placing of everydayness – by virtue of it being the fundamental aspect of temporality – in the centre of philosophical reflection serves a dual purpose. First, it indicates the context where we could grasp more adequately the simultaneous emergence of the ego, the Other and communal being (Ricoeur 1990: 124). Thus, Heidegger insists that the human subject is unthinkable without a world, as well as without others, while warning against a naïve ontologization of either the individual or the collective. He rather insists – and here, in my opinion, lies a very important aspect of his contribution – that both the individual and the collective should be treated, on the level of philosophical reflection, as fundamentally concealed (Heidegger 1962: 152), and the consequences of this point are also quite significant for the theoretical orientation of the social sciences. Second, it points to an understanding of historicity that wishes to go well beyond the context and scope – and, at the same time, establish beyond doubt the derivative character – of the science of history in a manner similar to that in which the concept of the worldhood seeks to unveil the derivative character of the modern interpretation of *physis* as nature.[6] This also involves an attempt to show how the triumphant progress of the natural sciences, which Heidegger sees as premised on the modern conception of nature, entails an obliteration of the primordial experience of the environing world and, consequently, a conditioning – and an impoverishment – of the historical horizon of modernity.[7] This often-criticized attempt to demarcate clearly the dimensions

---

6   See, for example, his contention that the modern 'narrowing of *physis* in the direction of 'physics' did not occur in the way we imagine it today. We oppose the psychic, the animated, the living, to the 'physical'. But for the Greeks it all belonged to *physis* and continued to do so even after Aristotle' (Heidegger 1959: 16). Indicative is also his attempt to arrive at a more originary interpretation of *physis* through the interpretation of Heraclitus's fragment 123, according to which '*physis kryptesthai philei*' and which he interprets as 'Being (emerging appearing) inclines intrinsically to self-concealment' (Heidegger 1959: 114).

7   Following Nietzsche, Heidegger traces this obliteration already in Greek antiquity in the interpretation of Being in terms of οὐσία and of human being as ζῷον λόγον ἔχων (Heidegger 1962: 47). This conviction must be the main reason informing Heidegger's motivation to unearth a primordial relationship with Being in the works of the pre-Socratics. Despite acknowledging the possibility of there being a different conception of 'life' in Greek thought, Heidegger covers this insight up, by identifying ζωή with *animalitas*. Consequently, for Heidegger, with '*animal, zoon*, an interpretation of *life* is already posited that necessarily lies in the interpretation of beings

of scientific research and philosophy proper (i.e., fundamental ontology)[8] is based on the previously drawn distinctions between *ontic/ontological* and *existential/existentiell* levels of enquiry and being. Since Being-with-others is conceived of as constitutive of Dasein, historicity as a fundamental attribute of Dasein also acquires a complementary – though equally important – relational dimension (162–63).

However, this promising conceptualization is followed by a surprising interpretative twist that equates 'the other' almost exclusively with the impersonal collective and which sees Dasein as oscillating between authenticity and inauthenticity in a constant process of partial detachments from its fundamentally in-authentically constituted[9] 'they-Self' (167–68). Thus, Heidegger is able to designate two modalities of individual and collective historicity based on the opposition between authenticity and inauthenticity. The key to the always incomplete passage from the inauthentic to the authentic historical comportment is Dasein's attitude towards the most important consequence of temporality, viz. death. With this move, the analysis focuses again on the non-relational elements of existence, since the deepest individuation of Dasein, and the concurrent disclosure of the possibility of its historical existence, are seen as the result of Dasein's authentic stance towards death. Although I do not wish to elaborate Heidegger's argument in detail here, it is important to notice that the category of *being-towards-death* functions as a

as *zoe* and *physis*, within which what is living appears' (Heidegger 1993: 227). Hans Jonas rightly alludes to a certain 'verbal sophism' in this argument of Heidegger's. Drawing on Plato's *Timaeus* (30c), Jonas concludes that 'life' in its Greek conception refers to any animated being, ultimately to the 'ensouled universe as a whole', and that consequently no '*lowering* of man is implied in placing him within that [cosmic] scale and the bogy of *animality* in its modern connotations is slipped in surreptitiously' (Jonas 1992: 333).

8 Axelos (1964) offers in his essay 'On Heidegger' an interesting support to this conception in indicating that, strictly speaking, it is incorrect to speak of fundamental ontology due to the absence of a systematically developed ontology in *Being and Time*. This entails that the tripartite distinction between fundamental ontology, traditional ontology and science should not be treated as some sort of objective model but that it primarily aims at the *uncovering* of the forgetfulness of being.

9 Everydayness and inauthenticity belong together in Heidegger's project. The 'everyday' is, furthermore, often described with the terms 'proximally' and 'for the most part', and it is strongly linked with the public, since it is said that the 'publicly manifest' belongs to everydayness. Furthermore, everydayness holds sway over human beings, since it is 'determinative for Dasein *even when it has chosen the they for its hero*', while even *in the moment of vision* 'indeed, and often just *for that moment*, existence can even gain the mastery over the *everyday*; but it can *never extinguish it*' (Heidegger 1962: 422; emphasis added). This shows the derivative character of authenticity in Heidegger's philosophy and the important role he ascribes to both the conscious and unconscious identification with a person or a collective for the performance of historical-political actions.

yardstick for the assessment of the authentic or inauthentic disclosure of historical worlds.

More specifically, authentic being-towards-death is theorized as grounded on Dasein's ek-static ability to be ahead-of-itself in projecting itself, and therefore on the existential-ontological phenomenon of care.[10] Now, this being-towards-death is understood as a mode of being whereby Dasein 'is dying factically and indeed constantly, as it has not come yet to its demise', and this dying has the character of an orientation towards an authentic or inauthentic stance with regard to death that allegedly defines Dasein's becoming at any point of time (Heidegger 1962: 303–04). Death's revelation as a possibility in this personal sense mentioned above results in an 'anticipation' of this possibility in terms of which Dasein discloses 'itself to itself' and wrenches itself away from *Das Man* (307).[11] In a direct agonizing with Kierkegaard, Heidegger sees authentic being as characterized by anxiety as opposed to fear, the latter allegedly being a defective or inauthentic mode of anxiety by virtue of its being always directed towards entities encountered within the world (234). The important element here is that the state of Dasein's being-anxious is conceived as disclosing the world qua world, while by virtue of this disclosure Dasein's Being-free for 'the freedom of *choosing itself and taking hold of itself*' becomes manifest (232). Here we encounter not only the acknowledgment of the existence of different modes of 'worlds' based on their emergence from inauthentic or authentic comportment, but also the assumption that the *authentic* disclosure of a 'world' incorporates in its very realization the consciousness of what it really means to disclose and to 'have' such a 'world'. In other words, if inauthentic being-

---

10 It is difficult to overestimate the importance of the concept of care (*Sorge*) for Heidegger's project in *Being and Time*. Care represents the fundamental structure of Dasein (Biemel 1993: 61), which cannot be traced back to 'some ontical *primal element*, just as being cannot be explained in terms of entities'. It follows that Care must be conceptualized as a state of being always already underlying Dasein. It is related to *perfectio*, to man's transformation 'into what he can be in Being-free for his ownmost possibilities', while it is also pertinent to Dasein as an entity surrendered or thrown to the world of its concern (Heidegger 1962: 240–44).

11 However, since care is an existential-ontological phenomenon, it must also apply to inauthentic modes of comportment, otherwise the whole conception of Dasein becoming authentic would be absurd. Accordingly, although Dasein's being-ahead-of-itself is primarily construed as a departure from the 'they-Self', even in being inauthentic Dasein is said to remain 'essentially ahead of itself ... in face of itself as it falls, [and it] still shows that it has the State-of-Being of an entity *for which its being is an issue*' (Heidegger 1962: 238). Biemel rightly suggests that since care is grounded structurally on temporality and its three ecstatic modes (i.e., past, present, and future), the *future* should play an important role also in the case of inauthentic Dasein. Unlike authentic Dasein, though, inauthentic Dasein concerns itself with everydayness and, consequently, the 'inauthentic future' has the character of an 'awaiting' (*gewartigen*) (Biemel 1993: 65).

towards-death results in the representation of the historical world as 'natural', 'given', or 'inalterable', its authentic modification should entail the awareness that the emergence of a 'world' in general is always an *achievement* of the incessant interplay between the already established interpretations of 'the-they', the possibilities inherent in tradition and the specific interpretation/enactment of these possibilities by an individual human being or by a collective.[12]

It is true that the commitment to authenticity characterizing Heidegger's early philosophy allows for – and has invited many – unfavourable interpretations that detect therein a relapse to metaphysics and to the solipsistic philosophy of the subject. It is equally true, though, that Heidegger speaks explicitly about *co-historicity* and *destiny* in an attempt to reintroduce a level of collective historical determination. Importantly in this respect, destiny signifies more than an aggregate of 'individual fates', since Heidegger contends that 'our fates have already been guided in advance, in our Being with one another in the same world and in our resoluteness for definite possibilities' (436). As I have tried to show, however, the most important loss in this conception of Heidegger's is arguably the – rather unintentional – delegation of the relational character of being-towards-death. As Levinas (1969) has convincingly argued, this entails a one-sided understanding of death[13] that seems to be premised on a passive understanding of Dasein, at least with regard to this specific issue. If this interpretation is correct, then the theme of death paints a picture of Dasein that leans towards the traditional model of consciousness that Heidegger attempted to overcome with some success.

Tradition and the Disclosing Qualities of Belonging

Gadamer is undoubtedly the thinker who saw it as his philosophical task to impregnate Heidegger's insights – before and after his so-called 'turn' – with a rigorous systematic critique of philosophy and the human sciences. In his most celebrated work, *Truth and Method*, Gadamer (1989a) discusses the importance

---

12 The authentic anticipation of death on Dasein's part and the resultant authentically resolute comportment are seen as providing Dasein with the possibility of choosing its goal among the many possibilities offered by tradition, by 'pushing' its existence into its 'finitude' (Heidegger 1962: 435).

13 Despite Heidegger's later attempt in his book *An Introduction to Metaphysics* (Heidegger 1959) to describe Dasein as fundamentally violent, there is still missing in Heidegger's text something even similar to Levinas's equation of death as nothingness with the will to annihilate the Other through murder: 'More profoundly and as it were a priori we approach death as nothingness in the passion for murder. The spontaneous intentionality of this passion aims at annihilation. Cain when he slew Abel should have possessed the same knowledge. The identifying of death with nothingness befits the death of the other in murder' (Levinas 1969: 232).

of Heidegger's conception of thrownness, for the overcoming of Dilthey's elaborations on historical understanding and for the surpassing of the model of consciousness characteristic of modern philosophy since Descartes. To cut a long story short, Gadamer's argument is that Dilthey's investigations were severely confined by his attempt to secure an epistemological ground for the human sciences (*die Geisteswissenschaften*) of the type that Kant allegedly furnished for the natural ones. As neither Heidegger nor Gadamer were willing to share the neo-Kantian perspective that sees Kant's works, and especially the *Critique of Pure Reason*, as primarily epistemological achievements, Gadamer's strategy is to show how the epistemological perspective in itself distorts not only our interpretation of Kant's oeuvre but also how it misses the fundamental aspects of human historicity by making it an 'object' of scientific analysis. In effect, Gadamer follows a path of argumentation already travelled by Heidegger in *Being and Time*, as he attempts to establish that Dilthey's approach culminates in psychologism due to its being plagued simultaneously by an inadequately formulated philosophy of life and by an indirect emulation of the understanding of method advanced by the natural sciences (Gadamer 1989a: 258). In Gadamer's view, Heidegger succeeded exactly where Dilthey failed (and also Husserl, who in his later works, despite his attack on scientific reason and his 'discovery' of the lifeworld, retained the traditional emphasis on the transcendental ego in the form of the *Ur-Ich*). The very concept of *thrownness* is interpreted as indicating the centrality of the experience of belonging to a tradition for both remembering and forgetting and, therefore, for experiencing and recreating the historical past. Belonging to a tradition and the projection towards 'future possibilities' of existence are seen as two inseparable aspects of Dasein's historical finitude and, in spite of Heidegger's intentions, this couplet is treated as the basis for the very development of a historical hermeneutics (Gadamer 1989a: 262).

Gadamer wishes to establish the inseparability of thrownness and understanding via an evaluation of Heidegger's discussion of the problem of the hermeneutic circle in *Being and Time*. Gadamer rightly suggests that the ontologically positive significance of the hermeneutic circle as established by Heidegger entails that the constant task of interpretation is explicitly seen as being dictated by the things themselves, while interpretation and understanding are explicitly formulated in terms of projecting. Heidegger is thus seen as describing an interpretative process where every revision of fore-projections is capable of generating another projection, thereby making possible both the coexistence of rival projections and the arrival at more suitable interpretations in accordance with the nature of things (Gadamer 1989a: 266–67). If Dilthey's discussion of the hermeneutic circle served as a means of separating his own position from 'the post-Schleiermacherian scientific epoch', then Heidegger's discussion of this problem, in being directed 'toward the structure' of being-in-the-world, is interpreted as concurrently pointing towards the overcoming of the 'subject-object bifurcation', which was the 'main thrust' of Heidegger's analytic of Dasein.

On another occasion, Gadamer draws on Heidegger's analysis of tools in the first part of *Being and Time* in order to show how the circularity of the hermeneutic understanding can be a productive rather than a limiting condition. In the same manner in which 'one who uses a tool does not treat that tool as an object', Gadamer argues, Dasein's understanding of itself 'in its Being and in its world' cannot be adequately grasped in terms of a comportment towards 'definite objects of knowledge', but has to be seen as 'the carrying out of Being-in-the-world itself' (Gadamer 1989b: 22–23). Gadamer understands, moreover, his own philosophical contribution as consisting in the discovery that 'no conceptual language, not even what Heidegger called the "language of metaphysics", represents an unbreakable constraint upon thought if only a thinker allows himself to trust language' (Gadamer 1989b: 23). In Gadamer's eyes, then, the task of hermeneutic understanding is not to effect a radical break with tradition in line with the premises of the Enlightenment, but rather to exclude everything that hinders the attempt to open up towards the elements carried through by tradition (Gadamer 1989a: 269).

The acknowledgment of the unavoidably prejudicial character of all understanding that Gadamer inherits from Heidegger, and which echoes also the Romantic struggle against the Enlightenment (see Ricoeur 1981a: 61), is therefore placed at the heart of the hermeneutic problem. With this move, Gadamer re-inscribes historicism within the conceptual framework of Enlightenment philosophy, despite historicism's critique of both rationalism and natural philosophy (Gadamer 1989a: 270). Gadamer furnishes a challenging and provocative interpretation of 'prejudice' through the weaving of a subtle and pervasive argument that discerns a 'prejudice against prejudices' at the core of all the currents of Enlightenment thought. Suffice it to say in the context of the present discussion that one significant 'prejudice' historicism shares with the whole Enlightenment movement is the witless – in Gadamer's view – conception of *historical distance* (1998: 126–27) as a hurdle that should be surpassed if the historian is to grasp interpretatively the past. It follows that, according to historicism's own premises, objectivity becomes attainable for the human sciences only to the extent that the historian manages to transcend the present in order to enter the horizon of a past epoch. In so doing, the historian would be able to think using concepts and collective representations pertinent to the epoch's spirit and thereby 'objectively' recreate this historical era. Gadamer wishes to show that this ideal of historicism is based on a conception of historical time that sees it in terms of a vacuum (empty time) that has to be covered, or as a breach that is always in need of being bridged. Such a conception has the further disadvantage of concealing the productive dimension of historical distance and the living continuity of the multiple elements that become parts of a tradition, in the light of which the *past* is itself always made available.

There is, though, one even more significant dimension of the beneficial consequences of historical distancing that Gadamer brings to the fore by using an example from the sphere of art, namely, that the very act of freeing oneself from the prejudices of the present is premised on the human ability to distance oneself ecstatically from the present. Thus, the work of modern art cannot be really judged aesthetically solely from the perspective of the present and the prejudices that, in Gadamer's view, conceal its authentic or inauthentic qualities, but has rather to be looked at from the wider perspective of the whole history of art. Tradition in this case functions as the indispensable element that effaces momentarily the relations of the present, and which therefore makes possible the transition to the universal (Gadamer 1998: 127). In this manner, temporality emerges as the precondition of universality and as the condition that provides the criterion for the demarcation between confining and productive prejudices, or, as Gadamer puts it, between prejudices that enlighten and prejudices that blind us. It is thus this historical distancing that makes possible the distinction between true and false prejudices which thereby grounds the critical functioning of hermeneutic philosophy (Gadamer 1998: 128).

Gadamer's attempt to renew the question concerning the meaning of tradition is premised on the demonstration of the impossibility of a complete liberation from tradition. This explains why, although he attempts to guard himself against a relapse into 'traditionalism' – of which he has been nevertheless often accused – and in consonance with the Romantics, Gadamer traces in tradition the veritable 'ground' of the force and validity of morals (Gadamer 1989a: 280–81). This does not mean that Gadamer would like to subscribe to the Romantic quest for the growth of traditions, which he repudiates as being a mere reversal of the enlightened preoccupation with reason. Although Gadamer does not wish to refute the normative claims of reason, he still senses the impossibility of maintaining an extra-temporal (ahistorical) conception of the latter. This becomes apparent in his rejection of the unconditional antithesis between tradition and reason and his critical remarks against Habermas's defence of undistorted dialogue, which he finds utterly idealist (281, 568). Indeed, the human sciences are for Gadamer the disciplines that are in principle capable of giving tradition its full value, since it is there that research cannot be conceived as antithetical to the very manner in which individual human beings relate to the past. Thus, the abandonment of the distinction between '*tradition and historical research, between history and the knowledge of it*' is placed at the centre of historical hermeneutics (282). This move signifies the acceptance of the essentially finite, conditioned perspective, from which the historical can be addressed and theorized (285). More importantly, it shows that tradition should not be regarded simply – or mainly – as an epistemological precondition, but rather as the ever-transforming product of acting human beings (293). We encounter thus a non-ossified and open conception of tradition[14] as the simultaneously conditioning and conditioned historical context of human action, premised on the open character of human understanding.

Two concepts are pivotal in this attempt to show the always-conditioned character of human understanding and existence,[15] viz. the *effective historical consciousness* and the celebrated but often criticized[16] *fusion of horizons*. Gadamer's main concern is to secure the very notion of the horizon from its being identified with whimsical and unjustified subjective interpretations, and mere caprice, by establishing its dependence on the wider contexts of tradition. In the concept of horizon we encounter the indication of the range of vision articulated from 'a particular vantage point', a state of affairs characterized by what could be termed the determinacy of finitude over thought. In the field of historical understanding, the idea of a horizon is often used to indicate the attempt to bypass the criteria and prejudices of the 'present', so as to enable the immersion into the 'past', wherefrom the traditionary text or the historical event addresses the historical consciousness. This prevalent understanding of horizons in terms of a transposition into the 'alien' is, in Gadamer's eyes, a legitimate, though by no means adequate conceptualization of the notion of horizon (302–03). Leaving aside his objections against the psychological aspect[17] of this

---

14 Although it is true that Gadamer focuses much more on tradition than even the early Heidegger, we still find in Heidegger an intimation of Gadamer's formulation when, for example, he argues that the 'assumption of the tradition is *not* necessarily traditionalism' and that the '*genuine repetition* of a traditional question lets its external character as a tradition fade away and pulls back from the prejudices' (Heidegger 1992: 138).

15 See Gadamer's insistence that reflection on the essence of humanity's historical being 'can never be completely achieved' and that correlatively '*to be historically means that knowledge of oneself can never be complete*' (Gadamer 1989a: 302).

16 Caputo even sees in the concept of the fusion of horizons a 'Hegelian streak' and a Platonic influence, which signifies the development of a 'conservative Heideggerianism' stemming from the 'right flank' of Heidegger's disciples, in spite of Heidegger's thought having 'moved forward' (Caputo 1987: 96).

17 This does not mean, though, that Gadamer fails to take into account the subjective aspect of this phenomenon. On the contrary, the centrality attributed to the dialogical process in Gadamer's thought suggests that the communicative experience of the individual human being – alongside the inter-subjective experience of dialogue that Gadamer attempts to wrest from its being

standard conception, Gadamer sees as extremely problematical the postulation of 'closed horizons', which supposedly enclose whole cultures (303–04). Gadamer capitalizes on the fleeting qualities of time in order to show the indeterminacy of the very notion of the horizon and, accordingly, that the postulation of a radical historicity of Dasein signifies the inability permanently to fix a standpoint wherefrom history is experienced and hence to conceive of a truly 'closed' horizon. Consequently, both the singular human being and the historical horizons that humans are immersed in are said to be in a state of constant movement. In the same manner that 'past', 'present', and 'future' are – at least since Heidegger – seen not as separated dimensions, but as ecstasies of time, the transposition of historical consciousness into 'alien' historical horizons does not merely imply the passage into alien historical, textual and artistic worlds. For Gadamer, this transposition rather reveals the fundamental dimension of the historical horizon, namely, that it consists of a single horizon, which in its movement embraces the past and the present, while keeping itself open to the future (304). It is thus altogether questionable whether it is proper to speak of a 'fusion of horizons' characterizing the historically effective consciousness and not of a 'fusion of the ecstasies of time' within a single historical horizon. How else could one interpret Gadamer's statement that *'understanding is always the fusion of these horizons supposedly existing by themselves'* (306)? Indeed, Gadamer acknowledges that the term 'fusion of horizons' is preferable to that of the 'formation of one horizon', mainly because the former discloses more explicitly the hermeneutic situation. To be more precise, the concept of the 'fusion of horizons' has the advantage of explicitly acknowledging that understanding 'becomes a scholarly task only under special circumstances' and that there is an acknowledged tension between the text – or the historical event – and the present.

However, the mediation Gadamer has in mind when speaking about the fusion of horizons is better grasped in relation to the hermeneutic-disclosing functioning of art, which, in being a fundamental hermeneutic dimension (along with the 'text' and the 'law'), allows Gadamer to bridge his philosophical position even with Heidegger's thought after the 'turn'. The intrinsically hermeneutic situation of historical existence and the concurrent disclosure of a world is the theme of Heidegger's (1975) meditation, 'The Origin of the Work of Art'. His masterful analysis of Van Gogh's painting starts from the

sublated in the conceptual framework of speculative dialectics – occupies a prominent part in Gadamer's construction of the very notion of the 'fusion of horizons'. This becomes apparent in Gadamer's description (1989b: 41) of the relation between text, interpreter and reader, to which I can only point the reader here due to limitations of space.

interpretation of a pair of peasant shoes as equipment that disclose, in Gadamer's (1994: 103) expression, the whole world of rural life – a world of anxiety about the acquisition of daily bread and the always present threat of death – in order to establish the status of art as an event of truth. Importantly, the event of the truth of art that Heidegger called 'clearing' is inaccessible to traditional thought guided by thing-concepts (Heidegger 1975: 35–38, 53), while it is characteristic of every mode of art and especially of poetry and tragedy. This means that Gadamer's concept of aesthetic non-differentiation should be seen as an explicit attempt to grasp, at the same time, the peculiar mode of being of historical worlds and the appropriate way of approaching the creations of human beings without reifying them.

Some Concluding Remarks

If Heidegger is remembered primarily for renewing the question regarding the meaning of being and for accusing metaphysics of nurturing the oblivion of Being, Gadamer would be certainly remembered for his attempt to cast into doubt our enlightened repudiation of tradition. Despite the differences in scope and the diametrically opposed intentions, these approaches share the commitment to develop non-reified conceptualizations of human beings and the worlds they inhabit and construct. Despite the tentative character of every attempt to theorize our social-historical existence, I think that Heidegger's and Gadamer's elaborations burgeon with instructive elements for anyone who wishes to study – and to act in – history. Their insistence on the fundamentally temporal/finite character of human understanding, on the possibility of an originary/authentic (Heidegger) or non-objectified (Gadamer) encounter with one's own – always already historical – self and with the always transforming and persisting socio-historical 'worlds' are exemplary in this respect. Certainly, the acknowledgment of human beings' immersion in their historical contexts does not remove the ambiguities and the tensions intrinsic in social-historical action. Rather, the pivotal place attributed to finitude by both thinkers – despite their differences in accent – successfully captures the conditioned character of historical being, the always incomplete nature of interpretation and the paradoxical and precarious elements that go together with the creation, renewal or even destruction of socio-historical worlds. Arguably, the shift from Heidegger's concept of thrownness in the world to Gadamer's notion of belonging to a tradition already signifies a taming of the often cruel, tragic character of historical-political action. However, I have attempted to show that the two thinkers share the same fundamental insights on the issue, as Gadamer's conception of the *fusion of horizons* grasps uniquely the contextual, relational, unpredictable and essentially open character of all creation. In this respect, it does not only account for the incessant interpretative appropriations of culture but it also uncovers the appropriative processes leading to the creation, maintenance and alteration of a variety of socio-historical worlds. More importantly, the interpretation of both Heidegger and Gadamer proposed here suggests that the main thrust of their works consists in establishing the acts of creation and their conditions as fundamental characteristics of both singular human beings and collectives, nay as *constitutive* of being human.

References

Axelos, Kostas, 1964, *Vers la pensée planétaire*, Paris, Les Editions de Minuit.

Berger, Peter L., and Thomas Luckmann, 1966, *The Social Construction of Reality. A Treatise in the Sociology of Knowledge*, New York, Penguin Books.

Biemel, Walter, 1993, *Heidegger*, (in Greek), trans. Th. Loupasakis, Athens, Plethron.

Caputo, John D., 1987, *Radical Hermeneutics: Repetition, Deconstruction and the Hermeneutic Project*, Bloomington and Indianapolis, Indiana University Press.

Castoriadis, Cornelius, 1997, *World in Fragments*, ed. and trans. David Ames Curtis, Stanford, CA, Stanford University Press.

Gadamer, Hans-Georg, 1989a, *Truth and Method*, 2nd edn, rev. trans. Joel Weinsheimer and Donald G. Marshall, London, Sheed and Ward.

— 1989b, 'Text and Interpretation', in Diane P. Michelfelder and Richard E. Palmer (eds), *Dialogue and Deconstruction: The Gadamer–Derrida Encounter*, New York, State University of New York Press, 21–51.

— 1994, *Heidegger's Ways*, trans. John W. Stanley, with Introduction by J. Schmidt, Albany, NY, State University of New York Press.

— 1998, Το Πρόβλημα της Ιστορικής Ευνείδησης (*The Problem of Historical Consciousness*), trans. into Modern Greek and prefaced by A. Zerbas, Athens, Indiktos, originally published in French, 1963, as *Le Problème de la Conscience Historique*, Publications Universitaires de Louvain.

Heidegger, Martin, 1959, *An Introduction to Metaphysics*, trans. Ralph Manheim, New Haven, CT, and London, Yale University Press.

—1962, *Being and Time*, trans. John Macquarrie and Edward Robinson, Oxford, Blackwell.

— 1975, 'The Origin of the Work of Art', in *Poetry, Language, Thought*, trans. Albert Hofstadter, New York, Harper Colophon.

— 1992, *History of the Concept of Time*, trans. Theodore Kisiel, Bloomington and Indianapolis, Indiana University Press.

— 1993, 'Letter on Humanism', in *Basic Writings*, ed. David Farrell Krell, London, Routledge, 213–67.

— 1998 [1949], 'Introduction to "What is Metaphysics"', in William McNeill (ed.), *Pathmarks*, Cambridge, Cambridge University Press, 277–91.

Jonas, Hans, 1992, *The Gnostic Religion: The Message of the Alien God and the Beginnings of Christianity*, 2nd edn, London, Routledge.

Levinas, Emmanuel, 1969, *Totality and Infinity: An Essay on Exteriority*, trans. Alphonso

Lingis, Pittsburg, PA, Duquesne University Press.

Ricoeur, Paul, 1981a, 'The Task of Hermeneutics', in John B. Thompson (ed.), *Paul Ricoeur: Hermeneutics and the Human Sciences*, Cambridge, Cambridge University Press, 43–62.

— 1981b, 'The Hermeneutical Function of Distanciation', in John B. Thompson (ed.), *Paul Ricoeur: Hermeneutics and the Human Sciences*, Cambridge, Cambridge University Press, 131–44.

— 1990, 'Ο Heidegger και το Ερώτημα για το Υποκείμενο' ('Heidegger and the Question of the Subject'), in Δοκίμια Ερμηνευτικής (*Essays on Hermeneutics*), Athens, Morphotiko Institouto Agrotikes Trapezes.

CHAPTER 13

Imperial Modernism and European World-Making

Peter Wagner

A European Variety of World-Making?

At the time of writing, it seems that the sceptics have been right. After the referenda on the constitutional treaty of the European Union in France and the Netherlands, the European political project is in disarray. Some of those sceptics will even insist that there never was such a political project anyway. The European Union, in their view, is nothing but an association of states to further their own interests, and the apparent acceleration of political integration over the past fifteen years did not really change its nature. The EU Charter of Fundamental Rights, so they will underline, explicitly does not strive to go beyond the existing rights at national level, but only aims to bring them together in a single document. And the constitutional treaty, if it were ever to come into force, is nothing but an exercise in institutional architecture, at best eliminating some incoherence in the historical layers of European treaties and at worst petrifying some dysfunctional co-operative mechanisms due to power-bargaining between the nation states.

Such a purely sceptical look fails to perceive the most significant novelty of the process, namely, the founding of a polity through the deliberate interaction of the members of that new polity. European political integration can fruitfully be seen as an attempt at world-making. Rather than start the analysis of such an attempt with an a priori emphasis on its limitations, which any such process will always have, it seems more promising to understand its nature by analysing the problems it tries to address, and this in a twofold way. On the one hand, European world-making takes place against the background of the historical experiences made and with the resources provided across the history of political ideas. The problems it addresses will be shaped by those experiences and the

247

available means with which to interpret them. On the other hand, it takes place in a given context, the present situation of 'globalization' or emerging 'empire', and it tries to place the new polity it aims to create in response to the problematic features of that situation.[1]

Most of the sceptics referred to above hold their view on what they think are 'realist' grounds (for further discussion, see Chapter 4 and Chapter 14 in this volume). In this view, politics is about power and interest, and states are the containers of power and interest in the global arena. One can, however, also be sceptical about the possibility and desirability of any specifically European self-understanding of political modernity for normative reasons. To those who try to identify normative underpinnings for European political integration, it has been objected that such European self-understanding is *either* entirely indistinct from the general self-understanding of the West, i.e., a commitment to human rights and liberal democracy, *or* highly problematic, because it is based on 'thick' presuppositions that are untenable against the background of European cultural diversity and risk to revive non-liberal European political traditions. Since the end of the Second World War and, in particular, during the past fifteen years, social and political theory has often assumed that there is a single model of 'modern society', to which all societies will gradually converge because of the higher rationality of its institutional arrangements. Similarly, political modernity is then equated with a single institutional model based on electoral democracy and a set of basic individual rights. It has often appeared as if there were a single scale of 'political modernization', on which the US and, possibly, the UK always figure at the top, and continental European polities – not even to speak of what is now often referred to as 'the rest of the world' – lag behind.[2]

If any general, universalist commitment to liberal democracy were indeed sufficient to understand Western polities, our discussion about varieties of world-making would have a very limited scope. One world only – a West based on this universalist understanding – could be normatively defended and all other varieties would need to be rejected. The argument is familiar in our times, but frequency of evocation does not make it any more valid. What its defenders fail to understand is the possibility that a basic commitment to personal liberty and collective self-determination can be interpreted in a variety of ways, none of which has any evident claim to superiority. This commitment can be called 'modern', but there is more than one way of being so.

Therefore, a concept of political modernity that can take account of a variety

---

1 For a first attempt at a more detailed historico-philosophical account of the political form of European modernity, see Wagner 2005b.
2 For a recent similar remark, see Dahrendorf 2001.

of truly modern political forms is needed to raise the level of debate. By modernity, I mean a situation in which human beings commit themselves to determine and master their lives, their relations with others and their ways of being in the world. By *political* modernity I mean, more specifically, the self-determination and mastery of life *in common* with others and the rules of life in common.[3] While such normative self-understandings may – and mostly do – contain general and universal elements, they are always specific and situated in the time and space of the social life to which they refer. Thus, modernity is marked by a tension between the decontextualizing move that is necessary to generate a normative argument of some reach and the requirement to link any justification to a situation for which it is adequate. In the current global contest over ways of world-making specifically, one of the sites in which this tension becomes visible is the European attempt at creating a self-understanding that forms itself in its particularity on the one hand, and, on the other, an approach that claims validity and applicability without regard for context, an approach that will here be called 'imperial modernism'.[4]

This contest over world-making will be discussed here by taking two rather tentative steps. First, a slightly schematic comparison of social and political thought in Europe and the US will be provided, showing the basic features of imperial modernism and indicating some – historical and contingent – reasons for its dominance in the US, even though its sources are to be found in Europe. This relation of current dominance to historical sources will be illustrated with the help of the well-known theme of conflict between two brothers, thus demonstrating a relation both of similarity and difference, and one marked by a struggle over its interpretation as either equal and symmetrical or hierarchical and asymmetrical.[5] Since this first step will show that individualism and instrumentalism are the key features of imperial modernism, the second step

---

3   For a broader discussion of the concept and the history of modernity, see Wagner 1994, 2001a and 2001b; for the concept of political modernity more specifically, see Wagner 2005a; for an attempt to identify the varieties of moral-political philosophies in France and the US, see Lamont and Thévenot 2000. Discussions of modernity sometimes focus on individual autonomy as a key feature (e.g., Taylor 1989); analyses of political modernity, in contrast, would always need to emphasize collective autonomy, collective self-determination and, therefore, democracy.

4   My use of the term 'imperial' draws on Hardt and Negri (2000) and accepts the observation of a novel 'aterritorial' form of (discursive) domination. Otherwise, however, as will become clear in the course of my argument, a different understanding of the novel imperial situation is proposed here, namely, one that sees imperial modernism as an interpretation of modernity that is inclined towards hegemony, for reasons to be detailed below, but that is only contingently related to the rise of the US (for a recent historico-sociological analysis of empire, see Mann 2003).

5   For related concepts applied to the relationships between Europe and its former colonies, see Karagiannis (2004).

will discuss the consequences for any future hegemony of such thinking by exploring how the question of the common has become problematic in political philosophy in the light of the rise of individualist and instrumentalist liberalism. In conclusion, I will briefly come back to the question of whether any elements of an alternative to such hegemony can be identified in European political integration.

Plural Interpretations of Modernity and the Meaning of Empire

When the late Pope John Paul II visited Israel some years ago, a process of rapprochement of the Catholic Church towards the Jewish religious community, which had started with the visit of the Pope to the synagogue in Rome in 1986, reached a high point. John Paul II, contributing to the general movement of reconciliation and pardoning that marked the 1990s, addressed his audience in Rome as 'Dear Jewish and Christian friends and brothers' and, turning explicitly to the Jewish listeners, he uttered a phrase that has often been quoted since: 'You are our favourite brothers and, in a certain sense we may say, our elder brothers.' On this occasion, as on many others, the speech was interrupted by sustained applause, as observers reported.

Some years later, there was a little uproar in Italian political-intellectual circles when historian Carlo Ginzburg (1998: 210–15) dared to pour some water into the wine. He recalled the fact that the term 'the elder brother' had a long history in Christian thought, even a constitutive semantic role in that history. It was used by Paul the Apostle in the letter to the Romans, when Paul referred to the Lord telling Rebecca, who was pregnant with twins, that 'the elder shall serve the younger' (Romans 9.12). And so it was: Jacob, the younger son, bought the rights of the first-born, Esau, for a lentil dish, after having cheated him about the legitimacy of the transaction.

This is not the place to comment on the interpretations of John Paul's speech or to intervene in any way in discussions about the relations between Christianity and Judaism in general. Rather, I want to suggest that we can think fruitfully about the relations between Americans and Europeans, and in particular about their intellectual or *geistige* – spiritual-intellectual – relations in analogy to this ancient story of the two siblings. I do not aim at the impossible: to make a comparison between American and European social and political thought in our time. Instead, I want to point to a structural feature in our ways of analysing the social world: a structural feature that exists on both sides of the Atlantic, but that finds observably different expressions on each side. And, with the rise of the younger brother to dominance, the story of the two siblings provides a way of describing that structure as a potentially imperial one.

The story suggests a relationship in which the elder brother (the European) could say that he was the rightful inheritor of great intellectual traditions, but that over time the younger brother (the American) appropriated this heritage, developed it but also changed it, and partly succeeded in turning it against his older brother, since he had grown much more powerful. The younger brother would admit that he had a debt towards his older brother, who had given him his major ideas and practices. But he would insist that he had improved on those ideas and practices and put them right, whereas his older brother still tended to get them wrong. In the younger brother's view, he had needed to lift these ideas out of their original context in order to be able to develop them into the powerful intellectual tools that they now are.

Such discourse, it should be recalled, especially from the point of view of the elder of the two brothers, was quite common in broad intellectual circles during the interwar period – that is, when Europeans first strongly experienced the presence of the US in terms of its superiority. That situation gave rise to a critical, self-reflexive discourse on the modernity of Europe (see Wagner 1999). But for current purposes I want to demonstrate, using four examples, how such a structure in intellectual relations can be detected in the social and political sciences.

First, *individualist liberalism as a political philosophy* gradually emerged in Europe during the seventeenth and eighteenth centuries. It became inescapable with the American and French revolutions, the onset of political modernity, as one might say, although it was not then widely accepted as a political philosophy. It began to flourish in political theory at American and at some British universities after the Second World War, and some time later John Rawls' *A Theory of Justice* (1971) became the landmark publication in the field. Since then, individualist liberalism has become the pivotal approach to political theory. The current situation can be described in an anecdote. Some years ago, an English philosopher, who specialized in so-called Continental Philosophy, went to Frankfurt on a Humboldt Foundation scholarship, hoping to live and work for a while in the Frankfurt School milieu. All he found, he reported, was discussion about Rawls and Michael Walzer and the dispute between liberals and communitarians.

Second, *rational choice* theorists do not normally endow their approach with a long history. In their view it began only in the middle of the twentieth century. However, a lineage can easily be traced back to Hobbes, which then leads to Condorcet and some other Enlightenment thinkers. Through political economy, the approach receives a clear place in moral philosophy, as well as an objective, i.e., an increase in the wealth of nations. Thus, it addresses issues of a theory of social order and of distributive justice at the same time. Modified and formalized in the neoclassical mode of economics, which emerged from the marginalist revolution in the late nineteenth century, it acquires the potential to become a *general theory of action*, a potential that is realized after the Second World War. This thinking is now widespread across the globe and across the disciplines of the social sciences, but nowhere as strongly as in the US.

Third, explicit moves towards *quantification as a methodology* in philosophy and the social sciences are normally dated to the seventeenth century and to political arithmetic in England and France, which worked with state-provided data. Statistics became a more refined and reflected tool in the late nineteenth and early twentieth centuries. But the key social scientist to mention in this context is a young Austrian socialist and mathematician, who tried to put his skills to good use in the socialist-led city administration of 'Red Vienna' after the First World War. He was Paul Felix Lazarsfeld, who later went into exile in the USA, where he founded the Bureau for Applied Social Research at Columbia University. After the Second World War, he was probably the leading methodologist in American social science.

Fourth, social scientists today naturally think about their fields of enquiry in terms of *disciplinary organization and professionalization*. There are, however, many ways of dividing up the modes to study the social world. The major social-science perspectives, such as the economic, sociological, cultural or statistical, were all well developed at the end of the nineteenth century. But in Europe they mostly did not give rise at that time to separated disciplines and professions with well-demarcated fields and boundaries. Current thinking about the disciplines of the social sciences is often based on a view that takes their American history as the model. In the US, a non-disciplinary, quite amateurish and politically oriented American Social Science Association (ASSA), which was founded in 1865, came under increasing pressure towards the end of the nineteenth century to develop a proper scientific and professional statute. Since it proved unable to reform itself, disciplinary associations were formed one after the other by breaking away from the ASSA, following the example set by the American Historical Association (AHA) in 1884. Thus, the American Economic Association (AEA), founded in 1885, the American Political Science Association (APSA), founded in 1903, and the American Society for Sociology (ASS, now the ASA), which split off from the AEA, were formed, providing by the beginning of this century the ideal picture of social-science disciplines that is still familiar today (Manicas 1987). Under the guidance of UNESCO, this model was globalized after the Second World War, not least by founding the international associations such as the International Sociological Association (ISA) and the International Political Science Association (IPSA).

Even in the absence of a comprehensive comparative study, few would contradict the statement that these four approaches and orientations are more widespread in the American than in the European social and political sciences. Rather than the comparative observation, however, another question is of significance here: how could the recent versions of these approaches make a claim to intellectual superiority with regard to the broader traditions from which they have emerged – that is, the superiority of the younger brother over the elder one? There is an asymmetry in the current intellectual constellation that is worth exploring because it provides the ground for thinking about empire.

It is not difficult to find explicit claims to such superiority in the approaches just described. One example from political philosophy may suffice to illustrate the nature of the claim. Speaking about some version of liberalism in terms of 'the growth of freedom' and 'the rise of liberal institutions and customs', an American philosopher recently claimed that 'Western social and political thought may have had the last conceptual revolution it needs'. One would think that this statement contains far too much vulgar philosophy of history to be seriously sustained at the end of the twentieth century. But the author was not Francis Fukuyama, it was Richard Rorty (1989: 63). This statement, just like any other claim to superiority, did not go uncontested and I do not want to move to a refutation now (although I will take steps towards it in the next part of this chapter). A particular vision of modernity is embedded in those approaches and it is first necessary to understand how this vision has come to be seen as unsurpassable.

The four approaches to the social and political sciences described above radicalize the modern orientation, the dual commitment of human beings to autonomy and mastery. As far as the organizational and methodological models – institutionalization of social sciences and quantitative research – are concerned, their ambition to order and master the world is rather straightforward. For the two theoretical approaches – the political philosophy and the theory of action – the relation between autonomy and mastery is more complex. Both individualist liberalism and individualist rationalism are theories of freedom, but they conceptualize freedom in a very particular way. Their specificity is to start out from the singular human being, defined as an individual, devoid of any specificity, rather than from social relations or from any form of collectivity of humans. From this starting point, they devise a relation of such an individual to the world in terms of instrumental or procedural rationality. They can hardly do otherwise, since all substantive features of social life were eliminated in their conceptualization of the individual.

This is a very specific interpretation of autonomy and mastery – autonomy as individual and mastery as instrumental. It is a somewhat dogmatic rendering of what modernity is about. That is why I prefer to call those approaches 'modernist' rather than just 'modern'. What this approach claims to accomplish is this: it removes all contaminations of history and sociality from analysis and so creates a distance from context and situation that is, so the argument goes, required for social and political theorizing.[6] In other words, modernism claims to create a purity that underpins universality (or, at least, 'universalizability'). By virtue of this move, it pushes everything else – the approaches of its critics – into the realm of the specific, the particular, or even, when a direction of history is implied, of a remnant of tradition. In this regard it is therefore different from all other approaches to understanding the social world. Even though, on account of such striving for purity, the superiority of this 'younger brother' may be questioned on good grounds (as we aim to do below), it is true that this move created an asymmetrical relationship between the 'brothers', the fact of which provided the grounds for an imperial claim.

Clearly, such a claim to hegemony cannot be accepted; its forceful existence, however, brings about a need to interpret its basis, although in other terms. To at least indicate the direction in which such an interpretation needs to go, Rémi Brague's *Europe, la voie romaine* (1999 [1992]) can be helpful, not least because it discusses the specificity of Europe by means of a related image of twinness. If the search for identity is a search for sources, for origins, Brague argues, it is characteristic for Europe to find its sources outside itself, to find itself secondary to something that it is not. If in cultural-religious terms Europe is predominantly Christian, we need to add that Christianity is historically secondary to Judaism. If in philosophical-political-institutional terms Europe draws on the heritage of the Roman Republic, we need to note that this republic derived its inspiration from the Greek polis and is secondary to it.

Brague's conclusion is that it is this 'secondarity' – the tension between the one and the other source (in both respects) – that provides for the specificity of Europe. This 'secondarity' gave Europe its historical dynamism, the searching and self-questioning nature of its philosophical and political life. A full appreciation of such a reading of Europe's intellectual history would require a detailed discussion for which there is no space here (and which would need to include a critique of Brague's emphasis on Roman Christianity). For the present purpose, I shall just suggest that European modernity may have created anew the tension between 'modernism' and its critics in political philosophy and in social theory and that this tension can to some extent – with all due caution, which also needs to be applied to Brague – be mapped onto the existing social

---

6 As will be shown in the second step of my argument, below, this emptying out of substantive concerns by conceptual means is seen as the core problem, rather than the main solution, in theorizing the modern polity.

world as 'America' and as 'Europe' (in the form of a geo-philosophy of 'the West', to employ and modify the term coined by Massimo Cacciari [1994]).

In this sense, the approaches briefly discussed above are expressions of the search for an identity of modernity, for the specifically modern solutions to socio-political *problématiques*. The quest for purity, as just discussed, can be understood as the search for the specificity of modernity, which, in the view of modernism, would generally and, thus, universally be found wherever the socio-political world turns modern. Such striving for purity, however, seems both necessary and futile.

The striving is necessary because its 'method' (to use the term broadly) of distancing from the context provides the intellectual means to deal with problematic historical situations. Thus, liberalism was originally developed to deal with religious wars and revolutions and with the diversity of human strivings that thus became politically visible. Individualist rationalism provided ways of dealing with the emergence of an industrial-capitalist mode of production and with 'the social question'. Quantification was developed as a means for dealing with the novel issues emerging with mass-democratic societies and welfare states. Clear-cut and coherent institutionalization of social-science disciplines reflects the quest for a well-ordered society, matched by a well-ordered set of knowledge forms.

But such striving is also futile, because these approaches (to political philosophy, social theory, methodology and institutionalization) do not provide self-sufficient modes of analysing the social world – self-sufficient in the sense of proceeding without regard for context or situation. Such striving means the attempt to overcome 'secondarity', and the tensions and ambiguities that come with it. But if it could succeed, the elimination of those tensions would do away with that which generates creativity and plurality in the interpretative struggles over what modernity is about. By implication, such a move would distance the others who do not follow it, treat them as 'less advanced' (as the elder, European, brother treated those whom he colonized during his age of colonization). It would signify an attempt to dominate the elder brother.[7]

By contrast, the space of reasoning that opens up between the purity of imperial modernism and its critics is of interest. This space provides the interpretative possibility to think of varieties of modernity as varieties of conceptualizing autonomy and mastery and of their relationship with each other. Then the relationship between America and Europe – and their respective social

---

7 And the elder brother, in turn, would resort to the counter-argument that these elaborations, while having sound roots, have gone too far, have mis-developed. That was the structure of the European argument towards America during the interwar period.

and political sciences – would not be the relationship of a younger, more energetic modernity that has outperformed the older one, but that of one interpretation of modernity to others – and yet others, outside the so-called West. Since the individual, seen as an atom linked to other human beings only through instrumental rationality, is at the centre of imperial modernism, I shall in a second step explore the consequences of the rise of this mode of thinking for political philosophy and in particular for the question of the common that is at the core of all things political.

Freedom and the Common: Rethinking Modernity Beyond Imperial Modernism

Under the impact of contemporary imperial modernism, the history of political philosophy is sometimes read in terms of a gradual but irresistible rise of individualist liberalism. Individualism and, increasingly, individualist liberalism, experienced renewed breakthroughs after major socio-political transformations, such as the end of the religious wars, the French Revolution and the rise of capitalism, and the end of totalitarianism. Such historical experiences seemed to strongly suggest that rights-based individualism was the only viable basis for political theory. In the aftermath of totalitarianism, for instance, versions of individualism have dominated the scene, reaching from Isaiah Berlin's (1969) famous defence of 'negative liberty' to John Rawls' (1971) individualist reasoning for limited policies of redistribution. To speak loosely, one could suggest that wars and revolutions were so destructive – or, at least, transformative – of the social bond that in their aftermath doubts were raised about the possibility of strong substantive ties between human beings that could sustain a sense of the common.

When, some two decades ago, communitarianism was proposed in the US as a response to this dominance, it provided the historically weakest argument ever in defence of holist and/or collectivist views of the social and political world – 'weak' in the sense of having most of all accepted the rise of individualism as at least a historical fact and context, or even as theoretically unavoidable. The European intellectual traditions of political Catholicism, nationalism, socialism and communism had all given stronger grounds for a 'thick' political life, or, we may say, they have upheld a strong conception of the common. With the partial exception of Catholicism, however, they all appeared rather discredited after the end of the Second World War and more so after the demise of Soviet socialism.

However, there are reasons to argue that individualist liberalism is insufficient in *theoretical* terms, because it lacks criteria for determining what members of the polity have in common, while necessarily remaining interested in the question. In the face of that absence it tends to resort to a concept of reason – a term meant to close an aporia far more than accept it – which tends to be interpreted as instrumental rationality. Furthermore, in terms of *political* experience, individualist liberalism tends to combine two potentially dangerous effects. Given that in this view the protection of negative liberty is all that the polity is about, it tends to withdraw political energy from the effort of determining what members of a polity have in common, thus mirroring the theoretical insufficiency in political life. The dedication to private affairs, which it encourages, is not problematic in itself, but under conditions of extended market relations it may be steadily transforming the world, thus increasing the worldlessness that further undermines action in common (see Wagner 2005c for an extended version of this argument).

Persistent criticism along both of these lines has made the debate between individualist liberalism and its critics continue, even though the former seems to become ever more dominant. At the same time, little advance can be noticed in this debate: the individualist-liberal tradition, defined most clearly by Locke and Kant, found its strongest contemporary representation in John Rawls' *Theory of Justice* in 1971. The first strong response that emerged historically towards this tradition, while accepting the idea of individual freedom, is Hegel's; and it has been taken up in our time by, among others, Charles Taylor in his *Hegel* and in *Hegel and Modern Society* during the 1970s. Across this period of more than two centuries, the basic constellation seems to have remained the same. Individualist liberalism is unable to develop an adequate concept of the common, but its alternatives, as will be shown in a brief reconstruction below, either entertain overly strong and thus normatively problematic conceptions of the common, risking violation of the commitment to personal freedom, or their concept of the common is too weak to sustain the self-understanding of a polity.

The question, then, is how to retrieve a concept of *the common* that goes beyond individualist liberalism but fully sustains the normative ideas of *personal as well as political freedom*. A retrieval is possible in principle by virtue of the fact that European political thinking, from its Greek origins, to republicanism and Romanticism, to critical theory and phenomenology, has often worked with rich conceptual registers that escaped the theoretical choice between the abstract freedom of individualism and the pre-definition of the range of permissible freedoms by a strong community. However, as political philosophy is itself a historical activity, the reworking of such intellectual traditions needs to live up to the demands of its time and to develop its perspectives on current political restructuring under conditions of so-called globalization and, intellectually speaking, imperial modernism.

Historically, one can observe two major ways of criticizing the individualist-liberal position: on the one hand, the claim was made that human beings forge strong links with each other before they enter into interaction as individuals in polity and society. Such attempts to theorize what may be termed *pre-political* bonds all start out from the critical observation that the human being who enters into political relations is not the kind of individual described by liberal political theory, and that the hypothesis of any original position would lead to serious flaws in the conclusions. This thinking emphasizes the rootedness of singular human beings in *contexts* from which stem their ways of giving *meaning* to the world. The broadest intellectual movement of this kind has been the *cultural-linguistic theory* of the boundaries of the polity, whose most significant representative is Herder, and which inaugurated culturalist thinking in the social sciences and also became one source of later nationalism. However, the contexts need not necessarily be defined in strong collectivistic terms. They can also be conceptualized as modes of *intersubjectivity* emerging from ideas of *primary sociality* and *interaction*, such as those in the early works of Hegel (for recent appropriations, see the work of Axel Honneth and Charles Taylor, for instance), or they can start out from an original condition of *being-in-the world* and of *being-with*, as developed by Martin Heidegger and his followers (for recent examples, see the work of Jean-Luc Nancy [1991] and the chapter by Angelos Mouzakitis in this volume). In both cases, though, such alternative assumptions do not lead as directly to ideas about the form of the polity as do collectivistic theories.

The other main line of socio-political thought started out from two major insights. The first is that once the basic individualist-liberal assumptions were cast into effective rules they would have durable and important *effects* on what social scientists would soon call the 'structure' of social bonds. In this sense we can consider those bonds as being conceived of as *post-political*. The second is that the question of such bonds was forced onto the agenda of social and political thought by virtue of the fact that the liberal assumptions on their own did not suffice to create and justify a political order (see Karagiannis in Chapter 8 in this volume). The observation of structures of representation was used to enhance stability and certainty in political procedures that otherwise could appear to be opened to all contingencies by the commitment to freedom and by the abolition of any legitimacy of preordained orders. There are then two main strategies for rediscovering certainties, systematic observation and reflective conceptual-ization. These two intellectual responses to the political *problématique* inaugurate three well-known modes of social theorizing: the *behaviouralist*, based on observation; and the *critical* and the *structural-functional* modes, both based on a social-interest theory of representation. The last two modes do not make individualistic assumptions, but aim at grounding socio-political life in purely social forms.

The critique of liberalism that focuses on pre-political human bonds has often been seen as politically right wing because it appears to rely conceptually on some notion of tradition and politically to want to uphold such a tradition, a position that literally appears conservative (but see Mouzakitis on Gadamer in Chapter 12). The alternative critique, which focuses on post-political social structures, has tended to be seen as left wing, because it often diagnoses problematic social results of the application of liberalism, not least in the version of market liberalism, and aims at remedying those problems by resorting to some form of collective intervention. With regard to this last critique, the intellectual distinction between mainstream social science and critical theories appears to resonate with the political distinction between reformist and revolutionary approaches.

More recently, however, such social-science thinking in both its main versions has come under strong attack, mostly because of its inherent determinism. Determined outcomes can only result from planned or routine activities – work and labour in Hannah Arendt's (1958) terminology – over which certainty can be established before they are started. In contrast, political action in a context of liberty must go along with contingency of outcome. From an Arendtian viewpoint, therefore, social science establishes an impossible connection. In their efforts to identify laws and regularities of human action and societal development, the social sciences necessarily abandoned the heritage of political philosophy, the emphasis on creative agency, irreducible diversity and the permanent possibility of unpredictable beginnings. From such viewpoints, there were no worlds to be made. The world as it existed determined what human beings would think and do.

It is in the light of such considerations that the closing decades of the twentieth century have witnessed a revival of political philosophies of freedom, many of which go beyond concepts of liberty as held in individualist-liberal political theory. These works, by authors such as Claude Lefort (1999), Pierre Manent (1995, 2001) or, more historically oriented, Quentin Skinner are not merely contributions to political philosophy or its history. Rather, they challenge the very separation of the social sciences from political philosophy. In their best versions, they offer elements of a retrieval of the relation between freedom and the common from the history of political philosophy, and they aim at recasting the issue in the light of our present society and the experiences it made with the relation between freedom and the common.

Highly valid though the critique of the social sciences from such a perspective may be, however, the mere return to political philosophy is no solution to the issues that are raised. Many of the contributions to the current debate fail to address the reasons for the historical decline of political philosophy and the concomitant rise of the social sciences. And those that do most often conclude with a normative rejection of the 'invention of the social' (Donzelot 1984) because of the implied move towards the 'administration of the social' (Arendt 1958), but without fully appreciating the ways in which politics were transformed in response to actually problematic situations rather than merely because of misconceptions of the political. What is needed, however, is a reconstruction of the historical separation of the political from the social with a view to the specific conceptions of the political and of the social bond (for more detail, see Karagiannis and Wagner 2005).

Any critical account of intellectual history will need to agree that some notion of equal liberty became central to political thought, and this for good normative reasons. If one immediately concludes from this observation that individualist liberalism is central to European (and North American) history of the past two centuries, however, one overlooks the openness of the assumption of equal liberty to a variety of interpretations. Dispute over the justification of a good polity does not stop at this point; rather, it is its starting point. In my reconstruction above, this assumption is also at the core of individualist liberalism, which, however, is not seen as straightforwardly hegemonic on normative grounds, but rather as the pivotal theory of political modernity in the sense that all other political philosophies need to relate to it. If such a position of individualist liberalism is accepted as in some way unavoidable, there are at least three ways to deal with this approach.

First, one can take individualist liberalism as self-sufficient for the normative underpinning of 'modern societies'. All one needs to posit is the equal freedom of rights-endowed human beings, and everything else can be left to the use of the liberties by those human beings. To this position, which is a central element of imperial modernism, applies the critique that was stated above: individualist liberalism conceives of only a thin political bond between human beings, and of no social bond of any interest at all.

Second, one can respond to the desire to know more about the bases on which humans interact by observing and conceptualizing their modes of interaction with various auxiliary means. This is the way the social sciences went, and it has been accused of socially over-determining human life. It works with a strong conception of the social bond, or rather with a variety of such conceptions, and it has largely forgotten about the political question that stood at its origins, because the assumptions about the social bond already provide an answer to the question of the common.

Third, one can argue that equal liberty is only the starting point for reasoning about a political modernity that is furthermore characterized by the communicative interaction between human beings with a view to determining what they need to regulate in common and how they should go about it. This is the republican position that has largely been found, even while attractive, implausible and unsustainable under conditions of large societies with complex forms of interaction. It works with a strong assumption about political bonds being woven and constantly rewoven in human interaction, but it says little to nothing about the nature of those bonds. It can be combined with 'open' conceptions of the social bond, as expressed in concepts such as primary sociality, inter-subjectivity or being-in-the-world/being-with. However, one needs to insist that such concepts should not be enriched with strong substantive meaning. Otherwise, as history has shown, the thinking of philosophers such as Herder, Hegel and Heidegger has lent itself to providing normatively problematic conceptions of the common.

Instead, to become of use for political analysis and for a diagnosis of society, the – broadly conceived – republican political philosophy needs to be underpinned by an analysis of the state of social bonds, not via an objectivist social science or an empty theory of rational communication, but through an investigation of the ways in which justifications for political decisions are provided for matters under dispute in given societal situations.

Situating Political Modernity: Europe in Context

Under conditions of political modernity, the rules of political life are always in need of justification, or, more broadly, they can be exposed to the requirement of justification. If this exigency, which has been emphasized in the work of Luc Boltanski and Laurent Thévenot (1991), for instance, is interpreted within the framework of a comprehensive political sociology, an analysis of justifications allows for substantive assumptions the application of which determines the outcome of interactions and the positions of human beings in society. In this sense it operates in social science mode. But it also holds that the application of such assumptions is itself a possible concern in terms of dispute and interpretation, thus requiring the kind of communicative deliberation that is in the centre of republican political philosophy. Thus, there is a possible theoretical position that reintegrates what was separated in the intellectual history of the past two centuries: the conceptualization of the political and of the social.

Historically existing polities can then be interpreted as institutionalized compromises of a variety of basic modes of justification. Individualist liberalism can be recognized as providing and sustaining the assumption of common humanity and, as a consequence, of equal liberty. It thus provides the background and also creates the basic *problématique* against which the other modes of justification are being deployed – but nothing more than that. It indeed

261

allows the issue of the constitution of a polity to be seen as a political one, as the foundation of basic agreement under conditions of liberty. The conceptual separation of the political bond from other bonds between human beings is the consequence of the rise of individualist liberalism as the pivotal philosophy of political modernity: first the call for freedom from non-legitimized intervention into personal lives, and second the call for collective self-determination against the reign of autocratic rulers, were grounded on an abstract conception of the individual and the collectivity with a view to elaborating a general, universalist claim beyond the specificity of the given situation.[8]

While such a normative-conceptual move can be understood against the background of the European historical experience of resistance against illegitimate domination, individualist liberalism proved, for the same reason of abstraction from context, to be insufficient and unsatisfactory as the guiding political philosophy of modernity whenever polities were to be founded. Political deliberation does not occur under a 'veil of ignorance', and a political theory that aims to address constitutional matters in the process of founding and refounding polities needs to provide tools to understand and conceptualize the positions from which political actors reason (see Chakrabarty in Chapter 6 in this volume for a discussion of meanings of the political under different conditions).

Assumptions about the social bond – such as the cultural-linguistic assumption or the structural-functional assumption – then stepped in to deal with the *problématique* thus created. These are not just social theories; they support repertoires of justification of immediate political relevance. They may be used to determine, as a matter of principle, whether a human being is a member of one polity rather than another, and her/his place within that polity. However, observations on cultural, economic and social relations should not be seen as providing an answer to the political *problématique* of human life, but rather as raising questions. Similarly, political theory should not fall into cultural, economic and/or social determinism, as much of political thinking did during the nineteenth and twentieth century, in response to the abstraction from any cultural, economic and social bonds that characterizes individualist liberalism. Conceptually speaking, the response to this double challenge – individualist abstraction versus social determination – lies in seeing observations on such bonds, or on cleavages and boundaries, as resources in political reasoning that can and should be brought in as arguments in favour of some institution or policy over another: they do not have compelling power on their own, but are in need of justification under conditions of a possible plurality of modes of justification.

---

8   For a critical history of (individualist) liberalism, see Manent 1995 [1987]; see also Manent 2001: Chapter 10; and Esposito 1998.

The question, then, is how political dispute can be adjudicated under such conditions of plurality. The answer cannot but be twofold. First, there is no solution to political dispute offered by political theory alone, because the universalist theoretical claims that can be made are insufficiently concrete to guide institutional design or policy-making. They are in need of specific interpretation. Second, saying this does not, however, amount to arguing that those claims are invalid. They have to be confronted with the situation in which policy deliberation takes place. And this situation is defined by two basic components: the problem of the moment that gives rise to deliberation in the first place; and the resources that political actors bring into this moment, based on their observation of the cultural, economic and social bonds and cleavages. The struggles about European political modernity across history therefore need to be interpreted with a view to grasping how the self-understanding of a modern polity evolved and changed through all of these features: by developing core universalist elements of a political philosophy of modernity; by experiencing changing problematic constellations that needed to be dealt with in common; and by elaborating a rich range of resources to guide the situation-specific interpretation of such philosophy with a view to solving those political issues.

Imperial modernism denies these questions any relevance, claiming that there is a singular – individualist-instrumentalist – interpretation of political modernity that, once identified and developed, can be applied and exported in any conceivable situation. That this is wrong not only in terms of political thinking but also in political history is evident at the moment, with disastrous consequences, in Iraq.[9] Political developments in Europe, slow and hesitant about their proper direction though they may be, exemplify the counter-claim, aiming at creating and instituting an alternative interpretation of political modernity based on a more elaborate balance of the exigencies for personal and collective freedom, at the same time making the broader case – which is of global significance – that more than one interpretation of modernity can be sustained.

While there is still some hope for success in the elaboration and construction of such an alternative in Europe, the struggle still suffers from the claim to superiority that the younger brother keeps making. The hesitations in the European developments could possibly be diminished if sustained intellectual efforts were made to oppose this claim to superiority. The two steps of the above reasoning were intended as contributions to such an effort.

---

9 There seems little doubt that the Anglo-American war in Iraq is also an example of robber capitalism aiming at accumulation by violent means. However, the justification it is endowed with by its commanders, with its emphasis on human rights and democracy, is an application of imperial modernism. As such it has created considerable havoc in political and intellectual debates in Europe and North America.

References

Arendt, Hannah, 1958, *The Human Condition*, Chicago, University of Chicago Press.

Berlin, Isaiah, 1969, 'Two Concepts of Liberty', in *Four Essays on Liberty*, Oxford, Oxford University Press.

Boltanski, Luc, and Laurent Thévenot, 1991, *De la justification*, Paris, Gallimard.

Brague, Rémi, 1999 [1992], *Europe, la voie romaine*, 1st edn, Paris, Gallimard.

Cacciari, Massimo, 1994, *Geofilosofia dell'Europa*, Milan, Adelphi.

Castoriadis, Cornelius, 1990, 'Pouvoir, politique, autonomie', in *Le monde morcelé. Les carrefours du labyrinthe III*, Paris, Seuil, 113–39.

Dahrendorf, Ralf, 2001, 'L'Europa unita, ultima utopia', *La repubblica*, September 5.

Donzelot, Jacques, 1984, *L'invention du social. Essai sur le déclin des passions politiques*, Paris, Fayard.

Esposito, Robert, 1998, *Communitas. Origine e destino della comunità*, Turin, Einaudi.

Ginzburg, Carlo, 1998, 'Un lapsus di papa Wojtyla', in *Occhiacci di legno. Nove riflessioni sulla distanza*, Milan, Feltrinelli, 210–15, first published in *La Repubblica*, October 8 and 9 1997.

Habermas, Jürgen, 2001 [1998], 'The Postnational Constellation and the Future of Democracy', in *The Postnational Constellation*, Cambridge, Polity, 58–112.

Hardt, Michael, and Antonio Negri, 2000, *Empire*, Cambridge, MA, Harvard University Press.

Karagiannis, Nathalie, 2004, *Avoiding Responsibility, The Politics and Discourse of European Development Policy*, London, Pluto.

Karagiannis, Nathalie, and Peter Wagner, 2005, 'Towards a Theory of Synagonism', *Journal of Political Philosophy*, 13(3).

Lamont, Michèle, and Laurent Thévenot (eds), 2000, *Rethinking Comparative Cultural Sociology. Polities and Repertoires of Evaluation in France and the United States*, New York, Cambridge University Press.

Lefort, Claude, 1999, *La complication. Retour sur le communisme*, Paris, Fayard.

Manent, Pierre, 1995 [1987], *An Intellectual History of Liberalism*, Princeton, NJ, Princeton University Press.

— 2001, *Cours familier de philosophie politique*, Paris, Fayard.

Manicas, Peter T., 1987, *A History and Philosophy of the Social Sciences*, Oxford, Blackwell.

Mann, Michael, 2003, *Incoherent Empire*, London, Verso.

Nancy, Jean-Luc, 1991, *The Inoperative Community*, Minneapolis, MN, University of Minnesota Press.

Rawls, John, 1971, *A Theory of Justice*, Cambridge, MA, Belknap Press of Harvard University Press.

Rorty, Richard, 1989, *Contingency, Irony, Solidarity*, Cambridge, Cambridge University Press.

Taylor, Charles, 1989, *Sources of the Self*, Cambridge, Cambridge University Press.

Wagner, Peter, 1994, *A Sociology of Modernity. Liberty and Discipline*, London, Routledge.

— 1999, 'The Resistance that Modernity Constantly Provokes. Europe, America and Social Theory', *Thesis Eleven*, 58, 39–63.

— 2001a, *Theorizing Modernity*, London, Sage.

— 2001b, 'Modernity, History of the Concept', in Paul Baltes and Neil Smelser (eds), *The International Encyclopedia of the Social and Behavioral Sciences*, Oxford, Pergamon.

— 2005a, 'Social Theory and Political Philosophy', in Gerard Delanty (ed.), *The Routledge Handbook of Contemporary European Social Theory*, London, Routledge.

— 2005b, 'The Political Form of Europe – Europe as a Political Form', *Thesis Eleven*, 80, 45–73.

— 2005c, 'The problématique of Economic Modernity', in Christian Joerges, Bo Strath and Peter Wagner (eds), *Economy as a Polity*, London, University College London Press.

CHAPTER 14

Global Governance and the Emergence of a 'World Society'

Friedrich Kratochwil

That nations dwell in eternal anarchy has been one of the defining assumptions that have shaped the socialization of several generations of students of international relations. While political struggle inside the state takes place in the shadow of the law (conceived as the sovereign's command), this mediation was thought to be absent in the international arena. However, the demise of the Soviet Union and the increase in the volume, scope and speed of transnational interactions challenged this traditional assumption of anarchy and non-co-operation. Departing from the presumption that war was now a less plausible defining characteristic of the international arena, and the subsequent subversion of the foundational distinction between 'internal' and 'external' arenas, it was naturally tempting to conceive of these fundamental changes as constituting a transformation of the international system into a global or 'world society'. This chapter will consider to what extent this argument is valid.

Several strands of argument converged to produce this new 'synthesis' of global change. First, so successful was realism's imposition of its own conception of the world system that, when the premises of anarchy were called into question, it seemed that no other vocabulary was as readily available as that of a 'society'. Second, the failure of socialism seemed to prove the impossibility of an alternative to the liberal political project and thus suggested the 'end of history'. Third, the 'sociological' vocabulary also pointed to a way out of the conceptual impasses of earlier debates, in which states were conceived of not only as rigid billiard balls but also as 'containers' for their respective societies. The focus on complex networks of policy-making, rather than clearly defined central decision-making centres, was thought to provide a more accurate picture of these processes in the internal and the international arenas than when they were observed through the conceptual lenses of sovereignty and the autonomy of the 'state'. Finally, it seemed possible to distinguish between government and the broader notion of 'governance', the former being only one specific historical form of the latter.

However, this sociological vocabulary masks some deeper conceptual problems. Issues of reference and self-reference are crucial in the discourse of 'society', since the meaning of terms in political and social discourses is derived from their relationship to other terms – to 'the state', for example, or the public, citizenship and participation – rather than from some 'correspondence' between a concept and the phenomenon thereby named. Precisely because 'constitutive' issues and explanations are thereby raised, their clarification cannot be reduced to empirical observations of the workings of dependent and independent variables in a causal pattern, or to a harder look at the 'facts'.

Thus a type of critical analysis becomes necessary that rests on conceptual clarification and the satisfaction of historical contextual criteria, rather than on the collection of further 'confirming' evidence or instances of refutation. As is the case with any analogy, the validity of the conceptualization – of the state as a 'contract', for example – depends on the similarity of certain relationships among the crucial concepts, and not on the discovery of some similarities through a point by point comparison. In other words, to find a similarity between A and B in two different domains is not enough to establish validation; what is required is to discover a similar *relationship* between A and B: as A : B, so C : D. This logical requirement points to the importance of the historical context. We have to understand the 'puzzles', of which the analogy is part, and which issues are thereby brought to the fore and which ones recede into the background. To that extent, the 'social contract' (and its distinction between 'society' and the 'state') arose from the dissolution of the estates society, in which 'rule' (*dominium*) was shared and 'belonged' to individuals as members of a certain status; now what was emphasized was the impersonal nature of the public order. It is also clear that the shift from the master metaphor of a 'body politic' to the metaphor of a contract cannot be understood as having reached greater descriptive 'accuracy' or fit with social reality (because a state is neither a 'body' nor a simple 'contract'). The new metaphor is part of a different political project, in which the nature of the association and the nature of 'rule' are fundamentally altered.

One could now argue that exactly the same conceptual moves are now under way when we consider the emergence of a global society. The first conceptual move implies, therefore, the severance of the notion of a 'society' from that of a state in order to allow for its reconstruction at a higher level. Here, the forces of globalization are invoked as having undermined the close connection between the territorial state and the existing political community. This move paves the way for the argument that for (democratic) rule to be effective, a 'cosmopolitan community' has to be established.[1] The opposition of state and society is thus transferred from the national to the global scale, whereby a differentiation between the steering or 'governing' and society (which has historically occurred through the formation of the state) is awaited: this is the cosmopolitan project. However, the problem with the analogy is that there is neither a world state in the offing, nor is there much evidence that the 'local' identifications of historical communities have lost their significance in practical life, as advocates of cosmopolitanism suggest.

As Hobbes pointed out, the 'state of nature' at the international level need not give rise to a Super-Leviathan, because the possibility of collective defence by the organized community alleviates the security dilemma considerably and thereby undermines the 'necessity' for a global government. But if no world state is necessary or likely to develop, it is unlikely that a world society will emerge. The issue is not only how the 'unity' or the horizon within which the interactions of states take place has to be thought of – typically as a 'system' or a community of a special kind such as a 'republic', or a 'society' of states – but also how a 'thicker' institutionalization of this particular common horizon can be achieved, even though its experience is (still) mediated by identifications with more circumscribed communities. After all, the state remains deeply ingrained in most of our political and social practices. It is the ever-present 'third person' Hobbes discerned in all bilateral transactions among the members of a society,[2] while no such systematic presence seems accorded in our political life to cosmopolitan concerns.[3] We see instead a variety of trends: the decay of the state and rule by intermediaries, as in many regions of Africa and the former Soviet empire, and a new type of 'sub' politics that not only involves a 'renaissance of political

---

1 In this context, see the arguments by Held (1998) and Linklater (1998).
2 Usually, we restrict this presence of the sovereign to the sanctions that are part of the legal order and that allow not only for the punishment of lawbreakers, but also the prospective ordering of a society in the 'shadow of the law'. Conceptually even more important is the fact that certain of our moral evaluations are deeply embedded in the institutional order of the state. Consider in this context the problem of corruption. That we expect from a public official a 'neutral' performance of his duties – instead of paying back his family or clan who enabled him to study, for example, and thus gain office – is the outcome of a 'conceptual revolution' into which we have all been socialized: that 'traditional' loyalties and personal ties have no place in the public realm.
3 It seems that only Martin Albrow suggests this 'global presence' by pointing out that all types of people and groups derive their ideas and values, as well as their identity, increasingly from global contexts and problems and no longer from nationally constituted communities. See Albrow (1996).

subjectivity' in the West, but also transforms traditional binding decisions on behalf of a community into 'options' for private individuals. This 'privatization' and the pervasive scepticism towards traditional structures and identities makes it difficult to interpret this new politics as the harbinger of a new form of global citizenship.[4] Finally, since even the most principled 'advocacy networks' have to pick and choose their fights carefully, their activities give rise to at best a spotty pattern in the pursuit of cosmopolitan concerns. Finally, the nature of public goods seems also relevant in this context. Consumption goods obviously invite transnational activity, and distributive goods might also spawn greater transnational activity, but when 'redistributive' public goods are at issue we seem trapped in classical national decision-making structures.

The concept of world society does not usually rely on a 'lowest common denominator' argument. Rather, as evinced by Meyer et al. (1997), it is a claim that an ensemble of cultural forms has become universal as part of a modernization process encompassing the whole globe and virtually all dimensions of social reproduction. However, even if it is true that the form of political associations, the enterprise of knowledge generation, family life, sexual practices and so forth have all been revolutionized, we still have to look at the practices that are informed by these forms but are hardly ever mere performances of a given script. Given the ample local variation and considerable blending of rather heterogeneous cultural forms that characterize the reproduction of the social world, a concept of a world society must identify two things if it is to help in the diagnosis of our present predicament. The first is *the important elements of the ongoing processes*, including the analysis of homogenization and the emergence of new patterns of differentiation – sometimes described problematically as the re-tribalization of primordial ties;[5] and the second, *the levers for action*, even if – or rather because – the 'projective' character of the term remains a part of its grammar.

The issues of discerning, defining and describing society emerge when we enquire into the understandings and practices of actors and of the 'boundaries', inclusions and exclusions that are always part of and form the background to our practices. They are also raised when we examine the increased density in scope and domain of boundary-transcending transactions and try to understand these processes within a larger whole, even if the actors themselves are not (or are only vaguely) aware of these influences. To that extent, the notion of a world society is a 'projection' of processes of transformative change that predates its actual emergence in the vocabulary of actors in the closing decades of the last

4 See, for example, the various formulations by Beck (1995, 1997).
5 See, for example, Barber (1995).

millennium. The term 'world society' ought not to be dismissed because of its 'fuzziness', because identical or quite similar problems will be encountered after substituting other terms – 'system' for 'society', for example, as in Wallerstein's approach, or after engaging once more in structural-functional analysis. Ultimately, the idea that the terms of political discourse function like 'labels' that more or less describe the elements of the social world rests on a mistaken assumption: that is, that we are dealing here with analogues to 'natural kinds' and that it is the 'fit' between concept and phenomenon that decides the question of truth and/or utility. However, while the notion of natural kinds is already highly contested and problematic in the sciences, the meaning of concepts in the social world is derived from their 'use', that is, what they do and how they function in practice, rather than what they designate. To that extent, these concepts are more like signals, telling us how to 'go on', rather than labels for things.

The most interesting question, therefore, is not whether a world society exists, but what the 'gap' between the practices and the vocabulary means, and what a critical reflection is able to disclose when we, because of this gap, can *no longer* 'go on'. To that extent, neither the projective anticipation of 'one world' as the last horizon of a common human consciousness, nor the processes of system integration and disintegration, are sufficient. Instead, we have to reflect critically on the links between these practices and their conceptualizations, without privileging either process, that is, viewing one as essentially determined by the other. Admittedly, this might not make for an analysis that satisfies or comes close to the ideal of a social 'science' that is concerned with the discovery of universal laws or constant causal mechanisms. Nevertheless, it might be all that we can do to capture the open-ended nature of mankind's 'history' and to provide a diagnostic for appraisal.

From these initial remarks the plan for this chapter can be discerned. The next part will be devoted to a discussion of global governance as it has emerged in debates over the claims of movements and international networks to be part of a newly emerging sphere – that is, a global civil society – and from the programmes and practices of international organizations. In the following, third part of the chapter, I attempt to show the paradoxes of global governance as a 'practice' that has replaced 'development', and to provide a preliminary assessment. The chapter concludes with a brief analysis of the 'diagnostic' limitations of this novel liberal universalism.

From Globalization to Global Governance

If one examines the discourse on globalization during the last two decades, one notices a decisive shift from a notion of an encompassing process that, like a tidal wave, casts aside anything in its way,[6] to a notion that emphasizes again the possibility of choice. For the latter, the rather amorphous notion of 'governance' becomes the dominant term of reference. Even in the industrialized world, the events of September 11 2001 shifted the emphasis away from earlier 'atopian' notions[7] of networks and exchanges, of transnationally organized movements and an emerging civil society, to an analysis of the 'performance' and (in)efficiency of intergovernmental networks – from courts to routinized police collaboration – and regulatory institutions[8] ensuring 'governmentality',[9] transparency and accountability. Instead of the former 'resistance' to globalization by societal groups and NGOs, their changing role as norm creators or service providers is now more often the focus.[10] Nevertheless, there seems to have emerged a substantive agreement on what 'globalization' is.

The most important element of the globalization discourse has been the nearly overwhelming recognition of change in all areas of social life. In fact, 'globalization' has become a container for various complex processes of transformative change. Although as such it cannot act or cause anything, it does become some 'actant', an acting unit, which is adduced to make the observed changes intelligible. Three specific aspects of change are associated with this sense of transformation. First, at the most basic level, there is the communications revolution engendered by digitalization and telematics (linking computers to new information networks[11]) that has resulted in the compression of time and space to an extent never before imagined. Without such a new way of handling information, the modern forms of 'flat' organizational structures, observable in many multinational corporations, just-in-time production and the global diversification of production and of products according to customer demand, could not be imagined.

6 For an interesting discussion of the imagery of 'globalization', see Mueller (2003).
7 This is the expression used by the German sociologist Willke (2001) in order to describe the non-localizable nature of modern interactions without attributing to them the 'non-existing' or imaginary nature that is part of the 'utopian' vocabulary.
8 In this context the notion of the 'internationalization of the state' has been used. See, for example, Wendt and Duvall (1989: Chapter 4).
9 I use here the Foucauldian notion that designates a particular form of power that is diffused throughout society but co-ordinated by a government that has disciplined society. Thus, in a way, although governments are no longer seen as an expression of the 'sovereign' facing the people or its subjects, but becoming themselves objects of scrutiny and assessment, they nevertheless reconstitute themselves as crucial nodal points for networks of control that transcend classical notions of the 'public' order, or of social control (discipline), or 'private' maximization strategies, exerting 'capillary control' rather than working on the basis of 'sanctions'. For a further discussion see, for example, Dean (1999).
10 On the role of private actors in world politics see, for example, the assessment by Hall and Biersteker (2002).
11 See, for example, Drake (1995).

Second, the development of financial markets and thus of credit creation on a global scale would not have been possible without the continuous and virtually frictionless linking of established financial markets into what is effectively a single institution operating on a twenty-four hour basis. This development, in turn, has raised two further problems. One concerns the explosive growth of financial transactions: for each dollar changing hands on the basis of trade, sixty are exchanged in financial transactions.[12] The other deals with the connection of markets and the rest of the political and social system; here 'liberalization' engendered a debate on the loss of 'steering capacity' by state institutions. Hence the fear that the classical welfare state is being undermined *from below* through its shrinking capacity to provide for 'redistributive public goods'[13] while it is also being hollowed out *from above*, since globalization has removed many policy issues from national institutions to international fora or bureaucracies (Zuern 1998).

The more sanguine view is that new forms of control and influence by the various stakeholders result in the internationalization of the state[14] which, in turn, makes its democratization necessary. The prospects for such developments are auspicious since the third process lumped together in the container 'globalization', namely, the circulation of ideas, has reached explosive proportions. Notions of individual rights, governmental accountability, minimum standards and so forth have not only been universally diffused, but also have acquired a virtually exclusive legitimacy in all societies.[15] Besides, as cultural optimists have suggested, new public spaces are likely to emerge that are no longer tied to territorially organized societies. Instead, common concerns are now founding new communities (Ekins 1992) existing in virtual space or linked transnationally through a network of 'movements'.[16] Thus, cosmopolitan ideals – until now limited perhaps to certain elite strata – appear in this interpretation as the logical conclusion of the democratic revolutions that formerly needed nationalism and the territorial state to integrate viable societies. However, nowadays looser but more complex formations typical of a global civil society might do (Falk 1998)[17] or, as James Rosenau has suggested, global civil

---

12 See, for example, Strange (1998).
13 See the discussion by Cerny (1995).
14 See, for example, Shaw (2000).
15 See here the importance accorded to norm entrepreneurs and the network in Keck and Sikkink (1998). See also Khagram et al. (2002).
16 See, for example, Tarrow (1998).
17 See also Kaldor (2003), who distinguishes between different types of movements that have emerged and different forms of civil society. Such a perspective contrasts sharply with one that is derived from notions of an empire in which a no longer identified 'multitude' takes over the empire from below (Hardt and Negri 2000).

society might become a 'functional equivalent' to the classical territorially defined democracy (Rosenau 1998: 41).

The *political project* associated with the issue of governance arose as the autonomy of these transformative forces was contested and the question of 'regulation' was raised. The identification of options for control and the search for levers for action marked the shift in focus from 'globalization' to 'governance'. Three factors have proved decisive in this shift. First, earlier claims about the inevitability and inexorability of globalization have been replaced by more fine-grained approaches. As the studies of Hirst and Thompson (1996) and Scharpf and Schmidt (2000) clearly indicate, choices and decisions are still available and they need to be made, even though, interestingly, the arena is no longer restricted to individual nation states alone. A second crucial factor has been the attempt to rescue both the failed states of the South, which experienced mass violence, and the 'transition states' of the former Soviet empire. The place for this debate has been the UN and the ever more complex missions of 'peacekeeping' and 'peacemaking' in which it has become involved. Here, 'governance' means, above all, a disciplining of state institutions – as long as they still function – through greater transparency and accountability. If state structures have ceased to work, alternative systems for the delivery of services and certain public goods such as health care, schooling and disaster relief must be established. NGOs have offered themselves as an alternative to the corrupt and inefficient delivery systems of states, and also serve as advocates for local, often silenced voices, which now can be heard because of their links to the internationally organized advocacy networks. As Paris (2002: 638) observes:

> Without exception peace-building missions in the post Cold War world have attempted to transplant the values and institutions of the liberal democratic core into the domestic affairs of peripheral host states … In this respect, the contemporary practice may be viewed as a modern rendering of the *mission civilisatrice* – the colonial era belief that the European powers had a duty to civilize their overseas possessions. Although modern peace-builders have largely abandoned the archaic language of civilized vs. uncivilized, they nevertheless appear to act upon the belief that one model of domestic governance – liberal market democracy – is superior to all others.

Here, two additional terms that are part of the governance discourse become important. One is the concept of 'transition'. It differs from earlier notions of political development because its broader scope for transformation includes institutions and practices in the public as well as the private realm. The other is 'transparency' (often meaning 'accountability' rather than merely the enhancement of visibility), which has become a major issue in social, political and economic realms, and which can also be fitted neatly under the term 'governance' when issues of *corporate governance* attain new salience. Thus 'governance' is reformist in a much wider sense than earlier attempts at establishing a functioning 'developmental state'. Its goal is not only the establishment of a viable democracy, but also human rights and a 'liberal market-economy', thereby subjecting large swathes of social and economic life to international scrutiny and discipline. Moreover, even though international governance programmes address mainly state institutions, the reforms rely for their legitimacy on arguments about the efficiency gains achieved by a 'lean' state, and on the disciplinary control of all aspects of social life through the creation of transparency, benchmarking and reporting. As politics is largely dissolved into *technique*, the problem of 'rule' (*dominium, Herrschaft*) is mystified, making it appear that it is all about 'rules' that either work by themselves – because they are 'clear' and 'precise' – or, if there is still the need for some form of 'direction' – politics consists in 'delegation'[18] to some form of dispute settlement 'mechanisms'. These range from the WTO to the ICJ, to the global 'network of courts'[19] or chambers of arbitration, so that the problem of the rule of law is 'operationalized', in a way, as rule by experts.

This 'removed' and neutral stance, however, hardly squares with the difficulties engendered by the complex problems of transitions, because the viability of local structures is decisive. Local knowledge therefore seems more important than expertise in, or familiarity with, procedures for 'helping' that have been developed in other contexts but are of little use, given local circumstances. Thus, a third factor accounting for the rise of a governance discourse is the result of the demise of development planning. The realization that projects based on the reigning orthodoxy had done little to achieve the goal of jump-starting economic development was sobering but incontrovertible. Feasibility studies notwithstanding, many grand projects of yesteryear, such as dams, turned out to be of dubious economic value, usually having quite a detrimental *environmental* impact, and leading to increasingly vocal and active local resistance. Likewise, the traditional structural adjustment loans of the IMF, which had already been connected with obtrusive interventionist policies of 'conditionality', did not prove effective. Despite the administration of many bitter pills, the IMF encountered again and again the problem of 'slippage': a noble circumlocution for the fact that the programme had failed to induce the changes thought to be necessary. Money disappeared into the coffers of local

---

18 Such an essentially misleading approach to law and its function in the (inter)national arena is exemplified by the work of Goldstein et al. (2000).
19 See, for example, Slaughter (2003).

'elites' and loans had to be rescheduled for political reasons. But neither the IMF nor the government could afford to admit failure. The government needed access to funds; the international financial institutions needed recognition of their expertise for legitimizing purposes. Mounting criticism of these practices finally led the World Bank to reconsider some of its programmes, introduce poverty reduction as an important objective, and institutionalize some form of 'dialogue' with local groups and transnational activist networks. Participation at both *planning* and *implementation* levels seemed to be a necessary, if not a sufficient, condition for success.

These ideas dovetail neatly with the argument that a global civil society is able to provide governance not only by outflanking the increasingly corrupt state structures but also by creating new forms of participatory politics and accountability. 'Governance' is seen as a new type of public management that increases accountability through local involvement and through the introduction of managerial and market-based methods into public service provision. Thus 'good governance' for the World Bank involves efficiency in public services, the rule of law with regard to contracts, an effective judiciary, respect for human rights, freedom of the press and a pluralistic social and institutional structure. These goals, in turn, require the marketization of public service, a reduction of public sector staffing, budgetary discipline, the decentralization of administration and the participation of local and transnational NGOs. The emerging structure is one of a network that straddles not only the classical boundary between the inside and the outside of the state but also the boundary between the public and the private realm.

The Paradoxes of 'Global Governance'

Strangely enough, little attention has been paid by the governance discourse to problems that arise from the multiplicity of goals that might work at cross-purposes, such as when an expansion of participation might make greater 'efficiency' a hard goal to achieve. Even more significant an oversight is the failure to take account of how the participation of elements from 'civil society', such as NGOs, in the governance project is affected by the introduction of 'market elements' – competitive tenders and short-term renewable contracts – for providing services in failed states or transitional countries. Competition in these contexts need not be a boon. With a plurality of bidders for the same project, there arises the 'multiple principals' problem of serving more than one master, while there can also be races to the bottom affecting the quality of services. Conversely, co-operation should not be treated as a consumption good, as those who are subject to mafia-like cartels of 'co-operating' local actors are likely to find out. Finally, having to compete incessantly for funding displaces the time and energy of NGOs, detracting them from their actual goals, for example health care or schooling. Not only will there be a disincentive to report problems with the programmes one administers, but the scramble for funding might also lead to dysfunctional behaviour, such as undermining a competitor, and clientelistic practices (via side payments) towards the recipients of the service.

Thus, a different picture of 'civil society' and of the chances for a new and more effective form of governance emerges. Unfortunately, it is not necessarily one of benevolence, burden-sharing and joint commitments to common causes. Arguments that competition among NGOs demonstrates the 'vibrancy' of civil society, and that the ever-increasing number of NGOs exemplifies the force of this civic vision and of a new form of cosmopolitan politics, are clearly exaggerated. They simply take no account of possible negative externalities. While it might be considered obscene to charge humanitarian or 'principled' organizations or activist frameworks with selfish interests, it would be ideological in the worst sense, not to say foolish, to assume that humanitarian organizations are *toto caelo* to other organizations because they pursue some ideals or goals of which we approve. As Cooley and Ron (2002: 17, 22) suggest, after having examined several aid projects with substantive NGO involvement:

> Calls for IO and INGO coordination are ubiquitous in the humanitarian aid literature, prompting the periodic creation of new UN coordination studies and agencies. Recurring coordination problems are, however, not caused solely by poor communication, lack of professionalism, or the dearth of coordinating bodies. They are also – and perhaps chiefly – produced by a crowded and highly competitive aid market in which multiple organizations compete for contracts from the same donors. Inter-organizational discord is a predictable outcome of existing material incentives ...
>
> The lack of coordination is not a product of ill will or poor organizational culture. Rather it is increasingly generated by the marketized environment in which IOs and INGOs feel required to demonstrate their ability to spend monies and win influence, regardless of broader project outcomes.

Hegel's inkling that civil society would not lead to integration on either the individual or the systems level, but that for such an integration the 'state' was needed, was perhaps not far from the mark, even though the first part of the sentence seems much less controversial than the second. After all, the 'mediation' by the state that Hegel himself proposed was largely entrusted to the 'bureaucracy', that is, a group with a special ethos and knowledge. Given the different trade-offs between competing policy goals, the differential impact a policy is likely to have on different groups, and the likely disagreements over the timing and implementation of the measures under consideration, the idea of 'one best solution' based on technical expertise quickly shows its phantasmagorical quality.

A good illustration of these problems is the example of help to Kyrgyzstan to reform its institutions in accordance with 'governance' benchmarks. During the discussion of how to privatize Kyrgyz Energo, the former state-owned energy monopoly, USAID wanted to dismantle the firm completely, whereas the European Bank for Reconstruction and Development wanted to keep it intact, provided a foreign partner could be found who could then initiate gradual reforms. The World Bank, which had sided originally with USAID, shifted later to endorse the European position. Meanwhile, the Kyrgyz officials stalled, as the donors vied for influence and proposed strikingly different strategies. Much of the disagreement among the agencies and contractors, who had developed their strategies essentially by placing different bets on the future, rested on the question of which monitoring and statistical data collection method should be adopted, making it appear that the basic difficulties were only 'technical' in nature.

The obvious lesson is, however, that since these problems are not technical in nature the appropriate strategy is to ensure that all stakeholders of a policy are brought together. This shifts the emphasis from expertise to political participation. Sometimes it was on the basis of this strategy – adopted enthusiastically by transnational social movements – that the emergence of new political spaces and participatory structures was expected. Again, the actual record is rather mixed and gives much food for thought. On the one hand, the establishment of the developmental dialogue by the World Bank, and the adoption of the WTO Council's Guidelines for Arrangements with Nongovernmental Organizations (1996), has increased the legitimacy of NGOs by allowing them to attend plenary sessions (but not formal or informal negotiating sessions). The meeting at Seattle (1999), which was attended by 739 accredited NGOs, who – aside from protests – organized a whole programme of workshops and symposia to which the WTO delegates were invited, represents the apogee of NGO activism.[20]

While these numbers are certainly indicative of a changing political landscape and a new agenda, the question remains whether spectacular events and even mass violence translate into political influence, or constitute the emergence of a new particular political space. The numbers alone should make us a little

20 At Doha only 366 had registered.

suspicious. How can one speak of a meaningful debate and participation with such numbers? True, many NGOs espoused similar positions, so that the problem of *quot capita tot sententiae* need not arise. However, how can one speak of participation and the emergence of a public if not even the agenda is known, or if access is not granted to the ministerial meetings where the decisions are being made? Given the entrenched position of the WTO and its success in representing issues of far-reaching social and political import as belonging to 'trade', one has to wonder whether the democratization of its procedures – weak as it is – is not bought at a heavy price, that is, by undermining both national and international politics. David Kennedy's laconic remarks about why anyone should be excited and celebrate 'the expansion of participation in an emasculated policy process' seem rather apt (Kennedy 1999: 54).

The real question is whether the potential for meaningful democratic politics is merely dependent on an increase in information or even of 'transparency', or whether such a strategy has perverse effects. Zizek's (1999: 388) suspicion that 'our deepest commitments to equality and participation bind us into practices whereby we submit to a global capital' may be very well founded. In other words, the institutions where the choices are actually made have successfully insulated themselves from public scrutiny and accountability by creating fora for endless debates and 'arguing' (Risse 2000)[21] but with no possibility of participation in or influence on decisions, or of exercising effective control over those in power.

Even if we admit that the inclusion of 'stakeholders' improves the input and possibly also the output legitimacy of a decision by opening up the process of deliberation and bringing to the negotiation relevant information that otherwise would not have been available, the unresolved issue remains that of how stakeholders are identified in the first place, and thus, whether or not the necessary level of representation has been achieved.[22] Furthermore, we know from the corporatist literature that diffuse interests, though extremely relevant for the viability and the welfare gains derived from negotiated settlements, are difficult to organize. Corporatist 'partnerships' are frequently subject to 'capture' by narrow but well-organized interests, particularly if one group has an important asset, such as information that others lack, or can provide the necessary *episteme*, which integrates otherwise separate issues and links them to particular strategies. Some studies of the influence of European business on EU trade policy – to the virtual exclusion of other groups of civil society – suggest that these two factors, that is, information provision and *episteme*-definition, are

---

21 For a more strategically oriented approach, see Schimmelfennig (2001).
22 See the assessment of Nölke (2000).

the most important ones in explaining actual policy outcomes.[23] Transplanting such 'corporate' arrangements from the national to the international level obviously does not by itself enhance either the quality of the decisions or their legitimacy. As Ottaway (2001: 266) has pointed out:

> Despite the claims that tripartite agreements will introduce greater democracy in the realm of global governance, it is doubtful that close cooperation between essentially unrepresentative organizations – international organizations, unaccountable NGOs and large trans-national corporations – will do much to ensure better protection and better representation of the interests of populations affected by global policies.

It is perhaps no surprise that, despite the high expectations from global policy networks, only very few of them satisfied the original criteria for public/private partnerships. And questions could be raised even in the 'satisfactory' cases such as the Apparel Industry Partnership (which was charged with formulating standards for the US apparel industry and its subcontractors), since only the presence of the US government was envisaged, but its participation was practically non-existent during the negotiations (Bobrowski 1999). Two other rather satisfactory projects were the World Commission on Dams (WCD), which resulted from a Workshop sponsored by the World Bank and the World Conservation Union, and the ISO 14000 Project (Clap 1989), tasked with developing standards for environmental management systems (EMS).

Evaluations of the democratic dimension of these projects are rather mixed, although the Dam project apparently fared much better (Dubash et al. 2001). But even here its identification of stakeholders and the confidentiality of its proceedings can be criticized. The ISO 14000 was, in effect, a closed meeting between governmental and industry representatives from the northern hemisphere. Although developing countries had to come on board and held an effective veto position, given the nature of the enterprise they lacked know-how and access to information, and therefore possessed no clout at the bargaining table. For many NGOs and developing countries, the process appeared to them, as Virginia Haufler states, 'opaque, expensive and industry led' (Haufler 1999: 25).

The bitter truth for much of the 'Third World' is that its traditional fear of exploitation and colonialism is increasingly being replaced by the practical

---

23 Thus van Appeldoorn (2002) shows that the notion of 'competitiveness' provided the European Round Table with an important framework to which further programmes such as job creation could be bolted and which allowed the business association to influence the Commission's policy decisively.

irrelevance of entire parts of the globe for the 'global' economy, while they increasingly create problems for the society of states and its public order. This can perhaps best be seen in the privatization of security and in the development of a new form of predatory state that we encounter in many regions of the world. Marauding militias and mercenaries at the command of sub-national actors and warlords who have access to globalized networks of (misused) aid, as well as to international crime, increasingly determine the life of many 'failed' or 'transitional' states.[24] When, with the failure of the 'developmental state', which attempted at least to integrate society and provide the structures for political and economic accumulation, the resources channelled through official structures cease, it is inevitable that the state apparatus decays. More and more officials take bribes and the system of clientelism and patronage, prevalent in many societies, quickly generates new parallel structures for social reproduction. The resulting pattern is that of rule by a variety of intermediaries – 'big men', traditional leaders, ethnic entrepreneurs, religious fundamentalists, and so on.

Examples abound, ranging from Pakistan and Uganda to the successor states of the former Soviet empire. Thus, a Ugandan 'minister' owned the central train terminal in the capital, had a private security service which protected embassies, TNCs and NGOs and, at the same time, did not hesitate to use his 'private' force to disperse and coerce protestors who had taken issue with his licensing practices for 'servicing' the railway station. In Pakistan, the military – the only remaining state institution that is still somehow functioning at the price of representing a state within the state – had, in 1999, to use 30,000 soldiers to collect water and electricity bills, restore the networks by capping illegal taps and arrest corrupt officials. When the public education system broke down, nobody even knew how many schools actually existed, as many teachers had jobs in phantom schools. Elements of 'civil society', such as the largely fundamentalist brotherhoods, filled the gap, providing their pupils more with indoctrination than education.

These last two examples clearly illustrate the serious problems that the new emphasis on 'governance' and 'civil society' hides. Attempts at curbing corruption and making the state more efficient by relying on the capacities of private actors and civil society were, of course, quite in tune with Western ideas about liberalization and a 'lean' state. However, the beneficial effects of such a retrenchment of the state could not be realized in most developing or transitional countries. Instead of improving the efficiency of the existing state apparatus, such a 'downsizing' contributed to its further decay and to the development of

---

24 For an interesting account of these developments, see Schlichte and Wilke (2000).

parallel networks of power. It curtails the chances for a politics in which the state as an arbiter can make legitimate and binding decisions. Contrary also to the hopes of anti-statists and the advocates of the democratic potential of civil society, who often insisted on the superiority of private ordering, we notice the re-feudalization of these societies and the emergence of an entrenched and internationally well-connected kleptocracy. This leads to predatory rule by intermediaries and warlords who have commoditized the main function of the state, namely, security (with all the implications for responsibility, legitimacy and accountability), and who have 'communalized' other traditional state functions, such as education and welfare, by transferring these responsibilities to local and international networks of civil society. Even if we put a more optimistic gloss on these rather sobering experiences and assessments, one thing is evident: no general emergence of a 'global public sphere', or of a space for cosmopolitan democratic practice, seems to be in the offing. Although we do notice the emergence of new actors and claimants attempting to establish some institutional framework, the appropriateness of the civil society analogy is rather doubtful.

Morals

The above analysis not only explains why homogenization and differentiation are part and parcel of the same process of transformative change but also suggests that the function of 'civil society' in both contexts is rather different. Increasing reliance on these NGOs by Western states and international organizations in the name of 'governance' is not likely to have the expected beneficial consequences, particularly if this involves dealing with 'big men' and contending with the networks and structures of kleptocratic regimes. Far from creating the conditions for a flourishing global civil society, the result could be the emergence of new para-statal forms of rule in which predatory elites are even less dependent upon their 'subjects' than before, precisely because they can link to international networks (criminal ones and legal ones) that provide them with the necessary resources. Similarly, the idea that, through the organization of all the stakeholders, new political spaces could be opened up, or at least more legitimate and effective regimes could be created, reflects a distorted optimism that ignores the difficulties involved in identifying the appropriate stakeholders and the problems with corporatism writ large.

Thus the question arises as to why the liberal project's promotion of the autonomy and legitimacy of civil society seems powerful and persuasive, despite its obvious flaws. There are several reasons that can, on their own and in conjunction, explain this. One is the inherent abstraction of the perspective that systematically eliminates differences, or declares them unimportant or in need of justification. Unsurprisingly, then, all the problems usually associated with social differentiation do not appear in the model, because they have been ignored in the first place. The most obvious problem is that, for a theory of democracy, the liberal paradigm has no way of providing a coherent account of the role of boundaries in establishing and maintaining existing communities. It either simply assumes that 'we, the People' exist, or that it does not matter whether or not people are constituted as 'a people'.

The shortcomings of this liberal perspective are best illustrated by Rawls' attempt to rely on either the specification of the transcendental conditions of a rational choice (behind the veil of ignorance) in order to derive the criteria for a just society, or on the assumption of an existing community. In the second case, some form of 'overlapping' consensus is supposed to provide the grounds for the establishment of an order that assigns precedence to the right over the good. Here, historical contingency enters the picture and the identification of an overlapping consensus means empirically examining which structures prove viable under what circumstances, an enterprise that undermines, however, both universalism and the notion of absolute foundations. Thus, given the contingent historical practice, the existence of societies that resemble those of free associations under the rule of law are extremely rare: they are exceptions rather than the rule. Furthermore, as Habermas (1998: 115) suggests:

> Since the voluntariness of the decision to engage in a law giving praxis is a fiction of the contractualist tradition, in the real world who gains power to define the boundaries of a political community is settled by historical chance and the actual course of events – normally, by the arbitrary outcomes of wars and civil wars.

A second and, of course, equally important reason for the success of the liberal project is the concept of the individual that is taken as the ultimate entity for the construction of the social world. Although such a move entails usually a naturalistic fallacy, there is an intuitive, even if mistaken, plausibility to this position. Here I do not want to renew the debate between communitarians and liberals. I simply want to point out that the construction of the individual who 'owns' himself, and is, therefore, the bearer of subjective rights, mystifies in the concept of 'property' the exercise of power that comes with the granting of subjective rights. In addition, it skews the discussion of a whole host of socially important questions about the nature of property rights, the limits of their exercise and their coercive character, by providing powerful 'trumps' in debates. In this way, a comprehensive rights discourse can be constructed in which virtually all problems can be recast as issues of subjective rights. Any interference with them, for instance by regulatory measures, can be 'debunked' as improper interference, as the recent controversy about the patents for AIDS medicine in developing countries shows.

The upshot of these remarks about the liberal project is that, by making it appear that certain social arrangements work like natural forces, the project in the end subverts itself and becomes ideological. It projects a universality that is neither normatively nor historically justifiable, as it discounts both the inherent potential for diversity and the existence of several paths to modernity. It also mystifies power and its need for legitimization and accountability by making it appear that the particular arrangements we have arrived at are somehow the outcome of nature's plan, and thereby deserve to be universally accepted. Furthermore, by selectively focusing on some aspects of global transformation, e.g. the spread of certain cultural forms, or on transactions, such as capital movements, and by not paying attention to the local mediations that occur, a curious narrative is created in which the elements of the Western tradition, from natural law to modernity, are reconfigured. To what extent they can still serve as templates for a world of our making remains to be seen.

References

Albrow, Martin, 1996, *The Global Age: State and Society Beyond Modernity*, Stanford, CA, Stanford University Press.

Barber, Benjamin, 1995, *Jihad v McWorld: How Globalism and Tribalism are Reshaping the World*, New York, Ballantine Books.

Beck, Ulrich, 1995, *Die feindlose Demokratie*, Stuttgart, Reclam.

— 1997, *Weltrisikogesellschaft, Weltöffentlichkeit und globale Subpolitik*, Vienna, Picas.

Bobrowski, David, 1999, 'Creating a Global Public Policy Network in the Apparel Industry: The Apparel Industry Partnership', case study for the UN Vision Project on Global Public Policy Networks, http://www.gppi.net/

Cerny, Philip, 1995, 'Globalization and the Changing Logic of Collective Action', *International Organization*, 49, 595–625.

Clap, Jennifer, 1989, 'The Privatization of Global Environmental Governance: ISO 14000 and the Developing World', *Global Governance*, 4(3), 295–316.

Cooley, Alexander, and James Ron, 2002, 'The NGO Scramble: Organizational Insecurity and the Political Economy of Transnational Action', *International Security*, 27, 5–39.

Dean, Mitchell, 1999, *Governmentality: Power and Rule in Modern Society*, London, Sage.

Drake, Bill (ed.), 1995, *The New Information Infrastructure*, New York, Twentieth Century Fund.

Dubash, Navroz, Mairi Dupar, Smitu Kothari and Tundu Lissu, 2001, *A Watershed in Global Governance? An Independent Assessment of the World Commission on Dams*, Washington, DC, Brookings.

Ekins, Paul, 1992, *A New World Order: Grassroot Movements for Global Change*, London, Routledge.

Falk, Richard, 1998, 'Global Civil Society: Perspectives, Initiatives, Movements', *Oxford Development Studies*, 26(1), 99–110.

Goldstein, Judith, Miles Kahler, Robert Keohane and Anne Marie Slaughter (eds), 2000, *Legalization and World Politics*, Special Issue of *International Organization*, 54(3).

Habermas, Jürgen, 1998, 'The European Nation State: On the Past and Future of Sovereignty and Citizenship', in C. Cronin and P. De Greiff (eds), *Inclusion of the Other: Studies in Political Theory*, Cambridge, MIT Press.

Hall, Rodney, and Thomas Biersteker (eds), 2002, *The Emergence of Private Authority in Global Governance*, Cambridge, Cambridge University Press.

Hardt, Michael, and Antonio Negri, 2000, *Empire*, Cambridge, MA, Harvard University Press.

Haufler, Virginia, 1999, 'Negotiating International Standards for Environmental Management Systems: The ISO 14000 Standards', case study for the UN Vision Project on Global Public Policy Networks, http://www.gppi.net/cms/public/

Held, David, 1998, 'The Transformation of Political Community: Rethinking Democracy in the Context of Globalization', in I. Shapiro and C. Hacker Cordon (eds), *Democracy's Edges*, Cambridge, Cambridge University Press.

Hirst, Paul, and Grahame Thompson, 1996, *Globalization in Question*, Cambridge, Polity Press.

Kaldor, Mary, 2003, *Global Civil Society: An Answer to War*, Oxford, Polity Press.

Keck, Margaret, and Kathryn Sikkink, 1998, *Activists Beyond Borders: Advocacy Networks in International Politics*, Ithaca, NY, Cornell University Press.

Kennedy, David, 1999, 'Background Noise? The Underlying Politics of Global Governance', *Harvard International Review*, 3, 52–85.

Khagram, Sanjeez, James Riker and Kathryn Sikkink (eds), 2002, *Restructuring World Politics: Transnational Movements, Networks and Norms*, Minneapolis, MN, University of Minnesota Press.

Linklater, Andrew, 1998, *The Transformation of Political Community*, Oxford, Polity Press.

Meyer, John, John Boli, George Thomas and Francisco Ramirez, 1997, 'World Society and the Nation State', *American Journal of Sociology*, 103(1), 144–81.

Mueller, Philip, 2003, *Unearthing the Politics of Globalization*, Muenster and New Brunswick, Lit. and Transaction Pub.

Nölke, Andreas, 2000, 'Regieren in transnationalen Politiknetzwerken: Kritik postnationaler Governance-Konzepte aus der Perspektive einer transnationalen, Inter-Organisationssoziologie', *Zeitschrift für International Beziehungen*, 2(2), 331–58.

Ottaway, Marina, 2001, 'Corporatism Goes Global: International Organizations, Nongovernmental Organization Networks, and Trans-national Business', *Global Governance*, 7(3), 265–92.

Paris, Roland, 2002, 'International Peace Building and the "Mission Civilisatrice"', *Review of International Studies*, 28, 637–56.

Reinicke, Wolfgang, 1998, *Global Public Policy: Governing without Government*, Washington, DC, Brookings.

Risse, Thomas, 2000, 'Let's Argue: Communicative Action in World Politics', *International Organization*, 54(1), 1–39.

Rosenau, James, 1998, 'Governance and Democracy in a Globalizing World', in D. Archibugi, D. Held and M. Kohler (eds), *Re-imagining Political Community*, Cambridge, Polity Press.

Scharpf, Fritz, and Vivien Schmidt, 2000, *Welfare and Work in the Open Economy*, 2 vols, New York, Oxford University Press.

Schimmelfennig, Frank, 2001, 'Liberal Norms, Rhetorical Action and the Enlargement of the EU', *International Organization*, 55, 47–80.

Schlichte, Klaus, and Boris Wilke, 2000, 'Der Staat und einige seiner Zeitgenossen', *Zeitschrift fuer Internationale Beziehungen*, 7(2), 359–84.

Shaw, Martin, 2000, *Theory of the Global State: Globality as an Unfinished Revolution*, Cambridge, Cambridge University Press.

Slaughter, Ann Marie, 2003, 'A Global Community of Courts', *Harvard International Law Journal*, 44, 191–220.

Strange, Susan, 1998, *Mad Money*, Manchester, Manchester University Press.

Tarrow, Sidney, 1998, *Power in Movement: Social Movements and Contentious Politics*, Cambridge, Cambridge University Press.

van Appeldoorn, B., 2002, *Transnational Capitalism and the Struggle over European Integration*, London, Routledge.

Wendt, Alexander, and Raymond Duvall, 1989, 'Production, the State and Change in World Order', in E. Czempiel and J. Roseanu (eds), *Global Changes and Theoretical Challenges*, Lexington, KY, Lexington Books, Chapter 4.

Willke, Helmut, 2001, *Atopia: Studien zur atopischen Gesellschaft*, Frankfurt, Suhrkamp.

Zizek, Slavoj, 1999, *The Ticklish Subject: An Essay on Political Ontology*, London, Verso.

Zuern, Michael, 1998, *Regieren jenseits des Nationalstaats: Globalisierung und Denationalsierung als Chance*, Frankfurt, Campus.

Index

absolutism 135–7
   liberal 135–6
Abu Bakr 92
Abu Ghraib 27, 79
Abu-Lughod, Janet 134
accountability 273–4, 275, 278, 283
action, general theory of 252, 253
activism, Islamic 98–9, 103
advocacy networks 273
Aeschylus 96–7
Afghanistan 23, 27, 76, 83
Afghan prisoners 27–8, 79
Africa 66, 77, 83, 146, 268
agon (strife) 159
agrarian classes 135
aid projects 276, 277
AIDS 283
AK Party 187, 189
al-Qaeda 18–19, 178
Ali, Hirsi 178–9
all-affected principle 203–5, 206, 208
alternative worlds 157
American Constitution, religious non-establishment clause 31
American Economic Association (AEA) 252
American Historical Association (AHA) 252
American Political Science Association 252
American Social Science Association (ASSA) 252

American Society for Sociology (ASS) 252
Americas
   and modernity 66
   see also United States
Amritsar 119–20
Anderson, J. 97–8, 99, 104
Anglo-Saxon cultural identity 44–5
Annan, Kofi 78, 80
anti-clericalism 47
anti-colonialism 118, 121–4, 127
anti-communism 148
anti-foreignism 80
anti-globalization 17
anti-liberal policy 149
anti-modernist tradition 176
Anti-Secession Law 81
anti-Semitism 183
Apparel Industry Partnership 279
Arendt, Hannah 2, 3, 24, 155, 156, 160, 161, 259
Argentina 46, 48, 49, 52, 56
aristocracy, European 135, 136, 146–7
Aristotle 159
armaments industry 143, 144–5, 148
army
   as institution 130
   mass citizen (Napoleonic) 138, 146
Arnason, Johann 5, 69, 70, 167, 171
art 1, 241, 243–4
Asia 66, 67, 146
   see also Central Asia; East Asia